This book passed
through Greenwood Ave
Little Free Library

Fairhope,
AL   #138334

World Trade Rivalry

World Trade Rivalry

Trade Equity and
Competing Industrial Policies

William A. Lovett
Tulane University

Lexington Books
D.C. Heath and Company/Lexington, Massachusetts/Toronto

Library of Congress Cataloging-in-Publication Data

Lovett, William Anthony.
   World trade rivalry.

   Bibliography: p.
   Includes index.
   1. Commerce. 2. Industry and state. 3. Competition, International. 4. United States—
Commercial policy. I. Title.
HF1008.L68   1987   382'.3   85-40388
ISBN 0-669-11027-2 (alk. paper)

Published simultaneously in Canada
Printed in the United States of America
Casebound International Standard Book Number: 0-669-11027-2
Library of Congress Catalog Card Number: 85-40388

The paper used in this publication meets the minimum requirements of American National Standard for Information Sciences—Permanence of Paper for Printed Library Materials, ANSI Z39.48-1984. ∞™

92 93 94 95 8 7 6 5 4 3 2

Contents

Figures and Tables

Figures

Tables

Preface

The world economy is in disarray. Recent stagflation strains, widespread debt overloads, large budget deficits in the United States and other nations, fluctuating and unrealistic exchange rates, massive U.S. trade deficits, increased migration of industry and jobs to low-wage countries, and the United States's shift from substantial net creditor to significant debtor raise awkward questions about the existing regime. Economic development, which spread fairly generally in the 1960s and 1970s, stalled in many nations, especially Latin America and Africa, with heavy debt overloads, capital flight, and political insecurities. How can the process of economic growth be revived more broadly to general advantage? What, if any, limitations should be placed upon international capital movement, investment, borrowing, industrial relocation, and job migration in the world economy? Will the framework of world finance, banking, and trade arrangements require some adjustment? Does a system built around a disproportionately strong post–World War II U.S. economy (which served as leader, primary creditor, and willing market for exports from most other countries) need revision to a new reality? How should the United States blend its own independent actions with international practice and negotiations?

Four major strategies are competing now in the world market. Free-market globalists seek a broader, more secure environment for enlarged private enterprise, investment, lending, and trading. Meanwhile, Marxists encourage structural reforms and revolutions to place more countries in the hands of socialist party elites, with carefully regulated commerce among socialist states, along with limited trade and borrowing from capitalist corporations and banks outside their orbit. Many developing nations call for a New International Economic Order, with a considerable role for state planning plus more systematic preferences and aids for the poorer nations to help them catch up more rapidly in prosperity. Recently, populist welfare state interests and labor parties seek to cushion somehow the severity of international market competition, and to slow down and mitigate the process of industrial relocation and job transfer to low-wage countries. Considerations of national security, preventing undue foreign influence, and achieving fairness in world trade, investment, and lending complicate matters further.

Within these broad tendencies, compromise policies can be employed, suitable to each nation's ideology, institutions, and current leadership. Japan, Switzerland, the Federal Republic of Germany, Taiwan, and South Korea currently arouse special interest for their strong, sustained performance of improving productivity and economic growth.[1] But within many nations, including the United States, there is controversy on the best way to proceed. Among the less successful nations, there is often greater discord and less continuity. For years, Britain has been a notable underachiever, with stop-go policies and worried debates.[2] But recently, other nations have become troubled, from the United States, Canada, France, and Scandinavia through Italy, Greece, Mexico, Brazil, Argentina, and many smaller countries.

Realistic observers know the existing world marketplace is extensively regulated. Most countries employ systematic industrial development and export-promotion policies to improve their economic prosperity, growth, and national security. Because international trade is important for economic growth, investment, and productivity, most governments try to foster helpful commerce. But, the extent of this regulation, subsidy, and encouragement is highly asymmetrical and differs considerably from country to country. (See figure P–1.)

The United States, in fact, is more open than other major industrial countries. Europe is fairly open, but protects its agriculture to a greater extent, subsidizes and supports more of its industry, and uses voluntary restraint agreements more widely. Japan is considerably less open, with strong traditions of industrial promotion, easier credit, cultural loyalties, administrative guidance, and language barriers which limit foreign imports in many areas. Most new industrial countries (NICs) in East Asia, Latin America, and elsewhere are frankly mercantilist, and have used discount financing, subsidies, and government support heavily to promote industrial growth. Most less developed countries (LDCs) use similar policies, although with less resources and fewer targeted industries for development at earlier stages of industrialization. The General Agreement on Tariffs and Trade (GATT) authorizes and tolerates such unbalanced openness. While tariffs have been reduced greatly among industrial countries, and nontariff barriers to a lesser extent, NICs and LDCs are allowed a general freedom under GATT for infant-industry tariffs, selective import restriction, export promotion, and related subsidies. In effect, GATT established a double standard for trade openness, which became deeply entrenched, with strong multinational enterprise, multinational bank and government interests (among NICs and LDCs) relying upon this system. (Finally, most communist countries are not even GATT members and, as state-controlled economies, provide only restricted access for trade and borrowing, yet they seek technology transfer with other nations.) This unbalanced system is increasingly unsound, and needs improvement toward better trade equity.

Communist and heavily socialist countries
Largely state-controlled economies—modest openness, tightly regulated access, substantial borrowing, and technology imports. Subsidized exports to earn foreign exchange.

Newly industrialized and less developed countries
Limited openness—substantial protection with widespread subsidies and mercantile regulation to encourage new industries, expand exports, and limit competing manufacturers. Technology transfer encouraged, but carefully regulated foreign investment.

Japan
Partly open markets—significant subsidies and export-oriented financing. Strong tradition of government–industry collaboration, administrative guidance, and national strategy for export manufacturing and imports of raw materials. Growing capital exports and skillful blend of new plants abroad, both for low-wage components and assembly in export markets.

European Economic Community and
European Free Trade Area
Substantially open markets, but protected agriculture, considerable subsidies for manufacturing, and growing use of voluntary restraint agreements to limit excessive imports and industrial job losses. Moderate capital exports, with diversified overseas investment.

United States
Most open and least regulated major market—occasional protection and limited subsidies. Manufacturing tending to relocate abroad in lower-wage countries. Serious trade deficits, with possible threat of excessive deindustrialization. Traditional capital exports offset recently by large borrowing and capital investments into United States.

Figure P–1. Asymmetrical Trade Openness in the World Economy

While these arrangements have encouraged the movement of branch plants and manufacturers to lower-wage countries, thus helping equalize worker wages over the long run, they can alter the distribution of incomes, jobs, growth, and opportunities within and among nations. (See figure P–2.) A crucial question is the extent to which net deindustrialization, income losses, and weakened economic growth may be suffered within mature industrial countries (MICs).[3]

In the United States, for example, increased international competition is a major cause of stalled real wages since the 1970s. (See table P–1.) While U.S. real wages have risen substantially since the 1930s (reflecting broad economic growth and productivity increases), real wages peaked in the early 1970s. (*Manufacturing* real wages peaked in 1978.) While inflation kept increasing, average worker incomes stopped growing in real terms. Wage-earning families could only improve themselves with more people working, and the percentage of women employed increased greatly. On the other hand, in regions with declining industries and reduced employment, many families lost real income, as high-wage manufacturing plants cut payrolls substantially (and often relocated to low-wage countries). What policies are desirable, if any, to minimize or ease these disturbances?

Figure P–2 illustrates the competitive challenges for mature industrial countries resulting from widespread movement of their high-wage, "sick" industries to newly industrial countries. In a world marketplace with free trade and capital mobility, this trend has increased (with active participation by multinational enterprises and multinational banks).

While this relocation process yields general (broadly shared) income gains for participating NICs, the income effects for MICs are mixed. Many wealthy capital owners and upper middle class people (those not directly hurt by relocation) benefit from cheaper imports and somewhat improved service sectors. Lower-income workers gain more service jobs and cheaper imports. But, those higher-wage workers directly hurt by closed plants, together with distressed communities and workers getting lower wages, suffer income losses.

A crucial empirical question for each MIC is the relative size and extent of upper-, middle-, and low-income gains, as compared to job displacement and distressed-income losses. When gains greatly exceed losses, MICs will accept relocation of industry more gracefully. But, if displacement losses are substantial, widespread, and offset only by modest income gains, then political resistance to the relocation process should be stronger and more effective.

The ratio and distribution of MIC income gains and losses will be influenced, in each country, by its overall growth rate, productivity trends, quality of R&D, savings and investment behavior, character and success of industrial development and trade policies, and adjustment and redeployment programs.

In recent years, Japan has enjoyed the strongest performance record, with a good growth rate, healthy productivity, strong R&D, ample savings and investment, and sophisticated collaboration between industry and government. The United States, Canada, and many European countries have been less successful.

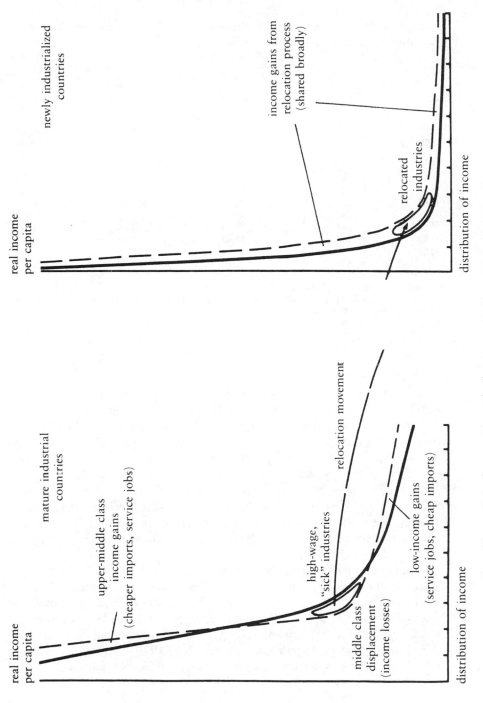

Figure P-2. Competitive Challenges and Industrial-Relocation Process

Table P-1
Average Weekly Earnings of U.S. Production or Nonsupervisory Workers
on Nonagricultural Payrolls, 1940–86

	Total Private		Manufacturing	
	Current Dollars	Constant Dollars [a]	Current Dollars	Constant Dollars [a]
1940	n.a.	n.a.	24.96	67.77
1947	45.58	123.52	49.13	133.14
1955	67.72	153.21	75.30	170.36
1965	95.45	183.21	107.53	206.39
1972	136.90	198.41	154.71	224.22
1978	203.70	189.31	249.27	231.66
1980	235.10	172.74	288.62	212.06
1981	255.20	170.13	318.00	212.00
1982	267.26	168.09	330.26	207.71
1983	280.70	171.26	354.08	216.03
1984	294.05	173.48	373.63	220.67
1985	301.16	171.60	385.56	219.93
1986 [b]	306.59	172.05	396.58	222.55

Sources: U.S. Department of Labor, Bureau of Labor Statistics, *Handbook of Labor Statistics* (June 1985), table 81. U.S. Department of Labor, Bureau of Labor Statistics, *Employment and Earnings* (monthly), table C–4.

Note: n.a. = not available.

[a]Constant dollars in 1977 base year.

[b]As of October.

Clearly, the world's manufacturing activities have relocated considerably over the past decades. After World War II, the United States was predominant in most areas (partly due to disruption in Europe and Japan). In 1946, the United States produced 60 percent of the world's steel, 80 percent of the automobiles, 71 percent of the petroleum, 48 percent of the coal, and 38 percent of the electricity, while operating 60 percent of the merchant shipping tonnage. The United States was ahead in most appliances and at the forefront in most technologies. By the mid-1980s, the U.S. share declined to 13 percent of steel, 25 percent of automobiles, 15 percent of petroleum, 25 percent of coal, 26 percent of electricity, and less than 5 percent of merchant shipping. The United States now imports a large part of its steel, automobiles, petroleum, and appliances, while relying heavily upon foreign shipping. While U.S. per capita income after the war was two to three times larger than in Northern Europe and ten times larger than in Japan, by the 1980s, Western Europe and Japan had largely caught up. Meanwhile, many NICs made rapid progress. Taiwan, South Korea, and Brazil were the most impressive, but even India and China (two of the world's poorest countries in the 1940s) have achieved strong and self-sustaining manufacturing growth since 1970. (See table P–2 and, in the appendix, tables A–1 through A–10.)

Table P–2
Per Capita Gross National Product by Nation, 1953–86
(in current U.S. $)

	1953	1960	1965	1970	1975	1980	1985	1986
U.S.	2,310	2,830	3,580	4,826	7,141	11,446	16,693	17,110
Soviet Union	—	1,600	1,900	2,300	2,700	5,730	5,749	—
Japan	230	460	900	1,964	4,481	9,069	11,024	16,121
West Germany	740	1,310	1.950	3,042	6,751	13,216	10,123	14,193
France	1,010	1,350	2,050	2,775	6,430	12,163	9,270	12,351
U.K.	940	1,380	1,840	2,213	4,162	9,470	8,039	9,363
Belgium	940	1,250	1,810	2,616	6,304	11,927	8,068	10,933
Italy	430	700	1,120	1,875	3,464	7,011	6,278	8,237
Sweden	1,120	1,740	2,660	4,139	8,843	14,938	11,975	14,816
Switzerland	1,150	1,600	2,330	3,308	8,477	15,920	14,194	19,883
Spain	—	340	680	1,086	2,952	5,665	4,340	5,426
Netherlands	610	990	1,570	2,567	6,364	11,970	8,525	11,727
Norway	870	1,260	1,890	2,883	7,100	14,121	13,953	16,895
Hungary	—	1,500	1,800	2,000	2,400	4,180	1,956	—
Yugoslavia	—	590	520	714	1,557	2,470	1,878	—
Poland	—	1,500	1,800	2,100	2,800	—	2,421	—
China	93	117	134	167	209	240	333	—
South Korea	—	152	115	266	583	1,620	1,986	2,271
Taiwan	100	150	199	227	910	2,260	3,140	3,750
India	62	74	103	100	147	210	255	—
Canada	1,710	2,090	2,460	3,870	7,213	10,800	13,096	13,253
Mexico	232	334	455	701	1,463	1,950	2,260	—
Brazil	—	208	236	505	1,219	2,060	1,623	—

Source: OECD, Department of Economics and Statistics, *National Accounts of OECD Countries, 1950–1968,* p. 10; *1960–1984,* comparative table 21. United Nations, Department of Economic and Social Affairs, Statistics Office, *Yearbook of National Account Statistics, 1969,* vol. II, table 1C; *1972,* vol. III, table 1A. *Geographical Distribution of Financial Flows, 1981–84* (Paris: OECD 1986), section C, pp. 274–75. *Worldmark Encyclopedia of the Nations, Vol. V: Hungary, Poland and USSR* (World Mark Press Ltd). Paul S. Shoup, *The East European and Soviet Data Handbook: Political and Development Indicator, 1965–75* (New York: Columbia University Press, 1981), table H–4. Willy Kraus, *Economic Development and Social Change in People's Republic of China* (New York: Springer-Verlag, 1979), table A1. Morgan Guaranty Trust Company, International Economics Department, *Morgan International Data* (June 1986), table A–1.

Note: 1986 GNP growth rates are based on "World Financial Markets" (Morgan Guaranty Trust Company, Oct./Nov. 1986), *OECD Economic Outlook,* Dec. 1986; and "Korea Business Brief," *Asia Wall Street Journal,* Jan. 5, 1987, p. 4; and they are adjusted for exchange rate realignments. The fluctuations in relative GNPs for 1980, 1985, and 1986 reflect a "low" dollar in 1980, a "high" dollar in 1985, and a "declining" dollar in 1986.

In response to this increasing competition from low-wage manufacturing countries, the United States tried to upgrade, produce higher-valued merchandise, and improve productivity. This march up the ladder of technology worked well enough through the 1960s, but less successfully in the 1970s. Currently, Americans face an even tougher challenge for world market competitiveness. By mid-1980s, the high tech edge of the United States was waning. In 1986, the United States no longer earned a net trade surplus in high technology production (see figure P–3), and highly efficient U.S. farms could not generate a large trade surplus. How would the U.S. economy earn its way in world markets? Could Americans enjoy increased standards of living without enhanced productivity? How should the United States meet the challenge of competing industrial and trade development policies in the world economy today?

Obviously, the United States is now a service-oriented economy.[4] Manufacturing absorbed 27 percent of those employed in 1952. By 1980, when 20.3 million workers found jobs in U.S. manufacturing, this required only 20 percent of 101 million employed. By 1986, manufacturing employment had declined to 19 million, but this represented only 17 percent of the 111 million employed. If trends toward increased movement of manufacturing jobs to low-wage countries continue, what will happen to the remaining U.S manufacturing, technology, and overall prosperity?

The United States and its multinational corporations (MNCs) led the world toward increased investment abroad and capital mobility in the 1950s and 1960s. Gradually, the Europeans, Japanese, and, more recently, a few NICs joined this trend toward more open capital movements. But, substantial asymmetry still operates in the regulation of capital markets, and many countries (including most of the developing nations) use heavy restrictions upon international investment activity.[5]

Western industrial countries (the United States, Europe, Canada, Australia, and New Zealand), Hong Kong, Singapore, and some smaller areas allow substantially free movement of funds, investment, and earnings in and out of their countries. Japan is becoming more open as well. Most NICs and LDCs, by contrast, use a mixture of regulated encouragements for foreign investment, with restrictions upon capital outflow, and often try to limit repatriation of earnings. Most developing nations (and many mature nations) also supervise foreign takeovers and investments to prevent undue dominance or influence upon key industrial sectors and to preserve more national autonomy and independence. Because the U.S. economy is considerably larger than other countries', it has felt less danger and need for regulation in this direction, at least thus far. Is this unbalanced regulation of capital markets desirable?

Unfortunately, substantial debt overloads in at least sixty countries, often aggravated by serious capital flight, also place great strain recently on world financial markets and multinational banks.[6] Many nations approached de facto default and set limits on their debt-service payments (unless granted generous new lending). New international liquidity is needed to maintain general solvency, revive economic development for many nations, and restore flagging growth in the international economy. How can all this be achieved without reigniting the excessive inflation of the 1970s? Are new regulations feasible or appropriate for world capital markets and finance?

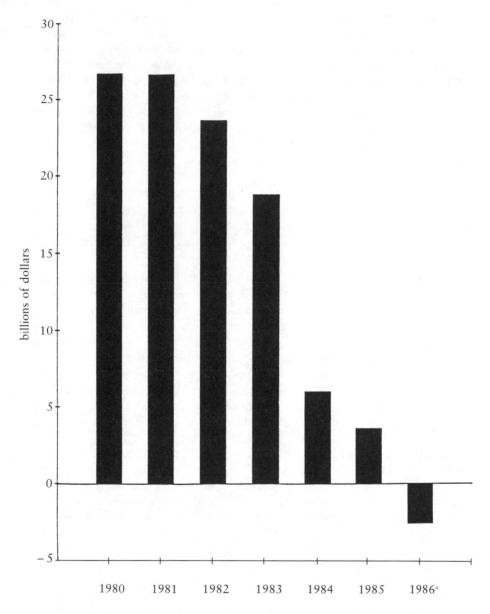

Source: W.F. Finan, Perry D. Quick, and Karen Sandberg, "The U.S. Position in High Technology: 1980–86," a report prepared for the Joint Economic Committee (Washington, D.C.: Quick, Finan & Associates, October 1986).

[a]Estimated.

Figure P–3. The U.S. Trade Position in High Technology, 1980–86

Big U.S. budget deficits, heavy borrowing from abroad, and its transformation from leading creditor to largest international borrower add further strains. The U.S. economy was the world's leader and "locomotive"; it still enjoys great confidence as a depository for flight capital and investment resources. Somewhat higher interest rates, resulting partly from U.S. deficits and government borrowing, reinforced this appeal. But, substantial overvaluation of the dollar resulted (especially in 1983–85), which crippled U.S. exports and enlarged U.S. imports. A moderate U.S. trade imbalance in the late 1970s–early 1980s became a massive trade deficit reaching $170 billion (4 percent of GNP) by 1986.[7]

	1986 (est.)	1985	1984	1983
U.S. imports	$387b.	$361.6b.	$341.2b.	$269.9b.
U.S. exports	$217b.	$213.1b.	$217.9b.	$200.5b.
Trade deficit	$170b.	$148.5b.	$123.3b.	$69.4b.

Although the dollar finally began to slide substantially from its peak in February 1985, experts were still unsure how much additional dollar decline might be needed. Meanwhile, most U.S. trade partners were reluctant to give up their export sales to the United States or to increase imports from the United States. They feared job losses, recession, and political strains. But, massive U.S. trade deficits are neither healthy nor really sustainable over the long run. Meanwhile, many interests in the United States complained about sluggish U.S. manufacturing industries, as well as slumps and recessions in agriculture, mining, oil, and gas, plus softness in real estate and many financial institutions. Stock traders and forecasters were concerned about slowed growth and uncertainties in U.S. and world markets.

Debate intensified about the best mix of U.S. industrial development, finance, tax, and trade policies. Should the United States continue more openness than other markets? What assistance, if any, should be given to U.S. manufacturing industries in distress which suffer severe (often subsidized) foreign competition? To what extent could foreign markets become more open for U.S. exports? How much could be expected from another GATT round? Must the United States act more independently to improve trade equity and to safeguard its own vital interests in finance, industry and trade? And, how would the world debt crisis, slowed growth in many countries, and the need for increased and more reliable international liquidity fit into the picture? What steps should the United States take independently? What might be done in collaboration with other nations and/or multinational institutions such as the International Monetary Fund (IMF), World Bank, and multinational banks)? These are the problems dealt with in this book.

Notes

1. For economic growth in many countries see table P-2. See also John Kendrick, ed., *International Comparisons of Productivity and Causes of the Slowdown* (Washington, D.C.: American Enterprise Inst., 1984); *1986 World Bank Atlas* (Washington, D.C.: World Bank, June 1986); Thomas K. McCraw, ed., *America versus Japan: A Comparative Study* (Boston: Harvard Bus. School Press, 1986); and Roy Hofheinz and Kent Calder, *The East Asia Edge* (New York: Basic, 1982).

2. For extensive controversy on the recent British economy, see Sidney Pollard, *The Development of the British Economy, 1914–67,* rev. ed. (London: E. Arnold, 1969); Charles Loch Mowat, *Britain between the Wars* (Chicago: University of Chicago Press, 1955); John F. Wright, *Britain: The Age of Economic Management: An Economic History since 1939* (Oxford, England: Oxford University Press, 1979); G.D.H. Cole, *The Postwar Condition of Britain* (London: Routledge & Paul, 1956); Andrew Shonfield, *British Economic Policy since the War* (Harmondsworth, England: Penguin 1958); J.C.R. Dow, *The Management of the British Economy, 1945–60* (Cambridge, England: NIESR, Cambridge University Press, 1960); John Richard Sargent, *Out of Stagnation: A Policy for Growth* (London: Fabian Society, 1963); Sydney Chapman and Keith Speed, *Blueprint for Britain* A Report on Behalf of the Young Conservative and Unionist Organization, 1965; Nicholas Davenport and Ernest Harold, *The Split Society* (London: V. Gollancz, 1964); Richard E. Caves et al. *Britain's Economic Prospects* (Washington, D.C.: Brookings, 1968); Samuel Brittan, *Steering the Economy: The British Experiment* (New York: The Library Press, 1971); James E. Alt, *The Politics of Economic Decline: Economic Management and Political Behavior since 1964* (Cambridge, England: Cambridge University Press, 1979); Alexander John Youngson, *Britain's Economic Growth 1920–66* (London: Allen & Unwin, 1967); Robert William Bacon, *Britain's Economic Problem: Too Few Producers,* 2nd ed. (London: Macmillan, 1978); Wilfred Beckerman, ed., *Slow Growth in Britain: Causes and Consequences*, Conference on Economics of the British Association for Advancement of Science at Bath (Oxford, England: Clarendon Press, 1979); Bernard Nossiter, *A Future that Works* (Boston: Houghton Mifflin, 1978); David Graham Hutton, *Whatever Happened to Productivity?* Tenth Wincott Memorial Lecture, London, Institute of Economic Affairs, 1980; Richard E. Caves and Lawrence B. Krause, *Britain's Economic Performance* (Washington, D.C.: Brookings, 1980); OECD *Economic Survey, United Kingdom* (Feb. 1980); OECD *Economic Outlook,* "United Kingdom" (Dec. 1980). See also Sir Nicholas Henderson, "Britain's Decline; Its Causes and Consequences," *Economist* (June 2, 1979); "Britain's Budget" (the first Thatcher Budget), *Economist* (June 16, 1979); "Britain: Rough Road Back to the Free Market," *Business Week* (Oct. 15, 1979); "Inflation's Sticky Path: Britain Is Not Winning Its Fight against Inflation," *Economist* (April 26, 1980); "Britain Isn't Working," *Economist* (Aug. 2, 1980); "How Labour's Left Took Power," *Economist* (Oct. 4, 1980); "In Thatcherland," *Economist* (Oct. 25, 1980); "Which of Her Promises Should Mrs. Thatcher Break?" *Economist* (Nov. 8, 1980); "Can Mrs. Thatcher Keep Her Present Cabinet Much Longer?" *Economist* (Nov. 29, 1980); "Embattled but Unbowed," *Time* (Feb. 16, 1981); "Here Endeth the Third Lesson. . . . Budget 1981," *Economist* (March 14, 1981). See also, Michael Stewart, *The Age of Interdependence: Economic Policy in a Shrinking World*

(Cambridge, Mass: MIT Press, 1984); C.B. McPherson, *The Rise and Fall of Economic Justice and Other Papers* (Oxford, England: Oxford Univ. Press, 1985); Bernard Elbaum and William Lazonick, *The Decline of the British Economy* (Oxford, England: Clarendon Press, 1986); Simi Lieberman, "Economic Socialization in the U.K.," in *The Growth of European Mixed Economies, 1945–70* (Cambridge, Mass: Schenkman-Halsted (Wiley), 1977); Nigel Lawson, *Thatcherism in Practice: A Progress Report*, Speech to the Zurich Society of Economics (London: Conservative Political Centre, Jan. 14, 1981); Nicholas Kaldor, *The Economic Consequences of Mrs. Thatcher* (London: Duckworth, 1983); Peter Riddell, *The Thatcher Government* (Oxford, England: Martin Robertson, 1983); P.G. Hare and M.W. Kirby, *An Introduction to British Economic Policy* (Brighton, Sussex, England: Wheatsheaf Books-Harvester Press, 1984); William Keegan, *Mrs. Thatcher's Economic Experiment* (London: Allen Lane, 1984); John Kay, ed., *The Economic and the 1985 Budget* (Oxford, England: Basil Blackwell, 1985); Martin Holmes, *The First Thatcher Government, 1979–83* (Colorado Springs: Westview, 1986); Joel Krieger, *Reagan, Thatcher, and the Politics of Decline* (Oxford, England: Oxford Univ. Press, 1986).

For other countries, see chapter 5 in William Lovett, *Inflation and Politics: Fiscal, Monetary, and Wage-Price Discipline* (Lexington, Mass.: Lexington Books, 1982).

For backgrounds and details of the Japanese success story, see the following: Mikoso Hane, *Japan, A Historical Survey* (New York: Scribner's, 1972); William R. Lockwood, *The Economic Development of Japan, 1868–1938* (Princeton, N.J.: Princeton University Press, 1954); Jon Livingston, Joe Moore, and Felicia Oldfather, *Imperial Japan, 1800–1945* (New York: Pantheon-Random House, 1973); *Postwar Japan, 1945 to the Present* (New York: Pantheon-Random House, 1973); Saburo Ienaga, *The Pacific War, 1931–45* (1968; reprint ed., New York: Pantheon-Random House, 1978); William R. Lockwood, ed., *The State and Economic Enterprise in Japan* (Princeton, N.J.: Princeton University Press, 1965); Hugh Patrick and Henry Rosovsky, eds., *Asia's New Giant; How the Japanese Economy Works* (Washington, D.C.: Brookings, 1976); Richard E. Caves and Masu Uekesa, *Industrial Organization in Japan* (Washington, D.C.: Brookings, 1976); Edward F. Denison and William F. Chung, *How Japan's Economy Grew So Fast, The Sources of Postwar Japanese Expansion* (Washington, D.C.: Brookings, 1976); Takoa Tsuchiya, *An Economic History of Japan* (Philadelphia: Porcupine Press, 1977); Chalmers M. Johnson, *Japan's Public Policy Companies* (Washington, D.C.: AEI, 1978); Isaiah Frank, *The Japanese Economy in International Perspectives* (Baltimore: Johns Hopkins University Press, 1975); Yuan-Li Wu, *Japan's Search for Oil: A Case Study on Economic Nationalism and International Security* (Stanford, Calif.: Hoover Institution Press, 1977); Saburo Okita, *The Developing Economies and Japan: Lessons in Growth* (Tokyo: University of Tokyo Press, 1980); Ezra F. Vogel, *Japan as No. 1: Lessons for America* (Cambridge, Mass.: Harvard University Press, 1979); James D. Hodgson, *The Wondrous Working World of Japan* (Washington, D.C.: AEI Reprint, January 1978); E. Van Helvoort, *The Japanese Working Man: What Choice? What Reward?* (Vancouver: University of British Columbia Press, 1979); OECD, *Economic Surveys*, (July 1977, July 1978, July 1980); OECD, *Economic Outlook* 28, "Japan" (Dec. 1980); William Manchester, "The Last Shogun: MacArthur and the Making of Modern Japan," *Atlantic* (July 1978); "Japanese Multinationals: Covering the World with Investment . . ." *Business Week* (June 16, 1980); "How Japan Does It: The World's Toughest Competitor," *Time* (March 30, 1981); Benjamin Higgins, "Three Success Stories—Japan: The Lone Graduate," in *Economic Development: Problems, Principles, and Policies*, rev. ed. (New York: Norton, 1968), pp. 617–35; "Rapid Growth but High Inflation" (graph comparing strong real growth with divergent inflation rates for Japan, Singapore, Taiwan, South Korea, Thailand, and Philippines), in *Euromoney* (May 1981).

For background on the strength of modern and postwar Germany's economy, see the following: Koppel S. Pinson, *Modern Germany: Its History and Civilization*, 2nd ed. (New York: MacMillan, 1966); Gustav Stolper, *The German Economy: 1870 to the Present* (London: Weidenfeld & Nicholson, 1967); Konrad Adenauer, *Memoirs*, trans. Beate Ruhm von Oppen (London: Weidenfeld & Nicholson, 1966); Constantino Brescianani-Turroni, *The Economics of Inflation: A Study of Current Depreciation in Postwar Germany* (London: Allen & Unwin, 1953); Kenyon Edwards Poole, *German Financial Policies, 1932–39* (Cambridge, Mass.: Harvard University Press, 1939); Albert Hahn, *Funfzig Jahre Zwischen Inflation and Deflation* (Tubingen: J.C.B. Mohr, 1963). See also OECD Economic Survey, *Germany* (June 1979, May 1980); OECD *Economic Outlook*, "Germany" (Dec. 1980). For a closely related collateral success in recent years, see Gottfried Haberler, *Austria's Economic Development: A Minor Picture of the World Economy* (Washington, D.C.: AEI Reprint, Jan. 1980). See also M.S. Mendelsohn, "Beating Inflation: The German and Swiss Experience," *The Banker* (London: Dec. 1979).

For the gradual increase in concern over the West German economy, see the following evolution; "Leading from Strength," *Time* (June 11, 1979); "Germany's Risky Antiinflation Strategy," *Business Week* (July 2, 1979); "Germany: Why It Thrives," *Dun's Review* (Dec. 1979); "Helmut Schmidt Walks the Tightrope," *Wall Street Journal* (April 3, 1980); "All Conservatives Now" (Oct. 11, 1980); "Starting Over: West German Economic Survey," *Economist* (Nov. 8, 1980); "End of the German Miracle," *The Banker* (London: March 1981).

For useful background on Switzerland, see Edgar Bonjour, H.S. Offler, and G.R. Potter, *A Short History of Switzerland* (Oxford, England: Clarendon Press, 1952); Christopher Hughes, *Switzerland* (London: Ernest Benn, 1975); Heinz K. Meier, *Friendship under Stress: U.S.–Swiss Relations, 1900–1950*; Emil Kung, *The Secret of Switzerland's Economic Success* (Washington, D.C.: AEI, 1978); Fritz Leutweiler, *Swiss Monetary and Exchange Rate Policy in an Inflationary World* (Washington, D.C.: AEI, 1978); Fritz Leutweiler, "Interview," *The Banker* (London: Feb. 1979); James Kelder, *How to Open a Swiss Bank Account* (New York: Crowell, 1976); OECD, *Regulations Affecting International Banking Operations of Banks and Non-Banks in France, Germany, Netherlands, Switzerland, and United Kingdom* (Paris: OECD, 1978); OECD, Economic Survey, *Switzerland* (April 1979, Oct. 1980); M.S. Mendelsohn, "The Swiss Turntable," *Money on the Move* (New York, London: McGraw-Hill, 1980); Silvio Borner, "Who Has the Right Monetary Perspective, the OECD or Its Monetarist Critics?" *Kyklos* 32 (1979), pp. 285–306; OECD, *Economic Outlook*, "Switzerland" (Dec. 1980).

Also see Shepard Bancroft Clough, *France; A History of National Economics 1789–1939* (New York: Octagon, 1970); Charles P. Kindleberger, *Economic Growth in France and Britain, 1851–1950* (Cambridge, Mass.: Harvard University Press, 1964); Francois Caron, *An Economic History of Modern France* (New York: Halsted-Wiley, 1975); John and Anne Marie Hackett, *Economic Planning in France* (Cambridge, Mass.: Harvard University Press, 1963); John Sheehan, *An Introduction to the French Economy* (Columbus, Ohio: Merrill, 1969); "Survey on France," *Economist* (Jan. 27, 1979);

OECD Economic Survey, France (May 1980); OECD, Economic Outlook 28, "France" (Dec. 1980); "Giscard Battles a Slump," Time (May 25, 1981).

For more background, see Eli Filip Heckscher, An Economic History of Sweden, trans. Göran Ohlin (Cambridge, Mass.: Harvard University Press, 1954); Kurt Samuelson, From Great Power to Welfare State: 300 Years of Swedish Social Development (London: Allen & Unwin, 1968); Steven Koblik, ed., Sweden's Development from Poverty to Affluence, 1750–1970, trans. Joanne Johnson (Minneapolis: University of Minnesota Press, 1975); John Fry, ed., Limits of the Welfare State: Critical Reviews on Postwar Sweden (Farnborough, England: Saxon House, 1979); Marquis W. Childs, Sweden: The Middle Way on Trial (New Haven: Yale University Press, 1980); OECD, Economic Survey, Sweden (April 1980); OECD, Economic Outlook 28, "Sweden" (Dec. 1980). See also interviews with Myrdal, Rehn, Hedborg, and Edin, "The Crisis of the Swedish Welfare State," Challenge (July–Aug. 1980) and "Forward to the 1890's Sweden: A Survey," Economist (Nov. 15, 1980).

Also see Shepard Bancroft Clough, Economic History of Modern Italy (New York: Columbia University Press, 1964); George H. Hildebrand, Growth and Structure in the Economy of Modern Italy (Cambridge, Mass.: Harvard University Press, 1965); Vera Lutz, Italy, A Study in Economic Development (London, New York: Oxford University Press, 1962); Muriel Grindrod, Italy (London: Oxford University Press, 1964); Josselyn Hennessy, Vera Lutz, and Guisseppe Scimone, Economic Miracles; Studies in the Resurgence of the French, German, and Italian Economies since the Second World War (London: IEA, A. Deutsch, 1964); Paolo Sylos-Labini, Trade Unions, Inflation and Productivity (Farnborough, England: Saxon House, 1974); Michael Arthur Ledeen, Italy in Crisis (Beverly Hills, Calif.: Sage, 1977); Henry Stuart Hughes, The U.S. and Italy, 3rd ed. (Cambridge, Mass.: Harvard University Press, 1979). See also "Italy: Business Shrugs Off the New Political Turmoil," Business Week (Feb. 19, 1979); "Which Italian Economy? Italian Industry Has at Least Three Economies. One of Them Is Doing All Right," (on the "underground" or black market economy) Economist (Dec. 8, 1979); OECD Economic Survey, Italy (March 1980); "Italian Economy: Putting the Boot In" (April 15, 1980); OECD Economic Outlook, "Italy" (Dec. 1980).

For extensive comparative data on Latin America, see reports of the Inter-American Development Bank, for example, Economics and Social Progress in Latin America, 1979 Report (Washington, D.C.: Inter-American Development Bank, 1979) and Economic and Social Progress in Latin America, 1976 Report (ibid., 1976). See also "Latin American Debt: Boosting Growth or Checking It?" Euromoney (Suppl.) (London: April 1981). For more general background on Latin American development and inflation, see the following: Hubert Herring, A History of Latin America, 3rd ed. (New York: Knopf, 1968); Joseph Grunwald, The Alliance for Progress: Invisible Hands in Inflation and Growth (Washington, D.C.: Brookings, 1965); Felipe Pazos y Roque, Chronic Inflation in Latin America (New York: Praeger, 1972); Susan M. Wachter, Latin American Inflation: The Structuralist–Monetarist Debate (Lexington, Mass.: Lexington Books, 1976); Jeannine Swift, Economic Development in Latin America (New York: St. Martin's, 1978); Gustav Donald Jud, Inflation and the Use of Indexation in Developing Countries (New York: Praeger, 1978). See also for general perspectives on the economic development process, Benjamin Higgins, Economic Development: Problems, Principles and Policies, rev. ed. (New York: Norton, 1968); Gerald

M. Meier, ed., *Leading Issues in Economic Development* (New York: Oxford University Press, 1976); William R. Cline and Sidney Weintraub, eds., *Economic Stabilization in Developing Countries* (Washington, D.C.: Brookings, 1981). See also Vicente Galbis, "Inflation and Interest Rate Policies in Latin America, 1967–76," *IMF Staff Papers* 26, no. 2 (June 1979), pp. 334–66; Donald J. Mathieson, "Financial Reform and Stabilization Policy in a Developing Economy," *J. Dev. Econ.* 7 (1980), pp. 359–95; E.J. Sheehey, "Inflation, Unemployment and Expectations in Latin America—Some Simple Tests: Comment," *So. Econ. J.* 45, no. 4 (April 1979), pp. 1292–98.

See the following on Brazil: Celso Furtado, *The Economic Growth of Brazil: A Survey From Colonial to Modern Times* (Berkeley: University of California Press, 1963); Werner Baer, *Industrialization and Economic Development in Brazil* (Homewood, Ill.: Irwin, 1965); Riordan Roett, *Brazil in the Sixties* (Nashville: Vanderbilt University Press, 1972); Georges Andre Fiechter, *Brazil since 1964: Modernization under a Military Regime*, trans. Alan Braley (London: Macmillan, 1975); Donald Eugene Syvrud, *Foundations of Brazilian Economic Growth* (Stanford, Calif.: Hoover Institution Press, 1974); Stefan Hyman Roback, *Brazil, A Study in Development Progress* (Lexington, Mass.: Lexington Books, 1975); Raouf Khalid, *Inflation and Economic Development in Brazil, 1946–63* (Oxford, England: Clarendon Press, 1973); Riordan Roett, *Brazil in the Seventies* (Washington, D.C.: AEI, 1976); William H. Overholt, *The Future of Brazil* (Boulder, Colo.: Westview, 1978); Sylvia Ann Hewlett, *The Cruel Dilemmas of Development: Twentieth-Century Brazil* (New York: Basic, 1980); Antonio Delfim Netto, *Some Aspects of Brazilian Economy* (Brazil: Public Relations Division, Ministry of Planning, Office of the Press, 1980). See also, Dimitri N. Balatsos, "How Brazil Will Stay Afloat in 1981," *Euromoney's Latin American Survey* (April 1981); interview with Pascal Salin, University of Paris, "O Monopolio da Moeda," *Visao* (Sept. 8, 1980); "A Riqueza dos Nacoes em Crise," *Visao* (Sept. 15, 1980); "As Politicos Salarias e O Progresso do Homem," *Visao* (Nov. 10, 1980); interview with Karlos Rischbieter, "O Brasil Perdue Um Ano," *Veja* (Jan. 14, 1981); "A Explosao dos Juros," *Veja* (Feb. 25, 1981).

See on Chile: Markos Mamalakis, *The Growth and Structure of the Chilean Economy: From Independence to Allende* (New Haven: Yale University Press, 1976); L. Edwards, *Economic Development and Reform in Chile: Progress under Frei, 1970–76* (East Lansing, Mich.: Michigan State University Press, 1972); Jere R. Behrman, *Chile* (New York: NBER, Columbia University Press, 1976); Barbara Stallings, *Class Conflict and Economic Development in Chile, 1958–73* (Stanford: Stanford University Press, 1978); Stefan De Vylder, *Allende's Chile: The Political Economy of the Rise and Fall of the Unidad Popular* (New York, Cambridge, England: Cambridge University Press, 1976). See also *Euromoney* (Latin American Suppl.) (April 1981).

See the following on Argentina: Arthur P. Whitaker, *Argentina* (Englewood Cliffs, N.J.: Prentice-Hall, 1964): Federico Pinedo, *Siglo y Medio de Economia Argentina* (Mexico: Centro de Estudios Monetarios Latin Americanos, 1961): Carlos Federico Diaz Alejandro, *Essays on the Economic History of the Argentine Republic* (New Haven: Yale University Press, 1970); Richard D. Mallon, *Economic Policymaking in a Conflict Society: The Argentine Case*, with Juan V. Sounrouville (Cambridge, Mass.: Harvard University Press, 1975); Laura Regina Rosenbaum Randall, *An Economic History of Argentina in the 20th Century* (New York: Columbia University Press, 1978); Gary W. Wynia, *Argentina in the Post War Era: Politics and Economic Policy in a Divided Society* (Albuquerque: University of New Mexico Press, 1978); (April 1981).

For Uruguay, see the following: Simon Gabriel Hanson, *Utopia in Uruguay, Chapters in the Economic History of Uruguay* (New York: Oxford University Press, 1938); George Pendle, *Uruguay, South America's First Welfare State* (London: Royal Institute of Economic Affairs, 1952); George Pendle, *Uruguay* (London: Oxford University Press, 1963); Russell H. Brannon, *The Agricultural Development of Uruguay* (New York: Praeger, 1963); Martin Weinstein, *The Politics of Failure* (Westport, Conn.: Greenwood, 1975); Edy Kaufman, *Uruguay in Transition: From Civilian to Military Rule* (New Brunswick, N.J.: Transaction, 1979).

For Mexico, see the following: Henry Bamford Parkes, *A History of Mexico,* 3rd ed. (Boston: Houghton Mifflin, 1969); Raymond Vernon, *The Dilemma of Mexico's Development: The Roles of Public and Private Sectors* (Cambridge, Mass.: Harvard University Press, 1963); William P. Glade and Charles W. Anderson, *The Political Economy of Mexico* (Madison: University of Wisconsin Press, 1963); Clark Winton Reynolds, *The Mexican Economy; Twentieth Century Structure and Growth* (New Haven: Yale University Press, 1970); Brian Griffiths, *Mexican Monetary Policy and Economic Development* (New York: Praeger, 1972); Roger D. Hanson, *The Politics of Mexican Development* (Baltimore: Johns Hopkins University Press, 1971); Leon Vincent Padgett, *The Mexican Political System* (Boston: Houghton Mifflin, 1976); John K. Thompson, *Inflation, Financial Markets, and Economic Development: The Experience of Mexico* (Greenwich, Conn.: JAI Press, 1979); Antonio Ortiz Mena, *Organized Labor, Wages and Inflation* (Washington, D.C.: Inter-American Development Bank, 1979); Robert E. Looney, *Mexico's Economy: A Policy Analysis with Forecasts to 1990* (Boulder, Colo.: Westview, 1978). "Mexico: Not by Oil Alone," *Euromoney* (Suppl.) (April 1981), describes the policy of gradual stabilization (aided by enlarged oil revenues).

More recent country reports can be found in various OECD *Country Surveys* (Paris: OECD); OECD *Economic Outlook* (Paris: semiannual); IMF *World Economic Outlook* (Washington, D.C.: biannual); World Bank country studies (Washington, D.C.); *International Currency Review* (London: bimonthly); and *The Banker* (London: monthly). See other country sources in chapters 1 and 2.

3. The industrial policy controversy (concern about slowed economic growth, international competitiveness, industrial decline, and structural unemployment) can be traced back to Britain's sluggish economy and worries in the early 1920s through the 1930s. See Keith Middlemas and John Barnes, *Baldwin: A Biography* (London: Macmillan, 1970), for an outstanding and detailed account of British leaders coping with industrial and trade problems, safeguarding, and tariff issues. An important early industrial policy package was Lloyd George's Liberal party proposal, *Britain's Industrial Future* (London: Ernest Benn, 1928), with its emphasis upon unequal trade openness (pp. 48–58). The Liberals admitted that trade barriers had grown significantly, but still hoped for freer trade. In contrast, the Conservatives in the 1920s (led by Baldwin and the Chamberlains, among others), argued that stronger safeguarding was more realistic and needed to rejuvenate British industry. Substantial British protection was legislated in 1931–32, with the Imperial Preference System, after the United States greatly increased protection with the Smoot-Hawley Tariff in 1930.

After post–World War II reconstruction of Europe and the increased prosperity of the European Economic Community (EEC), British economists became worried again in the later 1950s and 1960s about their own relatively sluggish growth.

Industrial policies were much discussed. (See sources cited note 2 and text of chapter 2.)

The U.S. industrial policy debates began somewhat later, after U.S. stagflation and recession in the 1970s. See Lovett, *Inflation and Politics* (cited in note 2), ch. 6, esp. note 25 (at p. 218); and William Lovett, "Competitive Industrial Policies and the World Bazaar", Staff Report, Subcommittee on Economic Stabilization, Committee on Banking, Finance and Urban Affairs, U.S. House of Representatives, 98th Cong., 2nd Sess., Nov. 1984, for an extensive bibliography. Highlights of recent U.S. literature include Barry Bluestone and Bennett Harrison, *The Deindustrialization of America* (New York: Basic, 1982); F. Gerard Adams and Lawrence R. Klein, ed., *Industrial Policies for Growth and Competitiveness* (Lexington, Mass: Lexington Books, 1983); Kevin Phillips, *Staying on Top: The Business Case for a National Industrial Policy* (New York: Random House, 1984); Robert Z. Lawrence, *Can America Compete?* (Washington, D.C.: Brookings, 1984); Otto Eckstein et al., *The DRI Report on U.S. Manufacturing Industries* (New York: McGraw-Hill, 1984); Report of the President's Commission on Industrial Competitiveness, *Global Competition: The New Reality* (Washington, D.C.: GPO, 1985); and Lester Thurow, *The Zero-Sum Solution: Building a World-Class Economy* (New York: Simon and Schuster, 1985).

4. According to recent U.S. Department of Labor sources (*Handbook of Labor Statistics, Monthly Labor Review, and Employment and Earnings*), the United States had a net loss of 1,200,000 manufacturing jobs between 1980 and 1986, nearly 400,000 mining jobs between 1981 and 1986, and 250,000 agricultural jobs between 1980 and 1986. This was offset by another 700,000 construction jobs between 1980 and 1986 and 8 million new private service jobs. Unemployment was 7 percent in 1980, surged to around 10 percent in 1982–83, and was back at 7 percent by the end of 1986. But, these are high levels of unemployment for the United States compared to the 1950s and 1960s. (See table 6–1.)

But, the AFL-CIO complains that these data understate real unemployment by excluding more than 1 million people no longer actively seeking work and by including nearly 6 million part-time workers (many of whom really want full-time jobs). Labor spokespeople also argue that millions of experienced workers have lost high-paying jobs and are unable to equal prior earnings in lower-wage service jobs. The full extent of this earnings loss (number of workers and income reduction) is not entirely clear. (See *The National Economy and Trade*, AFL-CIO policy recommendations for 1986.) But, a U.S. Department of Labor task force recently estimated that about 1 million experienced workers a year for the past seven years were victims of plant closings or long-term layoffs, many in the Rust Belt areas of older industry. David Broder, *New Orleans Times-Picayune* (Jan. 18, 1987), p. 9. See also "The Disposable Employee Is Becoming a Fact of Corporate Life," *Business Week* (Dec. 15, 1986), pp. 52–56.

For concern about the social costs of giving up higher-wage industrial jobs for lower-wage service jobs, with enhanced inequality of incomes, see Richard C. Michel et al., "Are We Better Off in 1984?" *Challenge* (Sept.–Oct. 1984); Bennet Harrison, Chris Tilly, and Barry Bluestone, "Wage Inequality Takes a Great U-Turn," *Challenge* (Mar.–Apr. 1986); and Ray Marshall, *Challenge* (May–June 1986). For conservative and free-market counterarguments, see Patricia E. Beeson and Michael F. Bryan, "The Emerging Service Economy," *Economic Commentary*, Federal Reserve Bank of

Cleveland (June 15, 1986). Yet, what about productivity? The *Wall Street Journal* reflects concern about negligible improvement in service-sector productivity. See Alan Murray, "The Service Sector Productivity Problem—The Outlook," *Wall Street Journal* (Feb. 9, 1987), p. 1.

    5. See chapter 3 (especially notes 11 and 19) and chapter 5.

    6. See chapter 4, especially surrounding table 4–1.

    7. See table I–1.

Acknowledgments

T his book evolved during 1982–86. Important assistance came from visits, teaching, lectures, and conversations in Britain, France, Germany, Switzerland, Italy, Greece, Japan, Korea, Taiwan, Hong Kong, Thailand, Philippines, Singapore, and Canada. Special thanks must be extended to Chuo University and The Institute of Comparative Law in Tokyo (for a sabbatical visit in 1983); to the Mitsubishi Bank Foundation and its sponsorship of a Japan–U.S.–Canada trade study group between 1983 and 1985 (conference papers edited by Professor Mitsuo Matsushita, Professor Thomas Schoenbaum, and Dorinda G. Dallmeyer, *Dynamics of Japanese–United States Trade Relations* [Athens, Ga.: Dean Rusk Center for International and Comparative Law, 1986]), to the Subcommittee on Economic Stabilization, Committee on Banking, Finance, and Urban Affairs, which printed and distributed an early draft (one of two papers written for the Japan–U.S.–Canada study group), "Competitive Industrial Policies and the World Bazaar" (November 1984); to *Stanford Journal of International Law* for its Trade Policy Conference in April 1985, which published an earlier version of chapter 5 as "Managing the World Debt Crisis: Economic Strains and Alternative Solutions," *Stanford Journal of International Law* 21 (Fall 1985); and to the University of Regensburg, Federal Republic of Germany, where I was a guest professor in the 1986 summer term and offered much of this book to students and colleagues in the law and economics faculties during classes and informal discussions. I have tried to understand and learn from the industrial developments and achievements in many of these countries. A desire for intelligent, selective emulation is the highest form of respect.

At Tulane University School of Law, where I have enjoyed eighteen years of teaching, research, and writing, there are many debts of gratitude for encouragement, stimulation, and counsel among friends, students, faculty, and staff. Particular appreciation must be expressed to Professor David Combe, Margareta Horiba, Alice Jones, and the cheerful, talented, and multilingual staff of the Tulane Law Library. No scholarship gets far without excellent library support. Valuable contributions were made by many student research assistants, including Will Allen, Cynthia Brosio, Douglas Brown, Manoj Chhabra, Steven Etkind, Antony Francis Julian, Chich-Heng Kuo, Arturo Lan Arredondo, Miyuki Miyazaki, Javier Parades, Anita Sippy, Reed Smith, Robert Tudor, Susan Micelli Tyler, Stuart Yaeger, and Meong Cho Yang. Finally, special thanks go to Dorothy Adams, Sherry Bacchus, and Stephanie Mitchell, for processing the manuscript, along with Roger Gardner and his lively crew, who reproduced it with speed and unfailing humor.

Acronyms

AEI	American Enterprise Institute
BIS	Bank for International Settlements
BIT	Bilateral Investment Treaty
CAP	Common Agricultural Policy (EEC)
CEPAL	Economic Commission for Latin America (also called ECLA)
CIF	cost insurance freight
CMEA	Council for Mutual Economic Assistance
COMECON	CMEA trade bloc
DITI	Department of International Trade and Industry
DITT	Department of Industry Technology and Trade
ECLA	Economic Commission for Latin America (also called CEPAL)
ECSC	European Coal and Steel Community
EEC	European Economic Community (Common Market)
EFTA	European Free Trade Area
EMS	European Monetary System
ERISA	Employee Retirement and Security Act
ESOP	employee stock-ownership plan
FAS	free-along-side
FDIC	Federal Deposit Insurance Corporation
FSLIC	Federal Savings and Loan Insurance Corporation
G-5	Group of Five (United States, United Kingdom, Japan, West Germany, and France)
GAB	General Arrangements to Borrow

GAO	General Accounting Office (U.S.)
GATT	General Agreement on Tariffs and Trade
GIC	Government Industry Council
GSP	generalized system of preferences
HMSO	Her Majesty's Stationery Office (U.K.)
IDA	International Development Association
IMF	International Monetary Fund
ITC	International Trade Commission (U.S.)
ITO	International Trade Organization
LDC	less developed country
LIBOR	London interbank rate
METO	Mid-East Treaty Organization
MFA	Multifibre Agreement
MFN	most-favored nation
MIC	mature industrialized country
MITI	Ministry of International Trade and Industry (Japan)
MNC	multinational corporation
MNE	multinational enterprise
NATO	North Atlantic Treaty Organization
NEDC	National Economic Development Council
NIC	newly industrialized country
NIEO	New International Economic Order
NIP	New Industrial Policy
NTB	nontariff barrier
OECD	Organization for Economic Cooperation and Development
OEEC	Organization for European Economic Cooperation
OMA	orderly marketing arrangement
OMB	Office of Manpower and Budget (U.S.)
OTA	Office of Technology Assessment (U.S.)
POSCO	Pohang Iron and Steel Company (South Korea)
SDI	Strategic Defense Initiative (U.S.)
SDR	special drawing right
SEATO	Southeast Asia Treaty Organization

SIBOR	Singapore interbank rate
UNRRA	United Nations Relief Rehabilitation Agency
URPE	Union of Radical Political Economy
USTR	U.S. Trade Representative
VAT	value-added tax
VRA	voluntary restraint agreement

Introduction:
The International Setting

During 1984 through 1986, the U.S. trade deficit surged to record levels, reaching $123, $143, and $170 billion, respectively, in these years. Imports increased from $250 to $387 billion between 1980 and 1986, while exports held at around $215 billion. (See table I–1.) Sources of this imbalance were greatly enlarged federal budget deficits exceeding $200 billion annually (nearly 5 percent of a $4,100 billion GNP), tight monetary policy and high interest rates (needed partly to offset increased deficits), and a seriously overvalued dollar (competing against an undervalued yen).[1] Unequal growth rates played a role, with faster U.S. recovery in 1983–84, and more sluggishness for other countries. In addition, many complained that U.S. markets were more open than most other countries', and that developing and newly industrialized countries, along with Japan and others, were subsidizing exports aggressively with favored financing, low interest rates, R&D support, and skillful export promotion. The United States suffered productivity problems in many industries, plus weakened competitiveness. While service sectors in the United States grew nicely, with employment increasing from 80 to 92 million, manufacturing suffered sluggishness and reduced exports, with employment declining from 20.3 to 19.1 million between 1980 and 1986, as shown in table I–2.[2] To what extent was deindustrialization coming to the United States? How, if at all, should government respond to this situation?

While many families enjoyed increased prosperity, others lost good salaries or had incomes cut, and some cities and towns endured heavier unemployment and demoralization. Smokestack America became the label for depressed or dying industries and decaying communities. During 1985–86, a political reaction grew stronger, combined with an overall recovery that slowed significantly from the 1983–84 revival that helped reelect Ronald Reagan's free-market–oriented administration in November 1984. By August 1985, political opponents started to smell blood in the water concerning the trade issue. In fall 1985, the Reagan administration began to change its tune, under Secretary of the Treasury Baker's leadership, by joining a growing chorus for greater fairness in international trade.[3]

Table I–1
Changing U.S. Regional Trade Balances, 1960–86
(in $ billions)

	1986ᵃ		1985		1984		1983	
	Imports	Exports	Imports	Exports	Imports	Exports	Imports	Exports
Western Europe	92	62	84	57	75	58	56.4	56
Canada	70	44	69	47	67	46	52.5	38.2
Japan	87	28	72	23	60	23	43.6	21.9
China	5.3	4	4.2	4	3.4	3	5.2	2.2
Southeast Asia	4.8	3.5	3.3	3	3.5	3.1	2.8	2.9
Other Eastern Asia	59	24	53	22	52	24	40.9	23
Latin America	42	29	45	28	44	26	37.3	22.6
Near East	11	8.5	6.6	9.7	9	11	7.5	13.8
Africa	10.5	6	12.5	7.4	15	9	15.2	8.8
Australia and Oceania	4	6.4	4.1	6.4	4	6	3.4	4.8
Eastern Europe, Soviet Union	2	2.1	2.1	3.2	2.4	4.2	1.5	2.9
Total	387.8	217.3	361	213	341	217	270	200

	1980		1976		1970		1960	
	Imports	Exports	Imports	Exports	Imports	Exports	Imports	Exports
Western Europe	48.9	67.5	24.3	32.4	11.2	14.5	4.2	6.3
Canada	42	35.4	27.5	24.1	11.1	9.1	2.9	3.6
Japan	33	20.8	16.9	10.1	5.9	4.7	1.1	1.3
China	1.2	3.8	3.3	1.63	.055	.053	.02	.11
Southeast Asia	1.6	2.7	1.02	1.7	.041	.093	.032	.83
Other Eastern Asia	30.2	21	15	8.56	3	3.1	.905	.86
Latin America	31.2	36	14	10.2	3.4	.4	1.3	1.5
Near East	18.3	11.9	10	9.2	.3	1.3	.3	.8
Africa	33.6	9	13.5	9	1.1	1.6	.5	.8
Australia and Oceania	3.8	4.9	1.9	2.7	.9	.9	.3	.5
Eastern Europe, Soviet Union	1.6	3.9	.9	3.5	.2	.4	.1	.2
Total	253	221	121	115	40	43	15	17

Source: 1976–85 figures: U.S. Department of Commerce, Highlights of U.S. Export and Import Trade, FT 990 (Dec. 1976, 1980, 1983, 1984, 1985, July 1986); imports: CIF., value basis; Exports: FAS. value basis. 1970 figures: U.S. Department of Commerce, U.S. Exports and U.S. Imports (Dec. 1970) (all customs value basis). 1960 figures: U.S. Department of Commerce, United States Imports of Merchandise for Consumption, Calendar Year 1960, ET 120, and United States Exports of Domestic and Foreign Merchandise, Calendar Year 1960, FT 420 (all customs value basis). 1986 figures: U.S. Department of Commerce Survey of Current Business (Dec. 1986); New York Times (Oct. 31, 1986, Dec. 10, 1986); Business Week (Dec. 15, 1986) Wall Street Journal (Feb. 2, 1987).
ᵃ Estimated.

Table I-2
U.S. Labor Force and Employment, 1952–86
(in millions)

	Total Employed	Resident Armed Forces	Agriculture	Construction	Mining	Manufacturing	Private Service	Civilian Federal	State and Local Government	Unemployment Rates
1952	62.6	2.4	6.5	2.6	0.87	16.2	25.4	2.4	4.2	2.9%
1960	67.6	1.9	5.5	2.9	0.71	16.8	28.8	2.3	6.1	5.4
1968	78.2	2.3	3.8	3.4	0.61	19.8	32.3	2.7	9.1	5.5
1976	90.4	1.7	3.3	3.6	0.78	19.0	41.2	2.7	12.1	7.6
1980	100.9	1.6	3.4	4.3	1.0	20.3	51.5	2.9	13.4	7.0
1981	102.0	1.6	3.4	4.2	1.1	20.2	49.6	2.8	13.3	7.5
1982	101.2	1.7	3.4	3.9	1.1	18.8	49.9	2.7	13.1	9.5
1983	102.5	1.7	3.4	3.9	0.96	18.5	50.9	2.8	13.1	9.6
1984	106.7	1.7	3.3	4.4	0.97	19.4	53.7	2.8	13.2	7.5
1985	108.8	1.7	3.2	4.7	0.93	19.3	56.3	2.9	13.4	7.1
1986	112.1	1.8	3.2	5.0	0.75	19.1	59.5	2.9	14.0	7.0

Source: U.S. Department of Labor, Bureau of Labor Statistics, *Handbook of Labor Statistics* (June 1985), table 63; U.S. Department of Labor, Bureau of Labor Statistics, *Monthly Labor Review* (monthly), table 13; U.S. Department of Labor, Bureau of Labor Statistics, *Employment and Earnings*, (monthly), table A–1.

Note: The 1986 figures are based on October and November 1986.

Trade policy was now a major issue. Linkages between imports, currency values, budget deficits, jobs, and prosperity were increasingly discussed. Interest groups were becoming aroused, including labor, farmers, business (domestic and those involved in foreign trade), multinational corporations, banks and financial institutions, and families with varied resources. Foreign governments and trade associations had become powerful lobbyists, too. In all of this, a widespread uncertainty was evident. How healthy was the U.S. economy? Was the world trade system in good order? Were corrective adjustments needed for trade equity, improved financing, and/or investment and development?

Meanwhile, U.S. trade balances turned adverse with major trading partners. The five major trade partners for the United States (Western Europe, Canada, Japan, the rest of East and South Asia, and Latin America) each swung into substantial trade surpluses against the United States between 1983 and 1985, as shown in table I–1.

None of these trading partners were eager to reverse the imbalances. Each felt more comfortable generating export surpluses with the United States, which could be spent on greater imports from other nations. How and when could a reasonable overall balance in trade be achieved? And, how would trade balances be affected with these major trading partners? Simple arithmetic suggested that a $25–35 billion swing in exports or imports with each major trading area might be needed to restore the overall U.S. trade balance. But, no major trading partner wanted any big changes in trade flows.

Aggravating these difficulties was a serious world debt-overload crisis, involving at least sixty nations, which greatly complicated matters.[4] Most overloaded debtors are developing new industrial countries, particularly in Latin America and Africa. These countries found it hard to increase imports from the United States and wanted more liberal rescheduling terms, along with renewed credits. Also, their exports needed growth to restore debt service. But, they already were overloaded with debts and tended to ration imports mainly to productive capital investments and consumption essentials. Hence, it seemed unlikely that the developing countries could do much to reduce the U.S. trade payments imbalance problems.

The world began heavy net lending and investment flows to the United States in the early 1980s, which led to the United States becoming a net debtor nation again during 1985, for the first time since World War I.[5] Much of the recent U.S. trade and budget deficits have been financed by foreign short-term borrowing, exploiting comparatively high U.S. interest rates and a reputation for financial security (including U.S. banks and thrift institutions, with generous FDIC and FSLIC insurance guarantees of $100,000 for each separate depositor). But, most observers realize this cannot go on indefinitely. Heavy foreign borrowing by the United States could be only a medium-term expedient.

The rest of the world, in effect, was financing big new U.S. deficits by accepting increased dollar balances, more securities, and bigger indebtedness from the United States at attractive interest rates. In the special circumstances of 1982–86, with recession followed by incomplete revival, uneven recoveries abroad, capital flight, and insecurities in many places, this could be tolerated, even to some extent welcomed. But over time, growing dollar balances and dollar-denominated interest payments would be a depreciating asset, especially if issued to excess in massive volumes. One way or another, these exceptional, large U.S. payments deficits, trade deficits, and budget deficits would have to be corrected and substantially eliminated reasonably soon.

Corrective Adjustments

The traditional adjustment mechanism for serious balance of payment disequilibria is exchange rate realignment.[6] For deficit countries, this means depreciation of their currencies, which reduces their ability to import from abroad and enhances export potential. Thus, according to international economics, a substantial deficit nation, such as the United States lately, should suffer a declining value in its currency. For the past several years, most observers have been expecting the dollar to fall, sooner or later, from its substantial recent appreciation. Between the previous low for the dollar (Summer 1980) and February 1985, the dollar appreciated 220 percent against the French franc, 160 percent against the British pound, 95 percent against the deutsche mark, and 82 percent against the Swiss franc, though only 22 percent against the Japanese yen. The dollar's roller coaster since 1967 is reflected in figures I–1 and I–2 and in appendix table A–11.

Finally, softening of the dollar began during Spring 1985. Then, a more substantial slump, reaching 5 to 10 percent against key currencies, occurred by July and August 1985. This was followed by further weakening, endorsed by the finance ministers and central bank governors from the Group of 5 (G-5) industrial nations—United States, Japan, Britain, Germany, and France—after their September 22, 1985, meeting in New York. Their joint statement recognized that "the U.S. has a large and growing current account deficit, and Japan, and to a lesser extent Germany, large and growing current account surpluses." They concluded that "exchange rates should better reflect fundamental conditions. . . . Further orderly appreciation of the main non-dollar currencies against the dollar is desirable."[7] In addition, the finance ministers and governors pledged collaboration to promote noninflationary economic growth, lower interest rates, open markets, resistance to protectionism, and continued financing of developing countries (appropriate to each case). They agreed that, "in countries where the budget deficit is too high, further measures to reduce the deficit [are] urgently required."[8] Most market analysts saw this G-5 undertaking as supporting a gradual, "soft-landing" scenario for a declining dollar, with reduced world market interest rates and improving economic growth. By the

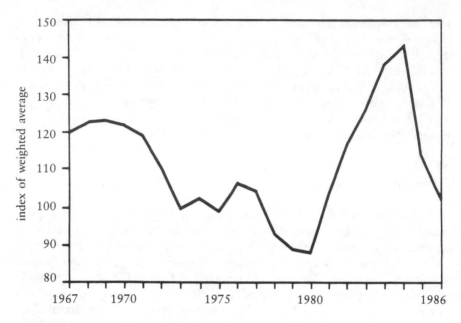

Source: Board of Governors of the Federal Reserve Board, *Federal Reserve Bulletin* (monthly); *Federal Reserve Statistical Release*, November 28, 1986.

Note: March 1973 = 100.

Figure I–1. The Exchange Value of the U.S. Dollar, 1967–86

spring of 1987, significant realignment had occurred, with substantial devaluation of the dollar against the yen, deutsche mark and Swiss franc.[9] But experts disagreed on how much more, if any, realignment of currencies would be desirable.

Unfortunately, large U.S. budget deficits were more difficult to eliminate than financial observers hoped. The Reagan administration has been reluctant to raise taxes, cut defense spending, or invite unpopularity by proposing significant reductions in social security and other specific outlays. Democrats sought, from the other direction, to force the blame for painful budget reductions on the administration; they preferred some tax increases and different spending priorities. A stubborn impasse has been developing since 1982, which might require a more decisive political resolution among conservatives, liberals, and moderates before the structural or excessive budget deficits in the United States can be seriously reduced. Although in November 1985, the U.S. Congress passed the Gramm–Rudman budget resolution which would mandate $36 billion deficit cuts every year between 1986 and 1991, this represented slow progress toward balanced budgets. And implementation proved difficult. With a Democratic Senate and House elected in 1986, and a major conflict ahead for the presidential election of 1988, few expected large deficit reductions

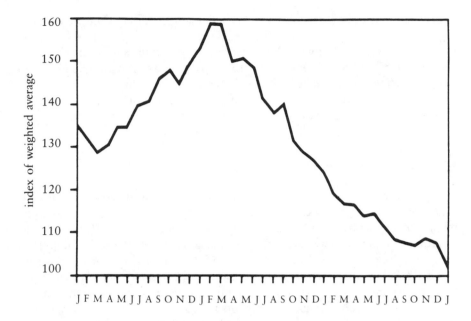

Source: Board of Governors of the Federal Reserve Board, *Federal Reserve Bulletin* (monthly); *Federal Reserve Statistical Release*, November 28, 1986.
Note: March 1973 = 100.

Figure I–2. The Exchange Value of the U.S. Dollar, Jan. 1984–Jan. 1987

quickly. Many domestic and foreign observers considered this leisurely progress toward fiscal balance to be irresponsible, although U.S. politicians found it difficult to do better.[10]

This means that substantial U.S. international borrowing, upward pressure on its interest rates, and large trade deficits may continue significantly longer than most economists believe desirable. Much should depend upon Federal Reserve monetary policies, which reflect conflicting pressures to ease interest rates and promote more economic growth, and, on the other hand, to resist any sudden collapse of the dollar's value or any significant revival of inflation. To some degree, this places U.S. monetary authorities in an awkward dilemma. Most observers want a soft-landing scenario for the dollar, though, with more or less gradual decline. Monetary authorities in other strong economies (such as Japan, West Germany, and Switzerland) also influence relative exchange rates, and their intervention probably would help limit any drastic, disruptive dollar decline (or rapid appreciation in their own currencies).

In these circumstances, slow exchange rate realignments to reduce the dollar, restrict U.S. imports, and expand exports may not bring prompt adjustments to eliminate the U.S. trade and payments deficits. Recent trends toward expanding imports from East Asia, newly industrialized countries, and less developed nations may continue, along with further import penetration into U.S. manufacturing sectors and movement of jobs to branch plants abroad. The extent to which growing service and distribution sectors can absorb such displacement is an important issue. In this situation, it may not be easy to keep protectionist and/or improved trade equity pressures in line.[11]

Competing Industrial-Trade Policies

Many economists emphasize the role of competing and divergent industrial-trade policies in the present world economy.[12] Certainly, most nations recognize that systematic industrial development, trade expansion, and economic growth are major objectives of government policy. Successful policies in Japan, Taiwan, South Korea, Singapore, and Hong Kong during the past few decades have attracted special interest. European and Commonwealth nations have employed industrial policies more recently, with somewhat mixed results. Most Latin American governments have stressed economic growth also, but typically with restrictive policies that limited foreign investment and competition; moreover, their government deficits and inflation were frequently excessive, with many inefficient state enterprises and performance that was often disappointing, particularly since the world recession and debt crisis of the early 1980s. Most African countries sought economic development after independence in the 1960s, but their results are even more divergent, often with excessive indebtedness, insecurity, and limited progress in many areas.

General industrial policy lessons are that productivity improvement, industrial expansion, and overall growth for the economy can justify helpful investments, tax relief, export subsidies, joint ventures, and infrastructure support, so long as net social benefit can be established. Infant-industry tariffs or import restrictions, special financing, and adjustment relief to promote improved technology and resiliency also may be appropriate within this framework. National security interests, within limits, can justify support for basic industries and services important to military strength and survival potential. On the other hand, sustained protection for inefficient industries that cannot survive world market competition makes little sense—except for essential national security interests.

Countries with limited economic development and low wages find broad opportunities for such infant-industry nurturing and support efforts, often more than their capital resources and labor talents effectively exploit. As they progress and prosper, however, greater potential can be mobilized. During the past fifteen to twenty years, many new industrial countries forged ahead this way. These nations, along with Japan, have gained a substantial share of the world's industrial markets, and this trend should continue. Inevitably, this competitive pressure impacts, in varying degrees, upon more advanced industrial countries, with some displacement effects for their labor and enterprises. Hopefully, these adjustment burdens may be eased by shifting into higher productivity industries, but increased world market rivalry, discount pricing, and technological progress bring awkward risks and complications.

Protectionist and Mercantilist Momentum

Systematic industrial expansion and export promotion policies among developing nations have been successful in many areas, but this challenge for mature industrial countries (and less successful developing nations) naturally leads to pressures for counterprotection and adjustment relief.[13] Even though tariffs have been substantially reduced for most industrial nations, nontariff barriers, widespread subsides and tax concessions, voluntary restraint agreements, and bilateral dealings (and countertrade requirements) for many nations remain very significant. Manifestly, trade liberalization is incomplete and, in some areas, stalled. For financial markets, the world debt crisis complicated recent trends toward multinational enterprise and makes these investment arrangements less secure. While most governments of industrial nations are eager to avoid any costly contractions of trade, finance, or credit, the present imbalances in world trade, uneven economic recoveries and growth, extensive budget deficits, and related debt overloads place significant strains upon the established system.

Accumulated progress toward multinational prosperity, trading, and investment flows could be reversed if there were any major spread of heavy protectionism, trade wars, bilateralism, and/or breakdown in credit financing. On the other hand, it seems clear that limited, reasonable safeguard relief and voluntary restraint agreements (VRAs) that ease excessive industrial displacement or rapid dislocations need not seriously impede the gradual diversification of world trade and economic prosperity. The more important questions that trade and finance experts face are how to sustain and, if necessary, restore healthier momentum toward more balanced, widely shared growth that characterized the world economy through the late 1950s, the 1960s, and much of the 1970s. This requires realistic evaluation of the present economic order, and incomplete consensus about these arrangements.

Incomplete Consensus on the World Trade-Financial Order

Among most economists, there is considerable agreement about the desirability of relatively open markets, comparative advantage, and international specialization as aids to efficiency and productivity.[14] The basic ideals of GATT (open and nondiscriminatory trading) seem to command substantial support. But, at this juncture in international economic relations, uneven recoveries, heavy trade imbalances, widespread debt overloads, and excessive budget deficits put stress upon the system and increase controversy on how to ease adjustments and cope with difficulties.

Most developing and Third-World countries complain of insufficient new credit lately, and many feel unable to make heavy debt-service payments now. In Latin America, IMF "disciplines" have become very unpopular, although multinational banks are unwilling to lend much additional credit without firm rescheduling and eventual repayment assurances. Most of these nations could use substantially more multinational credits from the World Bank and IMF, but multinational banks and the Reagan administration resisted—until Fall 1985—greater liberality (fearing excessive inflation, unsound state enterprises, and rivalry with private enterprise). However, at the September 1985 IMF meetings in Seoul, Korea, U.S. Secretary of the Treasury Baker proposed additional bank and multinational credits of $29 billion within the next three years. This was a more liberal outlook, favoring increased liquidity to sustain the rescheduling process. Whether this is sufficient remains doubtful, but most countries welcomed a new flexibility and pragmatism from the United States.

In retrospect, most experts agree that many developing nations borrowed too much in the later 1970s–early 1980s. The burdens of excessive debt loads— and their relief—must be shared, somehow, between borrowers and lenders amid the worldwide credit crunch, high interest rates, and recession of the 1980s. Unfortunately, the consequences of these debt overloads may reduce the pace of economic revival and development in the later 1980s and beyond, unless stronger bridge loans are mobilized to sustain world trade and prosperity—an issue discussed in chapters 4 and 5.

With respect to trade policies, important disagreements remain, as detailed in chapters 1 through 3. Most developing countries would like stronger, preferential access to export markets in advanced industrial nations; they worry about limits and resistance to these imports by threatened labor unions and domestic industries. But, present GATT arrangements already allow more latitude for LDC export subsidies, infant-industry tariffs and import restrictions, excises on imported consumer goods, and related policies among developing nations than for advanced industrial countries. Greater tolerance for subsidies, dumping, and mercantilist practices among the poorer LDCs seems likely to continue. And yet, increasing objections are being raised against these practices when employed by the more successful NICs, such as South Korea, Taiwan, Hong Kong, and Singapore. More open markets and trade liberalization may be expected for such middle-income, successful nations. Failure to improve trade balances by these nations could easily lead to some countermeasures from the United States, Europe, and other advanced industrial nations.

Advanced industrial countries mainly support broad trade, investment, and financial flows among nations, provided that they share adequately in this progress. But, significant elements within these countries that suffer displacement (such as declining industries, areas, and labor unions) naturally seek adjustment relief or protection from these adversities. Nations retaining more growth momentum suffer less of this malaise, but the weaker economies seek more protection or want reindustrialization policies comparable to those utilized by LDCs and NICs for industrial enhancement and export growth. The United States now reflects this range of views, with most MNCs and multinational banks supporting freer trade, while many domestic business, labor, and regional interests demand new industrial policies, improved trade equity, tougher trade bargaining, or even protectionism as means of restoring a healthier U.S. trade balance and strong economic growth.

With respect to Japan–U.S. trade, serious conflict has developed.[15] Among Americans, there is a widespread view that Japan's financing system (low interest rates, highly leveraged companies, and its tax structure) gives significant advantages to Japanese companies in export trade rivalry. Government R&D support, distress cartels, and other assistance is often strategic. Further advantage to Japan flows from a large, secure domestic market that is relatively impervious to substantial imports of unwanted foreign manufactures. While its tariffs are low (NTBs), cartelistic marketing restrictions, cultural loyalty, and language barriers limit foreign access to Japanese markets. Meanwhile, Japanese companies skillfully combine branch plant operations in low-wage countries with their own production to offer efficient, well-priced goods in world markets (at prices sometimes lower than in the home market). In addition, Japanese capital markets have been somewhat insulated from foreign participation, including restrictions against aggressive entry by U.S. multinational banks and securities firms. On the other hand, the Japanese do not see such practices as unfair or unreasonable, especially since their land area is small, with limited natural resources, while a high-skilled manufacturing-trade role is essential for them. Contemporary Japanese see their recent industrial growth and expansion as a well-deserved reward for hard work, efficiency, and sensible long-range planning.

If the overall U.S. trade imbalance were modest, little current account deficit existed, and less aggressive import penetration were occurring, U.S. trade policy would be less interesting. But, these problems along with large trade imbalances with Japan and East Asia are heavily discussed now. Among many financial analysts, the recent high dollar and big U.S. budget deficits are seen as major causes of imbalance, together with softness in parts of U.S. industry. But, higher U.S. wage levels have been a real problem, too, especially when exaggerated by an artificially high dollar. On the other hand, a significant slowdown in U.S. wage trends, weaker unions, lower taxes on business, and more productivity-related profit-sharing improvements are seen (by some) as constructive, strengthening developments for the long term (even though organized labor has felt aggrieved).

Now, the large U.S. trade and current account imbalances are appreciated as serious problems by most countries, because such imbalances cannot last indefinitely. U.S. capital imports and borrowing at $100 billion or more annually is a growing burden for the U.S. economy and diverts needed capital resources from less prosperous developing countries. One way or another, currency realignments and/or altered trade policies should try to restore substantial balance to the U.S. trade and payments accounts within a few years.

Lately, the Japanese, Korean, and Taiwan governments have been promoting greater imports from the United States and some capital market liberalization.[16] Whether much can happen without greater currency realignment (more significant dollar devaluation) is debatable. (But, the Japanese, Europeans, and many NICs fear the job losses associated with more drastic dollar devaluation, and more drastic devaluation could be disruptive for the United States, too.) Some capital market liberalization has occurred also, especially allowing larger short-term borrowing from Japan. But, whether East Asian governments are willing to allow major invasions by U.S. banks and securities firms on a large scale is doubtful.

In Western Europe, with greater influence from trade unions and higher unemployment levels (averaging 10 percent in many countries), protectionism and limits upon substantial import displacement have become a strong force in recent years.[17] Industrial policy traditions are stronger in Europe than in the United States. And, the recent entries of Greece, Spain, and Portugal into the EEC may accentuate a tendency for Western Europe, together with African and Middle Eastern nations, to become a natural, complementary trading area. From East Asia's viewpoint, Europe may be a less promising export-growth area than the Americas, because of tougher protectionism within Europe's trading area.

All this puts even greater emphasis upon the need for a more balanced, mutually reliable, and sustainable trading and finance environment for the United States and its friends. Trade among nations expanded greatly in recent decades, but recent imbalances and potential strains need careful attention. The entire world, along with most elements in U.S. society, have a great stake in improving U.S. fiscal and monetary policies, creating healthier trade balances, and achieving a more secure financing system.

Alternative Trade and Industrial Policies for the United States

Three main camps emerged in the growing United States debate over trade and industrial policies: (1) free market globalism, (2) improved trade equity and/or stronger industrial policy, and (3) protectionism, adjustment relief, and basic industry safeguards.[18] The first theme has been predominant in the post–World

War II era, but increasing support is developing for the other outlooks. Differences between them are rooted somewhat in ideology, but also in the interest group alliances being represented.

A serious reexamination of U.S. foreign economic policy is involved as well. Underlying this reassessment is increased awareness that the United States is no longer the dominating industrial and financial power of the world. Its extraordinary economic lead after World War II, with much of Europe and East Asia devastated or badly disrupted, could not last forever. And, with the revival of German industry and EEC prosperity in the 1950s–70s, the recovery and rapid growth of Japan, plus more recent industrial success in Taiwan, Korea, Singapore, Hong Kong, and other new industrial countries, the balance of industrial and financial power has shifted, with more competition and rivalry in most world markets. Even the Communist countries are significant for international trade and finance, with appreciable growth and a sizeable share of global production.

How, if at all, should U.S. trade, tax, and industrial policies be altered in this different situation? Should the United States continue to rely primarily upon free trade and open investment flows—even if most developing and newly industrialized countries restrict imports and investments by foreigners and subsidize industrial exports significantly—and even if European, Japanese, and other industrial markets are not as open as U.S. markets? Should the United States go it alone with faith in laissez faire?

Should the United States press for more equal openness in world trade and investment flows? Is it realistic to expect much change in foreign government policies? How much bargaining leverage does the United States enjoy? Would the United States be wiser to use more import and investment restrictions and/or export subsidies itself as bargaining leverage or to improve trade equity? What limits can and should be placed on these trade restrictions?

To what extent should the United States employ Japanese-style industrial and trade development strategies? How successful can government–industrial collaboration be for policy making, industrial development, and trade promotion? Are adversarial conflicts necessary or desirable? How can collaboration be improved with reasonable accountability? Why have some countries been more successful than others?

In recent years, most Americans have realized that productivity discipline, renewed technological progress, and overall efficiency are essential for prosperity. How can these traditional virtues be strengthened? What tax and spending policies are most suitable? How can frictions between capital, management, and labor be minimized to the general advantage of most citizens? Would improved access to profit sharing and/or employee stock ownership programs (ESOPs) be constructive? How should this be arranged? What are the best ways to restore healthy savings and productive investment disciplines?

To what extent is it a problem that countries select varied industrial, tax, and trade policies? Do divergent national policies create conflicts that require corrective adjustments or responses by other nations? To what extent are multinational corporations, investment flows, financial transactions, and tax havens desirable? How should they be regulated to mutual advantage by parent and host countries? How can multinational domicile be regulated and supervised?

What kinds of macroeconomic, fiscal, and monetary policies are most suitable? Are recent U.S. macroeconomic policies well adapted to the realities of world market rivalry? Are large U.S. budget deficits consistent with healthy stimulus for U.S. exports, industry, and trade? How can fiscal responsibility come more quickly to the United States? To what extent is the dollar's instability a roller coaster of unreliable and destabilizing liquidity for the U.S. itself and for its economic allies and trading partners?

How should debt overloads and rescheduling be dealt with in world banking and credit markets? How should additional credit and liquidity be infused into the system? To what extent are defaults likely? How can these burdens and risks be minimized? How can inflation be kept under control or even eliminated for those nations still suffering rapid inflation? What stabilization policies have been most successful? How can excessive government spending be brought into reasonable balance with revenues and noninflationary liquidity creation?

Prospects for Moderate Consensus

This book is based on prospects for an evolving U.S. consensus on these issues. While each of the foregoing problems leads to expert literature with diverse views, there is more common ground than many realize. What might seem to uninitiated observers of international economics to be a very complicated, perhaps unmanageable list of problems is now becoming more susceptible to substantial, coordinated resolution. And, in fact, the prospects—even necessity—for forthright attack on these problems of our world economy are stronger lately, especially after the September 1985 meetings of the G-5 powers and IMF meetings in Seoul, Korea, in October 1985. But the United States may take the lead in putting its own house in order. We should provide a more realistic example for other nations and thereby help achieve a more durable, better-balanced trade and finance regime.

Most international economists, bankers, and major corporate executives plus a growing number of government and political leaders now understand the mutual interdependence of world prosperity, finance, and trade. Able historians warn of the follies in past economic breakdowns and excessive national selfishness. The potential for a new, more realistic accommodation is gradually taking shape. This does not mean, of course, that a single, grand conclave of nations can or will gather to settle every outstanding question. Rather, what seems to be crystalizing is a revised framework for mutual accommodation, with an opportunity for stronger U.S. policy. The task of this book, accordingly, is to propose substantial improvements in U.S. national and international economic policy.

Notes

1. For U.S. budget deficits, see tables 6–1 and 6–2. For rapid growth in U.S. government debts between 1980 and 1986, see table 6–3. U.S. interest rates (discounted for inflation) were significantly higher than Japan's between 1978 and 1986 and also somewhat higher than West Germany's and Switzerland's after 1980. See table 4–3. These interest rate differentials attracted substantial foreign capital movements into the United States to help pay for its budget deficits and to cover growing trade and current account deficits. (See tables I–1, 5–1, and 5–2, and appendix table A–12).

An excellent graphic breakdown of the impact of higher U.S. interest rates between 1979 and 1986 is set forth in IMF, *World Economic Outlook* (Oct. 1986), p. 3 (chart 1). This shows how U.S. monetary policy and interest rates helped raise world market rates, with significantly higher U.S. real rates (rates discounted for inflation) between 1981 and 1985.

2. See sources cited in preface note 4.

3. The Plaza Agreement of September 1985 and the accord among Group of Five (G-5) (United States, Japan, West Germany, France, and Britain) finance ministers and central bank leaders to encourage a substantially lower dollar were triggered by increasingly strong protectionist pressures in the U.S. Congress. Rising U.S. trade deficits could have become even worse without significant realignment of currencies (and a substantial fall in the dollar). By early 1987, the yen, deutsche mark, and Swiss franc (the strongest foreign currencies) had appreciated roughly 40 percent against the dollar since the dollar's recent peak in Feb. 1985.

But, why did the U.S. trade deficit not improve significantly? First, NIC currencies and commodity prices are still pegged mostly to the dollar. This means that NIC exports are still strongly encouraged. Second, Japan, West Germany, and other strong industrial rivals of the United States benefit from substantially lower import prices (especially since their buying power improves with currency appreciation), which eases some costs of production and allows their exports to continue. Third, significant lags are common in the gradual adjustment process that follows currency devaluation in a country with substantial trade deficits (especially when foreign products enjoy advantages due to quality and reputation). Fourth, many U.S. manufacturers reduced their export activities in recent years after being discouraged by competitiveness problems.

4. See chapter 4, especially table 4–1 and extensive sources cited.

5. By the end of 1986, U.S. net external debt reached $200 billion. See Kenneth Gilpin, "What the Dollar's Latest Slide Means," *New York Times*, Jan. 15, 1987, p. 34. See also chapter 5, infra, especially tables 5–1, 5–2, and 5–3.

6. See, for example, standard texts in international economics such as Charles Kindleberger and Peter Lindert, *International Economics*, 7th ed. (Homewood, Ill.: Irwin, 1982), chapters 14–21.

7. See the text of the G-5 Plaza Agreement (or communique), *IMF Survey* (Washington, D.C.: Oct. 7, 1985), pp. 296–97.

8. Ibid, p. 296.

9. See figure I–2 and appendix table A–11 in this book. See also Peter Kilborn, "U.S. Upsets Allies by Seeming to Let Dollar Slump," *New York Times*, Jan. 15, 1987, p. 1 (and related stories).

10. For more details on U.S. budget problems, see chapter 6, around tables 6–1, 6–2, and 6–3.

11. The G-5 Plaza Agreement emphasized the dangers of protectionism. *IMF Survey*, Oct. 7, 1985, pp. 296–97.

12. See Adams and Klein (cited in preface note 3) for a balanced review of industrial policy experience in many countries, together with other sources cited therein. See also Bruce Scott and George Lodge, ed., *U.S. Competitiveness in the World Economy* (Cambridge, Mass.: Harvard Business School Press, 1985); Chikara Higashi, *Japanese Trade Policy Formulation* (New York: Praeger, 1983); David Yoffie, *Power and Protectionism: Strategies of the Newly Industrializing Countries* (New York: Columbia Univ. Press, 1983); Alexis Jaquemin, ed., *European Industry: Public Policy and Corporate Strategy* (Oxford, England: Clarendon, 1984); Robert Driscoll and Jack Behrman, *National Industrial Policies* (Cambridge, Mass.: Oelgeschlager, Gunn & Hain, 1984); Chalmers Johnson, *The Industrial Policy Debate* (San Francisco: Inst. for Contemporary Studies, 1984); Japan Productivity Center, *Measuring Productivity: Trends and Comparisons from the First International Productivity Symposium* (New York: Unipub, 1983); William Baumol and Kenneth McLennan, *Productivity Growth and U.S. Competitiveness* (New York: Oxford Univ. Press, 1985); Richard Rosecrance, *The Rise of The Trading State: Commerce and Conquest in the Modern World* (New York: Basic, 1986); Gunnar Sjostedt and Bengt Sundelius, eds., Swedish Institute of International Affairs, *Free Trade—Managed Trade* (Boulder, Colo., and London: Westview, 1986); John Culbertson, *International Trade and the Future of the West* (Madison, Wis.: 21st Century, 1984), and *The Dangers of "Free Trade"* (Madison, Wis.: 21st Century, 1985).

13. See, particularly, Culbertson (cited in note 2), Bluestone and Harrison (cited in preface note 3), and Mark Anderson, "America's Foreign Trade Crisis," *AFL-CIO American Federationist* (Washington, D.C.: October 13, 1984). In addition, see William Cline, *Trade Policy in the 1980's* (Washington, D.C.: Inst. for International Economics, 1983); S.M. Miller and Donald Tomaskovic-Devey, *Recapitalizing America: Alternatives to the Corporate Distortion of National Policy* (Boston and London: Rutledge & Kegan Paul, 1983); Milton Hochmuth and William Davidson, *Revitalizing American Industry: Lessons from our Competitors* (Cambridge, Mass.: Ballinger, 1985); Herbert Striner, *Regaining the Lead: Policies for Economic Growth* (New York: Praeger, 1984); Vernon Whitford, ed., *American Industry, The Reference Shelf* 55, no. 6 (New York: H.W. Wilson, 1984); and James Fallows, "America's Changing Economic Landscape," *The Atlantic Monthly* (March 1985).

14. See, for example, Cline (note 13), Johnson (note 12), and Kindleberger and Lindert (note 6).

15. Thomas McCraw, *America versus Japan* (Boston: Harvard Business School, 1986); Karel van Wolferen, "The Japan Problem," *Foreign Affairs* 65, no. 2 (Winter 1986/87), pp. 288–303; "Collision Course: Can the U.S. Avert a Trade War with Japan?" *Business Week* (April 8, 1985), pp. 50–59; "Will Japan Really Change?" *Business Week* (May 12, 1986), pp. 46–58; Basil Caplan, "No Easy Solution to the

Japan Trade Problem," *The Banker* (London: Sept. 1985), pp. 46–57; Robert Reich and Eric Mankin, "Joint Ventures with Japan Give Away Our Future," *Harvard Business Review,* no. 2 (Mar.–Apr. 1986), pp. 78–86; Thomas J. Schoenbaum, "Trade Friction with Japan and the American Policy Response," *Michigan Law Review* 82 (Apr.–May 1984), pp. 1647–61; Edward Fried et al., eds., *The Future Course of U.S.–Japan Economic Relations* (Washington, D.C.: Brookings, 1983); "U.S.–Japan Trade: The $30 Billion Gap," *Hearing,* Subcommittee on East Asian and Pacific Affairs, Committee on Foreign Relations, 98th Cong., 2nd Sess., Oct. 3, 1984; James Abegglen, *The Strategy of Japanese Business* (Cambridge, Mass.: Ballinger, 1984); Charles Yuji Horioka, "Why Is Japan's Private Savings Rate So High?" *Finance and Development* (World Bank, Dec. 1986), pp. 22–25; Mary Saso and Stuart Kirby, *Japanese Industrial Competition to 1990* (Cambridge, Mass.: Abt, 1982); Charles McMillan, *The Japanese Industrial System* (Berlin: Walter de Gruyter, 1984); C. Fred Bergsten and William R. Cline, *The U.S.–Japan Economic Problem* (Washington, D.C.: Inst. for International Economics, Oct. 1985); Thomas Pugel and Robert Hawkins, *Fragile Interdependence: Economic Issues in U.S.–Japanese Trade and Investment* (Lexington, Mass.: Lexington Books, 1986); "The Sun Also Sets: Currency Woes and Aging Industries Slow Down Japan's Growth," *Time* (Dec. 8, 1986).

16. And yet, despite these limited efforts, Japanese and other East Asian trade surpluses with the U.S. increased during 1986 (as shown in table I–1), even though the yen appreciated from about 240:1 to 150:1 with respect to the dollar between February 1985 and January 1987. (See table A–11.)

17. For extensive discussions of European protectionism, safeguards against import displacement, and various forms of relief and subsidization see, Adams and Klein (preface note 3); together with Sjöstedt and Sundelius, Jaquemin, and Driscoll and Behrman (cited in note 12); Cline, and Hochmuth and Davidson (cited in introduction note 13). Also, see Jagdish Bhagwati, ed., *Import Competition and Response* (Chicago: National Bureau of Economic Research, Univ. of Chicago, 1982); W.M. Corden, *The Revival of Protectionism* (New York: Group of Thirty, 1984); David Greenway, *Trade Policy and the New Protectionism* (New York: St. Martin's, 1983); Lynden Moore, *The Growth and Structure of Trade since the Second World War* (Brighton, Sussex, England: Wheatsheaf, 1985); Andre Benard, chairman, *A Europe open to the World: A Report on Protectionism and the European Community,* Spec. Rpt. no. 5 (London: Trade Policy Research Centre, 1984); William James Adams and Christian Stoffaes, eds., *French Industrial Policy* (Washington, D.C.: Brookings, 1986); R. Joseph Monsen and Kenneth Walters, *Nationalized Companies: A Threat to American Business* (New York: McGraw-Hill, 1983); Vincent Cable, *Protectionism and Industrial Decline* (London: Overseas Development Inst.-Hodder and Stoughton, 1983); Brian Hindley, ed., *State Investment Companies in Western Europe: Picking Winners or Backing Losers* (London: Trade Policy Research Centre; New York: St. Martin's, 1983); G. Shepherd, F. Duchene, and C. Saunders, eds., *Europe's Industries: Public and Private Strategies for Change* (Ithaca, N.Y.: Cornell Univ., 1983); and Harry G. Johnson, "Mercantilism: Past, Present, Future," presidential address, *The New Mercantilism* (New York: St. Martin's, 1974).

But, note that the unemployment rate in Western Europe increased from 5.8 percent in 1980 to 11 percent in 1986. Olivier Blanchard and Lawrence Summers, "Unemployment Must be Attacked; An Austerity That's Wrecking Europe," *New York Times* (Feb. 8, 1987), p. B-3.

18. Free-market globalists largely support continued openness in U.S. trade and markets, èven though most other countries do not fully reciprocate. Some comment, "If the rest of the world wants to subsidize us for a while, that's fine!" Although many would like greater openness abroad, they accept the restrictions, subsidies, and partial mercantilism of Japanese, European, NIC, and LDC governments, at least for the medium term. (Most realize that communist and strongly socialist societies will not open up to free international competition.) But, as U.S. trade deficits increased substantially in recent years, more serious U.S. competitiveness problems became evident; the ranks of those demanding improved trade equity and/or stronger industrial policy for the United States enlarged greatly (with much heavier Congressional support lately).

Those wanting protection from "excessive" competition are widespread in most societies. As an old saying goes, "Nobody really wants completely free competition except full professors of economics with tenure." But, many domestic interests (business, professional, and labor) have felt reasonably secure and confident, at least in prosperous times. Thus, except for aggravated recession, slump, or depression—or major increases in foreign imports—those directly threatened by international competition in the short run are a fairly limited minority (unless a nation suffers extended industrial sluggishness, limited growth, and relative economic decline).

But, with weak growth, extensive structural unemployment, and a sizeable minority stuck with poverty or limited wages and salaries, those seeking protection or adjustment relief easily multiply. Demands for safeguarding may flourish in these circumstances, especially for industries, employees, and communities hard hit by foreign competition, widespread discounting of prices, or excess capacity in world markets. A variety of foreign "unfair" trade practices—such as dumping; export targeting; subsidies (direct or indirect); infringement of trademarks, patents, or copyrights; disruptive selling tactics; or a failure to offer comparable openness to their home markets—lead to demands for relief, countermeasures, or corrective action in some way. As U.S. imports expanded substantially in the 1980s, with little growth in U.S. exports, while trade deficits grew massive for the United States, the chorus of complaints grew much louder and stronger politically. So long as big trade deficits continue, and much of the U.S. economy remains sluggish in comparison to faster-growing rivals abroad, trade equity and/or relief pressures will most likely continue.

The case for stronger industrial policy goes beyond these issues. Its adherents see a global challenge of broader industrialization, enhanced competition, and improving technology. To maintain prosperity, the United States must make more systematic efforts as a high tech, increasingly productive nation. While some retrenchment and leaner staffs may be needed in this effort for competitiveness, it would be unwise to dismantle and throw away too much engineering and industrial capacity. In this context, foreign mercantilism, export promotion, and import trade restrictions are a natural and unavoidable element of economic policy for many other nations. Accordingly, it would be foolhardy and naive for the United States to expect complete trade and investment openness from other countries. The real world does not present a choice between total free trade and total protection, but rather a continuum of partly mercantilist competition and rivalry between nations, in which some government support and restrictions are inevitable. For these reasons, industrial policy advocates condemn the more credulous spokespeople for completely free trade as being unrealistic or, in many instances, as merely using free-trade arguments to support the vested interests of importers, MNCs, and/or multinational banks involved in existing trade flows. While industrial policy enthusiasts insist upon improving technology and productivity, their strategy requires its application to many particular industries. This forces U.S. industrial policy (like those of Japan, West Germany, and other countries), to confront the realities of current world-market competition (a messy thicket of discount financing, tax subsidies, export encouragements, marginal cost pricing, special deals, bailouts, domestic-content preferences, countertrade, and widespread nontariff barriers). In this way, industrial policies require substantial efforts to improve trade equity, which became part of an ongoing process of national bargaining and rivalry for technological, industrial, and economic development.

1
From Mercantilism to the Multinationals

C ommercial rivalry among cities, nations, and empires goes back to ancient Mesopotamia, Greece, and the Mediterranean. Corinth, Athens, Carthage, and Rome achieved at least regional ascendancy, among many rivals, for maritime power and commercial influence. The Chinese empire enjoyed extensive commerce within its borders, too. In the medieval age, Constantinople and later Venice, Genoa, Pisa, Florence, and the Hansa towns vied for trade and prosperity. Various river or landlocked cities—including Baghdad, Damascus, Kiev, Milan, Cologne, Paris, Novgorod, and Moscow—also became commercially significant. In the early modern era, Portugal, Spain, the Netherlands, and Sweden became serious maritime or trading powers. More recently, Britain and France became powerful, with Germany a strong late bloomer. Most created substantial industries, naval empires, and extensive trade and commerce. Lesser powers, however, were not entirely eliminated, and many countries have shared, to some degree, the broadening competition and wealth of modern technology and industry. But trading countries normally have tried to promote and regulate commerce in their own favor, with more or less mercantilist restrictions, taxes, or financing.

During the past few centuries, leading European states spread colonial and trade networks into the East Indies, the Americas, India, the rest of Asia, and most of Africa. Europe enjoyed a technological edge, growing out of military and industrial progress between roughly 1500 and 1900. Gradually, the colonies became independent nation-states in their own right, which ultimately enlarged the expanding international trade system. Thus, the United States, significant already in the last century, was followed by Canada, Australia, New Zealand, and South Africa. Japan was the first major Asian country to catch up with Western technology. Russia, on the fringe of Europe, was catching up in the nineteenth century; it created the first great Communist industrial power and a rival social system after World War I. In the past few decades, many more "new" industrial countries (including Spain, Italy, Yugoslavia, Korea, Taiwan, China, Brazil, and Mexico) have been closing the gap rapidly. More than a hundred developing nations now complete the international trade roster.

A mixture of rivalry and economic collaboration continues today in the world economy. Nations strive through public and/or private investment, laws, and regulation to maximize growth, productivity, and beneficial exchange for their peoples. World markets became considerably more open during part of the nineteenth century, though more restricted by World War I, the 1930s, and World War II. But, trade and investment opened up again and broadened substantially, at least among non-Communist nations, in the last thirty years. The General Agreement on Tariffs and Trade, together with policies followed by the United States and most Western bloc industrial nations, have encouraged this expansion of world trade, investment, and banking activity. Nonetheless, every nation, within limits, tries to supervise and regulate its engagement with the world marketplace.

In this environment, many corporations, businesses, and families have prospered and become transnational or multinational enterprises (MNEs). Most remain attached predominantly to parent countries or their primary domicile; but others have achieved a degree of detachment or functional independence (rather like migratory birds or sea fowl, with assorted roosts of convenience). An interesting question is where, if at all, these multinational interests and corporations owe loyalties? Or are they simply devoted to the diverse individuals, staffs, and/or investors that make up MNEs? National regulatory policies naturally seek to attract, retain, exploit, supervise, and/or constrain MNEs for the benefit of host, parent, and customer countries. And, the MNEs often become linked to domestic industrial or financial interests to better secure themselves and their profitability. Transnational commerce is hardly unique in history, though it probably has flourished more recently than in other periods, when people, investments, and trade could move about less freely.

Competing models or outlooks on economic behavior are used to analyze international trade, investment, and finance. One view emphasizes a global marketplace.[1] It stresses the benefits to individual participants of optimal specialization plus extensive trade and factor mobility, while claiming that a substantial part of recent world prosperity is traceable to increased trade and investment openness. Other views place emphasis on the community obligations and performance of MNEs, trading, finance, and national economies—for peoples as a whole, business and/or investor interests, and working families. The socialist and Marxist outlooks place the greatest emphasis on benefits to community and worker, though others place importance on workers' welfare, too. Outlooks respecting capitalist property rights seek reasonable freedom for its enjoyment, investment opportunities, and favorable social institutions. Cultural, religious, ideological, and national loyalties complicate these assessments. Many affiliations transcend national boundaries and/or class lines, while leading to international alliances, connections, and antagonisms. These divergent viewpoints can be awkward for policy making, especially in pluralist or cosmopolitan nations.

Traditional Mercantile Rivalries

Economic historians trace the early roots of mercantilism. Human progress always involves teamwork. Community organizations—from primitive clans, small villages, broader tribes, towns, and city-states, through wider territories, kingdoms, and empires—have normally tried to regulate economic affairs, commerce, and trade with outsiders to promote their own interests. As Gustav Schmoller summarized mercantilism: "The soul of that policy is the putting of fellow-citizens at an advantage, and of competitors from outside at a disadvantage."[2] Tolls, tariffs, subsidies, licenses, and regulation of access or participation were typical means to these ends. Naturally, the gains from trade to outsiders could not be fully preempted without destroying or limiting external commerce. But, mercantilist regulation, navigation laws, and promotional policies were designed, within limits at least, to favor "one's own" and to foster the community's prosperity and security. Other polities and states presumably did much the same—to the extent that economic leverage and power allowed.

The history of cities and nations reveals a great deal of jostling, bargaining at cross-purposes, and not infrequent land or naval warfare. In periods when one or several powers are predominant, this leverage can be exploited with some harshness or at least used to sustain strength and advantages already enjoyed. When power is more diffuse and leaders enjoy much less leverage, trading might be more equal, balanced, and, perhaps, more freely accessible. But—even with many competing states—import tariffs, tolls, licenses, and regulation were usually employed as revenue sources and methods of control or supervision. Thus, regulation of commerce is a normal incident of sovereignty, and its exercise presumably favors the interests of states imposing these regimes.

As city-states and smaller territories are integrated into bigger nations and/or empires, many parochial and local restrictions tend to be rescinded to favor interests of the bigger polities and their influential merchants, enterprises, or governments. In this way, local mercantilist regulations are relaxed or eliminated, but often replaced with regulations developed in favor of larger states, federations, or empires. Thus, mercantilism is commonly expanded in its scale of operation, with a larger and more diverse citizenry and collection of enterprises within its borders to be favored and encouraged. Nonetheless, some local regulation and encouragement often continue. But, the remaining regulation tends to be more general and less protectionist against workers, traders, or enterprises from other parts of the enlarged territory.

U.S. Mercantile Policies

The U.S. Constitution prohibits restriction that unreasonably burdens interstate commerce, except for those legitimate "police" power regulations designed to promote general welfare, health or safety.[3] Local licensing of doctors, lawyers, taxi drivers, financial institutions, utilities, and many other industrial activities and regulations occur under this "federal" tradition, which often limits new entry or competition. Yet, objective standards, applied on an impartial basis, are supposed to allow new people or enterprises from other parts of the country to enter without undue prejudice. Likewise, local subsidies, tax concessions, or promotional support for new industry and economic development have become common in the United States and a considerable number of other countries. But, massive support of local interests to achieve the exclusion of all outside investor companies would be quite unusual. In fact, the normal goal is, rather, to entice new resources, companies, and jobs to benefit the local economy.

Tariffs as well as import, export, and customs duties have been a significant revenue source for trading states since ancient times. Under the U.S. Constitution, Congress has the "power to lay and collect taxes, duties, imposts and excises, to pay the debts and provide for the common defense and general welfare of the United States." Throughout most of U.S. history, at least revenue tariffs have been imposed, averaging roughly 8½ per ad valorem in the early years, but adjusted periodically thereafter.[4] The War of 1812 and its aftermath brought somewhat higher rates, with protective levies to favor New England industry. Further increases followed in 1824 and with the "Tariff of Abominations" in 1828, a generally protective measure. But, with extensive opposition, especially in the South, gradual tariff reductions followed until 1842, when the Whigs restored somewhat more protective duties. But, James Knox Polk's Democratic administration soon reduced them again with the Walker Tariff of 1846, which emphasized revenue primarily, with some protection for Northern iron, cotton, and woolen goods. Walker was a free-trader and this relaxation paralleled British free-trade policy and repeal of the Corn Laws (grain tariffs) in 1846. Modest further reductions followed in 1857, with some opposition from the new Republican party.

The Civil War and Republican majority brought higher tariffs and stronger protectionism, which coincided with greater industrial development. These increased tariffs were supported by northern industry, Midwestern farmers, and early labor unions. A mild reduction came in 1894 under Grover Cleveland, when the Democrats controlled Congress, but William McKinley's election brought the Dingley Act of 1897 and higher customs duties. While Woodrow Wilson's administration's Underwood Act of 1913 lowered tariffs somewhat, substantial protection remained intact for many industries, and sizeable revenues still flowed from customs levies. Increased tariffs were restored in 1922, and extremely high protective duties came with the Smoot-Hawley Tariff of 1930.

But, after substantial foreign retaliation to increased tariff rates under Smoot-Hawley and worsening of the worldwide depression, Franklin Roosevelt proposed, and a heavily Democratic Congress enacted, the Reciprocal Trade Agreements Act of 1934. This legislation was the beginning of a slow reversal of U.S. tariff policy. It authorized the president to reduce tariff rates by as much

The Republican Party was the champion of tariff protection when this cartoon was published in 1904. It shows the GOP elephant, labeled "protection," preventing the "free trade" donkey from upsetting turn-of-the-century U.S. prosperity, symbolized by the "full dinner pail." It was widely believed that protective tariffs had contributed to this prosperity.

Source: Library of Congress, Washington, D.C.

as 50 percent in return for reciprocal concessions from other nations. Because the most favored nation principle was included, mutual concessions could be established fairly rapidly. Although only limited tariff reductions were negotiated before World War II, the authority for gradual tariff reduction was renewed regularly after the war (with much larger reductions following in the GATT era), especially after the Kennedy Round in 1967.

Mercantile Policies in Other Major Countries

Most other modern nations have used revenue and protective tariffs in the course of their industrial development. Britain employed typical mercantilist policies, encouragements, duties, navigation laws, and aggressive naval expansion during the course of its modernizing and early industrial revolution. Elizabethan economic policies (1558–1603), Stuart and Commonwealth policies (1603–88), and subsequent policies until the 1820s were predominantly mercantilist in character. Britain was a "catching-up" nation in the earlier periods, and its many naval wars (against Spain, the Netherlands, and later France) and colonial expansion were part of this development process. Naturally, all of its significant rivals were mercantilist, too. Spain, Portugal, the Netherlands, France, Sweden, Prussia, Austria, and even Russia (from Peter the Great onward) were using broadly similar policies for national development (with unequal success) during most of the seventeenth and eigthteenth centuries.

Britain only began a gradual shift toward more open, freer trade when its naval, industrial, and commercial leadership was secure after Napoleonic France had been defeated, even though Adam Smith's *Wealth of Nations* appeared earlier (in 1776).[5] The French took the first modest steps toward somewhat freer trade in the 1780s under physiocrat influence. Of course, the French Revolution plus Napoleon's Continental System (a mercantilist attempt at European integration under French hegemony) interrupted this liberalization. Subsequently, the classical economists (free-traders) in Britain only achieved ascendancy gradually during the 1820s through the 1840s. In Britain, Huskisson's liberalizing reforms and tariff cuts in the 1820s, and Peel's more drastic reduction of tariffs (1842–46) finally brought substantial free trade to the home markets. Even so, many British colonial markets were, in fact, less open to outsiders, and British industry enjoyed substantial headstart and efficiency advantages in many areas. Hence, Britain could afford freer trade, with little risk of economic disruption or significant industrial decline through most of the nineteenth century.

Later, however, as German, U.S., and other competition became stronger, British protectionist sentiment revived. Shortly before 1900, a leading conservative, Joseph Chamberlain, urged more protection; in 1902, he formally proposed a network of Imperial Preferences, and this view gained increasing support among conservatives.[6] Until World War I, however, the British free-trade bloc still prevailed, with fears of increased food costs and disruption to established trade and finance interests if Britain followed protection elsewhere. But, the British outlook changed gradually with World War I. The Safeguarding of Industries Act of 1921 allowed gradual protective relief. Then, in the Great Depression, major tariff increases occurred (partly responding to Smoot-Hawley in 1930), and the Imperial Preference System was enacted in 1932. Thus, the remarkable British experiment toward freer trade and more open markets was, in actuality, based upon special circumstances and economic advantages in the nineteenth century that enabled its success.

For most major European countries, mercantilism had strong momentum and the period of freer trade was limited. French regulation of industry and commerce was restrictive under Richelieu, Mazarin, Colbert, and the Bourbons in the 1600s and 1700s, although internal barriers were greatly lightened during the French revolution.[7] But, external tariffs and regulations remained protective and mercantilist through the Bourbon restoration until 1848. Then, Louis Napoleon tried to reduce tariffs, despite substantial business opposition, from 1852 onward. French–British trade quintupled between 1850 and 1860. France negotiated the Cobden–Chevalier tariff-reduction treaty with Britain in 1860, an arrangement favorable to the French.

> [France] pledged to reduce at once its rates to a maximum of 30 percent ad valorem and within five years to a maximum of 25 percent, while [Britain] agreed to wipe most of its duties off the books and to lower the rates on wine and brandies.[8]

Because British industry had grown more extensive and efficient, however, this imbalance was not unreasonable. Even more significant, perhaps, was a most-favored nation (MFN) provision, and a series of French tariff treaties with other European nations (Prussia, Italy, Switzerland, Sweden–Norway, the Netherlands, Spain, Austria, and Portugal) between 1862 and 1867. Yet, after the Franco–Prussian War, a need for greater public revenues, an expanding colonial empire, and revived protectionist sentiment led to substantial tariff increases, especially between 1875 and 1910. The French retreated from MFN treatment as well. World War I, the 1920s, the Depression, and revived German militarism under Hitler helped to sustain considerable French protectionism.

Germany had long seen mercantilism and parochial restrictions among most towns and territories, even though a limited number encouraged more open trading.[9] The Thirty Years War (1618–48) was a setback economically, and frequent wars in the 1700s through 1815 were burdensome. But, Prussia helped lead Germany toward economic integration between 1818 and 1870, with a series of customs treaties and its Zollverein (1834–67) customs union *within* Germany. In this period, Prussia set moderate, revenue-oriented external tariffs that were less than many states', but more than others'. Soon after Bismarck's victory over France and creation of the new German Empire in 1871, however, they switched to greater protection. Frederick List's *National System of Political Economy* (1841), a classic argument for protectionist industrial expansion, became increasingly popular and influential. Distress to farmers in the 1873–77 depression, demands for higher tariffs from industrialists, and a desire for stronger military-industrial power led to increased duties between 1879 and 1906. Then, World War I and blockade of the Central Powers enforced substantial isolation. Heavy war costs, reparations, disrupted trade, inflation, and severe distress followed. Although the Dawes Plan (rescheduling of reparations and major foreign borrowing) in 1924 brought significant recovery, the 1929 Depression led to massive unemployment and the dictatorship of Adolf Hitler in 1933. Under the Nazis, rearmament and deficit financing revived the economy, but trade grew distorted with bilateral dealings and semi-autarky, as World War II approached. Germany had become an increasingly export-oriented economy with industrial success, but elements of mercantilism and protective regulation had been an important part of its modern progress.

The Austro-Hungarian Empire evolved from Hapsburg family holdings. Under Emperor Charles V (1519–56) it included Spain, Sicily, Naples, Belgium, the Netherlands, and much of Austria, but by 1815, it was "Austria–Hungary," which then included Bohemia, Slovakia, Transylvania, Galicia, Croatia, Slovenia, the Dalmatian Coast, and even Venice in Italy. This multilingual aggregation had never been fully integrated economically, and some parts remained relatively backward. Considerable liberalization followed, however, in the midnineteenth century, and most internal trade barriers were dropped.[10] But, like Germany, the Austro–Hungarian Empire became more protectionist externally in the late nineteenth and early twentieth centuries. Most of its dismembered parts, unfortunately, followed protectionist policies after independence in 1919. Apart from the most industrial area, Bohemia, which helped Czechoslovakia attain considerable prosperity between 1919 and 1938, economists believe that the breakdown of Austria–Hungary as an integrated trading area was a major setback, at least until Nazi Germany reorganized much of it into an exploited economic zone in the late 1930s.[11] In any event, Austria–Hungary was significantly mercantilist in its later external economic policies, in spite of the fact that Austrian neoclassical economists ranked among the most distinguished of this past century.

Italy had been the most prosperous, advanced area of Europe in the high Middle Ages and early Renaissance. Venice, Florence, Genoa, Milan, and other cities enjoyed flourishing trade, extensive craft industries, and financial prowess. Venetian fleets were generally strong in the central and eastern Mediterranean after the decline of Byzantine power. Mercantilist rivalry was a major theme of city-state policies. Unfortunately, the lack of Italian unity, growing Ottoman Turkish power, reduced Eastern trade, Portuguese diversion of trade around Africa, and foreign occupations in parts of Italy led to economic decline. Portugal, Spain, the Low Countries, France, and Britain in turn became more prosperous. Divided into small states, often with significant trade barriers, Italy failed to keep up with expanding prosperity in northwest Europe and become relatively backward. Between 1848 and 1870 economic integration and considerable liberalism came with *risorgimento* (national revival and unification), but more liberal trade with outsiders was eventually restricted, and substantial protection came in the late nineteenth century. Further limits followed after World War I and during the Fascist era between the two world wars. Thus, the predominant theme of earlier and more recent Italian commercial policy has been mercantilism.[12]

Spanish unification came in the late 1400s. Great ocean explorers and adventurers made it the world's largest empire by the early 1500s. But, though Mexico and Peru yielded a steady stream of bullion, most of their colonies were thinly settled; small Spanish elites governed primitive agrarian cultures. Under Charles V's successors—Philip II (1556–98) and later monarchs—Spanish military and naval strength declined. Its economic base, agriculture, industry, and finances were abused, with harsh taxes, unproductive restrictions, and unenlightened mercantilism. Even the Spanish population was substantially reduced. The Netherlands broke free and prospered. Then, France, Britain, and later Germany surpassed Spain in economic vitality. In the later 1700s,

Spain tried to liberalize internal trade and reform its empire, but this came late. Then, French occupation by Napoleon's armies was a burden, and most of Spain's colonies gained independence between 1810 and 1825. During most of the nineteenth century, Spain remained a protected economy, with slower industrialization than most of Europe. Modest progress occurred later, but tragic disruption and costly civil war in the 1930s left Spain an even more isolated and exhausted nation under the Franco dictatorship.[13]

Russia had come a long way from backwardness and Tartar domination in the thirteenth and fourteenth centuries. Gradually, mercantilist policies were imposed upon a feudal society. Since Peter I (the Great) in the early 1700s, Russia gradually began to encourage more modern industries, import Western technology, and establish bureaucratic administration. Taxes were onerous, however, and tariffs generally high until 1824. During the next fifty years, some tariff reductions were made to yield more revenue and to allow more imports of agricultural, industrial, and transport machinery. But after 1877, policy shifted to greater protection, culminating in an act of 1891 that systematized protection and extended it to many raw materials and semimanufactured goods (including coal, machinery, and steel). In the late nineteenth and early twentieth centuries, industrial growth became more rapid in Russia, although it was seriously disrupted by World War I and the Bolshevik revolution.[14] Bolshevik policies, war, communism, and subsequent planning emphasized heavy industries and self-sufficiency. State control is comprehensive, and foreign trade has been used mainly as a resource to improve technology and speed industrial growth. Russian development also illustrates a general theme of mercantilism. The Soviet Union's subsequent transformation into a planned, centralized communist society reflects the ultimate form of state control.[15]

Smaller or Less Developed Countries

In countries of smaller size or modest development, mercantilist protection was sometimes limited. Industrial progress was usually less comprehensive, especially for modern, large-scale industrial plants. Small nations might not justify big enterprises, unless substantial export growth could be relied upon. And, since larger countries were mostly mercantilist and protectionist, not many big export markets could be exploited (apart from situations or comparative advantage, distinctive raw materials, unusual crafts, or special technology). Britain was the big exception, a major, relatively open market in the later nineteenth and early twentieth centuries. Small countries might be more open markets, too, except where local interests or industries had enough clout to obtain their government's support through tariffs, subsidies, or other regulation.

Portugal, with only 1 million people in the late 1400s, created the first Western European naval and colonial empire. From the Azores, Madeiras, Brazil, coastal stations in Africa, India, the East Indies, and, later, outposts in

China and Japan, Portuguese shipping created an improved route to the East, which bypassed Venice and the Turks. Considerable trade prosperity followed for Portugal in the 1500s. But, Spanish occupation between 1580 and 1640 ultimately proved costly. And the Dutch, followed by the British and French, soon took over the major part of European trade with the East. Portugal was eclipsed by larger peoples in mercantilist rivalry and never developed much industry. Although left largely alone (except for limited, unsuccessful Dutch efforts to conquer Brazil), Portugal never recovered general economic vitality, and its empire became a backwater. In the later 1700s, gold and development in Brazil helped restore some trade, but British shipping and merchants took a heavy role in the revival. But then Brazil, the one big colony (one even larger than its parent), declared independence during the Napoleonic wars, soon becoming more important than Portugal economically. Portugal itself remained a rather undeveloped agricultural country. Being less protectionist and more open than some European countries helped keep Portugal a relatively weak, predominantly agricultural country, one dependent upon foreign manufacturers as the Industrial Revolution progressed.[16]

The Netherlands was a prosperous collection of provinces, cities, and countryside under Hapsburg suzerainty in the early 1500s. But later, Spanish misrule (including religious and political persecution) led to a successful war for independence. Quickly, the Dutch became aggressive ocean traders to the East, with outposts in the Caribbean, Africa, the Indian Ocean, and the East Indies. It established colonies in North America between 1621 and 1664, and in Brazil from 1624 to 1654. Explorations to Hudson's Bay, Australia, and the South Pacific helped round out their efforts to global proportions. Craft industries thrived. Dutch shipping, trade, and fisheries were the strongest in Europe for many years. In the early 1700s, when Peter the Great visited the Netherlands, it was probably the most progressive, enlightened, and prosperous area of Europe. Although having considerable competition among themselves, the Dutch were mercantilist in much of their external relations. But, while they enjoyed an era of commercial leadership, ultimately the rival mercantilism of Britain, France, and Sweden, together with Spain and Portugal, hemmed in the Dutch. The nation was too small to support a dominant naval power, and its territory was too easily exposed to land invasion. Thus, its role subsided to that of a secondary trading, industrial, and agricultural country with a limited empire. Its commerce suffered seriously under French domination in the Napoleonic era, and the South African and Ceylonese colonies were lost. Between 1815 and 1830, the Netherlands were united to Belgium, and it gave more protection to industries. This continued until the 1850s, when the Netherlands became a low-tariff country again, trying to facilitate manufacturers for export, transshipment, finance, and insurance activities.[17]

Since independence, Belgium's commercial practice has been relatively open to imports. Some agricultural protection came in the late nineteenth century, and the Congo became important for the economy. After World War II, the Benelux nations moved closer to economic integration with a customs union in 1948.[18]

In the Baltic area, Denmark and Sweden developed considerable commerce and used mercantilist policies.[19] During the 1600s, Sweden created naval and commercial dominance in the eastern Baltic, while Denmark dominated the Narrows and built a modest overseas empire (including the Faeroes, Iceland, Greenland, West Indian islands, and even an East India company). But Dutch (and later British) shipping had the bigger role in the Baltic, while Danish and Swedish exports were mostly raw materials (iron, lumber, fish, grain, and amber). Even so, considerable protection was the commercial policy of Denmark and Sweden until the midnineteenth century, when somewhat freer trade was used. But, protection increased again toward the end of the century and did not change appreciably until after World War II.

In Switzerland, trade and artisanry developed in some towns in the high Middle Ages. But, as in most of Germany and Central Europe, a patchwork of tolls and restrictions also limited commerce. While Geneva gradually became a small financial, trade, and crafts center, along with other Swiss towns, there were serious constraints. Internal tariffs were not fully eliminated until the Federal Republic of 1848, when the Swiss also shared in lower tariffs throughout much of Europe. But after 1870, Switzerland became somewhat more protectionist again, taking special care to maintain considerable self-sufficiency during World Wars I and II.[20]

In Eastern Europe and Turkey, meanwhile, economic backwardness prevailed, and there was less trade and commerce.[21] But, there was a degree of mercantilism and significant revenue tariffs for Balkan countries before World War I. Breakup of the Austro-Hungarian Empire created new states: Poland, Czechoslovakia, Hungary, a substantially enlarged Romania, and Serbia (which became Yugoslavia). But, a major problem in the interwar period was restricted trade, increased protection, and limited potential for economic expansion. These difficulties were aggravated in the Great Depression, with greatly reduced agricultural and raw material export prices.

Outside of Europe, the United States, and Japan (which developed rapidly from the late nineteenth century), there was little industrial development before World War II. In colonial countries, the "mother" country naturally dominated trade and greatly limited access for outsiders. India and China had failed to modernize, although they accumulated large populations with considerable commerce and aggregate purchasing power. India had become a British colony and was increasingly tied to the Empire economically. Afghanistan, Persia, and Arabia were isolated and backward, with little access to world trade. Southeast Asia was even more backward, mostly under colonial rule, and primitive in many places. Only China remained somewhat open in the nineteenth century as a large, independent empire free of direct colonial administration. But "treaty port" China became significantly weaker, subjected to foreign concessions, and exploited by foreign commercial interests. Britain led in exports and commerce to Asia (and dominated the Indian trade), but other leading European nations, the United States, and later Japan also enjoyed significant trade in China and elsewhere.[22] Commercial policy for China was substantially influenced by the Westerners. Imports from Europe or the United States were allowed rather freely in some parts of China, with little more than revenue tariffs. Exports from Asia generally comprised handicrafts or raw materials, for the most part.

Japan was the major exception in Asia.[23] It came out of Tokugawa isolation (1600–1868) into a rapid modernizing process under Emperor Meiji (1868–1912). More prosperous, generally literate, and better administered than any other Asian country, Japan quickly adopted Western technology, industrial techniques, and military organization. Japanese commercial policies were soon mercantilist, along European lines. Substantial modern industry was encouraged, with protective tariffs used in support. By 1894–95, Japan had an efficient, modern navy. It defeated China, seized Formosa, and invaded parts of Korea. In 1904–05, Japan beat Russia, occupied Korea, and won significant positions in Manchuria. During World War I and the 1920s, Japan extended its influence in China. During the 1930s, Japan tried to create a big new military-commercial empire, the Greater East Asia Coprosperity Sphere. But, the Chinese resisted domination, and a long war ensued. Japan joined Hitler's Germany in World War II, hoping for quick victory, but complete defeat and American occupation followed. In all this rapid expansion and imperial effort, Japan certainly emulated European-style mercantilism.

In Latin America, meanwhile, independence (won from 1810 to 1825) had brought uneven economic progress.[24] For most areas, the Creole elites shared in the improving technology and productivity of the nineteenth and early twentieth centuries, and many were substantial landowners, ranchers, or plantation developers. Many European immigrants and some foreign investors joined in this development process, especially for mining, plantations, railroads, and utilities. But, the native Indian (or former slave) populations remained largely backward, serving as a low-wage underclass. The Latin American governments used customs revenue as a major tax source, but tariffs tended to be oriented more for revenue than strong protection of local manufacturers. Because most countries were small, with limited purchasing power, local manufacturers did not receive much encouragement. Most of Latin America emphasized mining, food, or cash crop exports, and becoming dependent mainly upon imported foreign manufacturers. Limited industrial development was occurring in a few countries, especially Brazil, during the generation before World War II, and mercantilist protection was used to some degree. But, serious, broad efforts for industrial development came mostly later in the post–World War II era.

From an economic standpoint, Africa was the least developed, most isolated, and often most primitive area of the globe during the nineteenth century.[25] Beginning with scattered European coastal outposts, French occupation of North Africa, and a final scramble among Britain, France, Germany, Portugal, and Belgium to occupy the remaining inland territories, most of Africa had become colonized by 1902. Colonial administration was mildly exploitative and paternalistic, with only limited modern economic development, except for some European agricultural settlers in North Africa plus more extensive mining, agriculture, and modest industry in the white-dominated Union of South Africa. Each colonial power regulated trade to strongly favor its own nationals and commercial interests, though no large volume of commerce had accumulated before World War II (except in parts of North Africa and the Union of South Africa).

Expansion of Trade, Finance, Banking, and Capital Flows[26]

Sending goods by caravan or ship involved risk of loss. But, profits in longer-distance trade involving articles of serious value, gems, spices, or precious metal usually justified these investments (especially if risk pooling or insurance coverage could be obtained). Thus, trading and shipping cities normally brought together investor and merchant families with shipowners, caravan leaders, and overseas traders. When regular, large-scale trade flows became established, these merchant families often set up correspondent relations or marriages, or created branch offices or outposts to facilitate trade. By the late Middle Ages, fairly sophisticated short- and medium-term financing had become customary to cover the costs and risks of trade and shipping activities. Joint venture contracts, negotiable bills of exchange, and partnerships were employed. So long as trade suffered no serious disruption or slump in value, these financing investments would be reasonably sound.

From the standpoint of trading states, the process tended to finance itself. Initial and continuing profits would support further cargoes, expeditions, outlays, and inventories. The stronger trading centers normally took the initiative in these export-import operations, while providing most of the short- and medium-term financing. Not much long-term financing was extended for foreign operations, except to maintain outposts, factories, fleets, or forts abroad to help sustain profitable trade flows into the future. Early trading corporations (such as the Dutch East India Company or the British East India Company) were greatly enlarged, sophisticated financing partnerships which helped institutionalize and support these activities. Countries or city-states with strong networks abroad could have significant advantages this way. This helps explain why many European countries (including Spain, Portugal, the Netherlands, Britain, France, Sweden, Russia, and Denmark) made efforts toward colonization and trade expansion in the sixteenth through the eighteenth centuries. Not surprisingly, naval rivalry and warfare developed over conflicting interests abroad. The investments in naval forces, garrisons, and other support to sustain trade routes were social overhead costs to help maintain prosperous trade and finance activities.

Stronger trading powers might extract more of the gains from exchange to the extent that weaker bargainers had limited alternatives or were seriously dependent. Naturally, weaker parties might try to improve themselves and develop broader, less onerous alternatives. In this way, a certain logic toward more independent trade competition—and less extreme returns from trade or its financing—might be expected to operate. But, whenever new opportunities or markets opened up, initial gains could be generous for those with headstart or leverage advantages. And, the profits from protected leverage often encouraged trading states to fence off and divide markets among each other to achieve more secure, valuable spheres of influence or dependent territories. Colonies could be particularly profitable this way, if skillfully developed and exploited.

Limited financial flows began to occur, apart from trade finance, as mercantile and other wealth began to accumulate in liquid form (other than lands, castles, houses, equipment, or immovable assets). Wealthy families might relocate or transplant themselves to more favorable climates or seek refuge from political or religious persecution. The Canton of Geneva in Switzerland attracted Huguenot refugees this way, for example, which strengthened its local economy and boosted early banking entrepreneurship. During the French revolution and Napoleonic era, many noble families fled to safer places, often with liquid capital. But, for the most part, no great volume of capital moved in international commerce, except what people could carry with them as gems or specie, until the nineteenth century. Insecure travel and doubtful enforcement of transnational contract and debt obligations had made international credit rather limited— other than traditional short- and medium-term trade finance.

Gradually, capital transfers enlarged as the nineteenth century progressed. Shipping and communications improved in speed and reliability, and British naval dominance (with the support of other powers) sheltered a more secure world transfer system. International relations were more peaceful, with increasing worldwide respect for property, contracts, travelers, foreign residents, emigrants, and immigrants. Business enterprises increasingly took the corporate form, with broader ownership plus more reliable payment of stock dividends, debt servicing, and obligations to corporate bondholders. Governments began to issue debt in significant volumes with greater reliability of repayment. By the end of the 1815–1914 period, world finance had become partly internationalized.

Investment and portfolio management by and for prosperous families began to change during this period. Previously, there had been rather little movement of credit abroad beyond the expectation of payment for goods in transit or recently delivered (which normally yielded notes discounted to banks for liquidity). Thus, merchants and banking houses typically took short- and medium-term positions as creditors (or debtors) in foreign commerce, but these investments were really secured by the continued process or growth of trade flows. But, as the nineteenth century moved on, broader possibilities for international investment were established. Foreign government bonds, foreign corporate securities (ones involved in utilities, railroads, mining, industrial activities, or other commerce) and more business activities across international boundaries were available for investment, trade, and prosperity. Leading bankers helped to underwrite and distribute foreign bonds and stocks as well as enlarged loans to international business. Risks of default, delayed servicing, or reduced interest payments could not be totally eliminated. But, so long as the general system could be sustained and defaults or disruptions were relatively infrequent, investors could place considerable confidence in the international part of their portfolios, especially when premium interest rates or returns were offered.

Gradually, and somewhat unevenly, foreign credit and investment flows began to come from the wealthier countries of Europe, beyond traditional banking and short- and medium-term trade finance. Britain was the largest creditor country, France a strong second, and other nations, including Germany and the Netherlands, became sizeable creditors, too.[27]

The most important recipients of net foreign investment through government borrowing, corporate bonds, and stocks were the United States, together with other former colonies in Latin America (led by Argentina and Brazil), Canada, Australia, South Africa, India, and some other nations, to a lesser extent. Favored sectors included railroads, public utilities, mining and, occasionally, new industries. For some recipients, the proportion of net foreign investment in total capital formation was substantial, at least at times. For the United States, these new foreign investments had been considerable in the later 1820s and up to the panic of 1837, but slowed sharply after defaults by many states during the following depression. Net flows to the United States resumed in later boom periods, but were less important as a share of capital formation by the end of the nineteenth century. U.S. industry was providing much more of its own capital by then, but other investment areas in Latin America and European colonial empires were growing rapidly, attracting much immigration and foreign investment.

So far as major industrial country expansion was concerned, however, it is probably fair to say that most of their development was internally financed. Domestic manufacturing growth in the United States, Germany, France, and Japan (the big "catch-up" nations relative to Britain in the later nineteenth and early twentieth centuries) was mostly financed by their businesses through internal cash flow and local capital markets. In fact, some of these newer industrial countries (especially the United States and Germany) began to export considerable capital by the turn of the century. (Japan began this process after World War I to a modest degree.) The United States had become a net capital exporter shortly before World War I, and greatly increased its lending during that war and the 1920s.

Unfortunately, heavy borrowing for many countries during World War I brought substantial strains.[28] Severe inflation disrupted the economies of

Germany, Austria, Hungary, and Poland, and many others suffered considerable inflation. Although France, Britain, and other victorious nations wanted German reparations to help finance big war debts (as Germany had financed the Franco–Prussian War of 1870–71), as things worked out, this expectation was founded upon large U.S. loans (and the Dawes Plan rescheduling package of 1924). U.S. loans helped provide the basis for revitalizing Germany's economy and its long-term reparations payments. When world recovery slowed in the late 1920s, and the Wall Street stock market crashed in October 1929, a chain reaction of international business slowdown, reparations and debt defaults, competitive devaluations, and an overall crisis in confidence drastically reduced further foreign lending and investment. In addition, Latin America had borrowed heavily during the 1920s, especially from the United States, which became its major new creditor. But, with a collapse of commodity prices during the Great Depression, the Latin American economies suffered distress, most of this indebtedness could not be serviced, and many of these countries fell into default as well.

Because of widespread defaults, slump in many world markets, reduced trade, increased business risks, greater bilateralism, and restrictive exchange controls, international credit and lending contracted greatly during the 1930s. This disrupted international finance, along with heavily restricted trade flows, was seen as a major source of reduced world prosperity.

Lessons from Earlier Mercantile Development

Four helpful lessons can be drawn from this long history of mercantile policies. Cumulative economic progress was enormous for humanity, especially from, say, the 1400s to the 1700s and more rapidly through the 1800s, early 1900s, and now the later 1900s. But, the pacesetters of industrial and trade prosperity shifted substantially over time. Venice, Florence, Portugal, Spain, the Netherlands, France, Britain, the United States, Germany, and Japan (and, more recently, Taiwan and South Korea) have shared honors for the most rapid growth at various points. And, past success is clearly no guarantee of sustained future performance, although it helps to have a legacy of inherited capital, education, and technology.

First, the most important ingredients of rapid national growth are (1) technological progress and improved productivity, (2) expanding industries and trade momentum (at least internally, if not through export earnings and increased imports), (3) substantial saving and investment from productive enterprise, sustained over a long period, (4) moderate, bearable tax loads with no significant disincentive effects, and (5) sufficient sharing in improved prosperity to maintain social morale and teamwork. Adequate military security was essential to support this effort, and expanded territory and/or influence was often associated with (but not necessary for) success.

Second, most successful industrial countries used a mix of mercantilist encouragement for industrial development, revenue tariffs and/or consumption taxes, and selective protection to foster at least key industries. General foreclosure of foreign imports, by contrast, was much less successful; autarky tends to limit trade, inhibit export development, restrict useful imports, and reduce access to technology. At the other extreme, complete openness for importation was rarely employed, and not by any major industrial countries except for Great Britain in the 1850s through 1914. And, Britain adopted free trade only *after* its naval, commercial, and industrial ascendancy was securely established and after its strongest and most threatening rival, Napoleonic France, had been defeated.

Third, continuing access to new technology from other countries has been essential for industrial progress. Foreign investments and lending were helpful to some countries, especially the United States, at some stages in the nineteenth century. But, most successful leaders in industrial growth and development, at least before World War II, relied mainly upon their own internal capital, savings, and investment. Yet, access to the best available technology from other countries has been important for most leaders in industrial and commercial development.

And fourth, with World War I and the Great Depression, the importance of sustaining prosperity, trade, and finance was emphasized. Costly wars and conflict should be avoided, if possible, and aggregate demand, employment, and liquidity should be sustained. World War II reinforced these lessons, with another round of destruction and great loss of life. On the more optimistic side, however, full employment had been achieved through deficit finance in most major nations such as the United States, Britain, Germany, and Japan, which suggests that more aggressive government finance, within reasonable limits, could help to sustain prosperity and achieve more economic growth.

Post–World War II Development

The world economy has become substantially more industrialized, with highly productive technology and agriculture. Better living standards emerged for most peoples since World War II. International trade and finance are more competitive, and a much larger number of companies, from a considerable list of nations, are effectively multinational. The global marketplace is more integrated, in some respects, than during the Edwardian Age (before World War I) or the 1920s. And yet, national rivalries still operate, and the world's economy is divided ideologically and institutionally into three main patterns:

1. Predominantly free-enterprise economies
2. Mixed economies with substantial public and private enterprise
3. Predominantly socialist economies

These cleavages seem likely to continue.[29] This complicates intergovernment collaboration and imposes constraints upon the extent to which our world marketplace can be trusted by many nations.

The post–World War II settlement evolved through five phases. Each featured somewhat different economic circumstances. While the ultimate result is a more competitive world economy, the majority of nations retain considerable mercantilist regulation. All countries accommodate this international bazaar and try to promote their best interests.

Immediate Postwar Reconstruction, 1945–51

The initial period of postwar reconstruction and institution building was dominated by the United States and Britain. It began with plans developed during the war. John Maynard Keynes and Harry Dexter White led negotiations for Britain and the United States, which tried to achieve a postwar economic settlement. Determined to avoid mistakes of the past, they tried to fashion a more open trading system and multinational financing institutions—the International Monetary Fund (IMF) and International Bank for Reconstruction and Development (now known as the World Bank). They feared a recurrence of conflicts over war reparations, excessive economic nationalism, restrictive exchange controls, and beggar-thy-neighbor policies that weakened world prosperity and finance during the 1920s and 1930s.[30]

The IMF was designed as a mutual lending association (facilitating short- and medium-term loans) for member nations, with potential to create multinational liquidity over the long run. The IMF was capitalized by proportional contributions of gold, dollars, and national currencies from each member. (Initial capital was $10 billion, with a major U.S. contribution, substantial British contribution, and lesser amounts from other countries.) The IMF's mandate was to help stabilize currency relationships, as defined in terms of a gold–dollar exchange standard. Members were allowed to withdraw reserves and borrow from the Fund for the purpose of correcting a "fundamental disequilibrium" in their balance of payments, with additional drawings and credits subjected to conditions designed to encourage or maintain realistic exchange rates and adjustment policies. The IMF's initial capitalization and liquidity potential were rather modest, however, and direct U.S. loans and aid to Britain and other nations, plus additional assistance through UNRRA, the Marshall Plan, military support, and other aid programs proved to be more important financially in the earlier postwar years.

The International Bank for Reconstruction and Development (World Bank) was created to complement the IMF's role as a means for longer-term lending above and beyond what private investors, international banks, traditional export finance, and the IMF could support. Initial World Bank capitalization, however, was modest, proving quite inadequate to fund the immediate postwar reconstruction of Europe or to make a serious contribution to early development of the newly liberated countries of Asia (India, Pakistan, Burma, Ceylon, Indonesia, and the Philippines), the Middle East (Syria, Lebanon, Egypt, Iraq, Jordan, and Israel), or Latin America. Help from the United States through UNRRA, the Marshall Plan, Point Four programs, surplus agricultural commodities, military aid, and other assistance was more important in the early years. (In the 1960s, however, World Bank loans gradually became more significant, along with U.S. and European development aid programs.)

U.S. aid to allies during the war years through lend-lease financing of military equipment, aircraft, ships, munitions, and supplies had been large, being generously provided by Congress through wartime deficit finance.[31] But U.S. policymakers soon realized that major postwar support would be needed as well for healthy economic recovery in Europe. Recognition of this need was stimulated by aggressive communist efforts to consolidate and seize power in Eastern Europe. Poland, East Germany, Czechoslovakia, Hungary, Romania and Bulgaria had been "liberated" by the Soviet Red Army; Yugoslavia was liberated by its own communist-dominated partisans; and communist partisans were attempting to take over Greece. In China, communist forces threatened Kuomingtang control. Further pressure was applied through Soviet troops in Northern Iran and substantial communist parties in Italy and France. From the viewpoint of the United States and other Western governments, the new Cold War with Stalin's Soviet Union required big financial help to sustain weak and troubled governments. Without substantial U.S. aid in one form or another, an adverse and fundamental change in the world power balance would result. Much of Europe and many other countries could have fallen under communist rule rather quickly.

Military support and economic aid were used by the United States to contain communist expansion, proving reasonably successful in most areas (except China). Created in 1949, the North Atlantic Treaty Organization (NATO) integrated North American and Western European defenses, with firm U.S. commitments to allies if attacked. Similar collective security arrangements under SEATO (Southeast Asia Treaty Organization) and METO (Mid-East Treaty Organization) followed later. And, substantial U.S. aid (with modest British and French support) financed these efforts. The United States rallied to South Korea's defense after it was attacked by North Korea, and the United Nations allies won a costly defensive victory (1950–1953) after three years.

Meanwhile, the United States, and Britain to a lesser extent, gradually tried to fashion a more open trading system than had prevailed in the years before World War II. From the standpoint of earlier history, U.S. industrial, financial, and naval dominance was much like Britain's leadership after the Napoleonic Wars. German and Japanese industry were badly devastated. France, the Low Countries, Italy, Poland, Hungary, and Czechoslovakia were seriously exploited, disrupted, and weakened. British industry was somewhat stronger but tired, and its finances depleted. The Soviets emerged with a strong army and air force, though economically drained, and with considerable need for reconstruction. In these circumstances, U.S. industry accounted for nearly half the world's industrial output, had a large export surplus, and was financially much stronger than its prewar competitors (as reflected in appendix tables A–1 through A–10). Thus, like Britain in most of the nineteenth century, postwar U.S. leaders felt it could afford freer trade.

In addition, U.S. leaders (and many Europeans) believed that more open markets would help build a more prosperous and stronger Free-World economy, one better able to withstand aggressive pressures from the communist bloc. Leading bankers and industrialists saw economic opportunity for themselves, too. Mutual advantage could unite most of the world (including less developed nations) in this way. Economic, military and political logic meant that freer trade would be a cheaper, more productive form of assistance than sustained subsidies. Hence, "trade not aid" became a popular slogan in persuading Congress to alter gradually the country's long protectionist traditions.[32]

But, protectionist tariffs and outlooks could not be dismantled overnight, neither in the United States nor elsewhere.[33] Many U.S. economists urged a code for postwar international trade that would outlaw "unfair" trade practices and encourage most-favored–nation treatment, with negotiations toward reciprocal reductions in tariffs. A two-pronged strategy emerged along these lines. A draft charter for an International Trade Organization (ITO) was prepared in 1946–47 for the Havana Conference of 1948. But, while the proposed ITO included a permanent staff (as desired by U.S. negotiators), substantial compromises and exceptions were imposed by the British and most developing nations that substantially weakened the commitment to multilateral, open free trade, with insufficient safeguards for U.S. investments abroad. Congressional and business resistance was strong, however, to this much trade liberalization (especially since the terms were not particularly favorable to U.S. industry). Accordingly, an alternate track was pursued—a General Agreement on Tariffs and Trade, signed in April 1947, by twenty-three countries (including the United States, Britain, most Commonwealth nations, France, Benelux, Austria, Norway, and some Latin American countries). Part I of GATT established the most-favored–nation principle, while Part II articulated a standard for unfair trade practices (with major exceptions for countries in balance of payments difficulties and developing nations wanting protection for infant and growing industries). The GATT contemplated successive rounds of tariff reduction on a reciprocal basis. And GATT was merely an Executive Agreement requiring no Congressional approval or review (unlike ITO, which required treaty ratification by Congress). Although the Truman administration urged ITO ratification until winter 1950–51, it was thereafter abandoned. (Ultimately, though, GATT acquired a small executive secretariat in Geneva, became a continuing organization, and evolved into a stronger freer-trade lobbying institution than the initial compromise charter for ITO.) By 1982, 117 countries were GATT signatories or accepted it as former colonies of signatories.

Three successive rounds of tariff and trade barrier reduction negotiations were conducted between 1947–1951. Some initial progress was achieved at Geneva (1947), Annecy (1949), and Torquay (1950–51). With Europe not fully recovered economically or seriously integrated beyond Marshall Plan collaboration under the OEEC and the new NATO treaty, bargaining prospects were somewhat limited. Republican opposition in Congress also prevented major U.S. trade concessions. And yet, the institutional foundation for major, subsequent reductions in many tariff and trade barriers had been established in the GATT.

In this context, British and leading U.S. banks began to revive international finance as a handmaiden to European recovery. As industry and trade began to recover, bank finance and deposits shared in the growth. And, since business profits were often good in the postwar recovery (despite some inflation in many countries), internal cash flow also helped refinance gradual recovery. In this way, the basis was being laid for a stronger, sustained period of general Western prosperity in the 1950s and 1960s.[34]

Finally, contrasting mention must be made of developments in Eastern Europe and the Soviet Union.[35] Partly responding to Western recovery, and for their own economic needs as well, the Soviet Union organized an economic, trade, and military bloc of communist states (itself and Eastern Europe). The Council for Mutual Economic Assistance (CMEA) and Warsaw Pact were counterparts and rivals to the Marshall Plan and NATO. Within a few years, Eastern Europe switched most of its trade from West to East (under Soviet and Western pressures). Although Czechoslovakia and Poland had joined the IMF at the outset, they soon withdrew. Substantial industrial growth was encouraged later within this COMECON bloc, although heavy requisitions of plants and equipment had been extracted from East Germany and former Axis partners. The new Soviet satellites also complained of some economic exploitation as captive markets, but bloc discipline left few outside alternatives. While living standards were lower in the Eastern bloc, their starting levels had been more modest. Even so, the rate of heavy industry recovery and expansion was substantial, which supported a steadily growing military establishment.

When China became communist, it signed significant new trade and assistance agreements with the Soviets. But, Chinese dissatisfaction over the economic and military aid relationship with the Soviets led to a fairly rapid estrangement, and mutual suspicions then brought a virtual economic separation between them. This left China isolated and helped prompt its Great Leap Forward, a largely unsuccessful experiment with low-technology growth programs. This was followed by the Cultural Revolution, and some economic demoralization. (Ultimately, the weaker economic performance of Maoist China in the 1960s and 1970s helped erode confidence in Marxism for China in the

1980s, while opening the door to a more pragmatic era with greater market-oriented disciplines.)[36]

European Integration and Growing Prosperity,
1951–68

While substantial military budgets and NATO defense efforts continued through the 1950s and 1960s, recovery in Europe proceeded rapidly.[37] It soon encompassed most of Western Europe and benefited the United States, much of the British Commonwealth, and a considerable number of Latin American nations, together with Japan and some other countries in Asia. In Europe, trade was growing substantially. Earlier integration efforts, the OEEC and Marshall Plan (1947–52), European Payments Union (1948), and NATO (1949) had restored confidence in Europe. Closer economic integration was encouraged by the European Coal and Steel Community (ECSC) of 1951 and, most importantly, by the Treaty of Rome establishing the European Common Market (EEC) in 1957, with France, Germany, Italy, and Benelux as initial members. While Britain was reluctant to sever economic ties with Commonwealth nations, it favored considerable European integration (especially with EFTA countries). And, for the most part, the United States strongly supported European integration efforts. The United States had been pushing hard for Europe's unification since the late 1940s, primarily for military and political reasons. A united, more prosperous Europe could stand against communist pressures more effectively and be an equal ally for the United States.

Many U.S. corporations participated in European economic expansion and began to spread more widely to other parts of the world (beyond Latin America). Their capital outlays and enterprise added to the growing momentum of European prosperity. Gradually, many European (and later Japanese) corporations became equal in size and diversification to the U.S. multinationals and participated in the same trend toward global outreach. Leading U.S. banks joined the big British, German, and French banks in helping to finance this growth of industry and trade, and Swiss banking began to collect foreign deposits and trust accounts more extensively, becoming active in European and other international finance.

An important London innovation of the late 1940s, the Eurodollar deposit account, picked up increasing use in these years.[38] Traditionally, bank deposits were made in one's own national currency by individuals and domestic corporations. But, because dollars were a strong currency (with less risk of devaluation than, say, the British pound, French franc, or Italian lira) and were universally acceptable without exchange controls, increasing international dollar liquidity was held "offshore" in European or U.S. branch banks (and later in Asian banks or even in tax-haven branches anywhere). Eventually, through the later 1960s and 1970s, the Eurocurrency market grew massively, as a less regulated, more highly leveraged, and more profitable channel for international finance. Eurocurrency banking utilized and gradually reinforced the momentum of increasing financial and trade integration in Europe and the rest of the world.

Although Americans worried, for a while, that a more integrated Western Europe could wall itself off later with higher tariff barriers, the EEC's trade policy actually developed in line with U.S. policies toward freer, more open multinational trade. A basic reason was Western Europe's need for exports to purchase raw materials. While Britain tried to retain more Commonwealth connections, most EEC countries lacked comparable links to former colonies. And, the EEC gave French agriculture an assured market, a vital interest for them, so they collaborated more with their partners on industrial and trade policies. After de Gaulle returned to power in 1958, Franco–German cooperation on economic and trade policies was strengthened. Finally, to the extent that EEC and other European markets did remain somewhat protected, this encouraged U.S. firms to make branch plant investments and/or joint venture deals in Western Europe. Gradually, most of noncommunist Europe became more closely associated with the EEC, and most countries are now members. (The U.K., Ireland, and Denmark joined in 1973, Greece in 1981, and Spain and Portugal in 1984.)[39]

Additional steps toward trade liberalization were taken by the United States in this period, and GATT became more significant as a means toward reducing tariffs.[40] President Eisenhower broke with traditional GOP high-tariff policies and supported extensions of the Reciprocal Trade Agreements Act. Using the Randall Commission's recommendations for freer trade, Eisenhower said in 1953 that U.S. capital and trade must go to the developing countries, for "only in this way can they absorb our industrial and agricultural surpluses; only in this way can we get the vital raw materials we must have." By the end of Eisenhower's presidency, Republican and big business outlooks had shifted and largely accepted a more open trade policy. Meanwhile, GATT's administrative capabilities improved, with ad hoc working parties in the early 1950s, standing committees in 1955, regularized in 1958, and a permanent GATT Council organization in 1960.

The Dillon Round of tariff reduction negotiations under GATT auspices followed in 1960–62 (with somewhat broader latitude from Eisenhower on bargaining for the U.S. delegation). Even more significantly, the Kennedy administration then pushed aggressively (as expected) toward freer trade. The Trade Expansion Act of 1962 broadened greatly the negotiating mandate for across-the-board tariff reductions, created the Office of Special Trade Representative, and allowed opportunities for adjustment assistance resulting from freer trade. Much more sweeping trade negotiations followed between 1964 and 1967 in the Kennedy Round, involving the United States, EEC, Britain, Japan, and Nordic countries as key participants. This led to a substantial and widespread reduction of tariff barriers between industrial countries. While agricultural markets were left more protected, the Kennedy Round agreements probably represented the most substantial, far-reaching reduction in trade barriers among industrial countries since the 1850s. On the other hand, most developing countries were becoming more protectionist (at least selectively), which was allowed under the GATT (with further encouragement by part IV of GATT, which was added in 1965). And, many countries still used revenue tariffs extensively.

Thus, European economic integration and growing prosperity evolved into a broader world marketplace by the late 1960s. Significantly freer trade, expanding multinational corporations, enlarged foreign investment, and stronger international banks, with additional liquidity potential through Eurodollar deposit accounts, were part of greatly increased economic growth among industrial nations. During the 1960s, most less developed countries were beginning to improve their growth performance too. And, some were entering the take-off stage into more advanced industrial development. Many economists were becoming substantially more optimistic about the world economy in the later 1960s.

Meanwhile, expansions of IMF capitalization followed in the late 1950s and early 1960s, together with the General Agreements to Borrow (1963), which added appreciably to its resources in assisting countries (mostly developing nations now) with balance of payments difficulties.[41] World Bank resources were gradually increased in this period also, as was economic aid from Europe (in addition to the United States) for developing countries. While private foreign investment and trade financing substantially exceeded these multinational and government loans and assistance, development economists emphasized the complementary, mutually reinforcing character of these financial flows to the spread of economic growth and world prosperity.

And, in 1968, IMF liquidity expansion potential was further increased (at least for the long run) by authority allowing issuance of a new international reserve asset, the special drawing right (SDR). (In 1969, $3.5 billion of SDRs were issued, followed by $3 billion of SDRs in 1970 and again in 1971.) SDRs were created as an alternative to dollars and gold as international reserve assets, because more countries—even the United States itself—were becoming somewhat uneasy about a single national currency, the dollar, being the primary financial reserve asset for international commerce. This was a heavy responsibility and potential strain for U.S. macroeconomic, trade, and industrial policies. Some serious European doubts already were expressed about U.S. economic policies, Vietnam War outlays, and the possible dangers of inflation spreading from the United States to its European allies and elsewhere.

Inflation Strains, Dollar Devaluation, and Floating
Exchange Rates, 1968–74

Some of the increased world growth, trade, and international investment flows continued into the 1970s. But, serious complications with dollar devaluation, currency realignment, and major commodity price inflation (especially for feed grains, petroleum, and energy in 1973–74) later slowed real growth for most industrial countries.[42] And quite importantly, the fixed dollar–gold exchange rate system agreed upon at Bretton Woods in 1944 finally broke down and was replaced by the present system of floating exchange rates (with limited government intervention to prevent speculation, ease adjustments, or promote exports.)

In most of the post–World War II era, the U.S. dollar has been a strong currency, one greatly desired as a liquid asset by countries with weaker, more vulnerable, or depreciating currencies. The dollar was exceptionally strong in 1945, when vast gold reserves (magnified by foreign capital flight and borrowing) had accumulated, and the U.S. industrial machine dominated world trade. For Europe and Japan, along with most developing nations, there was a natural desire to enlarge exports to the United States and earn more dollars. U.S. economic aid, military assistance and bases abroad, together with growing private investment by the United States, sent more dollars into the world. The creation of Eurodollar deposits by leading international banks was adding even further dollar-denominated liquidity. By 1971, there was a huge overhang of liquid dollar balances, at least $100 billion, and the U.S. gold reserve had declined from its wartime peak of $16 billion to roughly $8 billion. The potential for a run on the dollar was quite serious under the Bretton Woods dollars–gold fixed exchange rate system.

There had been some forethought and institutional response to increasing reliance on dollars as the primary reserve currency in the years after World War II, and to strengthening the IMF currency stabilization-support system. The United States had fixed $35 per ounce for gold as its currency par value back in 1934 (after brief fluctuations following dollar devaluation in 1933). The strength of the U.S. economic base, growing foreign investments, military power, and security helped sustain confidence in the dollar through the 1950s (despite significant balance of payments deficits accumulating since 1950 thanks to U.S. aid and military outlays abroad, increasing investments overseas, and the need to allow more exports into U.S. markets). But in 1961, upward pressure on London gold prices (early speculation against the dollar) led to formation of the London Gold Pool. Britain, the EEC countries, and Switzerland agreed to provide half the gold necessary to support the dollar at $35 per ounce, with the United States providing the other half. For many years this reassurance seemed to suffice (at least in support of the dollar).

The British pound, however, as a secondary reserve currency, was more difficult to sustain.[43] The pound needed considerable U.S. help in the late 1940s, but still had to be devalued from $4.03: 1£ to $2.80: 1£ in 1949. The British economy (with depleted financial assets abroad, large sterling balances owed, and substantial deficits in payments) simply could not serve much longer as a major reserve currency. Things improved somewhat for the British and the pound during the 1950s, but substantial overseas defense commitments (and strains over failure of the Suez expedition in 1956) added burdens. Serious difficulties were union wage pressures, uneven productivity, stop-go fiscal stimulus and restraint, and fairly heavy tax loads. In contrast, German economic and industrial recovery was much stronger in the 1950s and 1960s. The deutsche mark was revalued upward already in 1961; shortly thereafter, speculative pressure weakened the pound. At this stage, leading industrial country central banks agreed in Basle to extend automatic emergency credits in support of currencies threatened with speculation. Britain borrowed $900 million from these central banks and drew $1,500 million from the IMF. Later in 1961, the Group of Ten announced their General Arrangements to Borrow (GAB) and pledged up to $6 billion for this purpose. All this helped for a while, but Britain became the initial GAB borrower in 1964 and suffered considerable economic strain and recurrent crises for the next three years. Ultimately, another devaluation of the pound from $2.80 to $2.40 was needed in 1967. A stronger British incomes (wage-price–restraint) policy followed, and this devaluation was more successful, at least for a few years.

Relief for the pound, however, meant direct exposure for the dollar. By 1967, the Johnson administration was preoccupied with the escalating Vietnam War, unrest in many cities, and a newly proclaimed War on Poverty. U.S. budget deficits were increasing. A policy of retrenchment and deflation to support the dollar was unthinkable and might not have helped much anyway, because of the massive dollar balances held abroad. Nor were U.S. exchange controls acceptable to business interests, because this would have undercut confidence in the U.S. economy and the dollar. (Half-hearted controls to limit capital investment abroad—the interest equalization tax—already failed earlier in the 1960s.)

The first U.S. response was a two-tier gold price system announced in March 1968 at a hastily called meeting of seven countries. The official price for transactions among the seven governments would still be $35 an ounce. But, the private price of gold in London, Zurich, and elsewhere was free to fluctuate with market forces (and speculation). This was, in large measure, a de facto devaluation of the dollar relative to gold, yet no other industrial country really wanted to risk slowing their export sales by an upward revaluation of their own currency.[44] For the time being, these measures eased the dollar problem, although U.S. balance of payments deficits increased during the early 1970s.[45]

Meanwhile, at the IMF meetings in 1967, agreement was reached to create additional international liquidity in the form of SDRs. Some $10.5 billion worth of SDRs were issued in 1969–71. And, although many Europeans were complaining that the United States was exporting Vietnam War inflation, relatively strong growth and expansion of international reserves (including dollar balances) were continuing for most nations. Many experts felt the key problem was to sustain world economic expansion, while gradually broadening international liquidity reserves (including other hard currencies and SDRs as well as the dollar).

But, in spring 1971, U.S. economic policies did not seem entirely successful, at least by contrast to the 1950s and, especially, the 1961–66 boom period. Despite somewhat tighter monetary policy, an increased inflation rate had cooled only slightly, growth had slumped, and unemployment remained significant. And, the U.S. balance of payments deficit remained serious. It appeared that the United States might be falling into stagflation like the British economy had earlier. In these circumstances, dollars began to flow to Germany, and the mark was revalued upward slightly; Japan, however, refused to revalue the yen, being afraid to risk losing export sales. In the summer, more substantial withdrawals of dollars for gold occurred, and by early August 1971, a run on the dollar was in progress.[46]

On August 15, 1971, President Nixon closed the gold window completely, ending dollar convertibility for the time being. He imposed a temporary 10 percent import surcharge (to force an upward revaluation of other hard currencies) and imposed stringent wage-price controls. These drastic measures greatly slowed inflation for a while and allowed some fiscal and monetary stimulation to improve economic growth and employment for Nixon's Nov. 1972 election victory. Meanwhile, U.S. allies had accepted a 10 percent dollar devaluation (after some initial objection) at the Dec. 1971 Smithsonian meetings, and the import surcharge was rescinded.

When Nixon began dismantling most controls early in 1973, another run on the dollar began. The pound, Canadian dollar, and yen were floating by this time, and in March 1973, the EEC currencies floated jointly against the dollar.[47] By summer 1973, another 9 to 18 percent appreciation of key currencies had occurred. While OPEC's oil price increase in late 1973 caused a substantial revival of the dollar (because the United States was less dependent on OPEC oil than Europe and Japan), by late spring 1974, the dollar declined back to its April 1973 levels, reflecting a 15 to 20 percent overall devaluation since August 1971.[48]

By 1975, eleven currencies (involving 46 percent of the trade among IMF members) were floating. While most small countries pegged exchange rates to key currencies (most frequently the U.S. dollar), major industrial nations (including the United States, EEC bloc, Britain, Japan, Switzerland, and some others) used floating exchange rates. The new "dirty floating" system involved selective currency intervention (part of the time) designed to prevent excessive speculation and, in some cases, to limit risk of loss in export sales. The U.S. used intervention sparingly, partly because the dollar was believed less controllable. (The U.S. monetary officials had less authority, and a substantial part of world dollar holdings were internationalized, i.e., involved in Eurocurrency bank accounts.) But, Japan and Europe were more willing to intervene.

The government of Japan has tried repeatedly to hold down the dollar value of the yen, apparently in order to give Japanese sellers of traded goods an extra competitive edge in international markets. In the process, Japanese official institutions have bought tremendous volumes of U.S. dollars that have nonetheless declined somewhat in yen value. The Japanese determination to resist the rise of the yen is a leading example of what has been called the "dirty float," a floating exchange rate involving considerable official intervention in one direction.

Governments of the European Economic Community strove to prevent movements in exchange rates among their currencies, setting up "the snake" within "the tunnel" in December 1971. They agreed on maximum ranges of movement for the most appreciated versus the most depreciated member currently (the tunnel), and on maximum bands within which pairwise exchange rates could oscillate (the snake).[49]

The performance of the floating exchange rate system has been reasonably satisfactory, though far from perfect.[50] Almost everyone concedes that the Bretton Woods fixed exchange rate system, with the dollar serving as the only reserve asset except gold (and limited SDRs) could not have operated in the special stresses of the early 1970s. (Nor could the world have permitted its liquidity to consist primarily of U.S. dollars indefinitely.) While many complain of excessive exchange rate variability or too much intervention with respect to key currencies (such as the Japanese yen, which some believe has been artificially undervalued to sustain exports), few believe a fixed exchange rate system could be restored today. Controversy centers today on more limited issues—the extent to which macroeconomic budget, fiscal, and monetary policies can be harmonized among major countries and the degree to which coordinated intervention by their central banks might be feasible to limit excessive variations or distortions in exchange rates. The G-5 undertaking of September 1985 represents an important step forward in that direction.

Naturally, the new floating exchange rate system involves a somewhat altered role for the IMF. Now countries suffering sustained balance of payments deficits can simply let their currency's float downward immediately and gradually, without having to draw upon IMF resources to defend fixed exchange rates until some fundamental disequilibrium becomes evident and allows a formal devaluation. IMF assistance is still helpful for distressed economies; it can be a valuable aid to their stabilization and recovery efforts. But, many economists believed that considerably less need for expanded multilateral liquidity might be involved under the floating exchange rate system. Furthermore, in view of growing inflation in the early 1970s (especially 1973–74), this was not a time to enlarge international liquidity (according to these economists).

Certainly, the world economy was suffering increased inflationary strain, particularly in 1973–74. The most immediate problems were a doubling of feed grain and meat prices, aggravated by European and Soviet crop failures and compounded by the OPEC cartel's trebling of oil and gas prices. But, this commodity price inflation had been aggravated by years of booming economic growth, bigger fiscal deficits for many countries, and a general expectation of increased living standards and incomes. In most industrial countries, unions had become very influential and wage-price spiral inflation had become common. In many countries, inflation had become serious and chronic, and the problem seemed to be spreading significantly worldwide in 1973–74.[51]

Such strong inflation, however, finally led to some deflationary discipline, slack, and greater unemployment, partly because the food, oil, and energy cost increases reduced real purchasing power for many people. Tougher monetary restraint and higher interest rates also reduced growth in many countries; substantial recession followed for the United States, Japan, and some European countries, among others. But, while the 1974–75 recession was widespread, unemployment increased substantially, and the world experienced its most serious economic slump since the 1930s, considerable inflationary momentum continued. For these reasons, economists found the term *stagflation* a good way to characterize the early- and mid-1970s economic performance of many nations.

Stagflation involves a blend of traditional *inflation* (excessive wage and price increases beyond real productivity) and *stagnation* (sluggishness, slowed growth, and significant unemployment). To many economists, this seemed paradoxical, because strong inflation normally had been associated with full employment and general overheating of an economy, while substantial unemployment was linked with widespread slack and soft prices generally. It was becoming evident that structural rigidities in wage and price setting (with powerful unions, corporations, lobbies, governments needing interest group support, and less competition in some sectors) were sustaining a momentum of wage-price increases in many nations, even when significant unemployment and slack in some areas were building up. Although earlier economic literature identified this as a potential problem, stagflation was not recognized as a widespread, important phenomenon until the 1970s. But, in this decade, stagflation came to be seen as a major economic problem of the world economy, with worrisome implications for trade, financing, and economic prosperity.[52]

Petrodollars, Stagflation, and Uneven Recovery, 1974–80

OPEC's trebling of oil prices in 1973–74 meant a substantial shift in price-income flows among nations. Almost overnight, leading oil-producing countries, including Saudi Arabia, Iran, Iraq, Kuwait, the Emirates, and Libya, received vastly increased petroleum revenues that could not be easily absorbed or spent domestically. This liquidity was deposited short-term or "parked," in interest-bearing Eurocurrency bank accounts (mostly in dollars). These "petrodollar" deposits greatly increased the lending resources of international banks. Loan portfolios of multinational banks grew beyond U.S. and European corporate clientele to include much more developing-country borrowing. Formerly, borrowers had been mostly private multinational corporations, but now governments, nationalized companies, and quasi-public enterprises were becoming substantial borrowers too. Some European governments and many non–oil-developing countries became significant borrowers in these years, partly to offset budget and economic strains resulting from the oil price shock, inflation, and recession. (It was estimated that three-quarters of the world's deficits in 1974–76 were financed by the banks, and external debts of nonoil LDCs went up from 13 to 18 percent of their GDP between 1973 and 1978.) In this way, petrodollars were recycled back to many countries that had been injured by the oil-energy price hikes imposed by the OPEC cartel.[53]

Eurocurrency banking was growing for other reasons. As multilateral trade and finance increased, more deposits and borrowing naturally took place in multinational banks and their branches and affiliates. And, with increasing mixtures of international components and services in business, it became possible, through skillful accounting and pricing arrangements, to locate profits increasingly in low-tax or tax-free countries. As sophistication spread more widely for these purposes, tax-haven banking and corporate affiliates were strongly encouraged. Multinational banks proliferated their branching and service networks in this environment. Thus, tax-minimizing strategies, and the avoidance of regulation generally, combined with convenience to greatly enlarge the use of multinational and Eurocurrency bank deposits, borrowing, and other activities. For all these reasons (including petrodollar recycling), Eurocurrency banking and deposits increased, on the average, nearly 25 percent a year between 1973 and 1981.[54]

Since Eurocurrency banking was lightly regulated, with thin reserves and high leverage, more bank liquidity was created in these banking channels. And, this liquidity went beyond (and was not fully included within) domestic money supplies. Some economists worried about additional world inflation from Eurocurrency banking, and they argued for tougher regulation. But, multinational bankers objected to such regulation, insisting that inflation was mostly a national economic mismanagement problem (based on, for example, excessive wages or government budget deficits). There was some concern for "country risk" (excessive borrowing by LDCs). But, most international bankers felt that diversification of lending among the many LDCs would be a sufficient precaution. And, many developing countries were enjoying solid economic growth (more than the majority of industrial nations), while seeming to be profitable, relatively high-yield loan customers.

In the 1970s, international liquidity reserves for most countries increased more rapidly than in the fifties and sixties.[55] Increased gold prices and dollar devaluation (relative to gold) were major factors. In addition, IMF quotas were increased by 32.5 percent in 1975 and 50 percent in 1978, and there was a gradual strengthening and broadening of facilities for IMF support to member countries. Thus, nations received somewhat more latitude to sustain progrowth, stimulative economic policies. (Some economists complained that too much liquidity growth, deficit finance, and international borrowing resulted, but the larger portion of this criticism came later, in the early 1980s, when the excesses of international inflation and debt overloads began to be more fully appreciated.)

Among major industrial countries, stagflation was a real concern. The United States, Britain, France, Italy, Sweden, Canada, and Australia all seemed to be suffering the disease. A substantial wage-price spiral continued, despite considerable slack and increased unemployment. Budget deficits had grown, partly in response to these strains. And, the politics of democracy made it difficult to crack down on inflation. Unions and their political parties resisted wage-price discipline. Business interests feared controls also. Some urged monetary restraint, but higher interest rates, greater slack, and more unemployment did not seem promising politically. Nor was stringent fiscal discipline popular in pluralist societies. Most industrial nations muddled through the mid- and late 1970s with appreciably more structural unemployment and inflationary momentum than they considered normal or desirable, but found it difficult to do better. Somehow the Phillips curve trade-off between unemployment and inflation had shifted outward, yielding more of both than was suffered in the "golden sixties" (years of relatively strong economic growth, full employment, and low inflation). And worst of all, productivity growth rates had subsided in most of these countries.

A few industrial countries were in better shape. Japan, West Germany, Switzerland, and Austria accepted stronger fiscal, monetary, and wage-price discipline. They had retrenched living standards more readily (due to increased food, fuel, and energy prices) and kept their export-oriented industries more competitive. Switzerland accepted the most deflation, expelled many foreign guest workers, and achieved the lowest inflation (though with less growth than other nations'). Japan enjoyed the best economic growth from its "export machine," but held inflation fairly low and was concerned as unemployment crept toward 3 percent (a rate most countries envied). West Germany and Austria suffered more unemployment, but also held inflation fairly low, while preserving limited growth. The secret to better performance in these countries was greater economic discipline, which reflected greater realism about export dependence for these crowded countries (and maybe wiser governments).[56]

Developing countries varied even more widely in their economic performance during the mid- and late 1970s. But many, led by Korea, Taiwan, and Singapore in East Asia (new industrial countries), maintained very high growth rates and export expansion. More slowed somewhat, with high energy costs and greater inflation. A limited number, with bad governments or civil disorder, actually fell behind. And yet, on the whole, developing nations did reasonably well in the 1970s. Aggregate borrowing of LDCs and NICs increased substantially, as they "leveraged up"—collectively borrowing, we might say, on the

collateral of economic growth prospects. But, there was somewhat greater optimism about economic growth, despite insecurities, among most NICs and
many LDCs.[57]

In addition, developing countries (as a whole) were becoming more assertive and making stronger claims for a larger slice of the world economic pie.[58]
For example, at the end of 1974, the U.N. General Assembly (with a solid
voting majority of developing nations) approved a Charter of Economic Rights
and Duties of States.[59] This broadly supported proposals for a New International Economic Order (NIEO) and was followed by a resolution on Development and International Economic Cooperation in 1975. The main proposals
were: (1) increased resource transfers to LDCs and the linkage of development
aid to expanded SDR liquidity from the IMF, (2) more favorable treatment, interest rates, and leniency by the IMF and international banks to developing countries, (3) more international commodity cartels (such as OPEC), with prices
indexed to manufactures from developing countries, and (4) an international industrial policy emphasizing every state's sovereignty over national resources and
economic activities, including wide latitude to nationalize foreign investments,
some redeployment of industry to LDCs, systematic technology transfers to LDCs,
and the preferential lowering of tariffs by advanced nations to allow more generous
developing-country exports. This agenda of goals was clearly aspirational—a
wish list—but it represents a fair consensus of developing-country views on the
evolving world economy. It should be taken more seriously by advanced industrial nations, not merely out of kindness to less affluent countries, but as
revealing bargaining objectives as well as possible constraints in future trade,
investment, and debt-rescheduling relationships.

It is in this context that multilateral trade negotiations during the 1970s
must be understood. The Kennedy Round had led to substantially reduced tariffs
among industrial nations in the later 1960s, but developing nations were becoming more protectionist to encourage industrialization, and they generally tried
to limit imports of consumer manufactures such as automobiles and expensive appliances. Exchange controls were common in developing countries that
suffered significant budget deficits and inflation.

Preparations for the seventh GATT negotiating session, the Tokyo Round,
began in the early 1970s (and were initially styled the Nixon Round). U.S. negotiating authority was established in the Trade Act of 1974. This act narrowed
traditional U.S. trade-relief provisions (the escape clause, antidumping and
countervailing duties), although enlarging (at least in theory) the potential for
adjustment assistance to injured U.S. companies and unemployed workers. In
addition, the legislation created, in somewhat reduced form, generalized preferences for LDC manufactures (a priority objective for developing nations).

The Tokyo Round, concluded in 1979, brought another major reduction
(roughly by one-third) in tariff rates among *industrial* countries. Agriculture,
however, remained largely exempt, and the EEC's Common Agricultural Policy

(CAP), objected to by the United States as restriction of a major export market, was not significantly changed. Attempts to deal with nontariff barriers were made through a series of Codes of Conduct (Subsidies and Countervailing Duties Code, Government Procurement Code, Anti-dumping Code, Customs Valuation Code, Standards Code, and Licensing Code).[60] Each code provides for GATT committees to help resolve disputes. Some U.S. experts view these codes as a further weakening of U.S. domestic unfair trade practice laws (such as remedies for subsidies, dumping, and other unfair distortions). And, while some applaud further progress toward freer trade (at least among industrial nations), others protest against the continued toleration of widespread protection among developing nations (especially the NICs) and the weakness of many codes. Meanwhile, most LDCs complained that the Tokyo Round did not go far enough in their direction, and many of them boycotted the signing ceremony.[61]

Even so, the great cumulative reduction of tariffs and other trade barriers among advanced industrial nations (especially via the Kennedy and Tokyo Rounds), with MFN protection for most developing nations, had in fact created a substantial, general preference for NICs and LDCs. Developing countries were still free to use infant-industry tariffs and significant industrial development subsidies; they often "dumped" goods at lowered prices in export markets. While trade among advanced industrial nations had become relatively balanced, with more open and mutual access (their labor costs are not too dissimilar), industrial expansion among LDCs and NICs was now more strongly encouraged by the GATT world trade regime. Labor unions in the United States and Europe were beginning to complain about "job flight" and branch plants moving to low-wage countries. The loss of good jobs and increasing insecurity gradually led during the late 1970s–1980s to a New Protectionism.[62]

The New Protectionism took many forms—orderly marketing agreements, voluntary export restraints, systematic filing of unfair trade practice complaints, and extensive lobbying for import restrictions, quotas, and countersubsidies. This reaction to free trade, increased low-wage manufactures from abroad, and the threat of job losses became more widespread in Europe in the late 1970s and early 1980s, and grew in the United States also. Among heavily affected industries were textiles, apparel, shoes, steel, automobiles, and electronic appliances. Since advanced industrial democracies are pluralist, impacted interest groups (labor and industries) often were successful in efforts to increase protection. Leading U.S. examples in the 1970s were the Multifibre Agreement (MFA), a multilateral orderly marketing agreement for textiles, the steel "trigger-price mechanism" (1978–80), a compromise to discourage steel imports at prices below "efficient" Japanese reference levels, and voluntary Japanese auto import restraints (1980–83), which set limits on the number of cars exported to the United States. Similar developments occurred in Europe and the EEC, and most experts believe the New Protectionism has been somewhat stronger and more effective in Europe than in the United States.

All this represents a backlash to more open markets for imported manufactures in Europe and the United States or, in other words, the tariff-reduction achievements of the Kennedy and Tokyo Rounds. The New Protectionism also reflects the growing industrial vitality of many developing nations, led by Hong Kong, Singapore, Taiwan, South Korea, Brazil, and others. The fact that only a minority of developing nations reaped the greatest export-growth dividends was a serious complication, though, because it meant that a New Protectionist reaction to freer trade might involve some overkill and that it was not easy to target on clearly unfair trade practices. The potential for low-wage competition and job flight was, in fact, pervasive and, many believed, not fully stoppable.

In any event, many developing countries managed to continue considerable growth in the late 1970s, partly because their low-wage manufacturers were expanding. Another factor was generously increasing loans from multinational banks. Many Latin American countries in particular (led by Mexico with its rapidly enlarging petroleum sales) went on a shopping spree for industrial expansion and consumer durables. And, much of Asia did reasonably well in these years, too, with expanding exports (though less involvement in borrowing).

But between 1979 and 1980, another doubling of oil prices (OPEC II) occurred. This aggravated substantial inflationary momentum in many countries, and real growth slowed again. Most of the advanced industrial democracies (including the United States, Britain, France, West Germany, Italy, Sweden, Canada, and Australia) were affected to some degree. In almost all of these nations, unions were still fairly influential, and strong wage restraint was impractical politically. Only the Japanese and Swiss seemed less affected, and each enjoyed a stronger economy than most, while managing better wage-price discipline.

In the United States, particularly, a growing inflation rate (despite expanding employment) was beginning to erode confidence. In Fall 1978, the Carter administration's response—a much ballyhooed "voluntary" wage-price guidelines program, with modest reductions in large budget deficits ($30 billion was then considered excessive)—was perceived as weak. Another run on the dollar began, and gold was moving up rapidly. Then, more drastic action followed—$30 billion of borrowing abroad in hard currencies (unprecedented for the time) to buy up dollars being dumped. This worked for a while, but by then, at least $600 billion of dollars was held as liquid, international reserves. But, the voluntary inflation restraint program failed (partly due to OPEC II and anticipatory price-wage increases before mandatory controls could follow), and the price indexes moved into double digits again, as in 1973–74. During 1979, international confidence in the dollar sagged, and the price of gold (in dollars) went from $230 an ounce in April to $430 in October (reaching a peak of $875 in early 1980). In October 1979, under Federal Reserve Chairman Paul Volcker's leadership, the Fed switched to a more restrictive money-supply–targeting policy and drastically increased interest rates. Even tougher credit controls followed in March 1980, which finally broke the inflationary spiral (which peaked at 20 percent), and a brief slump followed. The Fed released its brakes somewhat, but inflation was increasing again in the fall, along with higher interest rates.

In the November 1980 presidential election, Reagan defeated Carter. This brought a historic change in political direction to the United States, from a moderate-liberal (with considerable faith in modern welfare states) to a right-wing conservative (believing in free markets and a need to reduce taxes and government). Broad frustration over increased inflation (and associated bracket creep in income taxes) plus national humiliation over the Iranian hostage crisis had undermined confidence in Carter, and Reagan seemed rather reassuring (and more poised) in their TV debate. But from this election, more significant changes in U.S. financial policies followed, which brought still another distinct phase in international economics.[63]

Monetary Restraint, World Recession, Debt Overloads, and Strain, 1980–86

Monetary restraint had been greatly tightened in the U.S. since November 1979 (although a brief relaxation occurred in late spring–early summer 1980). U.S. interest rates moved up sharply, reaching short-term peaks of around 20 percent in early spring 1980 and again during late fall and winter 1980–81. Because U.S. money and credit markets bulk so large, this forced world market rates up to a substantial degree, too. (Other countries feared a short-term capital drain to the United States if they did not follow, at least to a substantial degree.) Because most short- and medium-term Eurocurrency lending involves floating interest rates, keyed to LIBOR or SIBOR (the London or Singapore interbank rates), this pushed up the debt-service burdens of borrowing countries significantly. These deflationary policies were endorsed by most conservative business and banking interests in Europe and the United States as a necessary medicine to crack down on excessive inflationary momentum.

Strong monetary discipline was endorsed by the new Reagan administration, which quickly implemented: (1) substantial personal and corporate income tax cuts (increasing over three years), (2) a major relaxation of business regulation, (3) a new toughness against labor unions (including dismissal of all striking air controllers), and (4) significant increases in defense spending. Hoping to reduce social security and welfare outlays, the president appointed a blue-ribbon commission to make recommendations for reforms in that area. (Subsequently, the Social Security Commission recommended, and Congress approved, a mixture of modest cuts, a gradual increase in retirement age, and a small increase in social security taxes.) While increased budget deficits were contemplated as useful leverage to force Congress into reducing civilian spending, administration leaders were reasonably optimistic about reviving economic growth (or at least were convinced that a substantial defense buildup was needed to match growing Soviet military forces).

Almost immediately, however, in summer 1981, divergent estimates developed on the impact of supply-side economics (the large tax cuts combined with increased defense outlays). The most enthusiastic supply-siders projected rapid economic growth, which would eliminate deficits quickly. Monetarists were divided, with some endorsing bigger deficits as leverage to shrink government, and others remaining doubtful and worried. Traditional bankers generally approved of lower taxes and improved incentives, but believed big U.S. deficits were dangerous and would renew inflation, unless offset with tight money and high interest rates. Many Keynesian liberals commented that Reaganomics was really deficit-spending stimulus, which reflected their own policies (except for considerably different spending and tax load priorities).[64]

In these circumstances, the Federal Reserve implemented a tougher, more restrictive monetary policy than many expected. The Fed greatly feared a renewal of inflation from rising budget deficits and kept real interest rates unusually high for about four years. This produced more deflation and a more severe, worldwide recession (some labeled it a moderate depression) than in 1974–75. Unemployment reached 11 to 12 percent in the United States during 1982 (a rate not seen since the late 1930s), and slack developed in most world commodity markets, from feed grains to raw materials, oil, gas, metals, and lumber. Not only was growth halted for many countries, but a considerable number suffered a decline in real income (partly due to shifts in terms of trade, reversing the "exploitation" complained of by manufacturing countries in 1973–74 and 1979–80).[65]

But, the momentum of worldwide inflation was greatly reduced.[66] The slump in world commodity markets, including a decline in oil prices by roughly 50 percent over five years, helped to alleviate inflationary pressures. In the United States, the wage-price spiral was largely broken or at least reduced to 3 to 4 percent per year (from previous highs of 12 percent in 1973–74 and 1980). Union labor accounted for only 18 percent of the U.S. work force by the mid-1980s and was much weaker in these circumstances than before. In many other major industrial democracies, unions were still stronger, and somewhat more wage-price spiral inflation continued, though at lower levels. To be sure, countries with large or aggravated budget deficits (5, 10, or even 15 percent of GDP), accommodating monetary policies, and "confiscatory" interest rates (rates involving real capital losses) tended to suffer substantially higher inflation and, often, some degree of capital flight. (While U.S. budget deficits were approaching 5 percent of GNP in 1984–85, they were being offset by restrictive monetary policies and high real interest rates. This brought increasingly heavy short-term capital flows from abroad, exceeding $100 billion in both 1984 and 1985. This might not continue too much longer, however, and a premium in U.S. interest rates had to be paid—one sufficient also to compensate for a likely dollar devaluation. The United States paid for the "political luxury" of large budget deficits, in other words, by substantially enlarging its national debt, increasing debt-service burdens, and becoming a net debtor nation in 1985, for the first time since before World War I.

Naturally, this much deflation and recession imposed costs. The main cost was forgone economic growth (in the worst post–World War II recession slump), with somewhat reduced employment (and enlarged unemployment). But, the majority of people still working at good incomes benefited from major reductions in inflation. Hence, the costs of deflation landed unequally, falling most painfully against those losing jobs and having reduced incomes (a relative minority in the advanced industrial societies).[67]

While U.S. deflation discipline was the most important, some other industrial democracies used comparable policies. Britain's Thatcher government (and, to a lesser extent, West Germany) employed tighter monetary restraint and higher interest rates, too. The major exception was France (under Mitterand's socialist government), which attempted stimulative Keynesian policies in the midst of general restraint. But after a couple of years, the French soon were forced to accommodate to the overall trend. France found it could not inflate and reduce interest rates alone, when the United States and its other industrial allies were using tight money and higher interest rates. (Most Europeans and others complained, of course, about excessive $200 billion U.S. budget deficits and tight money policies during 1983–85, which "needlessly prolonged deflation" and drained off large amounts of liquid capital to the United States. Many American economists agreed, yet U.S. budget and tax policies were caught in a bad three-way split between conservatives, moderates, and liberals. The Reagan administration, a Republican Senate, and a Democratic House simply could not agree on the spending and tax priorities for an early balanced budget. Both conservative and liberal wings were hoping to win the next election due to mistakes of the other side.)

Meanwhile, rapidly increased interest rates and serious recession in many world markets forced a growing number of large debtor countries into near default on their external indebtedness. Led by Mexico and Brazil (owing roughly $80 billion and $90 billion, respectively), in summer and fall 1982, it soon became evident that most of Latin America, many African nations, and some others, were seriously overloaded with foreign debt obligations. A large part of this debt was recent, being owed to international banks, with greatly enlarged interest obligations. Considerable assistance from the IMF (and, to some extent, from the United States, the World Bank, and even BIS), with substantial additional bank lending from the creditor banks involved, helped finance rescheduling of this debt over the medium term. But, after several years of crisis reschedulings, it became clear that a lot more time, substantially renewed economic growth, and, more than likely, lower interest rates would be needed before full debt service could resume. In the interim, however, finding the capital to restore solid growth and keep the multinational banks solvent (all without unduly weakening the depressed economies of the Third World) would require some "creative financing" and liberal accounting discipline.

Much of Latin America and many African countries were suffering from widespread recession, increased unemployment, and slowed growth (if not a decline in national income). Crop failures, famine, and overpopulation in parts of Africa were serious, too. With great reductions in new bank credit and foreign investment, plus, for some countries, substantial capital flight, there was a serious problem in priming the pump for renewed economic growth. Most of these nations were already using substantial budget deficits; enlarging domestic inflation with even bigger deficits was often counterproductive, aggravated capital flight, and did not foster an environment for renewed private investment activity. Much of East and South Asia (including South Korea, Taiwan, Malaysia, China, and India), however, suffered less recession, maintained more general economic growth, and was still attractive to foreign investment.

By 1985–86, it was becoming more evident to international bankers and economists that the worldwide recession and debt-overload crisis of 1982–84 were serious, long-term problems and not merely transient liquidity strains. While it was not easy to organize a multinational response, three major trends were observable:[68]

1. *Easier money and lower interest rates.* During 1985–86, Fed leaders (and most other major central banks) moved toward more accommodation and were accepting higher rates of growth in the monetary aggregates. So long as no significant revival of inflation occurred, this relaxation seemed likely to continue, because it would ease the Third World debt crisis and promote broader recovery. (Whether this easing would continue if the declining U.S. dollar brought some additional import inflation was an interesting question.)

2. *Increased multilateral liquidity and lending support.* A 50 percent expansion of IMF quotas came in 1983–84, along with additional borrowing authority; the World Bank enlarged its activities, too. This increase was more controversial than normal, with developing countries demanding more multilateral support, yet some conservatives and liberal populists in the United States opposed bailing out international banks and Third World governments. Nonetheless, in October 1985, U.S. Secretary of the Treasury Baker urged $9 billion (50 percent) increases in World Bank and Inter-American Development Bank lending to fifteen key debtor countries, plus $20 billion in new international bank loans to these countries during the next three years. Whether this would be sufficient was at issue, but most countries welcomed a new pragmatism and more flexibility from the Reagan administration on these matters. Baker also urged more encouragement for private foreign investment, as well as measures to achieve the repatriation of capital flight from insecure countries.

3. *Renewed growth in world trade and prosperity, with more balance and improved trade equity.* Many multinational interests (corporations, banks, and export-import operations) feared further strengthening of the New Protectionism and a breakdown in world prosperity, exports, and debt servicing. Yet, serious imbalances in trade (such as $387 billion in U.S. imports but only $217 billion

in U.S. exports) needed to be corrected in the next few years. The Reagan administration, Japan, and many European countries supported an eighth GATT Round for increased trade liberalization, at least as a defensive measure to resist any substantial revival of protectionism.[69] U.S. leaders strongly urged substantial liberalization in services (banking, insurance, and computer services) where U.S. comparative advantage might operate.[70] Developing countries were opposing significant foreign encroachment in this area, however, and still wanted more open access to U.S. and other industrial country markets. While hardly any nations wanted a decline in trade, and most favored trade expansion, the majority wanted export surpluses and did not favor sizeable incursions of foreign imports that might threaten domestic jobs and industries. In this context of greater defensiveness, with New Protectionist pressures becoming more significant in the United States and Europe, it was clear that another round of trade negotiations would be difficult and complex.[71]

Conflicting Outlooks on the World Economy

Five major outlooks on the world economy are contending for the mid-to-late 1980s and beyond:[72]

1. states and interests favoring free trade and multinational enterprise
2. states and interests wanting a "new international economic order" (NIEO)
3. states and interests wanting more self-reliant economies for reasons of national security
4. states and interests wanting extensive trade, but seeking limits to protect domestic labor, industrial, and other economic capabilities
5. states and interests seeking Marxist socialist development

Each commands the support of many nations and influential minorities within others, but none seems likely to become predominant (at least for a good many years). This means that international trade, finance, and banking must be carried on amid some continuing rivalry and a struggle for ascendancy among these contending policies. So long as a balance of military power and economic strength is maintained, however, extensive trade, investment, and cooperation will take place among many nations and, to some degree, across ideological and institutional boundaries.

The United States, Canada, Australia, New Zealand, Japan (to some degree), most of the EEC and Western Europe, much of Latin America (for many purposes), Hong Kong, Singapore, and some new island nations in the Caribbean and Pacific comprise the Free Trade-Multinational Enterprise block of sixty nations and 850 million people. These countries have increasingly integrated their economies with each other, allowing more or less open trade and investment across each other's borders (subject to limited tariffs, restrictions, and regulation.[73] Most of these countries are highly industrialized and generally use capital-intensive methods of agriculture. An increasingly prosperous network of MNEs and multinational banks operates within these countries, carrying on extensive trade, credit, and investment with developing nations in the NIEO bloc, many of the more self-reliant nations, and, to a modest degree, the Marxist nations.

Developing nations in the NIEO bloc include most of Latin America and the Caribbean, most of Africa, most Muslim countries, and much of Asia (including India, Sri Lanka, Burma, Malaysia, Indonesia, the Philippines, and some island states in the Indian and Pacific Oceans). For some purposes, China too belongs in the NIEO bloc, which totals 120 nations with 2,700 million people. These countries carry on extensive trade with advanced industrial nations (exporting mostly raw materials, handicrafts, semifinished goods, and labor-intensive manufacturers). This group is increasingly diverse and not very cohesive culturally or ideologically. The bloc includes oil-rich OPEC members, rapidly industrializing NICs, and many LDCs. Yet, most NIEO countries share suspicion about MNEs or at least believe that powerful foreign interests must be closely supervised, regulated, and prevented from exploiting NIEO members or their peoples. Accordingly, the MNEs are given only a limited, partial, and somewhat insecure welcome by NIEO countries. Even so, most of the NIEO bloc finds it necessary to attract and encourage MNE investment, lending, and trade within reasonable limits. A few of the most prosperous NIEO countries (South Korea, for example) in recent years, however, have integrated themselves more into the MNE world economy, with their own enterprises participating more equally in multilateral trade.

Some nations find greater need for self-reliant military independence, security, or even nonalignment. Presently included in this bloc might be China, Taiwan, India, Iran, Iraq, Israel, Yugoslavia, Albania, Libya, and South Africa (ten nations with 1,850 million people). Diverse culturally and ideologically, they share elements of mistrust for the outside world. This imposes special limitations on their trade for reasons of national security. But, since political or military circumstances could change for many countries (for some states rather quickly), a much larger list of nations may find it desirable, as a precaution, to achieve a limited degree of self-sufficiency, at least in basic food supplies, minimum energy sources, and essential manufactures (including military equipment and supplies). In this broader company can be included most of the major powers: the United States, Soviet Union, Japan, France, and Britain, together with Sweden, Switzerland, Turkey, Pakistan, Argentina, Brazil, and, perhaps, others (twelve nations with 1,000 million people).

For broad economic reasons (the desire to promote industry or to limit dislocation, deindustrialization, or harsh adjustments to important industries, labor, or agriculture), most countries find partial justifications to limit trade, investment, or credit dependence on other countries and the world market. Naturally, this outlook may support considerable protectionism, even semi-isolation, where necessary. In the present world economy, few nations find general protectionist policy appropriate. But, the great majority of nations, including most free trade-MNE states, almost all NIEOs, and all socialist societies (totaling 150 countries with 4,000 million people), now find at least selective protectionist regulation desirable and necessary. In times of major depression, severe inflation, or other breakdowns in the world economy (as during World War I, the 1930s, or World War II), many nations would use protectionist or other trade regulation more extensively. And as ultimate insurance or emergency planning, most countries should be prepared (within limits and maybe with key allies) to implement national or regional self-sufficiency policies. (This logic applies equally to the free trade-MNE bloc, NIEO nations, and socialist countries.)

Marxist countries form another great bloc. Led by the Soviet Union, Eastern Europe, Mongolia, North Korea, Vietnam, Cambodia, Aden (Yemen People's Democratic Republic), Ethiopia, Angola, Mozambique, Cuba, and Nicaragua together constitute a close-knit grouping of Leninist-style communist states, totaling eighteen nations with 430 million people. More independent socialist countries include China, Yugoslavia, Albania, Guinea, Tanzania, Madagascar, Zimbabwe, and Guiana—eight nations with 1,000 million people. Islamic socialist countries (but not close allies) include Syria, Iraq, and Libya—three nations with 26 million people. Lesser degrees of socialism apply to a considerable number of Third World countries, including many NIEO nations and even a few states in Western and Southern Europe. Marxist and socialist parties, however, have a substantial presence in many European and NIEO countries as minorities (dissident groups or even potential revolutionaries). Hence, the Marxist and socialist bloc claims considerable growth potential (while free-market enthusiasts insist the tide of world history is turning away from socialism).

Because Marxist ideology proclaims a need to transform "unjust" capitalist societies into socialism, Marxist countries (especially the Soviet-led states) form an alliance working (at least within limits) to encourage socialist revolutions in other nations. This zeal for extending Marxism has been a feature of the Soviet Communist party since 1917, more actively since World War II. The capitalist and other noncommunist states have responded defensively (under the leadership of the United States, major European countries, and others). This cleavage between the Marxists and the Free-World alliance is still a vital organizing theme in world trade and politics. Many African, Muslim, Asian, and Latin American states try to maintain a degree of nonalignment in politics, however, and seek a "mixed-economy" blend of socialism and substantial free-market activities.

Notes

1. Models of international trade theory that stress benefits from specialization, comparative advantage, and free movement of trade, capital, or labor tend to emphasize

the overall gains for their integrated systems. Generally neglected or given much less attention is the allocation of unequal or divergent shares in these gains from international trade, commerce, and investment activity. See, for example, standard works such as Kindleberger and Lindert (cited in introduction note 7); Wilfred Ethier, *Modern International Economics* (New York: Norton, 1983); Richard Caves and Ronald Jones, *World Trade and Payments,* 4th ed. (Boston: Little, Brown, 1985; John Williamson, *The Open Economy and the World Economy: A Textbook in International Economics* (New York: Basic, 1983); Jagdish Bhagwati (ed. Robert Feenstra), *The Theory of Commercial Policy: Essays in International Economic Theory,* vol. 1 (Cambridge, Mass.: MIT Press, 1983). Thus, why should Britain decline so much against Japan between 1953 and 1986, with four times more per capita income in 1953, and yet little more than half by 1986? (See table P–2.) Or, why should the United States or Latin America be sharing less in world economic growth than Japan and other East Asian countries? (See preface.) Some recent works are attempting to grapple with these tough questions. See John Letiche, "Introduction," *International Economic Policies and Their Foundations* (New York: Academic Press, 1982). But, mainstream trade literature does not adequately explain differential growth, varied success in industrial policies, and changing patterns of comparative advantage.

Economic development analysts since the 1950s have concentrated on differential growth to a greater extent. See, for example, standard texts such as Gerald Meier, *Leading Issues in Development Economics,* 4th ed. (New York: Oxford Univ., 1984); Bruce Herick and Charles Kindleberger, *Economic Development,* 4th ed. (New York: McGraw-Hill, 1983); W.W. Rostow, *Politics and the Stages of Economic Growth* (Cambridge, England: Cambridge Univ., 1971); Benjamin Higgins, *Economic Development: Problems, Principles, and Policies,* rev. ed. (New York: Norton, 1968); and W.R. Cline and S. Weintraub, *Economic Stabilization in Developing Countries* (Washington, D.C.: Brookings, 1981). See also Lloyd G. Reynolds, *Economic Growth in the Third World 1850–1980* (New Haven: Yale Univ., 1985). The industrial policy literature, cited extensively in preface note 3 focuses directly upon catch-up strategies and methods to improve growth. See also John Pinder, ed., *National Industrial Strategies and the World Economy* (London: Atlantic Inst. for International Affairs—Allanheld, Osmun, 1982). In addition, a growing literature on Japanese success (see introduction note 5) tries to develop explanations.

Meanwhile, recent writings for MNEs, international banking, and business tends to take a globalist and freer-market view (with some loyalty to headquarters countries). See, for example, Michael Porter, *Competition in Global Industries* (Boston: Harvard Bus. School, 1986); *Euromoney* (London); *The Banker* (London); *Harvard Business Review; Financial Times* (London); *Neue Zürcher Zeitung; Frankfurter Allgemeine; Wall Street Journal;* and in many respects, *The New York Times* (in business and international economics coverage). The Japanese business press, e.g. *Japan Times* has a multinational tint, but reflects a more ethnocentric outlook and greater national loyalty (an interesting cultural characteristic that separates Japanese from their American or European counterparts).

Outlooks within developing countries (apart from wealthy business interests with substantial overseas investments) are less free-market globalist and incline toward New International Economic Order thinking. Latin American and African economists have been more interventionist, favor stronger protection, and are preoccupied with exploitation by the major Western industrial countries. See, for example, *CEPAL Review* (Santiago, Chile: Economic Commission for Latin America) and various UNCTAD proceedings and publications. But, as Letiche explains rather skillfully, some movement toward greater market discipline and less faith in government has been evident in recent years among Third-World experts.

Marxists and the most committed socialists, however, still claim that private capitalism (whether involving domestic companies or foreign MNEs) tends to be inherently exploitative. Accordingly, they prefer structural reforms that socialize most large-scale enterprise with appropriate nationalization. While Marxists and other socialists see benefits associated with trade, investment, lending, and technology transfer from established capitalist nations and MNEs (when carefully regulated), these remain transitional arrangements or *modus vivendi* and are only considered to be needed until more fundamental social reforms toward socialism are implemented.

2. Gustav Schmoller, *The Mercantile System and Its Historical Significance* (New York: Macmillan, 1914; originally published in Germany, 1884). See also Eli Heckscher, *Mercantilism,* rev. ed. (London: George Allen & Unwin, 1955); Witt Bowden, Michael Karpovich, and Abbott Payson Usher, *An Economic History of Europe since 1750* (New York: American Book Co., 1937); Ernest L. Bogart, *Economic History of Europe, 1760–1939* (London: Longmans, Green, 1942); Walter Jennings, *A History of the Economic and Social Progress of European Peoples* (Lexington, Ky.: Kernel Press, 1936); Shephard Bancroft Clough and Charles Woolsey Cole, *Economic History of Europe* (Boston: D.C. Heath, 1941); Herbert Heaton, *Economic History of Europe,* rev. ed. (New York: Harper, 1948); Fernand Braudel, *Civilization and Capitalism, 15th–18th Cent.,* 3 vols. (New York: Harper & Row, 1981-84); Jean Gimpel, *The Medieval Machine: The Industrial Revolution of the Middle Ages* (New York: Holt, Rinehart and Winston, 1976); Colin McEvedy, *The Penguin Atlas of Medieval History* (Harmondsworth, Middlesex, England: Penguin, 1961), and *The Penguin Atlas of Modern History to 1815* (Penguin, 1972); and E.E. Rich, M.M. Postan, E. Miller, H.J. Habakkuk, and C.H. Wilson, eds., *The Cambridge Economic History of Europe, Vol. III: Economic Organization and Policies in the Middle Ages, Vol. IV: The Economy of Expanding Europe in the Sixteenth and Seventeenth Centuries,* and *Vol. V: The Economic Organization of Early Modern Europe* (Cambridge, England: Cambridge Univ. Press, 1963–67).

3. Constitution of the United States: Preamble, Article I, Section VIII (Powers of Congress), Section IX and X (Limitations upon Congress and the States), Article II, Sections I, II, and III (Presidential Powers). See also Edward S. Corwin, *The Constitution and What It Means Today,* rev. ed. (Princeton: Princeton Univ., 1973); Rexford Tugwell, *The Emerging Constitution* (New York: Harper & Row, 1974); Bernard Schwartz, *The Law in America: A History* (New York: McGraw-Hill, 1974); Stephen Breyer, *Regulation and Its Reform* (Cambridge: Harvard Univ., 1982); Thomas K. McCraw, ed., *Regulation in Perspective: Historical Essays* (Boston: Harvard Bus. School, 1981); and Charles A. Beard, *An Economic Interpretation of the Constitution of the United States* (New York: Macmillan, 1914).

4. For U.S. tariff history, see John M. Dobson, *Two Centuries of Tariffs: The Background and Emergence of the U.S. International Trade Commission* (Washington, D.C.: U.S. International Trade Commission, Dec. 1976); Caves and Jones (cited in note 1), esp. figure 13.1, pp. 237–39; Kindleberger and Linder (cited in note 1), esp.

figures 12.1 and 12.2. See also Ernest Bogart, *Economic History of the American People,* 2nd and rev. ed. (London: Longman, Green, 1938); Witt Bowden, *The Industrial History of the U.S.* (New York: A.M. Kelly Reprints of Econ. Classics, 1967); Thomas C. Cochran, *The American Business System: A Historical Perspective, 1900–1955* (Cambridge, Mass.: Harvard Univ., 1957); Chester W. Wright, *Economic History of the U.S.,* 2nd ed. (New York: McGraw-Hill, 1949); Harold U. Faulkner, *The Decline of Laissez-Faire, 1897–1917* (New York: Rinehart, 1951); Kenneth W. Rowe, *Mathew Carey, A Study in American Economic Development* (Baltimore: Johns Hopkins, 1933); Frank W. Taussig, with Harry D. White, *Some Aspects of the Tariff Question,* 3rd ed. (Cambridge, Mass.: Harvard Univ., 1931); *The Protectionist* (Boston: Home Market Club, Aug. and Sept. 1899); and George B. Curtiss, *Protection and Prosperity* (Binghamton, N.Y.: May 1896), reviewed with approval in *The Protectionist* (Aug. 1899).

5. See Bowden, Karpovich, and Usher as well as Clough and Cole, Heaton, and *Cambridge Economic History* (cited in note 2). See also John Clapham, *A Concise Economic History of Britain* (Cambridge, England: Cambridge Univ., 1949); W.H.B. Court, *A Concise Economic History of Britain, from 1750 to Recent Times* (Cambridge, England: Cambridge Univ., 1954); Phyllis Deane and W.A. Cole, *British Economic Growth, 1688-1959: Trends and Structure,* 2nd ed. (London: Cambridge Univ., 1967); E.J. Hobsbawm, *Industry and Empire: The Making of Modern English Society, 1750 to the Present Day* (London: Weidenfeld & Nicholson, 1968); Frederick C. Dietz, *An Economic History of England* (New York: H. Holt, 1942); and Bernard Semmel, *The Rise of Free Trade Imperialism: Classical Political Economy and Empire of Free Trade and Imperialism* (Cambridge, England: Cambridge Univ., 1970).

6. For good accounts of the gradual revision in British trade thinking (especially among business people and Conservatives) and the evolution toward imperial preference as trade policy, also see Richard Rempel, *Unionists Divided: Arthur Balfour, Joseph Chamberlain, and the Unionist Free Traders* (Newton Abbot, Devon, England: David & Charles-Archon, 1972); Charles Loch Mowat, *Britain between the Wars, 1918–40* (Chicago: Univ. of Chicago, 1955); Middlemas and Barnes, *Baldwin* (cited in preface note 3). See also Alfred E. Kahn, *Great Britain in the World Economy* (New York: Columbia Univ., 1946).

7. For French economic history, see the general European sources cited in note 2, together with Shepard Bancroft Clough, *France: A History of National Economics, 1789-1939* (New York: Octagon, 1970); Charles P. Kindleberger, *Economic Growth in France and Britain, 1851–1950* (Cambridge, Mass.: Harvard Univ. Press, 1964); and Francois Caron, *An Economic History of Modern France* (New York: Halsted-Wiley, 1975). See also, for special insights on French mercantilism, Charles W. Cole, *Colbert and a Century of French Mercantilism,* 2 vols. (New York: Columbia Univ., 1939) and *French Mercantilism, 1683-1700* (New York: Columbia Univ., 1943).

8. Clough and Cole, *Economic History of Europe* (cited in note 2), pp. 608–9.

9. With respect to Germany's economic and industrial development, as well as its changing trade policies, see the general sources cited in note 2, along with Gustav Stolper, *The German Economy: 1870 to the Present* (London: Weidenfeld & Nicholson, 1967); Werner Friedrich Bruck, *Social and Economic History of Germany From William II to Hitler, 1888–1938* (London: Oxford Univ., 1938).

10. See general sources on European economic history cited in note 2 and Arthur James May, *The Hapsburg Monarchy, 1867–1914* (Cambridge, Mass.: Harvard Univ.,

1951); R.J.W. Evans, *The Making of the Hapsburg Monarchy, 1550–1700* (New York: Oxford Univ., 1979); John Komlos, *The Hapsburg Monarchy as a Customs Union: Economic Developments in Austria-Hungary in the 19th Century* (Princeton: Princeton Univ., 1983); David F. Good, *The Economic Rise of the Hapsburg Empire, 1750–1914* (Berkeley: Univ. of Calif., 1984); and Alexander Gershenkron, *An Economic Spurt That Failed: Four Lectures in Austrian History* (Princeton: Princeton Univ., 1977).

11. See David Mitrany, *The Effect of the War in Southeastern Europe* (New Haven: Carnegie Endowment, Div. of Economics and History, Yale Univ., 1936); Victor Mamatey and Radomir Luza, *A History of the Czechoslovak Republic, 1918–48* (Princeton: Princeton Univ., 1973); and Charles A. Gulick, *Austria From Hapsburg to Hitler* (Berkeley: Univ. of Calif., 1948). See also, Bogart, Clough and Cole, Heaton, and Bowden, Karpovich, and Usher (cited in note 2) for general European economic histories.

12. See general European economic histories, especially Braudel, Heaton, Jennings, and Bowden, Karpovich, and Usher (cited in note 2). In addition, see Gino Luzzato, *An Economic History of Italy: From the Fall of the Roman Empire to the Beginning of the Sixteenth Century* (New York: Barnes & Noble, 1961); John Julius Norwich, *A History of Venice* (New York: Knopf, 1982); Stuart Joseph Woolf, *A History of Italy, 1700–1860: The Social Constraints of Political Change* (London: Methuen, 1979); Rene Albrecht-Carrie, *Italy from Napoleon to Mussolini* (New York: Columbia Univ., 1950); Benedetto Croce, *A History of Italy, 1871–1915* (Oxford, England: Clarendon, 1929); Frederico Chabod, *A History of Italian Fascism* (London: Weidenfeld and Nicolson, 1963); Serge Hughes, *The Rise and Fall of Modern Italy* (New York: Macmillan, 1967); and Shepard Bancroft Clough, *The Economic History of Modern Italy* (New York: Columbia Univ., 1964).

13 Martin A.S. Hume, *Spain, Its Greatness and Decay, 1479–1788* (Cambridge, England: Cambridge Univ., 1905); R.A. Stradling, *Europe and the Decline of Spain: A Study of the Spanish System, 1580–1720* (London: Allen & Unwin, 1981); Raymond Carr, *Spain: 1808–1939* (Oxford, England: Clarendon, 1966); Simi Lieberman, *The Contemporary Spanish Economy: A Historical Perspective* (London: Allen & Unwin, 1982); Robert Ergang, *Europe: From the Renaissance to Waterloo* (Boston: D.C. Heath, 1954); Jaime Vincens Vives, *An Economic History of Spain* (Princeton: Princeton Univ., 1969); Joseph Harrison, *The Spanish Economy in the Twentieth Century* (London: Croom Helm, 1985); and Clough and Cole, *Economic History of Europe* (Boston: D.C. Heath, 1941).

14. James Mavor, *An Economic History of Russia* (New York: G.P. Putnam, 1914); William L. Blackwell, *The Beginnings of Russian Industrialization, 1800–1860* (Princeton: Princeton Univ., 1968); Margaret Stevenson Miller, *The Economic Development of Russia, 1905–1914* (London: P.S. King & Son, 1926); George Vernadsky, *A History of Russia*, 4th ed. (New Haven: Yale Univ., 1954); and Jennings (cited in note 2). See also Robert Massie, *Peter the Great: His Life and World* (New York: Ballantine, 1981).

15. Alec Nove, *An Economic History of the USSR* (London: Allen Lane, 1969); Abram Bergson, *The Economics of Planning* (New Haven: Yale Univ., 1964); and Morris Bornstein and Daniel Fusfeld, *The Soviet Economy: A Book of Readings*, 4th ed. (Homewood, Ill.: Irwin, 1974).

16. See, from general histories, Heaton, and Clough and Cole (cited in note 2) along with George Young, *Portugal Old and Young; An Historical Survey* (Oxford, England: Clarendon, 1917); H.V. Livermore, *A History of Portugal* (Cambridge,

England: Cambridge Univ., 1947); Charles Ralph Boxer, *The Portuguese Seaborne Empire, 1415–1825* (New York: Knopf, 1969); James Duffy, *Shipwreck and Empire, Being an Account of Portuguese Maritime Disasters in a Century of Decline* (Cambridge: Harvard Univ., 1955); S. Sideri, *Trade and Power: Informal Colonialism in Anglo–Portuguese Relations* (Rotterdam: Rotterdam Univ., 1970); and Stanley G. Payne, *A History of Spain and Portugal*, 2 vols. (Madison, Wis.: Univ. of Wisconsin, 1973).

17. From general surveys, see Heaton, Jennings, and Clough and Cole (cited in note 2), together with John Motley, *Motley's Dutch Nation; Being the Rise of the Dutch People to 1908* by William Griffis (New York: Harper & Brothers, 1908); J. Ellis Barker, *The Rise and Decline of the Netherlands: A Political and Economic History and a Study in Practical Statesmanship* (New York: E.P. Dutton, 1906); Jan De Vries, *The Dutch Rural Economy in the Golden Age, 1500–1700* (New Haven: Yale Univ., 1974); J.A. Van Houte, *An Economic History of the Low Countries, 800–1800* (New York: St. Martin's, 1977); and George Edmundson, *History of Holland* (Cambridge, England: Cambridge Univ., 1922).

18. See Jennings (cited in note 2) and Van Houtte (cited in note 16) along with Guido L. De Brabander, *Regional Specialization, Employment and Economic Growth in Belgium between 1846 to 1970* (New York: Orno, 1981); Ernst Heinrich Kossman, *The Low Countries, 1780–1940* (Oxford, England: Oxford Univ., 1978); and F. Gunther Eyck, *The Benelux Countries: An Historical Survey* (Princeton, N.J.: Van Nostrand, 1959).

19. Eli Heckscher, *An Economic History of Sweden*, Goran Ohlin, trans. (Cambridge: Harvard Univ., 1954); Kurt Samuelson, *From Great Power to Welfare State: 300 Years of Swedish Social Development* (London: Allen & Unwin, 1968); Steven Koblik, ed., *Sweden's Development from Poverty to Affluence, 1750–1790*, Joanne Johnson, trans. (Minneapolis: Univ. of Minnesota, 1979); Thomas Kingston Derry, *A History of Scandinavia: Norway, Sweden, Denmark, Finland and Iceland* (Minneapolis: Univ. of Minnesota, 1979); J.H.S. Birch, *Denmark in History* (London: J. Murray, 1938); and relevant sections of *Cambridge Economic History of Europe*, Rich and Wilson, eds., (cited in note 2).

20. See Jennings (cited in note 2) along with Wilhelm Oechsli, *History of Switzerland, 1499–1914*, Eden and Edgar Paul, trans. (Cambridge, England: Cambridge Univ., 1922); Edgar Bonjour, H.S. Offler, and G.R. Potter, *A Short History of Switzerland* (Oxford, England: Clarendon, 1952); Christopher Hughes, *Switzerland* (London: Ernest Benn, 1975); Heinz K. Meier, *Friendship under Stress: U.S.–Swiss Relations, 1900–1950* (Bern: Herbert Lang, 1970); and *Cambridge Economic History of Europe* (cited in note 2).

21. For general surveys, see Jennings (cited in note 2). See also Antoni Maczak, Henry Samsonowicz, and Peter Burke, eds., *East-Central Europe in Transition: From the Fourteenth to the Seventeenth Century* (Cambridge, England: Cambridge Univ., 1985); John Komlos, ed., *Economic Development in the Hapsburg Monarchy in the 19th Century* (New York: Columbia Univ., 1983); Hugh Seton Watson, *Eastern Europe between the Wars, 1918–41* (Cambridge, England: Cambridge Univ., 1945); Mamatey and Luza (cited in noted 11); Robin Okey, *Eastern Europe, 1740 to 1980: Feudalism to Communism* (Minneapolis: Univ. of Minnesota, 1982); Charles Issawi, *The Economic History of Turkey, 1800–1914* (Chicago: Univ. of Chicago, 1980); Alphonse

de Lamortine, *History of Turkey*, 3 vols. (New York: Appleton, 1895); and relevant sections of *Cambridge Economic History of Europe*, Rich and Wilson, eds. (cited in note 2).

22. For background on the British, French, Spanish, Portuguese, and Dutch empires, see sources cited in notes 2, 5, 6, 7, 13, 16, and 17, respectively. With respect to China, see Wolfrom Eberhard, *A History of China*, 3rd ed. (Taipei, Taiwan, 1969); E. Stuart Kirby, *Introduction to the Economic History of China* (London: George Allen & Unwin, 1954); Chi-Ming Hou, *Foreign Investment and Economic Development in China, 1840–1937* (Cambridge, Mass.: Harvard Univ., 1965); Michael R. Godley, *The Mandarin Capitalists from Nanyang: Overseas Chinese Enterprise in the Modernization of China, 1893–1911* (Cambridge, England: Cambridge Univ., 1981); Sterling Seagrave, *The Soong Dynasty* (New York: Harper & Row, 1965); Grover Clark, *Economic Rivalries in China* (New Haven: Carnegie Endowment for Int'l Peace—Yale Univ., 1932); and Frank H.H. King, *A Concise Economic History of Modern China, 1840–1961* (New York: Praeger, 1969).

23. For extensive sources on Japanese history and economic development, see William Lovett, *Inflation and Politics*, chapter 5, note 4 (cited in preface note 2) and sources cited in preface note 3 and introduction note 19. Highlights of this literature include William W. Lockwood, *The Economic Development of Japan, 1868–1938* (Princeton: Princeton Univ., 1954); Jon Livingston, Joe Moore, and Felicia Oldfather, *Imperial Japan, 1800–1945* (New York: Pantheon-Random House, 1973); William R. Lockwood, *The State and Economic Enterprise in Japan* (Princeton: Princeton Univ., 1965); Takafusa Nakamura, *Economic Growth in Pre-War Japan*, Robert Feldman, trans. (New Haven: Yale Univ., 1983); Chalmers Johnson, *MITI and the Japanese Economic Miracle: The Growth of Industrial Policy, 1925–1975* (Palo Alto, Calif.: Stanford Univ., 1982); and Sumio Mikio and Taira Koji, *An Outline of Japanese Economic History, 1603–1940* (Tokyo: Univ. of Tokyo, 1979).

24. Hubert Herring, *A History of Latin America from the Beginnings to the Present*, 3rd ed. (New York: Knopf, 1968); E. Bradford Burns, *The Poverty of Progress: Latin America in the Nineteenth Century* (Berkeley: Univ. of Calif., 1980); Celso Furtado, *Economic Development of Latin America: Historical Background and Contemporary Problems*, Suzette Macedo, trans., 2nd ed. (Cambridge, England: Cambridge Univ., 1976). See also sources cited in preface note 2.

25. P.L. Wickens, *An Economic History of Africa from the Earliest Times to Partition* (New York: Oxford Univ., 1981); Thomas Reginald Batten, *Tropical Africa in World History*, 4 vols., 2nd ed. (London: Oxford Univ., 1964); Peter J.M. McEwan, ed., *Africa from Early Times to 1800* (London: Oxford Univ., 1968); Peter J.M. McEwan, ed., *Twentieth Century Africa* (London: Oxford Univ., 1968); and William E.F. Ward, *A History of Africa*, 2 vols. (London: G. Allen & Unwin).

26. See, generally, Bogart, Heaton, Clough and Cole, and Bowden, Karpovich, and Usher, cited in note 2. See also Charles Kindleberger, *A Financial History of Western Europe* (London: Allen & Unwin, 1984); George William Edwards, *The Evolution of Finance Capitalism* (London: Longmans, Green, 1938); Percy Ripley, *A Short History of Investment* (London: Pitman & Sons, 1934); E.B. Fryde, *Studies in Medieval Finance* (London: Hambledon, 1983); and Center for Medieval and Renaissance Studies, UCLA, *The Dawn of Modern Banking* (New Haven, Yale Univ., 1979).

27. See Kindleberger, *A Financial History of Europe* (cited in note 26) and Bogart, and Clough and Cole (cited in note 2). See also Herbert Feis, *Europe, the World's*

Banker, 1870–1914 (New Haven: Yale Univ., 1930); Paul Herman Emden, *Money Powers of Europe in the Nineteenth and Twentieth Centuries* (New York: Appleton-Century, 1938); Karl Erich Born, *International Banking in the 19th and 20th Centuries* (Leamington Spa, Warwickshire, England: Berg, 1983).

28. See Bogart, Heaton, Clough and Cole, and Bowden, Karpovich, and Usher (cited in note 2) and Kindleberger (cited in note 26). See also Paul Studenski and Herman Kroos, *Financial History of the United States*, 2nd ed. (New York: McGraw-Hill, 1963); John Maynard Keynes, *Economic Consequences of the Peace*, with introduction by Robert Lekachman (New York: Harper & Row, 1971).

29. Enthusiastic partisans for these strategies urge their respective merits and often claim historical trends are moving their way. But since the late 1940s, communist gains in Africa and Latin America have been offset by reduced ardour in China and parts of Eastern Europe. And, while free enterprise capitalism enjoys somewhat more energy in the United States, Western Europe, and some of Asia lately, mixed economies have substantial momentum in these countries, as in Latin America, much of Asia, the Muslim nations, Africa, and various island states. Few should expect an early resolution of this rivalry.

30. For a symposium of outstanding economists in the 1930s, providing various diagnoses of the Great Depression and alternative ways to reorganize the world's financial and monetary arrangements, see A.D. Gayer, *The Lessons of Monetary Experience: Essays in Honor of Irving Fisher,* presented on the occasion of his seventieth birthday (London: George Allen & Unwin, 1937; reprinted, New York: A.M. Kelley, 1970). Highlights include pieces by Mariner Eccles, John H. Williams, James W. Angell, Alvin Hansen, James H. Rogers, R.G. Hawtrey, J.M. Keynes, H. Schumacher, Erik Lindahl, Bertil Ohlin, T.V. Soong, Eigo Fukai, and Alexander Loveday. Their diversity and lack of consensus illustrates how difficult it would have been to settle the postwar environment in any general congress of eminent economists and bankers from many countries. What really emerged, instead, was a cohesive "deal" worked out by small teams of negotiators from the United States and Great Britain, but their particular outlooks shaped the post–World War II economic settlement.

For historical background on these postwar international monetary, finance, and trade arrangements, see Margaret Garritsen de Vries, *The IMF in a Changing World* (Washington, D.C.: IMF, 1986); Charles Kindleberger, *A Financial History of Western Europe* (London: George Allen & Unwin, 1984); W. Arthur Lewis, *The Evolution of the International Financial Order* (Princeton: Princeton Univ., 1978); Kenneth W. Dam, *The Rules of the Game: Reform and Evolution in the International Monetary System* (Chicago: Univ. of Chicago, 1982); James Foreman-Peck, *A History of the World Economy: International Economic Relations since 1850* (Totowa, N.J.: Barnes & Noble, 1983); Robert Solomon, *The International Monetary System, 1945–76: An Insider's View* (New York: Harper & Row, 1977); Michael Moffit, *The World's Money: International Banking from Bretton Woods to the Brink of Insolvency* (New York: Simon & Schuster, 1983); M.S. Mendelsohn, *Money on the Move: The Modern International Capital Market* (New York: McGraw-Hill, 1980); Steven I. Davis, *The Euro-Bank: Its Origins, Management and Outlook,* 2nd ed. (London: Macmillan, 1980); John W. Williamson, ed., *IMF Conditionality* (Washington, D.C.: Inst. for International Economics, 1983); John Dobson, *Two Centuries of Tariffs* (cited in note 4); F.V. Meyer, *International Trade Policy* (New York: St. Martin's, 1978); Karin Kock, *International Trade Policy and the GATT, 1947–1967* (Stockholm: Almquist

& Wiskell, 1969); John Evans, *The Kennedy Round in American Trade Policy: The Twilight of the GATT?* (Cambridge: Harvard Univ., 1971); Kenneth W. Dam, *The GATT: Law and International Organization* (Chicago: Univ. of Chicago, 1977); W.M. Scammell, *The International Economy since 1945* (New York: St. Martin's, 1980); John Jackson and William Davey, *Legal Problems of International Economic Relations*, 2nd ed. (St. Paul, Minn.: West, 1986). See also, Nove, Bergson, and Bornstein and Fusfeld (cited in note 15) and sources cited in note 35 infra.

31. U.S. lend-lease assistance to allies totaled $.74 billion (1941), $4.93 billion (1942), $10.36 billion (1943), $11.30 billion (1944), $5.56 billion (1945), and $.65 billion (1946), *Statistical Abstract of the U.S. (1946)*, (1948). In these years, U.S. GNP increased from $125 billion to $212 billion; lend-lease flows reached 5 percent of GNP in 1943 and 1944. (See table 6–1.)

32. A decisive shift in U.S. thinking toward freer trade occurred during the Eisenhower administration, as he led the Republican party to reverse its traditional protectionism for a more internationalist policy. See Dwight D. Eisenhower, *The White House Years, Mandate for Change, 1953–56* (New York: Doubleday, 1963), esp. pp. 208–11, 292–94, 498–99. See also *Commission on Foreign Economic Policy, Staff Papers* (Randall Commission Report, Washington, D.C.: GPO, Feb. 1954).

33. See, particularly, Scammell, Meyer, and Kock (cited in note 30).

34. See Davis, Kindleberger, and Mendelsohn (cited in note 30).

35. See Foreman-Peck (cited in note 30), pp. 275–78. See also Vladimir Sobel, *The Red Market: Industrial Co-operation and Specialisation in COMECON* (Aldershot, England: Gower, 1984); Giovanni Graziani, "Dependency Structures in COMECON," *Review of Radical Political Economics* 13, no. 1 (1981), pp. 67–75; Patrick Clawson, "The Character of Soviet Economic Relations with Third World Countries," *Review of Radical Political Economics* 13, no. 1 (1981), pp. 76–84; *East–West Trade and Finance in the World Economy: A New Look for the 1980's* (New York: St. Martin's, 1985); Marshall D. Shullman, ed., *Terrain of Conflict: East–West Tensions in the Third World* (New York: American Assembly-Norton, 1986); "East Europe," *Current History* 83, no. 496 (Nov. 1984); A.M. Burghardt and C.A. Kortvelyessy, *Comecon; Economies, Debt and Prospects* (London: Euromoney, 1984); "East–West Financial Relations: Developments in 1985 and Future Prospects," *Financial Market Trends* 33 (Paris: OECD, March 1986). See also Adam Zwass, *The Economies of Eastern Europe in a Time of Change* (Armonk, N.Y.: M.E. Sharpe, 1984).

36. See, W.W. Rostow, ed., *The Prospects for Communist China* (New York: Wiley, 1954); Thomas Rawski, *China's Transition to Industrialism* (Ann Arbor, Mich.: Univ. of Michigan, 1980); Lin Wei and Arnold Chao, *China's Economic Reforms* (Philadelphia: Univ. of Pennsylvania, 1982); Wolfgang Klenner and Kurt Wiesegart, *The Chinese Economy: Structure and Reform in the Domestic Economy and Foreign Trade* (Oxford, England: Transaction Books, 1985); Yu-ming Shaw, ed., *Mainland China: Politics, Economics and Reform* (Colorado Springs: Westview, 1986).

37. See table P–2. See also sources cited in note 30, particularly Foreman-Peck, Kock, Meyer, Scammell, Solomon, and Garritsen de Vries.

38. See Mendelsohn, Davis, and Foreman-Peck, cited in note 30.

39. The nonmembers of the EEC are Switzerland, Austria, Norway, Sweden, and Finland, which are substantially linked into European Trade—although Finland has more trade with the Soviets.

40. See Dam, *The GATT*, Dobson, Evans, Foreman-Peck, Kock, Meyer, Scammell, and Jackson and Davey, cited in note 30.

41. See Garritsen de Vries, Solomon, Moffit, Foreman-Peck, Williamson, and Dam, *Rules of the Game,* cited in note 30.

42. See Garritsen de Vries, Solomon, Moffit, and Dam, *Rules of the Game*, cited in note 30.

43. See, especially, Foreman-Peck and Solomon (cited in note 30). See also Caves, *Britain's Economic Prospects*; Brittan, *Steering the Economy: The British Experiment*; Bacon, *Britain's Economic Problem: Too Few Producers*; and Beckerman, *Slow Growth in Britain: Causes and Consequences* (all cited in preface note 2).

44. Nor did most U.S. allies want its defense commitments, overseas bases, foreign aid, or investment seriously reduced. The only major criticism from U.S. allies centered on the Vietnam War, which many felt was wasteful, unnecessary, and a commitment carried to excess.

45. See Dam, *Rules of the Game*, Garritsen de Vries, and Moffit, cited in note 30.

46. Ibid. See also, Lovett, *Inflation and Politics*, chapters 1, 2, 3, and 5 (cited in preface note 2); and Lovett, *Banking and Financial Institutions Law*, (St. Paul, Minn.: West, 1984), chapter 2.

47. Some economists had urged floating exchange rates for a generation already, and Canada's success with floating between 1950 and 1962 and from 1970 onward had convinced more economists that floating exchange rates would be viable.

48. See sources cited in note 46. See also, appendix table A-11.

49. Lindert and Kindleberger, *International Economics*, 7th ed. (Homewood, Ill.: Irwin, 1982), p. 396.

50. See Garritsen de Vries, Solomon, and Dam, *Rules of the Game* (cited in note 30). In addition, see Kindleberger and Lindert, Caves and Jones, and Williamson (cited in note 1) together with John Bilson and Richard Marsten, eds., *Exchange Rate Theory and Practice* (Chicago: National Bureau of Economic Research—Univ. of Chicago, 1984); Sven Arndt, Richard Sweeney, and Thomas Willett, eds., *Exchange Rates, Trade, and the U.S. Economy* (Cambridge, Mass.: American Enterprise Inst.—Ballinger, 1985).

51. See Lovett, *Inflation and Politics: Fiscal, Monetary, and Wage—Price Discipline* (Lexington, Mass.: Lexington Books, 1982), for a review of the 1970s worldwide inflation trend, with extensive citations to the stabilization policy literature and analysis of alternative treatments.

52. Ibid.

53. See Dam, *Rules of the Game*, Davis, Mendelsohn, Moffit, and Garritsen de Vries (cited in note 30). See also Darrell Delamaide, *Debt Shock: The Full Story of the World Debt Crisis* (Garden City, N.Y.: Doubleday, 1984); William R. Cline, *International Debt: Systematic Risk and Policy Response* (Washington, D.C.: Inst. for International Economics, 1984); John Makin, *The Global Debt Crisis: America's Growing Involvement* (New York: Basic, 1984); and William A. Lovett, "Managing the World Debt Crisis: Economic Strains and Alternative Solutions," *Stanford Journal of International Law 21,* no. 2 (1985).

54. See Davis, Mendelsohn, and Moffit (cited in note 30), along with Delamaide and Lovett (cited in note 53).

55. See Dam, *Rules of the Game* (esp. pp. 176–314), Solomon, and Garritsen de Vries, (cited in note 30). For earlier concern about the adequacy of international

reserves, see Robert Triffin, *Gold and the Dollar Crisis*, rev. ed. (New Haven: Yale Univ., 1961).

56. See Lovett, *Inflation and Politics: Fiscal, Monetary and Wage-Price Discipline* (Lexington, Mass.: Lexington Books, 1984), esp. chapter 5.

57. See Foreman-Peck (cited in note 29); Lovett, ibid.; *1983 World Bank Atlas* Washington, D.C.: World Bank, 1983); and Inter-American Development Bank, *External Debt and Economic Development in Latin America: Background and Prospects* (Washington, D.C.: Inter-American Development Bank, Jan. 1984). See also Lloyd G. Reynolds, *Economic Growth in the Third World, 1850 to 1980* (New Haven: Yale Univ., 1985).

58. See Foreman-Peck and Scammell (cited in note 30). See also for New International Economic Order literature and commentary: Harry G. Johnson, *Economic Policies toward the Less Developed Nations* (Washington, D.C.: Brookings, 1967); Robert Rhodes, *Imperialism and Underdevelopment: A Reader* (New York: Monthly Review Press, 1970); Jagdish Bhagwati, *Dependence and Interdependence* (Cambridge, Mass.: MIT Press, 1985); Jagdish Bhagwati, *Wealth and Poverty* (Cambridge, Mass.: MIT Press, 1985); Jagdish Bhagwati and John G. Ruggie, *Power, Passions, and Purpose: Prospects for North–South Negotiations* (Cambridge, Mass.: MIT Press, 1984); Dilip Ghosh, ed., *International Trade and Third World Development* (Westport, Conn.: Greenwood, 1984); Robert Girling, *Multinational Institutions and the Third World: Management, Debt and Trade Conflicts in the International Economic Order* (New York: Praeger, 1985); Karl Brunner, ed., *The First World and the Third World: Essays on the New International Order* (Rochester, N.Y.: Rochester Policy Center Publications, 1978); David B.H. Denoon, *The New International Economic Order: A U.S. Response* (New York: NYU Press, 1979); Axel Borrmann, Christine Borrmann, Manfred Steger, *The EC's Generalized System of Preferences* (The Hague: Martinus Nijhoff, 1981); Jerry F. Hough, *The Struggle for the Third World: Soviet Debates and American Options* (Washington, D.C.: Brookings, 1986); John W. Sewell, Richard Feinberg, and Valeriana Kallab, eds., *U.S. Foreign Policy and the Third World: Agenda 1985–86* (New Brunswick, N.J.: Overseas Development Council-Transaction Books, 1985).

59. An earlier version of this program appeared at the first U.N. Conference on Trade and Development (UNCTAD) in 1964, attended by 122 nations (about ninety of them LDCs). UNCTAD has since become a permanent U.N. agency, with staff at Geneva and regular meetings.

60. These codes were not integrated into GATT, however, and the number of signatories represents only a limited percentage of GATT members.

61. For literature on the Tokyo Round and its significance, see William R. Cline et al., *Trade Negotiations in the Tokyo Round: A Quantitative Assessment* (Washington, D.C.: Brookings, 1978); Stanley D. Metzger, *Lowering Nontariff Barriers: U.S. Law, Practice, and Negotiating Objectives* (Washington, D.C.: Brookings, 1974); Jackson and Davey (cited in note 30). A good summary of developing countries' complaints about the Tokyo Round and subsequent GATT negotiations is provided by Girling (cited in note 58), pp. 140–151.

62. For summary of these developments, see Caves and Jones, *World Trade and Payments*, 4th ed. (cited in note 1), pp. 247–59, and other cited note 22. In addition, see Bluestone and Harrison (preface note 3), Culbertson (introduction note 12), and Anderson, and Fallows (introduction note 13), together with Metzger (note 61).

63. See chapter 6, infra, along with Lovett, *Inflation and Politics* (cited in preface note 2), especially chapter 6; and Lovett, *Banking and Financial Institutions Law* (St. Paul, Minn.: West, 1984), pp. 63–97. See also Martin Mayer, *The Fate of the Dollar* (New York: Times Books, 1981).

64. Ibid. See also Bruce Bartlett, *"Reaganomics": Supply Side Economics in Action* (Westport, Conn.: Arlington House 1981); Paul Craig Roberts, *The Supply-Side Revolution: An Insider's Account of Policy Making in Washington* (Cambridge, Mass.: Harvard Univ., 1984); David Stockman, *The Triumph of Politics: How the Reagan Revolution Failed* (New York: Harper & Row, 1986); Herbert Stein, *Presidential Economics: The Making of Economic Policy from Roosevelt to Reagan and Beyond* (New York: Simon and Schuster, 1984); and William C. Melton, *Inside the Fed: Making Monetary Policy* (Homewood, Ill.: Dow Jones-Irwin, 1985).

65. Ibid. See also sources cited in note 53, on the growing world debt crisis (particularly Delamaide, Cline, Makin, and Lovett), together with Inter-American Development Bank, *External Debt and Economic Development in Latin America* (cited in note 57) and Sewell et al., *U.S. Foreign Policy and the Third World* (cited in note 58).

66. Ibid. See also Philip A. Wellons, *Passing the Buck: Banks, Governments, and Third World Debt* (Boston: Harvard Business School, 1987); and Irving S. Friedman, *Toward World Prosperity: Reshaping the Global Money System* (Lexington, Mass.: Lexington Books, 1987).

Between 1983 and 1986, annual inflation in the major industrial countries had come down substantially, from an average of 5 percent in early 1983 to 3 percent by the end of 1986 (in terms of GNP deflators). U.S. inflation came down from 4 to 3 percent in this period, while Japanese inflation averaged between 1 and 2 percent annually. IMF, *World Economic Outlook* (Washington, D.C.: Oct. 1986), p. 6. IMF projections for 1987 showed a slight increase, because oil prices reached bottom in 1986 and were expected to rise somewhat.

Despite a world commodity price slump followed by substantially reduced inflation in industrial countries, some nations still managed to suffer aggravated inflation (in some instances, even approaching hyperinflation). For these unfortunate nations, the basic problem was very large government budget deficits. To the extent that recent "shock" treatments and tough stabilization measures have any hope of lasting success, eliminating big deficits is essential. See, for example, Peter Knight, F. Desmond McCarthy, and Sweder von Wijnibergen, "Escaping Hyperinflation," *Finance & Development* (Washington, D.C.: IMF, Dec. 1986), pp. 14–17 (with respect to Argentina, Brazil, and Israel); "Hyper Inflation and Back: How Four Countries Escaped," *Economist* (Nov. 15-21, 1986), pp. 55–64 (concerning Argentina, Brazil, Israel, and Bolivia). But, see Alan Riding, "Brazil Economy: Faith Turns to Fear," *New York Times* (Feb. 9, 1986), p. 21.

67. The worldwide recession of the early-to-mid 1980s was the most serious and long-lasting since World War II. It was brought on and sustained by exceptionally high real interest rates imposed by the United States. It was also maintained by other major Western countries between 1981 and 1985. Whereas "real" interest rates had fallen to around zero (after discounting for inflation) between 1977 and late 1979, the U.S. Federal Reserve (under Paul Volcker's leadership) cracked down hard (with a pause during late Spring through Summer 1980) and raised "real" interest rates for the United States to record levels between 1981 and 1985. World market "real" interest rates averaged 6

percent short-term, and 7 percent long-term, while U.S. "real" rates averaged 2 to 3 percent higher than those in other major industrial countries. See IMF, *World Economic Outlook* (Washington, D.C.: Oct. 1986), p. 3. This deflationary discipline was more harsh than U.S. monetary authorities really wanted. But, Reagan's 1981–83 tax cuts were bigger than many believed prudent (although they became popular politically), and the Democratic House of Representatives and the Reagan administration soon began blaming each other for the excessive U.S. budget deficits that followed. A subsequent impasse over military and domestic government-spending priorities was partly to blame. The Democrats wanted less defense and more civilian spending, with some increased taxes; Reagan wanted more defense, less civilian spending, and no tax increases. A compromise emerged between 1982 and 1987, with more defense spending, modest cuts in civilian spending, and little increase in taxes. Between 1983 and 1987, U.S. federal budget deficits increased to an average of $200 billion annually, and at least $100 billion of this deficit was believed to be excessive by many U.S. economists and bankers. See Chapter 6, infra, and compare sources cited in note 64.

68. See Chapters 4, 5, and 6, infra. These trends were widely discussed in the business and financial press toward the later part of 1986 and early 1987. Assuming the world debt crisis could still be managed, with enough new lending and somewhat lower interest rates (with no increase in "real" interest rates), the most significant difficulty for the world's gradual economic recovery in the late 1980s and early 1990s was an awkward trade-imbalance problem (and the massive U.S. trade and current account deficits).

69. Most developing countries were already protectionist (or at least mercantilist) in many ways, so that a serious conflict of interest was growing between NICs and LDCs, and the mature industrial countries.

70. Agricultural markets were another thicket of conflicting interests, with the United States wanting more agricultural exports. But, in a period of expanding world food production, with many surpluses, this would be difficult.

71. See, for example, "Launching of the Uruguay Round," *GATT Newsletter FOCUS* (Oct. 1986); "Results of the GATT Ministerial Meeting Held in Punta del Este, Uruguay," *Hearing*, Subcommittee on Trade, Committee on Ways and Means, U.S. House of Representatives, 99th Cong., 2nd Sess. (Sept. 25, 1986); "Possible New Round of Trade Negotiations," *Hearing*, Committee on Finance, U.S. Senate, 99th Cong., 2nd Sess. (July 23, 1986). See also Gary Clyde Hufbauer and Jeffrey C. Schott, *Trading for Growth: The Next Round of Trade Negotiations* (Washington, D.C.: Inst. for International Economics, Sept. 1985); and "Economic Summit, Latin Debt and The Baker Plan," *Hearing*, Committee on Foreign Relations, U.S. Senate, 99th Cong., 2nd Sess. (May 20, 1986).

72. See Chapters 2 and 3, generally, and Chapter 5, note 1. See also *1986 World Bank Atlas* (cited in preface note 1) together with table P–2 and appendix tables A–1 through A–10.

73. Substantial interests in these countries, however, want to limit this dependence on "free" trade and seek stronger protection, regulation, and support against the world market and foreign "unfair" trade practices. Labor unions, farm lobbies, and many business interests favor limits on free trade.

2
Competing Industrial Policies

Industrial and trade development policies are common around the world.[1] They reflect a desire of most nations to broaden their industrial capabilities, expand output, increase exports, and improve living standards. Japan's sustained performance record after World War II is particularly impressive. More recently, other East Asian countries, including South Korea and Taiwan, have also achieved rapid economic growth, with government encouragement, financing support, some selective protection, and administrative guidance. Many other countries have used comparable policies with uneven success. As more nations employ systematic industrial development and export-promotion strategies to enlarge their manufactures and markets abroad, international rivalry intensifies, and awkward adjustment problems may ensue. In response, mature industrial nations are contemplating "reindustrialization" policies, and many are using more protectionist measures, including voluntary import restraints. With global recession in the early 1980s, a widespread external debt crisis, and heavy budget deficits, some economists worry that a drift back toward selfishly protectionist mercantilism could undermine world prosperity and weaken the general economic progress of the last decades. And yet, the evident success of industrial development and export promotion policies, especially in East Asia during the past fifteen to twenty years, has prompted widespread emulation.

But, what does this mean for international trade, finance, and banking? Can all countries productively employ comprehensive industrial promotion, selective protection, and export subsidies? Or should only LDCs use these special encouragements? Should most NICs continue such efforts or be more constrained in their use? What should be the response of mature industrial countries (MICs)? Should they reply in kind with similar policies? Should each nation's industrial policies depend upon its competitive strength, resources, and comparative advantages? And, how can industrial development policies (investment subsidies, R&D support, export promotion, and easy financing) improve a nation's comparative advantage and industrial capabilities?

If comprehensive industrial development policies become overwhelming practice, what are the implications for free trade, open markets, and easy movement of capital, technology, and know-how in the world marketplace? Some argue that a serious conflict exists between activist industrial policies and laissez faire in international commerce. But, how can we explain the evident success of some national industrial-trade development policies in a post–World War II context of gradually freer world trade, at least for most industrial countries?

One explanation is that broadening prosperity (and more open markets) in the United States, Europe, and elsewhere created the export opportunity for *some (but not too many)* dramatically successful NIC industrial policies (along with Japan's sustained export success). Whether all nations could have succeeded simultaneously with similar export promotion policies is more questionable. And, if all mature industrial countries now stress exports (while limiting imports), the mutual growth and expansion of the 1950s–1970s could be hard to restore. Thus, it might be reasoned that the strong success of Japan and some other NICs is best explained as a special situation—(a) preferential treatment under GATT that allowed aggressive protection and subsidy for some LDCs and (b) increasingly open, larger markets in the United States, Europe, and elsewhere, which created the opportunity for export success in a limited number of NICs plus Japan.[2]

Seen in this light, the problem for national and international policies becomes more perplexing in the later 1980s. Should most nations now use comprehensive industrial policies? What trade development consequences follow? Is it realistic to believe all nations would abandon industrial policies together and open their markets simultaneously? And if not, what should be the response of freer market nations such as the United States to comprehensive industrial policies among most NICs, LDCs, and some mature industrial countries seeking rejuvenation and strong recoveries?

Recent Industrial Policy Momentum

Industrial development policies stress rapid capital formation, productive investment, and technology enhancement and sharing. These efforts go beyond traditional free-market encouragements for business; they represent more productivity-oriented stimuli for industry, technology, and export development than protectionist (or defensive) subsidies for new (or established) factories and workers. In the most successful countries practicing this art of government–industry collaboration, there is healthy teamwork among top-level bureaucrats, technocrats, industrialists, engineers, and scientists. Work ethics are strong; savings rates high. There is a shared national commitment to industrial success and competitiveness in world markets; the importance of expanding exports and trade for prosperity is understood. To those believing in this technique of improving economic performance, "New Industrial Policies" clearly comprise a sharply differentiated strategy of policy-making from old-fashioned laissez faire on the one hand, or old-fashioned protectionism on the other. A first step in appreciating the New Industrial Policy literature, therefore, is to fully understand this novelty and emphasis.

Characteristic elements of New Industrial Policies include: (a) capital formation and savings, (b) investment financing, (c) technology sharing and enhancement, (d) work incentives, (e) rationalization measures for efficiency and exports, (f) selective protectionism, and (g) international arrangements for development and exports. Capital formation and saving can be encouraged by generous tax policies, relatively low interest rates, and government (or central bank) money creation. Investments in industrial expansion and export marketing can be fostered through access to lower-interest lending, equity-type seed money, and high-leverage profit prospects for enterprises in desired sectors. Collateral investments in infrastructure, roads, transport, power, and communications can be subsidized by government and foreign assistance (and borrowing at long term, if possible at concessionary rates).

Technology transfer comes through license regulation, joint ventures, and requiring major importers to provide foreign assistance, local partners, technology sharing, and training programs. Enhanced technology springs from collaboration between domestic industry, universities, research institutes, and government agencies, plus cooperation and study with foreign technology sources. As nations prosper and move into advanced industrial status, they participate more equally in technology markets, though leadership tends to be shared in each field among relatively few countries.

Work incentives are provided by generous sharing of growth and profits among employees. Stronger performance increases these rewards, thereby reinforcing the momentum of an established progress. Labor–management relations should facilitate productivity, not promote disharmony, cleavages, or disruption. Unions function better with considerable loyalty to their enterprises. Mutual confidence between companies and workers is desirable. Corporate organizations and employee treatment patterns should emphasize long-run partnership; partial employee ownership in companies is normally helpful in building cooperation.

Rationalization cartels can help in easing adjustments to reduced demand or shifts of capital and human investment. But, such cartels need to be supervised closely by government antitrust agencies and limited in time, function, and financing to social goals of increased productivity for their companies and workers.

Selective, limited protection can be useful for infant industries, markets regulated by adjustment cartels, or sectors receiving reindustrialization support.[3] (Tariffs, quotas, or domestic-content laws may serve this purpose.) Ideally, these arrangements should be considered temporary and function under limited-duration mandates. In sectors where many countries use subsidies, support, or protection of one sort or another (international airlines, shipping, agriculture, and steel, for example), complications arise. In these sectors, prices across international boundaries tend to be somewhat distorted or affected by marginal cost discounts applied selectively. Surpluses, instability, discounting, dumping, and multiple track pricing are typical. (See figure 2–1.) Particularly when large fixed plant outlays and substantially declining marginal costs are involved (as in steel, heavy equipment, and transportation), sizeable price

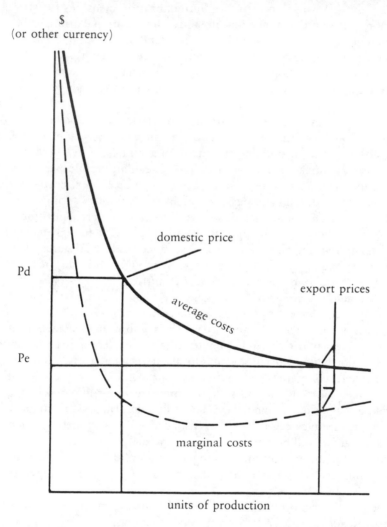

Note: Many countries use tax concessions, subsidies, export promotion, and adjustment assistance for their industries. This combination of widespread subsidization and discounting in world markets can be considered a significant form of market failure. It reflects the fact that many countries do not trust laissez faire to regulate important heavy industries.

Figure 2–1. Typical Costs for Heavy Industry

discounts are commonly used as export or sales promotion strategies. In these sectors, special international arrangements (such as the Multifibre Agreement or voluntary import restraints) or offsetting import tariffs may be constructive, even necessary to sustain viable participation in world markets. Care should always be taken, however, to ensure that each country's participation meets standards of genuine national interest (and not merely parochial benefit to special interest groups).

Just what patterns of collaboration or protection are best will vary regionally and reflect political, cultural, and economic alliances among states. But, each country normally benefits from a wider choice of trading partners and seeks enough latitude to make the best possible deals in the international bazaar of export and import operations. In this regard, we see that a broadened, competitive world market has substantial tendencies toward durability, because once it becomes reasonably well established, this marketplace serves the interests of most nations in the world community. Thus, if international arrangements (whether among a few or many countries) significantly restrict market forces, they tend to break down over time. Output-restricting cartels (such as OPEC) that artificially increase prices tend to stimulate greater production and encourage substitution and conservation behavior, which reduces demand. Cartels that artificially raise prices directly without controlling supply eventually find that additional supply (from new producers and added output) will squeeze into the market, while buyers respond to bargains available elsewhere. The ultimate strength of world market competition through increased numbers of suppliers, buyers, and alternatives can be reinforced by successful national industrial policies.

Some commentators, nonetheless, fear misuse of New Industrial Policies, particularly a danger that traditional protectionist forces (domestic industries, unions, and farmers) could rationalize crude protectionism. It is certainly true that productivity-oriented New Industrial Policy is not equivalent to sustained sheltering of weakness or losers. Few should support the protection of old, inefficient plants with weak management, or lazy, unproductive, or outmoded employees under such false colors. No wonder "lemon socialism" enjoys few explicit adherents. And yet, many free-trade advocates and lobbyists insist that such outcomes are common under the banner of New Industrial Policies, at least among older industrial countries.[4]

There should be no surprise that policy controversies are enmeshed in a web of conflicting interests and professional spokespeople. Lobbies for domestic industries, farmers, and workers threatened by expanding trade will be fought by the lobbies for exporters and importers, MNEs, branch plant investments, and international banking. The balance of bargaining power varies within each country and may shift over time. In the United States, in the early-to-mid-1980s, the foreign trade-international banking lobby seemed to be much stronger (on the whole) than the domestic labor-industry lobby, and the New Industrial concept was still struggling for broader recognition and respectability. In other advanced economies, the industrial policy idea was better established, but implementation remained controversial. For most NICs and LDCs, industrial policies are now conventional wisdom, even though performance ranges from strong to mediocre to weak. Such diverse experience reveals that talent, judgment, and the administration of governments and enterprises are key variables in determining the success or failure of new industrial policies.

Japanese Growth and Industrial Policies

Japan is widely regarded as the most successful long-term practitioner of modern industrial policy.[5] Its accomplishments have roots in Japanese history, cultural cohesion, and a tradition of strong government under the Tokugawa Shogunate (1600–1868). By the midnineteenth century, Japan was the most disciplined, literate, and regulated society outside of Europe. A prosperous mercantile network existed, with a well-integrated economy of farming, fishing, artisanry, and local manufactures. Although self-imposed isolation for more than two centuries left serious lags in technology, the potential for a strong catch-up effort was in place.

When the Meiji transformation (1868–1912) got underway, its leaders aggressively fostered new industries with state enterprises, subsidies, guarantees, and bank loans. Exports, coal, steel, shipbuilding, armaments, and munitions received emphasis along with railroads and power. Western-style education, engineering, and civil service were established. Government revenues were enlarged substantially. Feudal rights to income in rice were transformed into negotiable bonds and liquid capital, part of which helped to capitalize commercial banking. Additional government resources capitalized the Bank of Japan and other industrial development banks that reinforced commercial banks and provided further credits for expansion of industry and shipping. National output, war potential, and military strength increased rapidly, allowing expansion into Korea, Formosa, and China in 1894–95, 1904–05, and 1915–19. Japan quickly became a great power widely respected, and somewhat feared.

Although prosperity was incomplete and shared unequally, with considerable poverty for many peasants and urban workers, Japan was becoming a modern nation in many ways. Constitutional democracy was established formally in 1889; gradually, political parties took shape. Imperial expansion was popular, though, and militarism grew in influence. Until the late 1920s, Japan's evolution was somewhat like Europe's, but militarism became dominant in the 1930s. A stronger industrial policy was implemented, with deficit finance, credits for banking and industry, and skillfully coordinated development efforts (including colonial territories and Manchuria). War mobilization after 1937, especially from 1940 to 1945, added momentum. While disastrous naval and shipping losses plus massive damage to cities and industry followed in

1944–45, Japan's industrial progress had been a dramatic economic achievement, reflecting skilled and productive industrial policy as well as government–industry collaboration.

Occupation between 1945 and 1951 brought liberalizing reforms. Increased fairness, broadened education, better status for women, partial divestiture of Zaibatsu conglomerates, and company-style unionism improved incentives and morale. But, budget stimulus, bank credits, and government–industry cooperation were used for industrial reconstruction, export promotion, and rapid development of new industries. Technology transfer from major foreign companies was encouraged, along with joint ventures. The Ministry of International Trade and Industry (MITI), created before the war, became more influential in promoting economic success through consensus collaboration. As success picked up momentum during the 1960s and 1970s, skillful upgrading of industrial technology, marketing overseas, and selected investments abroad received government support or approval. Although OPEC's oil price shock slowed progress in 1974–75, the Japanese industrial machine and prosperity proved resilient—Japan was more successful than any other advanced nation in the late 1970s and 1980s. Japan's exports continued growing, and its technological excellence has become firmly established.

In recent years, Japan began shifting some manufacturing activities into branch plants in low-wage countries, while retrenching some aging industries (with distress cartels supervised by MITI and the Fair Trade Commission). Meanwhile, renewed emphasis was placed upon technological progress, further export development, and improvements in infrastructure, housing, and the environment. Close collaboration between government and industry continues, with greater attention to trade relations and enlarging investments around the world.

In terms of sustained economic growth and consciously orchestrated progress, Japan is increasingly studied as a model by NICs and LDCs; even Europe and North America see features worth emulating. Many foreign observers view "Japan, Inc." as a serious economic challenge, though they may not fully understand that its success is a skillful blend of increasingly competitive, export-oriented enterprises and banks, with unique government–industry collaboration. In fact, Japan is moving toward somewhat freer markets, even though social insurance and public-sector budgets are growing with affluence (and may approach Western European and U.S. levels in time).

Other East Asian Industrial Policies

South Korea is a more recent and even faster growing illustration of successful industrial policy since the early 1960s. Land reform, government financing and central bank credits, infant-industry protection, restrictions upon luxury imports, and foreign investment and borrowing were employed skillfully in forcing economic progress. Korean business enterprises (led by their conglomerate *chaebol* corporations) developed self-sustaining growth and became successful in many areas, including construction, steel, shipbuilding, transportation, trucks, buses, and automobiles. Its industrial growth rate was among the world's fastest during the past twenty years.[6]

Taiwan has been another success story since the early 1950s, with land reform, government finance, some state industries and banking, selective protection, strong foreign investment, and a light industry boom. One of their leading economists characterizes its formula for rapid progress as a "planned free market," a neat expression for the essence of market- and productivity-oriented industrial policies (with strong education, public-sector infrastructure, and national security outlays helping to support growth efforts).[7]

More recently, Singapore became successful as a trading and manufacturing city-state, with a unique blend of liberal incentives for business, careful government supervision, and more welfare state insurance than most developing economies seem able to achieve. Hong Kong has also been successful in terms of business growth sense, though it is more laissez faire and significantly less egalitarian. Moreover, it suffers the time limit problem of reversion to mainland China by 1997.

These four countries, plus Japan, constitute a New East Asia Challenge, reflecting vigorous dynamism in industry, exports, and economic growth, that offers strong competition (enhanced through new industrial policies) against the older industrial countries of Europe and North America.[8] In the coming years, more new industrial countries may be expected to follow this pattern of successful industrial development and rapid growth. Lower wage structures have been important in enabling this export-oriented economic growth. But, much more was needed to enable these East Asian countries to achieve stronger productivity, reliable and quality manufacturing, and rapid economic upgrading. Like most major human and social achievements, art and nature combined to create success via systematic, well-administered economic policies together with natural vitality, energetic peoples wanting higher living standards, and cultures with responsible morality and work ethics.

European Industrial Policies

Europe's industrial revolution in the eighteenth and nineteenth centuries (particularly in Britain, France, Germany and the Low Countries) led the world. A mixture of freer trade and mercantilist policies were used over this long period, but generally, most economic historians could agree that, within limits, each approach proved constructive. Freer trade tended to be associated with rising prosperity, expanding markets, and economic growth. Yet, infant-industry protection and commercial encouragement, research and innovation, public investments in transport and communications, and most sponsorship of exports were helpful and frequently employed to catch up with leaders. War potential, armaments, munitions, and shipbuilding received special support, which represented another category of government intervention. Warfare could become costly, though, at least for losers, and the heavy destruction of World Wars I and II suggested that peaceful rivalry would be less dangerous and consistent with greater overall prosperity.

During the immediate postwar period (1945 through the mid-1950s), reconstruction and recovery included a considerable role for government. Mixed economies and indicative planning were popular in many countries, along with social insurance. Yet, West Germany emphasized more free-market vitality in its recovery, which was the most successful industrial and export growth. The Common Market also provided freer trade stimulus for West Germany, France, Benelux, and Italy, and most of Europe shared in their broader prosperity. Britain grew more slowly, however, with problems of labor discipline, less vigor in some sectors, and recurrent trade payments difficulties. By the early 1960s, Britain felt a need for greater economic growth and industrial progress.

The Conservatives began a limited industrial policy with National Economic Development Councils (NEDC), which institutionalized government, management, and labor discussions for major industries. Harold Wilson's Labor government, between 1964 and 1970, began a more systematic industrial policy, with efforts to improve overall economic performance in Britain. It created a Department of Economic Affairs, Ministry of Technology, Industrial Reorganization Corporation, and incomes policy (for restraint of prices and wages) and it implemented a program for helping declining regions and industries. The Conservatives reduced these efforts between 1970 and 1974, but Labor revived many between 1974 and 1978. More recently, Thatcher's Conservatives switched to a more free-market philosophy, largely (though not completely) dismantling the industrial policy apparatus. Results of all this effort remain controversial, but many insist its major shortcomings were emphasis on job protection and propping up companies rather than productivity, innovation, and new industries. Among critics, British-style industrial policy was called "lemon socialism." Thatcher's Conservatives, in its place, have been preaching free-market disciplines and have accepted much higher unemployment as a step toward greater productivity.[9]

On the continent, the swings of economic and industrial policy have been less dramatic for the most part. Social Democrats and socialist parties tend to use explicit industrial and technology promotion policies, while more conservative parties de-emphasize them. It would be apt to characterize most of Europe as having employed systematic industrial and export-promotion policies with mixed results, during the last twenty years. Like Britain, however, there often has been a defensive emphasis, with concern for maintaining employment and strengthening weaker sectors.[10]

General lessons drawn by most observers and scholars seem to be that productivity-oriented industrial policies have frequently been worthwhile, though by no means required for successful industries. On the other hand, most

agree that subsidies designed merely to prop up companies and their employment tend to be wasteful and often fail in the end. These conclusions can be
upsetting, however, for those who fear a steady loss of production opportunities
and employment to low-wage NICs with successful, productivity-oriented industrial policies. This logic may suggest an inevitable decline in real wages for
production workers exposed to world market competition and a tendency
toward leveling of per capita incomes around the world. This trend implies
that real per capita incomes should reflect real productivity levels for their
respective populations, an outcome that makes sense to most believers in free-
trade economics (even though this places strain upon high-wage industries in
Europe and North America).

The bottom-line test for industrial policies should be like that for any other
public or private investment program. Can such efforts, outlays, subsidies, or
regulations justify themselves by a positive net contribution to production, exports, innovation, and living standards for the countries employing them? If
they can be managed responsibly to these ends, systematic industrial development policies make sense. Thus, an important dimension of industrial policy
potential is the integrity, talent, and long-range soundness of government administrators, the political process that supports them, and their collaboration
with productive enterprises in the market place. For the United States (and other
countries), therefore, the crucial questions are not merely whether systematic
industrial policies have worked in Japan, East Asia, or elsewhere, but the extent to which such policies can be transplanted successfully, in a different
political situation, and with different administrative capabilities.

U.S. Industrial Policies and Proposals

In the United States, federal and state government efforts to promote banking,
finance, industry, corporations, canals, turnpikes, and railroads began soon after
independence.[11] Substantial economic development followed, stimulated by
vigorous flows of immigrants and considerable foreign capital (especially in the
early-to-mid-1830s boom). This prosperity quickly became self-sustaining. The
United States was an NIC by the 1820s. From the midnineteenth century onward, it was among the pacesetters of industrial progress. Although patents,
tariffs, easy bank credit, and railroad subsidies (mainly through land grants)
helped foster this subsequent development, most of it seemed to be the fruit
of free enterprise, strong incentives, low taxes, and rapidly growing market demand in an underpopulated territory blessed with generous productivity and
resources. By the twentieth century, the United States was admired as a new
industrial giant—Europe's child and cultural heir—and respected for innovative
vitality. Energies seemed to be renewed steadily through new immigration and
native American enthusiasm. The world saw the United States as a land of
economic promise, where dreams could come true for ordinary people.

Considerable tariff protection was still employed for many industries (with doubts among some economists as to their impact on productivity for society). Some progressive antitrust, public utility, and consumer protection regulations came in the Theodore Roosevelt and Woodrow Wilson eras to limit the excesses of big business. The New Deal brought more of this regulation, along with depression relief, widespread unionization, and social security programs. World War II gave stronger stimulus to many branches of industry, metals, machinery, shipbuilding, aircraft, and armaments. Since many other industrial countries suffered substantial war losses and devastation, U.S. industry enjoyed special competitive advantages for a while. Its industrial system continued growing for many years, partly because of scale economies and technological momentum.

In the postwar era, large U.S. corporations expanded their marketing activities internationally and began to locate branch plants and component manufacturing abroad. Declining U.S. tariff barriers, growing European markets, lower wages abroad, and protected markets in many LDCs and NICs provided stimulus. Leading U.S. banks followed corporate clientele overseas and (especially in the 1970s) participated in a great expansion of multinational and tax-haven–related banking. Meanwhile, increasingly in the 1960s and even more during the 1970s, foreign corporations based in Europe, Japan and, recently, a number of other areas, grew rapidly to provide tougher competition in many markets—including steel, automobiles, machinery, electronics, and many other consumer articles.

Economic growth slowed somewhat in the United States after the 1960s, with stagflation and increased structural unemployment. Many industries prospered, such as agriculture, oil and gas, computers, semiconductors, aerospace (unevenly), and service activities (including health care), while others declined, including steel, automobiles, some machinery and machine tools, and portions of clothing manufacture. Tax loads increased with income tax bracket creep, higher social security levies, rising state and local taxes, so that marginal tax rates on upper middle class and salaried people became significantly more burdensome. Gradually, a tax revolt developed, first with respect to state and local property taxes and then with the Reagan administration income tax cuts of 1981–83. Corporate and business taxes were cut substantially, though some complained about excessive giveaways. Social security taxes remained high, though, and actually increased a little bit.[12]

Regulatory burdens, paperwork, and compliance expenses had increased considerably since the mid-1960s, particularly with respect to environmental protection, occupational safety and health requirements, consumer regulation, and greater tort liabilities. These burdens were more controversial by the late 1970s, and the Reagan administration greatly relaxed consumer protection, environmental and antitrust enforcement during the early 1980s.

Reagan's administration espoused a more free-market and business-oriented philosophy of government, hoping to reduce the size of government spending and social welfare programs. Congress was divided between 1981 and 1986, with a Democratic House resisting major slashes and the Republican Senate taking an intermediate line. But, Reagan's defense outlays (largely accepted by Congress) grew from 5 to 7 percent of GNP; this combined with tax cuts and impasse over civilian spending to generate record budget deficits, reaching $200 billion annually or roughly 5 percent of GNP between 1983 and 1987. Congress made little effort to close this budget gap before 1986, and most observers believed this fiscal impasse could only be resolved after the 1986 and 1988 elections (with eventual compromises keyed to the election outcomes).[13]

Meanwhile, big budget deficits (at record levels for peacetime) placed serious strain upon monetary policy and sustained upward pressure on interest rates. Prime business borrowing rates in the United States were 9 to 10 percent compared to 5 to 6 percent for Germany, Switzerland, and Japan during Spring 1984, and despite rates trending downward with slowed inflation, by Fall 1986, U.S. prime rates were still 7 to 8 percent compared to 5 to 6 percent for Germany, Switzerland, and Japan.[14] Higher U.S. interest rates, along with insecurities abroad (partly related to the LDC debt-load crisis) led to a substantial short-term capital flow into the United States and an artificially high dollar value. The dollar reached a peak of 60 to 70 percent appreciation above 1980 levels in February 1985. This helped U.S. imports grow substantially (despite a slump in oil prices), while U.S. exports remained sluggish. The U.S. trade deficit was growing much larger, approaching a record $170 billion in 1986, and its current account deficit exceeded $100 billion (as net imports greatly exceeded service, investment, and banking income). The dollar finally started to decline substantially in 1985, and had lost most of its recent appreciation by late fall 1986. But, the course of further dollar devaluation and eventual benefit to the balance of payments (or the trade balance) remained uncertain. Only limited improvement in the trade balance occurred by spring 1987. In this situation, U.S. concern for increased foreign imports, reduced export markets, and trade policy was understandable. Inevitably, these matters would be discussed extensively during the 1986 and 1988 election campaigns and possibly for years thereafter.

Proposals for a more comprehensive U.S. industrial rejuvenation policy began to appear in the later 1970s. This reflected a delayed response to European (and earlier Japanese) industrial policy efforts. American thinking was more free-enterprise–oriented than most of Europe's (where mild socialist ideology was fairly well established). The U.S. economy was still more prosperous in the later 1970s and early 1980s, with a stronger agricultural and natural resource base. And, U.S. MNEs had developed a strong stake in the GATT-encouraged multilateral trade-investment-banking regime. But, what provoked new interest in a U.S. industrial policy was increasing concern over declining industries, the smokestack sector (steel, auto, machinery, and machine tools) which had been a crucial part of earlier U.S. industrial success. Would it be wise to let these industries decline further? Could similar weakening spread to other industries? When would this process of displacement by low-wage foreign workers and industries come to an end? What should be done to deal with these structural challenges?

Viewpoints differed, naturally.[15] Organized labor, politicians, and scholars sympathetic to the companies, workers, families, and cities threatened with low-wage competition and displacement problems wanted substantial relief. Common suggestions were domestic-content legislation, quotas or tariff protection, or voluntary trade restraints on an ad hoc or multilateral basis. Other groups were seriously concerned, but preferred to facilitate adjustments and accept more free trade in their version of industrial policy. More conservative and free-market economists, with most MNEs and multinational banks, often denounced the new industrial policy movement as anticompetitive protectionism. Although some conservatives accepted elements of technology- and productivity-oriented industrial policy, they feared countermeasures abroad if the United States embarked upon widespread new protectionism. Some took a pure free-trade view and insisted that any form of protectionism (even antidumping and countervailing duty proceedings under U.S. law) was undesirable. Others replied that few nations abroad went so far as the United States in opening large markets to foreign manufactures, agreed that tougher U.S. trade bargaining was now desirable, and worried that a totally free-trade outlook would be naive and self-destructive. Through the 1980s, an extensive literature on industrial and trade policies emerged.

Among the more interesting features of this controversy was a reversal of positions in the political parties. Now, more Democrats tended toward protectionist views, with more Republicans and big business (MNE) interests favoring freer trade. Traditionally, most Democrats (from Jefferson through Jackson, Cleveland, Wilson, Franklin Roosevelt, Truman, Kennedy, and even Carter) supported freer trade, whereas the Whig and Republic parties supported more industrial protection (from Henry Clay through Lincoln, McKinley, Taft, Harding, Coolidge, and Hoover). Underlying this shift was growing unease about lower wage levels and unemployment among Democrats, while big business (MNE) interests were more involved in world trade, investment, and banking. Consumers might be expected to support relatively free trade and lower import prices, so long as their own family incomes were not threatened by displacement or declining wage levels.

In any event, the following kinds of measures were under discussion as possible elements in U.S. industrial policy during the 1980s:[16]

1. Stronger administrative emphasis
   a. A new Department of Industry Technology and Trade (DITT) to coordinate trade policy with industrial development.
   b. A stronger U.S. trade representative (USTR) with a mandate for tougher bargaining and improved trade equity.

    c. Systematic organization of Government Industry Councils (GICs) for significant industries

    d. Special task forces for industries under stress (such as steel, machinery, machine tools, automobiles, electronics, appliances, shipbuilding, textiles, and shoes) that need improved productivity to meet international competition

2. Stronger R&D, technology improvement, and more efficient engineering

    a. Additional funding for engineering schools, technology monitoring, and enhancement programs, with emphasis on industries lagging in productivity

    b. Technology sharing, transfer, licensing, and joint venture encouragement

    c. Special revenue tariffs, licensing fees, and royalty charges to finance technology enhancement, research, sharing, and licensing programs

3. Improved financing for industrial development

    a. Greatly reduced government deficits, eased pressure on monetary policy, and lower interest rates via Federal Reserve, Treasury Department, and Congressional action

    b. Reduction in takeovers and disruptive stock market speculation by investment banks and corporate enterprises

    c. General tax reform

        (1) Encouragement of increased savings with lower taxes on middle- and upper-level incomes

        (2) Encouragement of productive investments

        (3) Elimination of unproductive tax subsidies

        (4) Shift of some tax burden from saving and investment to consumption

        (5) Improved equity with mild progressivity in marginal income tax rates

4. Profit sharing and employee stock ownership for companies participating in technology enhancement and rejuvenation and retrenchment programs and for most industries

    a. Improved incentives for work force

    b. New mandate, tax incentives, and regulations to encourage employee stock ownership and profit sharing generally

5. Rejuvenation and retrenchment programs for industries facing serious competition from more efficient foreign suppliers

    a. Special rejuvenation, retrenchment, and consolidation plans developed by Special Task Forces for basic industries under stress (e.g. steel, machinery, machine tools, automobiles, electronics, shipbuilding, textiles, clothing, shoes, etc.) that need improved productivity to meet international competition (approved by DITT and antitrust agencies)

    b. Job retraining and relocation assistance available from Department of Labor to employees laid off in retrenchment plans

    c. Funding for retraining, relocation, and rejuvenation efforts obtained from special tariffs on imports

    d. Employee stock ownership and profit sharing encouraged as part of rejuvenation, retrenchment, and consolidation plans

6. Selective protection from foreign competition for limited periods under rejuvenation, retrenchment, and consolidation plans

    a. Special tariffs, quotas, or voluntary trade restraints for industries under significant stress

    b. Limited periods for special tariffs, quotas, or voluntary trade restraints (sunset restrictions)

    c. Performance accountability to relevant government agencies

7. Selective protection and support for essential elements of basic industries needed for national security, technological vitality, and industrial mobilization capacity ("core industrial base")

    a. Special tariffs, fees, quotas, or voluntary trade restraints for elements of basic engineering, materials, and defense industries important for technological vitality, national security, and continuity in the event of war or disruption of imports

    b. Limited subsidies and financing support, primarily through import fees and domestic production excises

8. Improved trade equity and more equal trade openness

    a. Stronger unfair trade practice remedies

    b. Tougher trade bargaining

    c. Improved openness for U.S. exports of goods, services, and investments

    d. U.S. revenue tariffs and/or foreign VAT waiver correctives (import levies)

    e. Increased use of import restrictions to match and offset foreign industrial policies, subsidies, and targeting (especially in distressed U.S. industries)

    f. Increased use of reciprocal import restrictions to match and offset foreign tariffs, quotas, and NTBs

Some elements of this agenda already have been proposed by the Reagan administration. A Department of International Trade and Industry (DITI) proposal of June 1983, is still pending. Established Congressional committees resisted the idea, perhaps wanting to keep more of the crucial power over import restrictions to themselves. Nor did the U.S. Trade Representative's staff show enthusiasm, since they feared weakened influence if they were merged with the Department of Commerce. With respect to profit sharing, employee stock ownership, and retrenchment, some of these are occurring now in the ailing steel and automobile industries, and a trend toward more employee stock ownership profit-sharing seems in progress. But, these reforms are merely occasional, ad hoc results and have not been systematically encouraged (beyond limited tax advantages already enjoyed by ESOPs). Likewise, recently relaxed antitrust enforcement allows some retrenchment plus merger and consolidation activity, but no systematic encouragement or supervision has developed that could be compared to the Japanese distress cartels (supervised by MITI and their Fair Trade Commission). Similarly, greater leeway for international joint ventures is allowed (for example, Toyota-General Motors) by the Antitrust Division of the Department of Justice and FTC. A limited further exemption for international joint research ventures was enacted in 1984. Also, the Reagan administration grudgingly endorsed occasional protection for a few industries, including some textiles and Harley-Davidson motorcycles. There were also voluntary auto import restraints. But, Reagan administration proposals fall considerably short of the comprehensive industrial policy efforts proposed by many others.[17]

Instead, the Reagan administration favored a supply-side free-market strategy, emphasizing mainly tax cuts, increased business incentives, and the elimination of nonproductive tax sheltering (to the extent politically feasible). The administration largely welcomed foreign competition as a discipline for U.S. industry and to keep wage costs (and inflation) reasonably low. For these reasons, the administration generally opposed all relief for industries threatened by imports and preferred (or at least hoped) to open more trade, services, and investment opportunities abroad. While the administration began to talk a little tougher with major trade partners about unequal openness in 1985–86 and sought somewhat greater openness abroad in the next GATT round, it seemed evident that the principal objective was mainly to keep U.S. protectionism contained and minimized. (Whether any significant increase in openness for U.S. exports, services, and investment was actually feasible or likely in the short run was doubtful, at least to most observers.)

In contrast, leading Democratic politicians saw increasing major issue potential and interest group appeal in trade policy; they complained about the "export of U.S. jobs" to low-wage countries. Reagan's campaign response in 1984 was to resist broader efforts, as illustrated by chapter 3 (Industrial Policy) in *Economic Report of the President, 1984*, which discounted the likely gains from industrial policies abroad. Yet, most Democratic contenders in 1984 developed more extensive industrial policy proposals. A major Democratic-sponsored trade bill (the Comprehensive Trade Policy Reform Act of 1986) sought also to strengthen U.S. unfair trade practice law and to somewhat restrict foreign imports.[18] It seems inevitable that prospective Democratic platforms would articulate these themes in a general way and offer to do more than a Republican administration is willing to suggest at this stage. Yet, we should not forget that considerable support for international trade still exists among many Democratic economists, consumer advocates, export-import interests, and the MNE and banking lobbies. Both parties are really a disorderly melange of free-trade and protectionist interests, even though presidential politics might create greater differences for the future.

Pressures for some kind of U.S. industrial policy (involving most of the foregoing agenda) could well increase if many basic industries continue to experience substantial (or increased) stress from enlarged import levels or if significant job displacement continues. A further decline in the dollar's value, which had boosted U.S. imports and discouraged U.S. exports, might be helpful, of course, and gradually ease these pressures. One way or another, the next few years would reveal more about the intensity of support for a New Industrial Policy in the United States and/or more traditional protectionism. A growing concern among mature industrial countries, such as the United States and much of Europe, is that industrial relocation to NICs around the world may accelerate substantially, creating continued, if not enlarged, displacement effects upon the higher-wage, skilled manufacturing or blue collar industries and labor of MICs. (See figure P–2.)

Threats to basic industries needed for long-run industrial strength and technological capacity are another important source of industrial policy support. To some degree, it can be said that most major industrial countries should preserve significant basic capacities, engineering talent, production labor, and facilities in almost every significant branch of technology. This core capability represents part of their mobilization base for national security in a world that is never completely secure in terms of trade flows, and political relationships. This industrial capability is also crucial for faster economic growth and to participate in overall technical progress as prosperous, scientific cultures. These requirements are evident for basic steel, machinery, machine tools, shipbuilding, aircraft, electrical equipment, computers, chemicals, pharmaceuticals, armaments, munitions, and direct war requirements, among other industries. While partial imports can be accepted in these areas—and should be welcome as efficiency challenges, prods to upgrading, and sources of technology sharing and transfer—these basic needs for national technology, security, and political independence should not be neglected. The awkward problems are to decide how much core industrial capacity is desirable in each sector, and how much support, protection, and/or regulation is useful and appropriate to achieve these objectives.

Economic Justifications for Industrial-Trade Development Policies

To the extent that economists accept a legitimate role for subsidizing industries and/or protection, five arguments are utilized:[19] (1) infant industry development, (2) increased economic growth from the industrialization process, (3) adjustment relief to distressed industries for their recovery, rejuvenation, or redeployment, (4) sustaining national security industries and essential military and survival capacity, and (5) response to unfair foreign trade practices or distortions (subsidies, discounting, dumping, exploitative cartels or monopolies, restraint of trade, fraud, and deceptive practices).

The infant-industry and industrial-growth arguments are employed widely by developing nations. (But, even mature industrial nations can use this reasoning to foster high tech industries and to maintain and improve comparative advantages.) Broad latitude for protectionist and mercantilist quotas, tariffs, subsidies, and other restrictive practices is entrenched in the present GATT regime, which allows use of these practices by developing nations generally. Freer-trade and open–foreign investment advocates, multinational corporations, and multinational banks have adopted and accommodated to this major, growing loophole in the free-trade system. A desire to spread prosperity to the less developed world is involved, together with expanding market potential in extractive industries, branch plants, component making, sales outlets, and financing and other service activities around the world. A substantial network of mutual interdependence has been woven together this way.

Advanced industrial countries, because of their higher levels of prosperity, education, and accumulated industrial enterprise, were felt less deserving of infant-industry or economic-development protectionism. Accordingly, under the GATT, the United States, Western Europe, Canada, Australia, New Zealand, and later Japan accepted a double standard: (1) lower tariffs, more open markets, and freer, nondiscriminatory trade as a goal for industrial nations and (2) mercantilism and industrial development strategies for the poorer nations, allowing them to catch up gradually with advanced countries. This reasoning made sense for the world, provided that sufficiently increased prosperity follows for most countries (even though the poor grow more rapidly). Although partial retrenchment might occur within some sectors of advanced industrial nations, continuing overall growth, shifting resources, and labor retraining were believed to be better adjustment strategies than extensive protectionism.

Until recent years, this outlook commanded general support in advanced or mature industrial democracies. But as stagflation and partial deindustrialization afflicted many advanced nations, doubts and protectionist pressures have increased. The demand for relief against the adjustment costs (and job losses) in spreading world trade and industrial relocation could involve a limited slowdown (or a regulated easing) of imports and job substitution from lower-wage countries. (See figure P–2.) Moderate relief of this type through voluntary restraint agreements, tariffs, or other devices need not be a fundamental challenge to the GATT system and could be a means to facilitate longer-run adjustments.

A more serious question is presented by industrial nations and areas that suffer net decline or very slow growth as a result of expanding world trade and weakened comparative advantage. In these nations, political pressures are strong to provide wider relief because stagnant or reduced living standards are unexpected. Where previous industrial and export markets and profits are lost and ready substitutes and alternatives seem to be lacking, protectionist relief for the remaining domestic markets is commonly sought. But, such relief can be a burden for the remainder of these sluggish societies. Protectionist trade barriers often become entrenched politically. Painful choices are imposed upon countries with significant sectors of industrial inefficiency or decline. In the long run, it is normally wise to use world market competition and adjustment relief, including moderate restraints and/or tariff subsidies, as a prod to greater efficiency and more productive adjustment than to coddle increasingly outdated, inefficient operations that cannot survive in world trade.

In more aggravated situations of industrial setback or decline, it makes sense to allow some LDC-style latitude for selective revival efforts. For depressed areas with extensive unemployment, such policies make sense, too. A liberal interpretation of GATT would seem to provide authority since its fundamental idea is to broaden and generalize world trade and prosperity.

Strictly speaking, the potential for government encouragement, subsidy, and selective protection should be available to mature industrial countries (MICs) in addition to NICs and LDCs. If mature countries are to maintain economic growth and technological progress, some outlays along this line are probably essential. Japan, West Germany, and France all employ active programs and support for industrial R&D, and the U.S. even more so, if one takes a proper accounting for national defense, aerospace, NASA, and health-medical research and technology efforts. The main question for Americans is not really *whether* the government should contribute support, but rather *how* this effort should be organized and allocated among competing interest groups and industries, in a general context of excess government spending and retrenchment needs. Enforcing productivity and monitoring results becomes more important in these times.[20]

In this way, the rejuvenation-and-adjustment relief argument can be accommodated to the infant-industrial growth arguments and confined to a reasonable scope that does not basically challenge healthy industrial development, comparative advantages, or the social economies of world market efficiency. But, allowing adjustment or rejuvenation relief to become permanent protection from the world market really taxes one's own society for special interest groups' survival. To the extent that countries insulate themselves from world market bargains in this way, protectionist policies can be costly and self-defeating; they should become unpopular and resented as price discrepancies become aggravated between protected domestic suppliers and the cheaper alternatives abroad.

National security and survival arguments present a more restricted justification for protectionism. Within reasonable limits, it makes sense to protect essential military, food, energy, transport, communications, and other basic production capacity. Greater ability to withstand disrupted economic or political relations can be achieved. Access to friendly supplies may be unreliable, and a cushion of domestic survivability may be important. Even in the nuclear age, frequent wars occur, and leading nations such as the United States are likely to be involved in limited war, support for allies and client-states, police actions, and vulnerability to terrorism.

But, national security interests hardly ever justify total reliance upon domestic supplies. In fact, sensible procurement for manufactured equipment, weapons, and technology should exploit and keep abreast of foreign producers to some degree. Skillful protection of national security interests should include a high technology, new industrial policy orientation. Collaboration with allies and friendly states is helpful; within carefully supervised limits, even weapon exchanges and trading with adversaries can be beneficial.

For these reasons, supervision techniques should be used for defense procurement, strategic materials stockpiling, and safeguarding long-run security interests. Domestic-content and supplier requirements, quota restrictions, and limits on foreign sources are proper for these purposes. Export controls can be used for sensitive materials, special equipment, and technology not readily available in the world market. The Department of Defense and other security agencies should monitor these aspects of import-export trade carefully. Economic analysis is required to evaluate the benefits of such regulations, domestic supplier programs, and budgetary outlays involved. Where major discrepancies are involved between domestic and foreign prices, the possibility of contractor fraud, penalties, and alternative domestic suppliers should be investigated. Within reasonable limits, foreign arms purchases and/or components supply is useful for competition and cost-accounting discipline, provided that strict quality control is maintained.

In a somewhat different rationale coupled with new industry-industrial process arguments, major nations (such as the United States, Japan, West Germany, France, and Britain) with strong technology traditions can justify retaining a reasonable minimum of enterprises and core production capacity in important basic industries and most branches of engineering technology. To participate equally for the longer run in complex engineering rivalry among advanced, well-educated nations, the United States and its peers cannot afford to suffer major gaps in technological capacity. Eventually, wage rates will become more equal around the globe, and major industrial nations such as the United States would be foolish to abandon entire branches of technology or areas of engineering. However, sound implementation of this policy requires good technology monitoring efforts, long-range goals, and more systematic collaboration between U.S. industry and government agencies. (Naive faith in short-term stock market prices as the sole test for long-run national performance is misleading and dangerous. The sad story of British de-industrialization and decline in the post–World War II era must be a warning for all.)

Finally, protectionist remedies, tariff duties, quotas, or other restrictions may be appropriate responses to foreign "unfair" trade practices, mercantilist industrial policies, or widespread international discounting (dumping) in excess capacity industries like steel. (In the argot of free-enterprise economics, these circumstances may involve significant "market failure.") Authority for government response and access to private remedies for injured domestic interests has long existed under U.S. trade law. In recent years, however, U.S. trade law remedies have been weakened significantly by amendment and interpretation. As a result, these "unfair" trade practice remedies are not very helpful to vulnerable U.S. industries, at least as administered by the president, International Trade Commission, and Department of Commerce. Remedies are rare and unreliable, and they have not seriously limited the flow of imports. Nor has any significant or coherent program of adjustment relief or rejuvenation been developed in the United States.

Two factors explain the difficulty of U.S. response. First, there is inherent ambiguity and an investigational problem in documenting foreign subsidies and discount pricing. It is hard to develop data from abroad in foreign languages; there may also be foreign resistance to any serious inquiry. More awkwardly, it is conceptually difficult to draw a reasonable line between tax incentives, easier financing, and encouragements for economic development, and significant subsidies to exports. This becomes especially difficult with large fixed costs, plus declining average and marginal costs (which are typical in modern manufacturing). (See figure 2–1.)

Mature industrial countries (the United States, Japan, and Europe), NICs (such as Korea, Brazil, Mexico, and Taiwan), and LDCs (China, India, Malaysia, and Egypt) all experience declining cost curves for big steel plants or other establishments with significant economies of scale. In these situations, to the extent that foreign competition is limited in the home market (as is normal for most NICs and LDCs as well as some MICs), domestic prices will be higher than in highly competitive and more open export markets. Does this imply that subsidy, dumping or "unfair trade practices" are taking place? U.S. manufacturers (with higher wages and average costs) are quite vulnerable to this competition and have trouble matching low foreign export prices. This is a grave difficulty for many U.S. exports and threatens the survival of some basic industries (such as steel). Furthermore, U.S. markets are significantly more open than most markets elsewhere.

Second, since World War II, the United States has assumed a leadership role for the free world as a champion of liberal democracy and helper of economic development for friends and allies. This led to unusual forebearance and a lack of retaliation to foreign industrial policies, subsidies, discount pricing (or dumping). Other MICs and NICs were tougher in response. Such kindness and asymmetrical openness for the U.S. market became entrenched custom. Europe, Japan, Canada, Latin America, many NICs, and most LDCs now regard any unilateral change in U.S. trade policy toward more equivalent tough-ness or countersubsidy as somewhat threatening, harsh, or even unfair.

And yet, if we think realistically, a massive surplus of U.S. imports over exports (currently $387 billion over $217 billion) is simply not sustainable. Somehow, the United States and its major trade partners (Canada, Europe, Japan, the rest of Asia, and Latin America) must achieve more balanced trade flows. (See table I–1.) A gap of $170 billion must be closed. (In fact, if the United States is to service its growing net foreign debt of the later 1980s, a trade-services surplus must soon replace a $170 billion U.S. trade deficit.) Foreign countries must buy far more from the United States, the United States must cut foreign imports sharply, or there must be a blend of substantially increased U.S. exports and reduced imports.[21]

Notes

1. Most countries (and most states and major cities in the United States) make efforts to promote economic development, support industrial expansion, and encourage exports from their area. The benefits from economic growth (net of environmental losses, which are supposedly limited by skillful regulation) are normally irresistible. Nations (whether capitalist, socialist, or mixed economies) can only improve them-selves by enlarging the volume of useful production and services. Societies often try to learn from each other, within limits, and seek to share technology and organiza-tional tricks that improve economic performance and enhance the quality of life for their citizens.

Industrial and trade-development policies illustrate these principles. Good ex-amples of industrial policy literature are the sources cited in preface note 3 (especially Adams and Klein, Phillips, Eckstein, and Thurow). See, more generally, Lovett, "Com-petitive Industrial Policies and the World Bazaar," and sources cited in preface note 3 and introduction notes 12, 13, and 15. See also "The Corporate Tax Code as Indus-trial Policy," Subcommittee on Economic Stabilization, Committee on Banking, Finance, and Urban Affairs, U.S. House of Representatives, 98th Cong., 2nd Sess. (Dec. 1984). But, this literature forms only part of economic policy "wisdom and controversy." More generally, see chapter 6, infra.

The question is not really *whether* government policies deserve a role along with competitive, world market forces, but rather *how* this government–industry–marketplace collaboration should be organized. *What kinds* of government encourage-ments are most helpful for sustained technological progress, productivity improvement, healthy expansion of industries and services, and beneficial international trade? And, *how* should each country regulate its engagement with the world market for goods, services, technology, investments, borrowing, and lending? To answer these questions, we must evaluate the relative success of industrial and trade policies around the world.

Finally, we must avoid a common and naive misconception about systematic industrial development policies, namely, that they mostly involve government bureau-crats picking winners and displacing sound marketplace competition. Nonsense! The most successful industrial policies in the post–World War II era (Japan's, Taiwan's, and South Korea's) are mainly concerned with (1) strengthening incentives, savings, and productive investment and (2) adding rational encouragements (taxes, tariffs, trade restrictions, favorable financing, infrastructure, and R&D support) for these purposes. (These countries differ with each other in institutions and implementation, but they illustrate the general theme.) In contrast, the less successful performers are likely to simply bail out losers or weaknesses. Ultimately, as also illustrated by the strong recent performers in Europe (West Germany and Switzerland, for example), there is no substitute for efficiency, quality engineering, and avoidance of significant waste, industrial strife, inflation, corruption, or weak incentives. (Table P–2 compares growth in per capita GNP around the world.)

2.   This does not mean Japan–Taiwan–South Korea–style industrial growth strategies are outmoded. They are helpful models of how to maximize industrial investment and expansion. But for three reasons, predominantly export-oriented strategies may not be successful for other NICs and LDCs in the coming years: (1) Many more nations are now emphasizing export-oriented growth, which produces more bunching or crowding effects in this direction. (2) U.S. imports grew much larger than U.S. exports between 1980 and 1986, which caused a massive U.S. trade deficit. The United States can no longer absorb rapidly enlarged imports from developing nations until its trade deficit eases substantially. (3) Europe seems more concerned with preserving its industrial base and jobs, and it is unlikely to be as open or generous in allowing itself to rapidly expand imports from developing countries. More balanced and integrated industrial and trade expansion will now be required for successful imitators of Japanese, Taiwanese, and South Korean rapid industrial development policies.

3.   Mercantilism was predominant in earlier political economy with respect to international rivalries, maritime and military strength, colonial networks, and international trade. But, even British classical economists (including Adam Smith, Thomas Malthus, David Ricardo, and John Stuart Mill) were pragmatic and somewhat qualified their support of freer trade. Arguments on behalf of infant-industry protection (including increasing returns to scale), national defense requirements, and reciprocity constraints upon unilateral lowering of tariffs) were accepted to some degree. See, for example, Henry William Spiegel, *The Growth of Economic Thought* (Englewood Cliffs, N.J.: Prentice-Hall, 1971), pp. 98–118, 360–61, 417–19; Joseph Schumpeter, *History of Economic Analysis* (New York: Oxford Univ., 1954), pp. 335–76, 505–506, 516–18. Other late eighteenth and nineteenth century economic writers (including Alexander Hamilton, Mathew Carey, Henry Carey, and Friedrich List) gave more emphasis to these exceptions (especially the infant-industry, increasing-returns, and learning of industrial technology themes) in their support for tariffs and protectionist policies. See Spiegel and Schumpeter, ibid. Also see Forrest McDonald, *Alexander Hamilton: A Biography* (New York: Norton, 1979); Jacob Cooke, *Alexander Hamilton* (New York: Scribner's, 1982); Kenneth Wyer Rowe, *Mathew Carey: A Study in American Economic Development* (Baltimore: Johns Hopkins, 1933); Frederick List, *The National System of Political Economy* (U.S. ed.) (Philadelphia: Lippincott, 1856); W.O. Henderson, *Friedrich List: Economist and Visionary 1789–1846* (London: Frank Cass, 1983).

Post–World War II economists specializing in international trade theory have tended to favor a system of multilateral and freer trade (and capital movements), with reasoning similar to British classical economists'. Broader international specialization and comparative advantage would allow mutual gains to freer trade, provided that reasonable reciprocity operates, and that "cheating" can be minimized among the nations. While standard trade textbooks concede some latitude for the "traditional exceptions" (infant-industry, industrial-development, and national security arguments), the majority of trade theory scholars like to construe them rather narrowly. See, for example, Lindert and Kindleberger, *International Economics,* 7th ed. (cited in introduction note 6), pp. 111–242; Caves and Jones, *World Trade and Payments,* 4th ed. (cited in chapter 1 note 1), pp. 203–80; and Ethier, *Modern International Economics* (cited in chapter 1 note 1), pp. 165–245.

But, modern specialists on the economic-development process tend to favor substantially more latitude for the infant-industry and increasing-returns–to-scale arguments. They approved the GATT's double standard on tariffs and protectionism, and many support greater generalized preferences (GSP) for LDCs. See sources on economic development cited chapter 1 note 1 (particularly Meier, Higgins, Pinder, and Herick and Kindleberger). See also W. Arthur Lewis, *Development Planning: The Essentials of Economic Policy* (New York: Harper & Row, 1966), esp. pp. 25–55; Hla Myint, *The Economics of the Developing Countries* (New York: Praeger, 1964), esp. pp. 102–64; Hollis Chenery, "The Role of Industrialization in Development Programmes," in A.N. Agarwala and S.P. Singh, eds., *The Economics of Underdevelopment* (Oxford, England: Oxford Univ., 1958), pp. 450–71; and Eugene Staley, *The Future of Underdeveloped Countries,* rev. ed. (New York: Council on Foreign Relations-Praeger, 1961); and Albert O. Hirschman, *The Strategy of Development* (New Haven: Yale Univ., 1958), pp. 120–25.

The results of post–World War II institutional development are an interesting blend of these two strains of thinking. GATT evolved as an institution dedicated to the ideal of freer trade, particularly among industrial nations. The United States, Western Europe, Canada, Australia, and New Zealand were included–as was Japan somewhat later, at least in theory—as the freer trade club. Gradually, the less developed countries (growing out of prewar "imperial preference" regimes for British, French, and U.S. colonies and dominions), generally were given access to U.S. and most European markets. Meanwhile, Latin America (along with many other developing countries) was becoming more strongly protectionist. Under the intellectual leadership of Raul Prebisch and other economists associated with CEPAL—the Economic Commission for Latin America (ECLA) located in Santiago, Chile—many developing nations began to emphasize more or less import substitution as a means to infant-industry development, increasing returns to scale, and improved national wealth and security. Export manufacturing industries were often cultivated as well through protected home markets, favorable financing, export promotion, and, in some instances, discount pricing and multiple exchange rates.

Thus, freer trade for advanced industrial nations was combined with greater mercantilism and protectionism for many developing nations (especially the NICs). This strategy has worked well when combined with conservative finance and competent administration (as in Japan, Taiwan, and South Korea). But, this approach often failed with massive government deficits, high inflation, business demoralization, corruption, and/or poor administration.

As Europe began to suffer more manufactured import penetration, the EEC countries (and some others) began to use more safeguard measures, mostly through voluntary restraint agreements or other nontariff barriers in the later 1970s and 1980s. Meanwhile, the United States reduced its usage of safeguard measures and greatly increased the dollar's value (through budget deficits and higher interest rates), which were major factors behind a massive enlargement of U.S. trade deficits.

4. Some recent free-trade writing tries to dismiss all New Industrial Policy proposals as mere protectionism. But, this overstates legitimate complaint against the misuse of NIP arguments as camouflage for old-fashioned protectionism (and the defense of inefficient technology, excess labor utilization, and/or inferior product quality). Properly understood, New Industrial Policy does not justify nonviable operations. Instead, the whole point of New Industrial Policy is to emulate use of the best available technology, organizational strategies, government encouragements, and marketing efforts used by other countries (and to offset foreign subsidies, restrictions, or unfair trade practices). Reasonable reciprocity and countermeasures may be appropriate to deal with foreign industrial policies.

5. See sources cited chapter 1 note 23 and introduction note 15. Among the most important works are Lockwood, Chalmers, and Nakamura (cited in chapter 1 note 23) and McCraw, Wolferen, Abegglen, Horioka, McMillan, and Saso and Kirby (cited in introduction note 5), together with Kozo Yamamura, ed., *Policy and Trade Issues of the Japanese Economy* (Tokyo: Tokyo Univ., 1982); and Yoshio Suzuki, *Money and Banking in Contemporary Japan* (New Haven: Yale Univ., 1980). See also Yutaka Kosai, *The Era of High Speed Growth: Notes on the Postwar Japanese Economy,* trans. by Jacqueline Kaminski (Tokyo: Tokyo Univ., 1981, trans. 1986); Jon Woronoff, *Japan's Commercial Empire* (Armonk, N.Y.: M.E. Sharpe, 1984).

6. See Chang Chul Suh, *Growth and Structural Changes in the Korean Economy, 1910–40* (Cambridge, Mass.: Council on East Asian Studies, Harvard Univ., 1978); Charles R. Frank, Jr., *South Korea* (New York: National Bureau of Economic Research–Columbia Univ., 1975); David Chamberlin Cole and Princeton N. Lyman, *Korean Development: The Interplay of Politics and Economics* (Cambridge, Mass.: Harvard Univ., 1971); Hon guk Kaebal and Yon Guwon, *Korea's Economy: Past and Present* (Seoul: Korea Development Inst., 1975); Leroy P. Jones, *Government, Business and Entrepreneurship in Economic Development: The Korean Case* (Cambridge, Mass.: Council on East Asian Studies, Harvard Univ., 1980); Parvey Hasan and D.C. Rao, International Bank for Reconstruction and Development, *Korea: Policy Issues for Long-Term Development* (Baltimore: Johns Hopkins Univ., 1979); Norman Jacobs, *The Korean Road to Modernization and Development* (Urbana: Univ. of Illinois, 1985); Susan Chira, "South Korea: The Next Wave," *New York Times Magazine* (Dec. 14, 1986).

7. See George W. Barclay, *Colonial Development and Population in Taiwan* (Princeton: Princeton Univ., 1954); Neil Jacoby, *U.S. Aid to Taiwan; A Study of Foreign Aid, Self Help and Development* (New York: Praeger, 1967); Samuel P.S. Ho, *Economic Development in Taiwan, 1860–1970* (New Haven: Yale Univ., 1980); Ralph Clough, *Island China* (Cambridge, Mass.: Harvard Univ., 1978); John C.H. Fei, Gustav Ranis, and Shirley W.I. Kuo, *Growth with Equity* (New York: Oxford Univ., 1978); Hungdau Chiu, *China and the Taiwan Issue* (New York: Praeger, 1979); "Taiwan (ROC): Making the Move into Quality Market," *Euromoney* (May 1981); Yuan-Si Wu, *Becoming an Industrialized Nation: ROC's Development on Taiwan* (New York: Praeger, 1985); Shirley W.Y. Kuo, *The Taiwan Economy in Transition* (Boulder, Colo.: Westview, 1983).

8. See Theodore Geiger and Frances Geiger, *The Development Progress of Hong Kong and Singapore* (London: Macmillan, 1975); Lim Loo-Jack et al., *Foreign Investment in Singapore: Some Broader Economic and Social Ramifications* (Singapore: Institute of South-eastern Asian Studies, 1977); Riaz Hassan, *Singapore: Society in Transition* (Kuala Lumpur and New York: Oxford Univ., 1976); "The Sovereign Municipality," *The Economist* (December 29, 1979); and Pang Eng Fong, "Employment Development and Basic Needs in Singapore," *International Labor Review* 119 (July-August 1980) pp. 495–504; Peter S.J. Chen, *Singapore; Development Policies and Trends* (Oxford, England: Oxford Univ., 1983).

For Hong Kong, see Geiger and Geiger, ibid.; Keith Hopkins, *Hong Kong: The Industrial Colony; A Political, Social and Economic Survey* (Hong Kong: Oxford Univ., 1971); William F. Beazer, *The Commercial Future of Hong Kong* (New York: Praeger, 1978); A.J. Youngson, *Hong Kong: Economic Growth and Policy* (Oxford, England: Oxford Univ., 1982); A.J. Youngson, ed., *China and Hong Kong: The Economic Nexus* (Oxford, England: Oxford Univ., 1983); Alvin Rabushka, *Hong Kong: A Study in Economic Freedom* (Chicago: Univ. of Chicago Graduate School of Business, 1979); "Is Hong Kong Still a Stomping Ground for Foreign Devils?" *Economist* (October 4, 1980); David G. Lethbridge, *The Business Environment of Hong Kong,* 2nd ed. (Oxford, England: Oxford Univ., 1984); Basil Caplan "Hong Kong: Ten Years to Go," *The Banker* (London: Dec. 1986).

Most recently, India is becoming a large new industrial country with a more liberalized economy, yet it retains significant elements of regulation, selective protection, and favorable financing and encouragement for development. See V.N. Bolasubramanyam, *The Economy of India* (London: Wiedenfeld and Nicholson, 1984).

9. For British industrial policy efforts since World War II, see Michael Davenport, "Industrial Policy in the United Kingdom," Adams and Klein, eds., *Industrial Policies for Growth and Competitiveness* (cited in preface note 3); Sidney Pollard, *The Development of the British Economy, 1914–67,* rev. ed. (London: E. Arnold, 1969); John F. Wright, *Britain: the Age of Economic Management: An Economic History since 1939* (Oxford, England: Oxford Univ., 1979); G.D.H. Cole, *The Postwar Condition of Britain* (London: Routledge & Paul, 1956); Andrew Shonfield, *British Economic Policy since the War* (Harmondsworth, England: Penguin, 1958); J.C.R. Dow, *The Management of the British Economy, 1945–60* (Cambridge, England: NIESR, Cambridge Univ. 1960); John Richard Sargent, *Out of Stagnation: A Policy for Growth* (London: Fabian Society, 1963); Sydney Chapman and Keith Speed, *Blueprint for Britain, A Report on Behalf of the Young Conservative and Unionist Organization,* 1965; Nicholas Davenport and Ernest Harold, *The Split Society* (London: V. Gollancz, 1964); Samuel Brittan, *Steering the Economy: The British Experiment* (New York: Library Press, 1971); James E. Alt, *The Politics of Economic Decline: Economic Management and Political Behavior since 1964* (Cambridge, England: Cambridge Univ., 1979); Robert William Bacon, *Britain's Economic Problem: Too Few Producers,* 2nd ed. (London: Macmillan, 1978); Wilfred Beckerman, ed., *Slow Growth in Britain: Causes and Consequences,* Conference on Economics of the British Association for Advancement of Science at Bath (Oxford, England: Clarendon, 1979); Bernard Nositer, *A Future That Works* (Boston: Houghton Mifflin, 1978); David Graham Hutton, *Whatever Happened to Productivity?,* Tenth Wincott Memorial Lecture (London: Institution of Economic Affairs, 1980); Richard E. Caves and Lawrence B. Krause, *Britain's*

Economic Performance (Washington, D.C.: Brookings, 1980); OECD Economic Survey, *United Kingdom* (February 1980); OECD Economic Outlook, *United Kingdom* (December 1980). See also Sir Nicholas Henderson, "Britain's Decline; Its Causes and Consequences," *Economist* (June 2, 1979); "Britain: Rough Road Back to the Free Market," *Business Week* (October 15, 1979); "Britain Isn't Working," *Economist* (August 2, 1980); "How Labour's Left Took Power," *Economist* (October 4, 1980); "In Thatcherland," *Economist* (October 25, 1980). See also sources cited in preface note 2.

For controversy about the wisdom and terms of British entry into the Common Market, see also the following: Harry G. Johnson, et al., *Economics: Britain and The EEC* (London: Longmans, Green, 1969); William Wallace, ed., *Britain in Europe* (London: Heinemann, 1980); Roy Jenkins, ed., *Britain and the EEC* (London: MacMillan, 1983); C.D. Cohen, ed., *The Common Market: An Economic Review of British Membership of the EEC 1973–1983* (Deddington, Oxford, England: Philip Allan, 1983); Peter Robson, *The Economics of International Integration,* 2nd ed. (London: George Allen & Unwin, 1984); Jacques Pelkmans, *Market Integration in the European Community* (The Hague: Martinus Nijhof, 1984); Stuart Holland, *The Uncommon Market: Capital, Class and Power in the European Community* (London: Macmillan, 1980).

10. See C. Andrea Bollino, "Industrial Policy: A Review of European Approaches," Francois DeWitt, "French Industrial Policy from 1945–1981: An Assessment," Gerhard Wagenhals, "Industrial Policy in the Federal Republic of Germany: A Survey," and C. Andrea Bollino, "Industrial Policy in Italy: A Survey," in Adams and Klein, eds., *Industrial Policies for Growth and Competitiveness* (cited in preface note 3).

See also Francois Caron, *An Economic History of Modern France* (New York: Halsted-Wiley, 1975); John and Anne Marie Hackett, *Economic Planning in France* (Cambridge, Mass.: Harvard Univ., 1963); John Sheehan, *An Introduction to the French Economy* (Columbus, Ohio: Merrill, 1969); "Survey on France," *Economist* (January 27, 1979); OECD Economic Survey, *France* (May 1980); OECD, *Economic Outlook,* no. 28, "France" (December 1980); "Giscard Battles a Slump," *Time* (May 25, 1981). See also, more recently, Jacques Melitz and Charles Wyplosz, *The French Economy: Theory and Policy* (Colorado Springs, Colo.: Westview, 1985); Howard Machin and Vincent Wright, eds., *Economic Policy and Policy Making under the Mitterand Presidency* (New York: St. Martin's, 1985); Volkmar Lauber, *The Political Economy of France: From Pompidou To Mitterand* (New York: Praeger, 1983); Philip Cerny and Martin A. Schain, *Socialism, The State, and Public Policy* (New York: Methuen, 1985).

See also, with respect to Germany, Gustav Stolper, *The German Economy: 1870 to the Present* (London: Weidenfeld & Nicholson, 1967); Konrad Adenauer, *Memoirs,* trans. Beate Ruhm von Oppen (London: Weidenfeld & Nicholson, 1966); Constantino Brescianani-Turroni, *The Economics of Inflation: A Study of Currency Depreciation in Postwar Germany* (London: Allen & Unwin, 1953); Albert Hahn, *Funfzig Jahre Zwischen, Inflation and Deflation* (Tubingen, West Germany: J.C.B. Mohr, 1963). For a closely related collateral success in recent years, see Gottfried Haberler, *Austria's Economic Development: A Minor Picture of the World Economy* (Washington, D.C.: AEI Reprint, January, 1980). See also M.S. Mendelsohn, "Beating Inflation: The German and Swiss Experience," *The Banker* (London, December 1979); Andre Markowatz and George Romset, eds., *The Political Economy of West Germany: Modell Deutschland* (New York: Praeger, 1982).

For more background on Italy, see Shepard Bancroft Clough, *Economic History of Modern Italy* (New York: Columbia Univ., 1964); George H. Hildebrand, *Growth and Structure in the Economy of Modern Italy* (Cambridge, Mass.: Harvard Univ., 1965); Vera Lutz, *Italy, A Study in Economic Development* (London and New York: Oxford Univ., 1962); Muriel Grindrod, *Italy* (London: Oxford Univ., 1964); Josselyn Hennessy, Vera Lutz, and Guisseppe Scimone, *Economic Miracles; Studies in the Resurgence of the French, German, and Italian Economies since the Second World War* (London: IEA, A. Deutsch, 1964); Paolo Sylos-Labini, *Trade Unions, Inflation and Productivity* (Farnborough, England: Saxon House, 1974); Michael Arthur Ledeen, *Italy in Crisis* (Beverly Hills, Calif.: Sage, 1977); Henry Stuart Hughes, *The U.S. and Italy,* 3rd ed. (Cambridge, Mass.: Harvard Univ., 1979). See also "Italy: Business Shrugs Off the New Political Turmoil," *Business Week* (February 19, 1979); "Which Italian Economy? Italian Industry Has at Least Three Economies. One of Them Is Doing All Right" (on the underground or black market economy), *Economist* (December 8, 1979); John Fraser, ed., *Italy, Society in Crisis, Society in Transformation* (London: Routledge & Kegan Paul, 1981). Italy's economy now suffers substantial government deficits, some inflation, and only modest real growth. Its thriving underground economy is a saving grace.

With respect to Sweden, see Eli Heckscher, *An Economic History of Sweden,* trans. Goran Ohlin (Cambridge: Harvard Univ., 1954); Kurt Samuelson, *From Great Power to Welfare State: 300 Years of Swedish Social Development* (London: Allen & Unwin, 1968); Steven Koblik, ed., *Sweden's Development from Poverty to Affluence, 1750–1970,* trans. Joanne Johnson (Minneapolis: Univ. of Minnesota Press, 1975); John Fry, ed., *Limits of the Welfare State: Critical Reviews on Postwar Sweden* (Farnborough, England: Saxon House, 1979); Marquis W. Childs, *Sweden: The Middle Way on Trial* (New Haven: Yale Univ., 1980); OECD Economic Survey, *Sweden* (April 1980); Barry Bosworth and Gary Burtless, eds. *The Swedish Economy* (Washington, D.C.: Brookings, 1987).

For recent Spanish developments, see Sima Lieberman, *The Contemporary Spanish Economy: A Historical Perspective* (London: Geo. Allen & Unwin, 1982); Joseph Harrison, *The Spanish Economy in the Twentieth Century* (London: Croom Helm, 1985). With respect to Greece and Yugoslavia, see Roy Macridis, *Greek Politics at a Crossroads: What Kind of Socialism?* (Stanford, Calif.: Hoover Institution, 1984); Zafiris Tzannotos, *Socialism in Greece: The First Four Years* (Aldershot, England: Gower, 1986); Nicholas Gianoris, *Greece and Yugoslavia: An Economic Comparison* (New York: Praeger, 1984); Fred Singleton and Bernard Carter, *The Economy of Yugoslavia* (New York: St. Martin's, 1982).

11. See Robert F. Wescott, "U.S. Approaches to Industrial Policy," in Adams and Klein, eds., *Industrial Policies for Growth and Industrial Competitiveness* (cited in preface note 3). After some stagflation in the early 1970s, substantial recession in the mid-1970s, and incomplete recovery with growing inflation in the later 1970s, the United States began to realize that it suffered industrial and productivity problems, too. See Gail Garfield Schwartz and Pat Choate, *Being Number One: Rebuilding the U.S. Economy* (Lexington, Mass.: Lexington Books, 1980); "Plugging in the Supply Side," Joint Economic Committee Report, Joint Economic Committee, 96th Cong., 2nd Sess., March 1980; "The Reindustrialization of America: Special Issue" (showing Uncle Sam holding a monkey wrench), *Business Week* (June 30, 1980); "Special Project: American Renewal," *Fortune* (March 9, 1980); "America's Restructured Economy:

Special Issue," *Business Week* (June 1, 1981); Edward N. Wolff, "The Magnitude of the Recent Productivity Slowdown in the United States: A Survey of Recent Studies," in William Baumol and Kenneth McLennan, eds., *Productivity Growth and U.S. Competitiveness* (New York: Oxford Univ., 1985).

Accordingly, U.S. industrial policies were proposed from many perspectives in recent years. For references, the following would be a convenient tracing of their evolution: Lawrence R. Klein, "The Supply Side," *American Economic Rev.* 68, no. 1 (March 1978), pp. 1–7; "A New Economic Era," Report of the Joint Economic Committee on the January Economic Report of the President (February 1980); "Plugging in the Supply Side," *The 1980 Joint Economic Report,* Joint Economic Committee, 96th Cong., 2nd Sess (March 1980); "The Wreck of the Auto Industry," *Harper's* (November 1980); "Industry Outlooks 1981: A Multi-tiered Economy—Growing, Information–Oil; Solid, Chemicals–Machinery–Paper; Ailing, Auto–Food–Steel," *Business Week* (January 12, 1981); *Economic Report of the President* (January 1981), chapters 2 and 3, pp. 127–130; "Special Project—American Renewal," *Fortune* (March 9, 1981); "The New Industrial Relations: Special Report," *Business Week* (May 11, 1981).

The Reagan economic program was set forth in *America's New Beginning: A Program for Economic Recovery* (Washington, D.C.: White House, February 18, 1981). This Reagan package consisted of: (1) a presidential message to Congress, (2) a White House report, (3) a budget reform plan, and (4) tax-reduction proposals. For explanatory appraisal, see "The Ax Falls: Reagan's Plan for a 'New Beginning',", *Time* (March 2, 1981); "The Team and the Plan: An Appraisal, *Time* (March 23, 1981); "Budget Director David Stockman: The President's Cutting Edge," *New York Times Magazine* (March 15, 1981). Economic thinking similar to the Reagan package was outlined in more detail by George Gilder, *Wealth and Poverty* (New York: Basic, 1981); and Bruce Bartlett, *Reaganomics* (Westport, Conn.: Arlington House, 1981). For contrasting commentary, see Alice Rivlin, "Making the Budget," *Challenge* (March-April, 1981); "An Analysis of the Kemp-Roth Tax Cut Proposal," Congressional Budget Office (October 1978); Report of the President's Commission for a National Agenda for the Eighties (a group appointed by President Carter on October 24, 1979), "The American Economy: Employment, Productivity and Inflation," in *A National Agenda for the Eighties* (New York: Mentor, 1981); *Economic Report of the President* (January 1981); and *Report of the Joint Economic Committee on The January 1981 Economic Report of the President.* "A Statement by the Research and Policy Committee of the CED," in *Fighting Inflation and Rebuilding a Sound Economy* (Washington, D.C.: Committee for Economic Development, September 1980). See also Phillip Cagan, ed., *The Impact of the Reagan Program: Essays in Contemporary Economic Problems* (Washington, D.C.: American Enterprise Institute, 1986).

12. See, for example, Lovett, *Inflation and Politics* (cited in preface note 2), pp. 185–228, including notes 1–70.

13. See tables 6–1, 6–2, and 6–3, together with surrounding text, infra.

14. See tables 4–2 and 4–3 as well as the comparison of interest rates among major industrial countries (1978–August 1986) *World Economic Outlook* (Washington, D.C.: IMF, Oct. 1986), chart 1 on p. 3.

15. For labor-oriented views, see Bluestone and Harrison (cited in preface notes 3 and 4), Mark Anderson (cited in introduction note 13), and AFL-CIO, *National Economy and Trade* (cited in preface note 4). Culbertson (cited in introduction note 14) favors better managed and balanced trade. Howard Smith urged broad but limited

protection against imports in the *Collegiate Forum* (Princeton, N.J.: Dow Jones, 1983). Douglas Lamont, *Forcing Our Hand: America's Trade Wars in the 1980s* (Lexington, Mass.: Lexington Books, 1986), sees a danger of excessive deindustrialization from Third-World imports and unequal openness; he urges tougher reciprocity, and, if necessary, restricting access to U.S. markets as a means to obtain access for U.S. exports abroad. Rimmer de Vries and Derek Hargreaves (Morgan Guaranty Trust Company), "The Dollar's Decline and Trade: Mission Accomplished?" *Challenge* (Jan.–Feb. 1987), stress the severity of U.S. trade deficits, but want further dollar decline, more yen and deutsche mark appreciation, greater fiscal stimulus and monetary ease in surplus countries, faster U.S. budget deficit reduction, and a stronger U.S. industrial policy keyed to improved competitiveness. Many experts are troubled now about weakened U.S. exports (including in agriculture and high tech) and unequal openness. While the Reagan administration still hopes for freer trade abroad, doubts have been increasing about the sufficiency of that strategy. Even President Reagan's State of the Union Address (Jan. 27, 1987) conceded that the United States should not let itself be a "trade patsy" and displayed a new toughness in rhetoric about trade relationships. free-trade lobbyists felt defensive in this situation, but they largely resisted significant protectionism. While consensus was emerging for improved U.S. competitiveness (a newly popular buzz word), the content of U.S. industrial-strengthening policy remained unsettled and, in some respects, rather controversial.

16. This collage of U.S. industrial policy and competitiveness proposals represents an eclectic, fairly exhaustive listing of serious ideas and specific recommendations offered during the 1980s. Many business and financial leaders, economists, political scientists, and legal scholars have been refining their suggestions in this period. While details of U.S. policy remain at issue, a broader and bipartisan consensus is emerging toward (1) a need for improved U.S. industrial competitiveness, (2) a productivity-oriented U.S. policy, and (3) greater fairness, balanced openness, and more reciprocity in world markets. See, for example, "Flocking together on trade: Congress and Reagan Moved toward a Bill on competitiveness," *Time* (February 2, 1987), p. 24. While initial legislation may be limited, a long-haul effort (with strong legislation later) seems likely if large U.S. trade deficits and competitiveness problems persist.

17. See Republican dissenting views, H.R. 4750 (cited in chapter 3 note 8). See also Alan Murray, "Reagan's 'Competitiveness' Package for Congress Is Viewed as Patchwork of Mostly Old Proposals," *Wall Street Journal* Feb. 12, 1987, p. 52.

18. Originally H.R. 4750 (later H.R. 4800), which is summarized in more detail in chapter 3.

19. This represents a sophisticated synthesis, updating, and broadening of the traditional exceptions allowed by most trade theorists. See notes, 1, 2, and 3, supra.

20. Sadly, it seems, high labor and overhead costs, sluggishness, and defensive-mindedness often impair the performance of MIC catch-up efforts. But, this misfortune does not really destroy the logic of systematic rejuvenation. Rather, these difficulties merely accentuate the overall urgency of industrial and technology renewal and the importance of standards for productivity and improved efficiency.

21. The most important adjustment lag in dealing with the U.S. trade deficit for the late 1980s is mental. Most U.S.trade partners (and many influential elements in U.S. business, finance, and politics) have not yet grasped the magnitude of trade-flow reversals necessary to eliminate the massive U.S. trade deficits.

3
U.S. Responses to Foreign Industrial Policies

Seven major alternatives are urged as U.S. responses to foreign industrial policies, massive trade deficits, and increased imports from abroad: (a) more open foreign markets and expanded U.S. exports, (b) tougher U.S. trade bargaining, (c) stronger U.S. trade law remedies, (d) increased U.S. adjustment assistance, (e) offsetting or equivalent U.S. trade restrictions, (f) more drastic dollar devaluation and appreciation of surplus country currencies, and (g) stronger U.S. industrial policy. No single response, by itself, within presently feasible limits, is likely to be sufficient as a corrective policy. But, all or most of these measures, if applied together, within manageable limits, can eliminate aggravated deficits and produce a healthier, more competitive U.S. economy. A sensible blend, geared toward the realities of world politics and national rivalries, should help restore a stronger, more balanced international recovery and prosperity.

More Open Foreign Markets and Expanded U.S. Exports

Greatly increased foreign openness could help enlarge U.S. exports, service earnings, repatriated profits, and interest income. U.S. MNCs and international banks endorse this effort, and it enjoys American public support. But crucial limitations include strongly entrenched foreign industrial policies, worries abroad about giving up jobs and prosperity, and the fear of economic domination by the United States and/or MNCs in many countries.[1]

Defensive-minded thinking operates in most of Europe, which already suffers fairly high unemployment. These nations have little enthusiasm for expanding imports of U.S. agricultural products or manufactures or giving up jobs to U.S. industry. Japan is gradually learning that export success must imply more imports, but most U.S. goods are still priced too high for Japanese consumers. And Japan is unwilling to allow U.S. financial and service institutions more than a limited role. For the short run, Japan prefers mainly to expand its foreign investments with export earnings rather than to greatly increase imports. The rest of Asia is even less able to buy expensive U.S. manufactures and more likely to buy Japanese goods. Latin America has had to reduce imports from the U.S. substantially to make some effort at servicing swollen international debts. Africa is too poor and overloaded with debt to enlarge imports, nor can the Middle East do any better. For most developing nations, significant inhibitions and nationalism also limit greatly the role for U.S. investors, banks, insurers, and service companies. For these reasons, no great trade, service, or investment opening can occur quickly that would yield appreciably larger U.S. exports or services income. And, a U.S. switch to substantial net debtor status further undercuts U.S. hopes for increased financial and service earnings in the medium term.

Few deny that more balanced openness for U.S. exports, finance, and services might eventually help its current account and trade balances. But for the near term, the feasible foreign concessions toward more open markets are rather modest and unlikely to yield more than limited results. While ample lip service and cosmetic assurances can be delivered up for U.S. negotiators, this will not accomplish much to quickly enlarge U.S. exports or reduce the U.S. current account deficit. Stronger action—through U.S. import restrictions in one form or another, a comprehensive U.S. industrial policy, a more substantial dollar devaluation, or some blend of these measures—will probably be necessary.

Tougher U.S. Trade Bargaining

Americans feel they have been generous with trade openness and foreign aid in the post–World War II era, and tolerant with respect to foreign protection, subsidies, and industrial development policies. Many American development economists, officials, and academicians encouraged and helped formulate industrial and export-promotion policies for NICs and LDCs. U.S. government policy often supported these efforts, along with GATT (and latitude for developing-country mercantilism) and the EEC (with more protectionist agricultural policies).

Although some U.S. labor unions and domestic industries protested the increasing incursions of foreign imports, for the most part, the U.S. Department of Commerce, U.S. International Trade Commission, and the White House have provided little relief or assistance. Imports have grown steadily, and U.S. manufacturing seems sluggish or in relative decline (as compared to Japan's, South Korea's, Taiwan's, or even West Germany's). The Reagan administration is particularly staunch in defense of free trade and the right of U.S. industry to shift jobs overseas. For all these reasons, a belief has grown among the U.S. public that the time has come for tougher trade bargaining.

But, while the public is ready and supports tougher trade bargaining, it will be difficult to achieve significant results in this direction quickly.[2] First, most U.S. trade and investment flows are mainly private enterprise decisions and not subject to U.S. government influence (under present policies). This means modest leverage, in the short run, for U.S. government negotiators. Second, because the U.S. acquiesced in the established asymmetrical trade–investment regime (and actually helped create the system), most foreign governments regard their status quo "privileges" as normal and the basis for further trade negotiations and mutual concessions. Third, few nations abroad fully appreciate that the current, severe imbalance in U.S. trade, with $387 billion imports and $217 billion exports for 1986, is a major disequilibrium that is not really sustainable. Fourth, most Latin American and other overloaded debtor nations cannot significantly increase imports from the United States (although they might accept additional U.S. loans and, perhaps, supervised foreign investments).

Accordingly, the potential for tougher trade bargaining is not a matter for big short-term trade breakthroughs (in reduced U.S. imports or expanded exports and services). The major scope for tougher trade bargaining lies in some blend of (1) long-run opening up to U.S. exports in some countries (mostly Japan and the more successful NICs), (2) strengthening U.S. unfair trade practice remedies, (3) offsetting or equivalent U.S. trade restrictions that achieve greater equity, and (4) a stronger, more systematic U.S. industrial policy. Public attitudes in the United States, with a massive $170 billion U.S. trade deficit (and major trade surpluses for key trade partners), allow stronger action now, without so much concern for mutuality of concessions. In this situation, the United States has substantial justification and latitude for independent corrective action, particularly in dealing with countries that enjoy big trade surpluses vis-à-vis the United States.

But the United States will have to supervise, monitor, and influence trade and investment relations with its significant trade partners and allies more carefully.[3] A large part of the U.S. problem, asymmetrical trade–investment openness and now drastic U.S. trade–current account deficits, is that other countries (especially Japan, many NICs, and even the EEC, to some extent) systematically "influence" their trade and economic relationships with the United States. This was understandable, and the big American market constitutes the most open, profitable market in the world. In contrast, the U.S. government increasingly left "hands off." As a result, seriously unbalanced relationships have developed, aggravated badly by the overvalued dollar— especially between 1983 and 1985. (See appendix tables A–11, A–14 and A–15.)

It would be naive to think foreign industrial policies, trade supervision, and influence will cease or be cut back in any great degree.[4] For most nations, their trade, investment, and service flows are vital national interests, affecting labor, employment, industries, and the political fate of governments. This means inherent limits on the potential for major trade opening or a completely free global marketplace. Therefore, to respond and survive in this real world, the United States must gear up, with more careful monitoring, supervision, and influences (of one form or another) to cope with a "dirtied" international marketplace, where most governments use "hands-on" policies. Substantial elements of competitive discipline can still operate in this world bazaar. But, people who idealize an immaculate, neutral, untrammeled world market—free of all government influences, taxes, licensing, administrative guidance, or corruption—are imagining a dream world. As a part of stronger U.S. trade bargaining, Americans must understand the need for more effective industry-government-financial supervision, and try to emulate their strong economic adversaries in the world market.

A final complication deserves emphasis. Because of serious debt overloads among many developing nations (see table 4–1), such as Brazil, Mexico, Argentina, Venezuela, Philippines, Indonesia, Nigeria, Peru, Colombia, Costa Rica, and other NICs and LDCs, economists now question the reliability of many international bank loans, foreign investments, interest-dividend repayments, and other services income flowing to creditor nations. Even though IMF-sponsored reschedulings attempt to salvage short-term liquidity and long-term solvency, this debt crisis and uncertainty could last five to ten years and more.[5]

Understandably, trade bargaining between advanced industrial-creditor nations and developing nations will be entangled in the debt-investment reliability problem. For leading creditor nations (such as the United States, United Kingdom, West Germany, Switzerland, and Japan), the need to protect creditor interests (banks, MNEs, and other investors) becomes an important priority today. For NIC and LDC debtor nations, on the other hand, alleviating debtor-interest burdens becomes a major priority. In many respects, these debt–interest–investment conflicts add serious strain to already contentious trade relations between North and South, or, more accurately, between the leading creditor nations and most developing nations in the world trade bazaar. Expectations of reliable debt repayment and returns on investment from developing nations are rather uncertain today. This should weaken the relative value of interest, dividend, and related service earnings from NICs and LDCs in the balance of payments for advanced industrial countries. This has an important implication for trade bargaining.

As leading creditor nations can no longer rely on as much interest, dividend, and related service earnings from NICs and LDCs (situation applying with special force to the United States lately), they should correct their trade imbalances and achieve more balanced trade flows with such countries. Thus, the debt-overload–rescheduling crisis should encourage more careful, equal bilateralism in the coming years, and weaken the tendency to substitute investment and bank interest income for exports of goods and other services in international trade.

Stronger U.S. Trade Law Remedies

U.S. trade law represents an evolving compromise between older traditions or protectionism, more recent policies (including GATT) to reduce tariffs and trade barriers, efforts to limit unfair trade practices, and occasional attempts to alleviate significant injury to domestic interests from enlarged imports. (See table 3–1.) Because U.S. trade law is a compromise, it has been criticized by free traders and traditional protectionists alike.[6] But, the present trade law compromise is now weighted heavily toward the free-trade/GATT-oriented philosophy rather than other viewpoints. Consequently, most protectionists (along with the AFL-CIO) and some New Industrial Policy advocates want stronger U.S. trade law remedies against increasing or disruptive foreign imports.

Existing U.S. trade law remedies constitute an extensive (though not complete) list of countermeasures directed against foreign unfair trade practices, and safeguard relief against injurious or disruptive imports. Countervailing duties can be imposed against imports when material injury is caused by foreign subsidies or dumping, as determined by the U.S. Department of Commerce and U.S International Trade Commission (ITC). But, under current administrative interpretations, these "unfair" practices must be demonstrated and traceable to particular countries and/or suppliers. It has not been sufficient to show widespread discounting, excess capacity in world markets, or disorderly pricing conditions in which some U.S. companies find competitive survival difficult. Exclusion orders also can be obtained against foreign importers using unfair methods of import competition (Section 337 proceedings), although this relief has been confined almost entirely to patent or trademark infringement situations. Market disruption from communist-country imports can be remedied (Section 406 proceedings), subject to presidential approval, but only limited volumes of such imports have come from communist sources thus far. Under any of the foregoing unfair trade practice situations, remedies can be ordered without need for consultation or compensating concessions to other countries.

In addition, the president may take all appropriate action (under a Section 301 proceeding), including retaliation, to obtain removal of any act, policy, or practice of a foreign government, which is found to violate an international trade agreement or is found to be unjustifiable, unreasonable, or discriminatory, and that burdens or restricts U.S. commerce. This drastic, sweeping authority can be helpful leverage in trade bargaining. But, it has been used rather sparingly, thus far. U.S. economic policies led the world toward greater trade openness in the 1960s through the 1980s, and no major problems in adjustment were evident, at least until recently. Other U.S. foreign policy and alliance interests normally limited the vigorous assertion of domestic trade, industrial, or labor concerns by presidential action (under Section 301 or other U.S. trade law remedies).

Apart from unfair trade practice remedies, limited economic safeguard measures, adjustment relief, and economic emergency action is authorized under

Table 3–1
Current U.S. Trade Law Remedies for Unfair Trade Practices, Relief for Injurious Imports, Adjustment Assistance, and Trade Restrictions

Remedy	U.S. Law	GATT Counterpart
Presidential authority to terminate international agreements	Trade Act of 1974, Section 125	GATT Articles XXII and XXXI
Escape clause power to restrict imports causing serious injury	Trade Act of 1974, Section 201	GATT Article XIX
Voluntary trade restraints for serious injury	No formal authority	Not formalized in GATT
National security problems	Power to curtail imports threatening national security under Trade Expansion Act of 1962, Section 232	GATT Article XXI
Trading with the enemy	Trading with the Enemy Act	No GATT counterpart
National emergency powers	International Emergency Economic Powers Act	No GATT counterpart
Balance of payments emergencies	Trade Act of 1974, Section 122	GATT Artilce XII
Antidumping Act of 1921	As amended by Trade Act of 1974, Section 321	GATT Article VI and Antidumping Code
Countervailing duties for subsidies	1930 Tariff Act, Section 303, as amended by Trade Act of 1974, Section 331	GATT Article VI and Subsidies Code
Response to unjustifiable or unreasonable tariffs, import restrictions, or discriminatory policies employed by foreign governments	Trade Act of 1974, Section 301	Compensation and retaliation under GATT are more limited
Unfair practices in import trade	Tariff Act of 1930, Section 337 as amended by Trade Act of 1974, Section 341	No GATT counterpart
Import relief for orderly adjustment	Trade Act of 1974, Sections 201–84	No GATT counterpart
Market disruption from communist countries	Trade Act of 1974, Section 406	
Buy American Act of 1933	As amended	GATT Government Procurement Code
Agricultural Adjustment Act of 1935	Section 22 as amended and Agricultural Act of 1956, Section 204	Exemption under GATT
Customs and import procedures		GATT Customs Valuation Code, GATT Licensing Code
Standards legislation	As amended by Trade Agreement Act of 1979	GATT Standards Code
Tariff Act of 1930		

Note: U.S. law prevails over GATT, but substantial efforts have been made to conform U.S. law to GATT over the years.

U.S. trade law. Under the long-existing escape clause (narrowed since 1974 in Section 201 proceedings), trade restrictions may be ordered (in the form of tariffs, quotas, or orderly marketing agreements) when increased imports are a substantial cause of serious injury to domestic industry. Normally, the president must approve an ITC finding and recommendation to this effect, a now rare event. (Congress may also order the ITC's recommendation into effect by a majority vote in both Houses, subject to presidential veto, but no such congressional action has occurred.) Even more limiting has been U.S. acceptance since 1974 of GATT Article XIX constraints upon the escape clause, which require consultation and compensating concessions to exporting nations significantly affected by safeguard restrictions—all the more reason for virtual "nonuse" of Section 201 restrictions recently.

But, this forced use of another escape hatch, which has become more significant. These are voluntary restraint agreements (VRAs) with exporting countries, for example Japanese auto producers, and foreign steel producers, and international textile agreements (since 1962 in one form or another). European countries use VRAs more extensively. Some political flexibility, room for maneuver, and responsiveness to badly hurt domestic interests are still needed. But, free-trade advocates and lobbies greatly prefer occasional escape "under the table" through VRAs to any explicit, broader legitimation of "protectionism."

In agriculture and textiles, however, tougher safeguard restrictions are built into U.S. law. The Agricultural Adjustment Act of 1933 (Section 22) authorizes restrictions to protect U.S. agricultural price supports, marketing controls, or other programs, and Section 204 of the Agricultural Act of 1956 authorizes international agreements to regulate trade in agricultural commodities, manufactured products, textiles, and textile products. Most countries have found that food supplies, the instability of farm prices (recurrent surpluses or shortages), and powerful farmer, agricultural, and sometimes textile lobbies need regulation, price support, subsidy, and/or control. U.S. law merely follows a general pattern for trade in this area, along with the International Multifibre Agreement (developed since 1962).

More general economic emergencies, balance of payments strains, or serious national security needs can be pressed into service to justify trade restrictions, import surcharges, or exchange controls under U.S. trade laws (or emergency powers of the presidency). The International Emergency Economic Powers Act authorizes foreign exchange controls, bank and currency regulation, or the freezing of property transactions for threats to the national security, foreign policy, or economy of the United States. (An example is the Iranian assets freeze of 1979–81.) Balance of payments emergencies can be used to justify nondiscriminatory quotas under GATT Article XII and the Trade Act of 1974 (Section 124). In 1971, President Nixon imposed a 10 percent surcharge on imports as part of an emergency economic and wage-price control program. National security needs can justify trade restrictions under GATT Article XXI and the Trade Expansion Act of 1962 (Section 232). More controls on trade are authorized under the Trading with the Enemy Act, but these require Congressional action or a state of war. While these laws and precedents provide latitude for emergency presidential action in aggravated circumstances, serious national security interests are a political requirement. In this category of drastic actions, one final step is also available, that is, termination of U.S. participation in GATT–Articles XXII and XXXI and the Trade Act of 1974 (Section 125), but this could be rather disruptive. Less severe measures (such as the foregoing) might normally suffice, and are more readily justified in serious economic emergencies or to protect essential national interests.

But, how much of this battery of U.S. trade law remedies is really useful and appropriate to deal with the problems of serious American trade imbalance in the late 1980s? And, what further legislation or amendments might be desirable and feasible?

Much depends upon the outlook of each U.S. president. In the hands of an administration devoted to free trade, protecting the interests of multinational banks and corporations, and encouraging the relocation of many manufacturing operations to low-wage NICs and LDCs (such as the Reagan administration), U.S. trade law provides little relief to domestic industry or labor interests affected by world market competition and foreign imports. With an administration sympathetic to labor and domestic industries, but kind to developing countries and unwilling to seriously limit international business or finance (such as the Carter administration), more frequent relief might be granted in certain areas, without appreciably changing the asymmetrical openness of the existing world trade network. But, in the hands of an administration committed to a New Industrial Policy (rejuvenating U.S. manufacturing and exports) and Trade Equity (equivalent openness and/or restrictions), even the existing U.S. trade law regime could achieve considerable results. The president, USTR, and Department of Commerce (or DITT) could collaborate systematically with industry and labor groups to share information and coordinate bargaining. Soon, the U.S. government could achieve, informally, more of a "hands-on" promotion of U.S. exports, and insist upon substantial increases in U.S. exports or services income as the equivalent "price" for large-scale access to its import markets.

Whether such a strong shift in U.S. trade policy is likely or desirable is debatable. But, if only a more limited change in outlook occurs (the Carter administration), then the potential for limiting foreign imports and expanding U.S. exports through trade law remedies will be modest. Only the next presidents of the United States, their cabinets, and Congressional leadership can resolve this problem in the coming years. But, most journalists, political observers, and foreign analysts expect some drift or evolution, at least, toward greater trade equity and tougher U.S. trade bargaining.

In any event, U.S. trade law is a battleground for conflicting interests. The multinational and foreign import lobby wants to keep these remedies relatively weak, emasculated, and administered largely by its own appointees. The domestic industry and AFL-CIO lobbies seek, on the other hand, a Trade Equity and New Industrial Policy orientation, stronger trade law remedies, and sympathetic administrators. Increasingly, the Democratic party is moving in the latter direction, although the majority of Republicans remain fairly steadfast in a free-trade, globalist orientation.

Recently, House Democrats developed the Comprehensive Trade Policy Reform Act of 1986 (H.R. 4750, later H.R. 4800).[7] Quite revealing are its trade policy guidelines and objectives: (1) Fair and Open Trade, (2) Reciprocity, and (3) GATT Reform. Main features include broader scope for antidumping, antisubsidy, and Section 301 remedies, along with greater investigative authority (directed in part toward improving trade openness abroad). The ITC would cumulate increased imports from different countries, together with multiple instances of dumping. The definition of subsidy would expand to cover the provision of capital, loans, loan guarantees, discounted goods or services, and resource input subsidies. Tougher trade bargaining by the USTR would be mandated, along with greater balance against major trade partners. New Section 301 remedies would be added against countries using industrial targeting to expand exports and against nations with excessive trade surpluses. In addition, there is a proposed Code for Internationally Recognized Worker Rights, and shortcomings in this area could be considered unfair trade practices. Denial of intellectual property rights could be an unfair trade practice, and special efforts would be mandated to open telecommunications and agricultural markets. In the hands of an administration committed to improve Trade Equity and New Industrial Policy, these measures would be stronger leverage and could somewhat further reduce foreign unfair trade practices, industrial targeting, and big trade surpluses earned against the United States.

But, those seeking improved trade equity would want a broader definition of subsidies to include cheaper financing costs, low interest rates, and past support against failure or periodic bailouts for losses. Antidumping relief could be broadened to cover disorderly international markets, widespread discounting, and marginal cost pricing, even where no particular country or supplier is identifiable as the initiating or primary cause of a breakdown in price levels. Even where private parties find it difficult to prove unlawful subsidies or dumping practices, the government should bring industry-wide investigation—relief proceedings, under liberalized standards, so that distressed industries could obtain tariff, orderly marketing, and/or retrenchment relief packages. A convenient method for achieving this result would be for the Department of Commerce (perhaps joined by the Department of Labor) to develop consolidated investigations under the countervailing duty (antisubsidy and antidumping) statutes, combined with consolidated Section 301 and 201 investigations. The antitrust agencies should be included in the review process, if any mergers, rationalization, or distress cartel arrangements are included. (Strong antitrust supervision should be required if domestic competition is reduced.) In these ways, stronger safeguarding could be achieved.

Most important, however, would be a new outlook in government policy that actively tries to help U.S. domestic industry and workers facilitate and strengthen their productivity and competitiveness in a rough world market. U.S. government should become a reliable friend of its domestic industry (like most governments abroad).

Meanwhile, Republicans offered (with Reagan administration support) a substitute for the House Democratic trade bill H.R. 4750, which reflected their response to greater public and industry demands for improved trade equity.[8] The Republican substitute was much narrower in scope, with a considerably different emphasis for improving trade openness. No significant enhancement of U.S. trade law remedies was offered, although a few minimal changes were a cosmetic effort in this direction. Instead, the administration merely proposed up to five years of antitrust exemption to distressed industries suffering foreign competition. But, more significantly, the administration wants eight years of negotiating authority for a new Reagan GATT round, which seeks trade openings primarily in services, high tech industry, software, intellectual property, finance, insurance and investment opportunities. This strategy accepts continued foreign imports in other areas, and ratifies, for the most part, the current industrial relocation process, and gradual shifting of manufacturing jobs to lower-wage countries. This reveals the administration's industrial and national security priorities and its sense of U.S. comparative advantage for the coming years.

By contrast, the Democratic trade policy reflects a desire to help more of U.S. manufacturing industry, protect organized labor, maintain higher wage levels, and save more jobs, but with less emphasis upon financial services, foreign investment, and their contributions to the trade and current account balances. In this way, we see how the major U.S. political parties represent somewhat divergent alliances, and express significantly different views on sound industrial and trade policy.

Increased U.S. Adjustment Assistance

Another response to increasing imports, relocation of industries to low-wage countries, and job losses is adjustment assistance to the companies, workers, and/or communities involved.[9] This can take the form of special credits, subsidized lending, loan guarantees, or new equity capital to companies and communities, along with severance pay, grants, or loans to the workers laid off or terminated. Retraining and relocation loans and/or aid may also be helpful. The big questions with adjustment assistance are: (1) how much funding to allocate for these purposes, (2) the distribution of support among companies, communities, and workers directly, (3) the share of direct grants or aid versus subsidized lending or credit guarantees, and (4) how closely to supervise this assistance to foster more productive enterprises and more productive, higher-earning workers over the long run.

Competition for government funding is intense, especially with substantial excesses in federal budget deficits. States and localities most hard hit by increased imports, foreign competition, and job losses often suffer awkward retrenchment pressures themselves. For these reasons, loan guarantees (such as the Chrysler bailout package, modernization loans to companies, and retraining and relocation loans to workers) will normally provide more cost-effective, broader-scale assistance, with better financial disciplines and incentives, than direct subsidies or doles to companies or workers. States and localities can be given some subsidized credits (on a matching basis) to mobilize their own resources along these lines, too, and further enlarge assistance efforts.

It is important to supervise any adjustment assistance, however, so that improved productivity can be enforced. Unsupervised aid or loans to companies in trouble easily degenerate into continuing doles or "lemon socialism." Worker retraining or relocation loans are somewhat less of a problem this way, mainly because troubled enterprises have already failed or been forced into retrenchment, and substantial job reductions have already occurred. At least, nonviable plants are not being propped up with worker loans. The most recent, marginal employees may not qualify for aid or loans, but longer-term workers, with a bigger stake and more reliance interests, probably deserve some subsidized lending (at least) to ease their often painful adjustment problems. But, sensible standards and disciplines are still essential to make sure worker assistance does not become long-lasting handouts.

Drawing lines among deserving companies and/or individual workers or families is not easy, however. Nor is defining the proper distribution formula among different states, industries, cities or towns. (Most states and Congressional districts would like "their share.") Scarcity of funds, along with difficulties in making these allocations, help explain the modest efforts made thus far. The recent impasse between Reagan Republicans and Democrats in Congress over federal spending priorities also contributed to adjustment assistance receiving a low priority, with minimal allocations recently. But an ideological preference among many conservatives for free-market discipline is operating as well.

Somewhat more effort toward adjustment assistance could be made, though, especially if specific revenues were developed for these purposes. A new idea that makes considerable sense is to impose special "adjustment fees" or import charges (tariffs) for industries suffering considerable distress, job losses, and displacement. In this way, foreign importers pay some of the external costs of displacement associated with their imports. These levies or adjustment fees are not really protectionist, but simply facilitate healthier trade adjustment (and operate more like user charges to capture external costs).

Adjustment fee levies of this type could be an additional provision for each of the traditional U.S. trade law remedies. Accordingly, it makes sense to add this significant remedial option to the relief available to countervail foreign subsidies, foreign dumping, discriminatory or unreasonable practices (Section 301), threats to national security (Section 232), or imports causing serious injury (Section 201). In this way, adequate funding for adjustment relief can be mobilized from the foreign countries, industries, and importers involved in the displacement of domestic industries and workers.

Without special import levies or tariffs to finance adjustment assistance, however, it is doubtful that Congress and the Executive branch would make much effort in this direction.[10] (The basic problem is that import displacement and job losses are bunched rather unevenly, which makes it harder for Congress to be generous out of general revenues.) Of course, general revenue tariffs can be employed as an offset to foreign industrial policies and widespread mercantilism abroad (as discussed in the next section). Revenue tariffs also yield substantially larger revenues. These additional tax revenues can be used for broader, general funding, and to help eliminate excessive federal budget deficits. And, the rationale for general revenue tariffs goes well beyond the more limited, well-known case for adjustment assistance.

Offsetting or Equivalent U.S. Trade Restrictions

The case for offsetting or equivalent U.S. trade restrictions rests upon an increasing belief that current trade with most foreign countries is not conducted upon a level playing field.[11] In other words, a major problem and significant source of large U.S. trade deficits is asymmetrical trade and openness. The established GATT regime is a double standard: protectionist mercantilism and industrial policies for LDCs and NICs (the large majority of countries) and an "ideal" of free trade for about 25 mature industrial countries (MICs). But, even among MICs, there is really considerable asymmetry in trade openness. Europe is frankly protectionist in agriculture (the United States's strong suit for comparative advantage) and uses VRAs and industrial subsidies more widely. In Japan, language, cultural loyalties, and administrative guidance form trade barriers, and its industrial policies skillfully promote expanded manufacturing exports, while greatly limiting its manufactured imports. Few would maintain that Japan is equally open to U.S. exports and investment, although they are moving lately in the direction of somewhat greater openness. Even Canada, the United States's neighbor (with only a tenth of the U.S. population) makes no real pretense of equivalent openness for trade and investment. Everyone realizes that Canada must protect itself to some degree from economic dominance by its giant neighbor below.

This does not mean that Europe, Japan, or Canada are unreasonable, nor are the NICs or LDCs. Quite the contrary—the policies of most nations stem from logical political and economic imperatives. This point is rather that U.S. policy must adapt intelligently to this situation, and consider offsetting or equivalent restrictions.

While it seems clear that some U.S. offsets might be appropriate (above and beyond U.S. unfair trade practice remedies), selecting them is not so simple. Among the alternative offsets are *general* responses that apply without discrimination between trade partners, and *graduated* responses that attempt to differentiate between LDCs, NICs, Japan, Europe, Canada, Latin America, and other relevant groups of countries, where appropriate.

Three general offsets are most interesting: (1) general revenue tariffs (say, in the 10 to 15 percent range); (2) VAT waiver correctives (to deal with a widespread practice of countries with value-added taxes (VATs) to waive such levies for exports); and (3) emergency import surcharges (say, 10 to 20 percent) until a reasonable U.S. trade balance is restored. Each makes considerable sense, but all three together may be an excessive offset, at least from psychological and political points of view. One other offset (for industries threatened by substantial imports), domestic-content laws that require 50 percent (or more) of sales in the United States to be manufactured in this country, could be even tougher. But, domestic-content laws can be more substantially protectionist and are quite controversial (even though organized labor supports them).

General Revenue Tariffs

The case for general revenue tariffs reflects a number of arguments, ranging from revenue enhancement to offsetting widespread trade restrictions and export subsidies from newly industrialized countries, and trade imbalances with Japan, Europe, and Canada. Historically, revenue tariffs were long the dominant tendency in U.S. trade history, with occasional periods of higher, more prohibitive tariffs. Such tariffs were employed during most of the United States's industrial growth and expansion. Only since the later 1960s has the United States used minimal or negligible tariffs. It is interesting that more competition problems for U.S. industry have developed in these recent years.[12]

From an economic welfare sense, tariffs (particularly moderate revenue levies) are less distortive than import quotas or voluntary trade restraints, and the nation using them recaptures more of the profits or artificial scarcity rents resulting from trade restriction.[13] The extra revenues from general tariffs will be helpful relief for aggravated U.S. budget deficits, and they are consistent with increased consumption and/or value-added taxes. Since most foreign countries use value-added or consumption taxes and rebate them on exports to the United States, a tax equalization argument can be used as well.

A further argument is that no other general relief can ease the strain of growing labor- and industry-displacement problems coming from low-wage, newly industrialized countries, most of which use strong infant-industry protection, luxury-import excises, and substantial export-promotion efforts. A moderate revenue tariff would reduce somewhat the incentive for shifting branch plants to these countries, and help offset their industrial policies and targeting programs.[14]

Finally, an argument can be made, more for the United States than for other advanced nations, that revenue tariffs could help Japan and many other U.S. allies contribute more of a fair share to the tax burdens associated with the U.S. defense establishment, foreign bases, alliance support, naval commitments, nuclear umbrella, and responses to the Soviet military and its potential menace.[15] (See table 3-2.)

Some may object that GATT limits U.S. freedom of action for revenue tariffs or at least that Japan, Europe, and Canada might respond with equivalent revenue tariffs of their own. (NICs and LDCs have less latitude in this regard, since they already use protection or excises of equivalent or greater degree for the most part.) But, GATT only mandates nondiscrimination and MFN treatment; it does not specify tariff levels (whether "moderate revenue"—say 8 to 15 percent—or "minimal"—say, 0 to 2 percent). The United States does enjoy freedom of action under GATT, especially with massive U.S. trade deficits, and manifest asymmetry in trade openness for world markets.

But the United States, Europe, Japan, Canada (and the rest of the world) would have to live with revenue tariffs under this policy (or accept *true* and *complete* trade, service, and investment openness, with more closely coordinated, and mutually disciplined fiscal and monetary policies—like the EEC today). Moderate revenue tariffs (in the 10 to 15 percent range) would be an entirely bearable world, with extensive trade (ample imports from low-wage countries would still flow), but the rate of deindustrialization could be slowed appreciably. The United States, Europe, and Japan already lived through such a world in the prosperous 1950s and 1960s, a period with substantial trade expansion and international investment.[16] In fact, assembly plants and licensed foreign affiliates would be somewhat further encouraged under this regime. Technology transfer, foreign investment, and lending would still flourish. But, the flow of jobs in MICs to NICs and LDCs would be somewhat reduced, and the discounting (or "dumping") of industrial surpluses could be significantly discouraged.

VAT-Waiver Correctives

The justification for value-added tax waiver correctives is strong, but more restricted. It is based upon the widespread practice, for most countries using VATs, of waiving this tax for exports.[17] U.S. states and cities do the same for sales taxes, with similar reasoning. These concessions help boost export sales and promote local manufacturing and jobs. Obviously, this represents an export subsidy (like export credit guarantees, government export promotion, and other widely employed export encouragements).

For VAT-using countries, export waiver is nearly universal, so almost all *collect the VAT on imports*. In the end, therefore, among the VAT club (now comprising Europe, Japan, and some NICs), a VAT is charged as a kind of *import* tax (to offset VAT export waivers). Among most LDCs, a comparable result is reached through excise taxes and tariffs.

But, this means that the Unives States, which does not yet employ the VAT, is not charging a normal, customary tax on imported manufactures of 10 to 15 percent ad valorem which most other industrial countries levy. This constitutes a significant disability for U.S. manufacturers, because they must compete against foreign companies paying less tax on their U.S. sales, and the U.S. manufacturers must still pay VAT taxes in most significant export markets.

It really makes no sense for U.S. tax policy to impose this disability on U.S. manufacturing, especially with its massive trade deficit and widespread sluggishness in many industries. There are two simple ways to correct the VAT-waiver problem:

1. Charge a 10 to 15 percent VAT-waiver corrective tax on all imports from VAT-using countries (either employing each foreign country's own VAT rate or a standard 10 to 15 percent average foreign VAT rate).

2. Alternatively, the United States should adopt its own VAT of 10 to 15 percent.

At the very least, the United States should adopt a VAT-waiver corrective tax. This can be done immediately as a tax-harmonization measure. It could generate $15 billion or more in additional revenue. but, many American economists believe the current U.S. fiscal deficit ($200 billion or so annually) cannot be closed without more substantial revenue enhancement.[18] A U.S. VAT of 10 to 15 percent now makes considerable sense. The federal government could share its VAT revenues with state and local governments (say, on a 50–50 percent sharing formula), because VATs are consumption-oriented taxes (competing with state and local sales taxes), and the federal government should not be allowed to preempt or overload this rich revenue source. A national U.S. VAT (along these lines) could net another $100 to 135 billion, which might substantially close the federal budget deficit gap, properly offset the foreign VAT-waiver export subsidy, and remove a disability for U.S. manufacturers.

Import Surcharges

Import surcharges have a somewhat different rationale, based more upon balance of payments disequilibria and misalignment of exchange rates. The Nixon administration forced revaluation of exchange rates (and appreciation of major European currencies) in 1971 through a 10 percent import surcharge, and GATT-Article XII contemplates the use of trade restrictions for balance of

Table 3–2
Comparative Defense Budget Burdens, 1984

Country	GDP ($ billions)	Defense Budget ($ billions)	Defense Budget as a Percentage of GDP
United States	3,619	258	7.1
Other NATO Nations	2,750	97	3.5
Canada	331	7	2.0
U.K.	400	22	5.5
Norway	55	1.6	3.0
West Germany	613	20	3.3
Denmark	59	1.2	2.0
France	492	20	4.1
Belgium	78	2.5	3.2
Italy	348	10	2.9
Portugal	20	1.7	8.5
Spain	161	4	2.5
Netherlands	122	4	2.5
Greece	33	2.2	6.7
Turkey	48	1.7	3.5
European Neutrals			
Sweden	99	2.7	2.7
Finland	51	.8	1.6
Switzerland	97	2	2.0
Austria	64	.8	1.2
Yugoslavia	58	1.6	2.8
Eire	17.5	3	1.7
Middle East			
Israel	23	3.6	15.6
Egypt	33	4.1	12.4
Jordan	4	5	12.5
Syria	20	3.3	16.5
Saudi Arabia	108	17.8	16.5
Soviet Union	1,806	289	16
Warsaw Pact Nations	560	24	4.3
East Germany	135	8	5.9
Poland	180	6	3.3
Czechoslovakia	115	5	4.3
Hungary	45	2.2	4.9
Romania	52	1.4	2.7
Bulgaria	32	1.5	4.7
Other Communist Nations			
China	362	n.a.	n.a.
Cuba	16	n.a.	10
Nicaragua	3.6	n.a.	9.7
Asia and the Pacific			
Japan	1,163	12.5	1.1
Taiwan	56	3.5	6.3
South Korea	83	5	6.0
Singapore	160	1.0	6.3
Australia	158	4.8	3.0
New Zealand	23	1.2	5.2
India	190	6.1	3.2
Pakistan	31	2.0	6.5

Table 3-2 continued

Country	GDP ($ billions)	Defense Budget ($ billions)	Defense Budget as a Percentage of GDP
Latin America			
Brazil	283	1.3	1.3
Argentina	69	2.7	3.9
Mexico	174	.7	.4
Chile	24	1.6	6.7
Peru	20	1.3	6.5
Venezuela	69	1.0	1.4

Source: *The Military Balance, 1985–1986* (London: International Institute for Strategic Studies, 1985).

n.a.=not available.

payments disequilibria. With greatly increased trade and current account deficits for the United States in 1984–86 (associated with an overvalued dollar, big U.S. budget deficits, and insufficient appreciation of currencies from countries with export surpluses), some suggested another round of U.S. import surcharges (in the 15 to 20 percent range) as a corrective adjustment and also as leverage to force more trade equity and balanced openness in trade, investment, and service activities.[19]

While smaller countries normally suffer substantial currency depreciation when they accumulate large deficits in their balance of payments and/or current accounts, this traditional corrective mechanism has not worked so well lately for the United States. Special factors explain the anamoly: (1) continued reliance on dollars as the major reserve currency, (2) confidence in the United States as a safe haven for increased investment and short-term liquidity (especially with its higher interest rates in the 1980s), (3) widespread insecurities abroad recently and limits on foreign investment opportunities, (4) comfortable acceptance of large U.S. deficits through net lending and investments into the United States for the medium term (between 1984 and 1987 and perhaps somewhat later), and (5) insufficient appreciation of export-surplus country currencies (fearing losses in their export markets). While some banking, securities, investment, and import interests in the United States benefit from this situation, its domestic manufacturers and high-wage labor suffer from continued large imports, weak exports, and relocation of manufacturing jobs to NICs and LDCs. (If heavy U.S. borrowing continues over an extended period, most of the nation could suffer from much larger U.S. external debt loads, and reduced industrial activity.) How much longer can these exceptional U.S. current account deficits (3 percent or more of GNP) be tolerated by the U.S. and world markets?

During 1984 and 1985, when many saw the dollar to be substantially overvalued, the logic for import surcharges was appealing (although foreign countries were saying that excess U.S. budget deficits were the main cause for this currency misalignment). But, a very considerable dollar decline followed during 1986, with significant appreciation of the deutsche mark, Swiss franc, and yen (close to 1980 levels for the DM and SF and even more for the yen). While some believe further currency realignment is essential, many are unsure, and the Japanese and Europeans seem unwilling to encourage any further, rapid dollar devaluation that might endanger their own exports. Meanwhile, most NICs (including South Korea, Taiwan, and Brazil) have experienced little, if any, currency appreciation, and their exports are improving. Some NICs (such as Taiwan) with strong export surpluses could be pressed into somewhat greater currency appreciation, but this would not greatly reduce their exports. As this situation evolved, the argument for currency misalignment as the major source of the U.S. trade-payments deficit is not so clear. This may undercut, to some degree, the balance-of-payments justification for import surcharges.

But, this leaves a secondary rationale for import surcharges as a powerful medium-term leverage to encourage more trade equity and improved openness. If Japan, Europe, Canada, Latin America, and other parts of the world could change their industrial-trade policies, alter trade flows, and accede to U.S. pressures this way, the import surcharge makes sense for leverage. But, if these other countries established their industrial, agricultural, financial, and international trade-investment policies for good political and sound economic reasons, the United States might be wise to accept these facts more gracefully. Thus, asymmetrical trade-investment openness should be met with more equivalent, offsetting U.S. restrictions, and America's own industrial policy.

Finally, the two arguments can be blended as a medium-term response (let us say for 4 to 6 years) to the severe U.S. trade imbalance problem of mid-to-late 1980s. Thus, steady pressure for exchange rate alignment can be combined with steady pressure for improved trade equity. In this way, a general corrective or offset through import surcharges would be sustained for a while as a medium-term policy. (This contrasts with moderate revenue tariffs—at somewhat lower rates—justified on a long-term basis for enhanced revenue, and as a more permanent offset to well-entrenched foreign industrial policies, broader use of trade subsidies, and extensive mercantilism.)

Domestic Content Laws

Domestic content laws have been employed in many countries, and more widespread use is urged by organized labor (and some industrial groups) for the United States.[20] The most extreme versions include "buy American" (or national purchase) laws to require local equipment or supplies in sectors associated with national security, public utilities, or government enterprise (with limited waivers allowed). If high-percentage domestic purchase requirements are imposed, this kind of legislation is frankly protectionist. It can be justified on national security and infant-industry (or rejuvenation) grounds, but probably makes sense only for the most crucial portions of the industrial network. But, with lower-percentage (say, 50 percent) domestic content requirements, this approach is less severely protectionist, and can be useful leverage upon MNCs from abroad to locate assembly plants in the importing or host country.

Both versions of domestic-content legislation make sense for many countries, within limits, and are unlikely to disappear from the world trade scene. Whether it makes good policy for the United States to expand use of these laws, however, is a more controversial question. The best argument for domestic content laws in response to foreign mercantilism, subsidies, and/or discounting, is as a strong safeguard measure. A moderate domestic content law (one in the 50 percent range) could save more of a domestic industry and its employees from displacement than moderate revenue tariffs. But, its impact is also more protective, and somewhat more distorting. Therefore, free-trader opposition to domestic content laws, especially with high percentages required for local purchases (say, 75 to 90 percent or more) is intense.

Because opposition to domestic content laws is influential and widespread, such restrictions are probably best confined to a fairly narrow category of key industries that are important for national security or part of a country's vital industrial base (including technology). But, in unfair trade practice situations, domestic content relief also may be appropriate. Hence, domestic-content options could be added to antidumping and subsidy relief, along with remedies under Sections 301, 406, and 201 of the Trade Act of 1974. But, more general use of domestic laws would be excessive, too protectionist, and not really justifiable.

Graduated Offset Responses

Another way to offset foreign mercantilism and achieve more trade equity are graduated responses tailored to individual countries or major regions.[21] While somewhat appealing, this response is not easy for the United States to administer. While GATT involves a double standard for trade relations (that is, more openness among MICs, with mercantilism allowed for developing nations), fundamental GATT principles are nondiscrimination and MFN treatment. More importantly, it is hard for the United States to play favorites in trade and investment policy among allies and friends. In many respects, MFN is a natural tendency for the United States in leading a Free-World alliance, which seeks friendly relations with as many nations as possible (even neutral and communist states).

Some elements of alliance relations (military bases, foreign aid budgets, visits among leaders, and political details) are necessarily localized. But for a free-enterprise country like the United States, most aspects of trade, investment, and banking relations with allies and friends are left for decentralized contracts among U.S. and foreign firms. This commercial activity, normally beneficial to the countries if agreeable to participating companies, flourishes under broad freedom and limited constraint. Except for occasional, special circumstances, the U.S. government finds it difficult to intervene in trade or lending relations (except to discourage government discrimination or default that injures U.S. interests). This is why the U.S. government has found it hard, over the years, to intervene in matters arising under U.S. trade laws (cases involving foreign subsidies, dumping, or proceedings under Sections 337, 301, 406, or even 201).

If the U.S. government finds it difficult to support American companies or unions under the U.S. unfair trade practice laws, should it be any easier to develop graduated, ad hoc responses in trade relations policy with most countries? It would seem that highly discriminatory U.S. trade policy is unrealistic. For these reasons, it seems better for the United States to develop general offsets to most foreign industrial policies and to fashion a stronger U.S. industrial policy of its own. This would be a more realistic response to problems of asymmetrical trade openness in world markets today.

But, it must be noted that U.S. trade deficits are bunched rather heavily among ten to fifteen countries. (See table 3–3.) In 1986, Japan and Canada enjoyed trade surpluses with the United States of $58 and $25 billion, respectively. Four EEC countries (West Germany, Italy, France, and Britain) shared another $25 billion. Three nations in Asia (Taiwan, South Korea, and Hong Kong) had a $25 billion surplus. And, Mexico, Brazil, and Venezuela earned a $15 billion trade surplus. How much pressure (some might say "trade bashing") can be developed against selected friends and allies? With a $170 billion trade surplus expected for 1986, where should the United States draw lines in a "hit list" for retaliation? All these trade partners claim need to earn surpluses from the United States to obtain essential raw materials and/or achieve their best comparative advantage in trading.

Each U.S. trade partner would resent being bashed with discriminatory tariffs or import surcharges. Certainly, Japan, Taiwan, Hong Kong, and South Korea invite more U.S. questions lately, and their combined trade surplus is about $85 billion (or 50 percent of the $170 billion total U.S. trade deficit). How eager is the U.S. government for trade conflicts with Canada, West Germany, Mexico, Brazil, Italy, France or Britain? A total of $70 billion trade surplus (or about 40 percent of the U.S. deficit) is concentrated among these seven allies. While most observers concede latitude for U.S. trade pressure against the bigger surplus countries (especially Japan), unduly harsh responses risk overkill and awkward political repercussions. On the other hand, for trade partners in the substantial surplus category (especially Japan, Canada, Taiwan, and West Germany), stronger objections can and should be made to unrealistic exchange rates and the failure to import larger amounts from the United States.

Clearly, there should be some pressure against the major trade-surplus countries (especially Japan, Canada, West Germany, Italy, France, the United Kingdom, Taiwan, South Korea, Hong Kong, Mexico, and Brazil) and even

Table 3–3
U.S. Trade Deficits and Surpluses by Trading Partner, 1984–85
(in $ billions)

	1985			1984		
	Import	Export	Balance	Import	Export	Balance
Japan	72.38	22.63	−49.75	60.37	23.58	−36.79
Canada	69.52	47.25	−22.27	66.95	46.52	−20.43
Europe						
West Germany	21.23	9.05	−12.18	17.81	9.08	−8.73
France	9.96	6.10	−3.86	8.52	6.04	−2.48
U.K.	15.57	11.27	−4.30	15.04	12.21	−2.83
Italy	10.38	4.63	−5.75	8.50	5.38	−4.12
Denmark	1.80	0.71	−1.09	1.52	0.61	−0.91
Sweden	4.34	1.92	−2.42	3.43	1.54	−1.89
Switzerland	3.58	2.29	−1.29	3.20	2.56	−0.64
Other Western Europe	17.34	20.80	+3.46	16.90	21.90	+4.70
Eastern Europe (Including Soviet Union)	2.11	3.22	+1.11	2.35	4.19	+2.16
Asia (other than Japan)						
South Korea	10.71	5.96	−4.75	10.03	5.98	−4.05
Taiwan	17.76	4.70	−13.06	16.09	5.00	−11.09
Hong Kong	8.99	2.79	−6.20	8.90	3.06	−5.84
Singapore	4.41	3.48	−0.93	4.12	3.68	−0.44
Indonesia	4.93	0.79	−4.14	5.87	1.22	−4.65
Rest of Asia	20.92	20.40	−0.52	22.67	22.02	−0.45
Latin America						
Brazil	8.15	3.14	−5.01	8.27	2.64	−5.63
Mexico	19.39	13.64	−5.75	18.27	11.99	−6.28
Venezuela	6.83	3.40	−3.43	6.82	3.38	−3.44
Rest of Latin America	11.12	7.68	−3.44	10.92	8.29	−2.63
Africa						
Algeria	2.43	0.43	−2.00	3.77	0.52	−3.25
Nigeria	3.11	0.68	−2.43	2.61	0.58	−2.03
Congo	0.65	0.02	−0.63	1.05	0.01	−1.04
South Africa	2.18	1.21	−0.97	2.58	2.27	−0.31
Rest of Africa	4.18	5.06	+0.88	4.99	5.45	+0.46
World total	361.63	213.15	−148.48	341.18	217.89	−123.29

Source: U.S. Department of Commerce, *Highlight of U.S. Export and Import Trade,* FT 990/Dec. 1985, B-22, table 5; p. C-26, table 8. Exports: F.A.S. value basis; Imports: C.I.F. basis.

smaller countries with disproportionate surpluses. These countries will be more receptive to switching some imports to the United States, though, than to cutting back on their exports into the big U.S. market. Alternate export markets are not so readily available, and serious export reductions mean painful job losses and increased unemployment for them. All this means that selective, graduated responses cannot be expected to produce more than limited, slow benefits to the U.S. trade and current account balances. But, sustained pressures of this type will be more helpful for the long run and are definitely worth the effort involved for U.S. trade officials such as the Secretary of Commerce and USTR.

Stronger U.S. Industrial Policy

Increasingly, it seems that a more complete effort toward competitiveness will be required for the United States. While stronger trade law remedies, tougher trade bargaining, and adjustment assistance may be helpful for some U.S. industries, a more general strengthening of the U.S. industrial and technological base is required for the long run.[22] Realignment of exchange rates can encourage U.S. competitiveness, but this only works gradually. Japan, Germany, and other strong rivals will resist any rapid or drastic further appreciation in their currencies, and many NIC currencies will remain pegged fairly closely to the dollar. Clearly, a sustained effort to open more export markets for U.S. goods and services is important, but major results cannot be achieved quickly and will need a competitive, well-capitalized, high technology industrial plant to earn the way for U.S. exports.

Accordingly, many believe that U.S. trade policy should be combined with a New Industrial Policy that tries to match, at least in some degree, Japanese-style trade expansion, economic growth, and technology upgrading success.[23] Key elements of such a policy were outlined in chapter 2. They comprise: (1) stronger administrative coordination, (2) stronger R&D and technology sharing, (3) better macroeconomic discipline (with greatly reduced budget deficits and lower interest rates), (4) sound tax reform (to encourage saving and *productive* investment and to eliminate wasteful tax shelters and needless giveaways), (5) improved labor relations, better teamwork, more profit sharing, and widespread employee stock ownership, (6) rejuvenation packages for vital industries in distress (such as steel, machine tools, and electronics), including special tariffs to raise necessary funds, (7) sensible antitrust policy (to maintain competitive discipline and responsible oversight, but facilitate orderly retrenchment where necessary), and (8) significantly improved trade equity (with better trade balance, more trade openness, and offsetting restrictions to correct asymmetry). A recommended New Industrial-Trade Policy for the United States is set forth in chapter 6.

Recent American attitudes on industrial-trade policy reflect growing consensus, with greater understanding that a serious challenge of competitiveness and productivity faces the nation. New Industrial Policy (NIP) enthusiasts are multiplying, and significant trends toward achieving some elements in this agenda are underway. Many NIP advocates are business-, high tech–, and export-expansion–oriented. Some NIP supporters are more defensive, perhaps, and concerned mainly with rejuvenation and maintenance of key U.S. industries under stress. But, a clear distinction must be drawn between old-fashioned protectionists, who simply want isolation from the rigors of world market competition, and up-to-date NIP advocates who see the modern world marketplace as an arena of rival national industrial policies (with a need for sophisticated government–industry collaboration).

While most conservatives remain loyal to free-market thinking, conservatives generally accept much of the NIP agenda—especially items (2), (3), (4), and (7). Many conservatives also share concern about the need to preserve some strength in key industries and to achieve greater trade equity and balance with U.S. trade partners—items (6) and (8). The main problem for sincere conservatives is their fear of government planning—a fear that politicians, bureaucrats, and foolish committees will try to target and control industrial development. But, this worry should not be overstated. Japanese-style industrial policy is not "lemon socialism" or government domination over industry. Rather, skillful NIPs emphasize industry–government collaboration, with a stress on technology enhancement, improving productivity, and export expansion. These views are not antibusiness, but quite the contrary. New industrial policies of this emerging tradition actually fostered business opportunities and more rapid economic growth.

Some elements within organized labor fear New Industrial Policy, especially if they are not substantially represented in government-industry councils. But, the AFL-CIO really has no other viable alternative for the long run. A strategy of defensive bailouts for "losers" (noncompeting companies, inefficient plants, and excessive staffs) cannot succeed; such a strategy enjoys rather limited public support. European policies along that line are justly condemned as "lemon socialism." Survivors must be lean and flexible, meet world market rivalry, and not try to shelter themselves from efficiency. On the other hand, working people, employees, and families with a commitment to their companies should expect reasonable consideration in return. Mutual loyalty, teamwork, and respect is a two-way street. This is why profit-sharing and employee stock ownership trends should be welcomed by labor, and not resisted by the AFL-CIO. Organized labor must accept a more collaborative teamwork relationship with industry. Older styles of adversarial, class-oriented unionism tend to weaken a nation's industrial competitiveness against countries with a more realistic, wholesome partnership spirit.

Every nation must, of course, evolve its own new Industrial Policy, institutions, and habits of thought. While we must learn from each other and pick up on useful innovations (in organization, programs, and/or technology), government programs usually need some skillful adaptation to be transplanted successfully. Vested interests often defeat sound innovations and improvements, if lessons from abroad are presented naively. Successful transplants require careful planning to minimize resistance, and to co-opt most of the local players and arrangements. Ultimately, each NIP must fly national colors, suitable to the main traditions of a culture, and to the roles of its own leadership and professional elites.

In the U.S. case, presidential leadership is required for a truly comprehensive New Industrial Policy with sufficient Congressional support.[24] But, a skillful policy effort should mobilize lobbying assistance, market information, and technical help from domestic industries. "Elite" federal agencies and coordinating councils could foster active government–industry collaboration, though continued antitrust watchdog efforts are needed. Within a few years, a vigorous program along these lines could be implemented, provided there is enough political will in the executive branch. While the Reagan administration wanted a more limited industrial-trade promotion policy (tax reductions and reform, trade-opening efforts, and gradual exchange rate realignment, with a little tougher trade bargaining), subsequent administrations are likely to move toward a somewhat stronger New Industrial Policy (and greater Trade Equity). How much so will depend on the next several presidential elections along with the relative success (or failure) of U.S. industry in meeting the world competitive challenge.

Notes

1. Increased openness abroad is an obvious slogan for U.S. multinational corporations and financial institutions. Their self-interest supports this strategy and it is consistent with the most optimistic formulations of free-trade theory. But, Americans must be realistic about the constraints of history, self-interest, nationalism, and ideology in most other areas of the world. Foreign industrial policies enjoy established bureaucratic momentum backed by strong business, labor, and political interest groups.

The "American challenge" from U.S. multinationals has been seen as a major threat in Europe since the early 1960s, and their role and access was limited carefully. See Jean Jacques Servan-Schreiber, *Le Défi American* (Paris: Denoel, 1967; or English translation by Ronald Steel, *The American Challenge* (New York: Atheneum, 1968).

In Latin America and most other developing nations, the fears of U.S. and MNC dominance and excessive dependency are generally stronger. Japan skillfully limited U.S. corporate influence in its early postwar recovery and subsequent industrial boom. Most socialist and communist states set strict limits on trade dependency and foreign investment by U.S. corporations and banks, except for highly desired capital equipment, technology, and some borrowing.

2. Tougher trade bargaining is rather easy to simulate with rhetoric or symbolic gestures given wide publicity. But, serious implementation of tougher trade bargaining can only be measured in results (namely, by substantially changing the flows of imports, exports, investments, and earnings for investment and service operations). But, enacting significant offsets to foreign subsidies, restrictions, and mercantilism and/or stronger U.S. trade law remedies would constitute greater toughness.

Even tougher bargaining strategy would be for the United States to announce its withdrawal from GATT. Under GATT Article XXXI, six-months notice is required. During this six-month period, the United States could renegotiate renewed access to markets on more favorable and equal terms. This approach would be comparable to Richard Nixon and John Connally's firmness in forcing a more realistic alignment of exchange rates between 1971 and 1973. See chapter 6 note 63. Perceptive observers might argue, even now, that the GATT's unbalanced trade regime is foundering and may require major modification toward improved trade equity.

3. If the United States continues a largely hands-off, laissez faire response to foreign industrial policies, targeting, and export subsidization (direct and indirect) as well as mercantilist import restrictions, performance requirements, countertrade, domestic-content regulation, and forced technology sharing, it can expect sustained difficulty in closing the large gap between its growing imports and crippled exports. The strongest commercial bargaining leverage the United States enjoys with many countries is its huge excess of imports and the opportunity for access to the giant U.S. market. It would be unwise for the United States not to use this leverage purposefully; most other nations would use their buying power without hesitation in comparable circumstances.

But, more complete government data collection, records of imports and exports, and various financial and service flows are desirable for more effective, sensible monitoring and bargaining supervision. A modest beginning was the first annual trade-barriers report, *Annual Report on National Trade Estimates, 1985* required by Section 303 of the Trade and Tariff Act of 1984 (Washington, D.C.: Office of the U.S. Trade Representative, October 1985). Much more needs to be done.

4. During this author's extended Japanese sabbatical in 1983, the question of MITI's influence and Japanese industrial policy arose in many discussions and lectures. The Japanese were often eager to downplay MITI to foreigners, even though this agency enjoys great prestige in their consensus-based evolution of improving industrial, technology, and trade performance. I discovered the best response to such talk was not accusatory recrimination, but rather to suggest, with some knowing innocence (in the Japanese way, with understatement), "Well, if MITI is not really so important, it may soon be abolished." At this point, a Japanese audience would break up with friendly laughter.

For cross-references to extensive literature on the well-entrenched character of foreign mercantilism, restrictive practices, and subsidization, see note 11.

5. See chapter 4.

6. Current U.S. trade law and its rather ineffectual relief against foreign imports are summarized by Peter Ehrenhaft and Charlotte Meriwether, "The Trade Agreements Act of 1979: Small Aid for Trade?" *Tulane Law Review* 58, no. 5 (May 1984), pp. 1103–57. See also *A Preface to Trade* (Washington, D.C.: Executive Office of the President, United States Trade Representative, 1982); "Overview of Current Provisions of U.S. Trade Law," Subcommittee on Trade Committee on Ways and Means, U.S. House of Representatives, 98th Cong., 2nd Sess. (Dec. 4, 1984); and Robert Baldwin and Anne Krueger, eds., *The Structure and Evolution of Recent U.S. Trade Policy* (Chicago: National Bureau of Economic Research—Univ. of Chicago, 1984). In addition, see Jackson and Davey (cited in chapter 1 note 19), especially chapters 9 and 10.

For strong criticism of established U.S. trade law, see Anderson and Culbertson (cited in introduction notes 13 and 12, respectively); "Background and Purpose," Comprehensive Trade Policy Reform Act of 1986, *Report*, to accompany H.R. 4750, U.S. House of Representatives, 99th Cong., 2nd Sess. (May 6, 1986), pp. 2–6. For other views, see Lamont (cited in chapter 2 note 15) and Gary Clyde Hufbauer and Howard F. Rosen, *Trade Policy for Troubled Industries* (Washington, D.C.: Inst. for International

Economics, March 1986), which both reflect a growing realization that established U.S. trade law is insufficient. Lamont favors tougher U.S. trade bargaining and working toward more genuine free trade (beginning with Canada, the Caribbean, Mexico, and some Latin American nations). Hufbauer and Rosen recommend substantially more liberal adjustment assistance, with financing broadened to include special tariffs or excises in industries suffering import dislocation. All this suggests movement toward greater safeguard and/or adjustment relief in U.S. trade law. For more suggestions and remedies (most indicating a need for stronger U.S. action), see House Ways and Means Subcommittee on Trade, *Hearings* (cited in note 7, infra).

7. See *Report*, together with dissenting views to accompany H.R. 4750, Comprehensive Trade Policy Reform Act of 1986, from the Committee on Ways and Means, 99th Cong., 2nd Sess., U.S. House of Representatives (May 6, 1986). See also, "Trade Reform Legislation," *Hearings*, parts 1 and 2, Subcommittee on Trade, Committee on Ways and Means, U.S. House of Representatives, 99th Cong., 2nd Sess. (March 20–April 17, 1986).

8. See *Report*, together with dissenting views (to accompany H.R. 4705), Comprehensive Trade Policy Reform Act of 1986 (cited in note 6), pp. 353–65. See also Alan Murray, cited in chapter 2 note 17.

9. Many free-trade advocates support adjustment assistance, partly as a sop to protectionist sentiments and to alleviate worries about job displacement from increasing imports. They contend the gains from trade (even if unbalanced) outweigh deindustrialization losses. In their view, adjustment assistance can be cheaper than trade limitation, and the market ultimately sorts out winners and losers. But, it has been difficult politically to mobilize and distribute much funding for adjustment assistance. Awkward issues complicate matters. Is the assistance primarily *relief* for import-related injury or displacement, or is it a *subsidy* for relocation, retraining, or reinvestment in more productive activities? Which "victims" (workers, companies, communities, and/or investors) deserve assistance and how much do they deserve?

The AFL-CIO supports generous adjustment assistance targeted mainly upon workers and/or job-saving activities. But, organized labor seeks through import limitation to prevent undue injury. Advocates of improved trade equity normally do not oppose adjustment assistance, but are more concerned with offsetting foreign mercantilism, subsidies, and import restrictions. New Industrial Policy tries to maximize net industrial productivity and combine assistance with rational upgrading and redeployment. Retrenchment of labor is often appropriate in distressed industries, but complete dismantling and elimination of most manufacturing capacity will be unwise and socially costly in the long run. With widely divergent views about adjustment assistance plus difficult problems of emphasis and allocation, it is not surprising that these efforts have been hesitant and rather limited so far.

U.S. adjustment relief to displaced or laid-off workers is modest to date. Some proof of import-trade injury has been required, with petitions filed and certified. Between 1975 and 1984, petitions covering nearly 2.8 million workers were filed; roughly half of them were certified. Their assistance cost $4 billion altogether and mostly consisted of supplementary weekly income payments (average duration being twenty-four weeks). The program was expanded considerably in the Carter administration, reaching a peak in 1980 and 1981, but it was cut back heavily in the Reagan period. Only 75,000 workers received any retraining; only 10,000 obtained relocation assistance; and 7,300 got job-search assistance. See "Background Material and Data Programs within the Jurisdiction of the Committee on Ways and Means," Committee on Ways and Means, U.S. House of Representatives, 99th Cong., 1st Sess. (Feb. 22, 1985); *OECD Adjustment for Trade: Studies on Industrial Adjustment Problems and Policies* (Paris: OECD, 1975); C. Michael Aho and Thomas O. Bayard, "Costs and Benefits of Trade Adjustment Assistance," in Robert Baldwin and Anne Krueger, eds., *The Structure and Evolution of Recent U.S. Trade Policy* (Chicago: Univ. of Chicago, 1984); Robert Lawrence and Robert Litan, *Saving Free Trade: A Pragmatic Approach* (Washington, D.C.: Brookings, 1986), esp. pp. 34–62.

10. For a recent suggestion of tariffs or import fees to fund adjustment assistance, see Gary Clyde Hufbauer and Howard Rosen, *Trade Policy for Troubled Industries* (Washington, D.C.: Inst. for International Economics, March 1986), pp. 77–80. For a similar proposal, see Robert Lawrence and Robert Litan, *Saving Free Trade: A Pragmatic Approach* (Washington, D.C.: Brookings, 1986), pp. 98–101. This approach could be expanded to provide tariff or import-fee financing for extensive rejuvenation efforts to companies and/or industries under stress from world market competition, widespread excess capacity, discount pricing, disruptive imports, or unfair trade practices.

11. See sources cited in note 19, infra, and in chapter 2 notes 5–7 and 9–10, and note 15 (Lamont, Culbertson, Anderson, and Bluestone and Harrison); Chapter 1 notes 35, 53, and 58; Preface note 3 (Phillips, Eckstein, Adams and Klein), note 12 (Scott and Lodge, Yoffie, Jacquemin, Driscoll and Behrman, Rosecranz, Sjostedt and Sundelius), note 13 (Fallows, and Hochmuth and Davidson), note 15 (McCraw, Wolferen, and Reich and Mankin), and note 21 (Corden, Cable, Greenway, Walters, Hindley, Shepherd, Duchene, and Saunders). In addition, other works emphasizing the many existing limitations upon free trade and nontariff barriers constitute further demonstration of the fact that presently established international trade is not a level playing field. See Hufbauer and Schott, *Trading for Growth: The Next Round of Trade Negotiations* (Washington, D.C.: Inst. for International Economics, Sept. 1985); Harry Shutt, *The Myth of Free Trade: Patterns of Protectionism since 1945* (London: Blackwell-Economist Books, 1985); Robert Middleton, *Negotiating on Non-Tariff Distortions of Trade: The EFTA Precedents* (New York: St. Martin's, 1975); Stanley Metzger, *Lowering Non-Tariff Barriers: U.S. Law, Practice, and Negotiating Objectives* (Washington, D.C.: Brookings, 1974); and Gary Clyde Hufbauer and Joanna Shelton Erb, *Subsidies in International Trade* (Washington, D.C.: Inst. for International Economics, 1984). See also *General Agreement on Tariffs and Trade*, particularly part IV (with its explicit endorsement of preference for LDCs) and the relatively weak constraints upon subsidies (as narrowly defined under GATT Articles VI and XVI and the Subsidies Code), dumping (as narrowly defined under GATT Article VI and the Anti-Dumping Code), and government assistance to economic development (GATT Article XIX) authorizing LDC infant-industry protection and LDC restrictions dealing with balance of payments problems. Most nations (including almost all developing countries) employ some currency restrictions and exchange controls, reflecting the fact that monetary and exchange-rate policies, along with differential credit, financing, and lending rates, are utilized to support economic and industrial development plus selected export promotion programs. (See chapters 1 and 5.) For additional sources on widespread export promotion and subsidies, see chapter 6, infra, note 35. See also

Richard Goode, *Government Finance in Developing Countries* (Washington, D.C.: Brookings, 1983). Finally, see sources cited in chapter 6, infra, note 45 (for the impact on U.S. manufacturing) and note 61 (for U.S. problems in agricultural trade and high tech industries).

12. See the sources cited chapter 1 notes 4, and 29 (especially Dobson, Evans, Kock, and Meyer).

13. Moderate revenue tariffs (say, in the 8 to 12 percent range) have only modest trade-distortion effects. The gains from trade forgone are relatively small. For references to calculation techniques, see Jackson and Davey (cited in chapter 1 note 29), pp. 31–34. And, very importantly, the modest price increase from moderate revenue tariffs becomes public revenue; quotas or VRA restrictions on imports, by contrast, often have larger price-increase implications, and the increased prices and profits all go to protected interests and foreign importers.

For the United States, for example, revenue tariffs of 10 percent in 1986 might apply to roughly $250 billion of competitive imports out of $380 billion total imports. (The remaining imports would be noncompeting raw materials or products not made in the United States.) Let us say that $50 billion of imports would be diverted by the 10 percent revenue tariff to domestic products, with a "gain forgone" in cheaper (or otherwise preferable) foreign goods of $5 to 8 billion. This would be the *net* welfare lost to society from a moderate revenue tariff–a worthwhile investment in limiting deindustrialization, saving valuable industrial capacity and trained labor, and boosting economic stability. (These revenue tariffs can be justified as offsets to foreign mercantilism, widespread export subsidies, extensive price discounting, and unfair trade practices.) Meanwhile, society gains the $20 billion of tariff revenue on the $200 billion of imports still coming into the United States (on a 10 percent revenue tariff ad valorem). But, if quotas or VRAs are used to achieve the same restrictive result as 10 percent revenue tariffs (namely, a 20 percent marginal import reduction), then the $20 billion of extra prices paid on these imports goes entirely to fatten the profits of domestic protected interests and foreign importers benefiting from this price increase. From a social welfare standpoint, economists properly condemn the quota or VRA restriction as socially inferior to a tariff as a trade restriction. If a nation decides that it is in the national interest to restrict imports (for infant industries, rejuvenation, economies of scale, national defense, or other legitimate objectives), the best way to do so is normally a tariff (which yields social revenue instead of windfall private profits).

14. For industries with significant fixed capital, R&D distribution, and marketing costs (which represent a large part of modern manufacturing costs), a moderate revenue tariff (8 to 12 percent) eliminates much of the labor-cost differential that might otherwise accelerate the migration of U.S. plants to low-wage countries. Also, data regularly collected on such revenue tariffs would make enforcement of U.S. unfair trade practice laws (including antidumping laws and countervailing duties on subsidies) much easier and more effective. In this connection, see also Peabody (cited in chapter 6 note 45).

15. The Japanese national defense absorbs roughly 1.1 percent of its GNP, whereas U.S. defense absorbs 7.1 percent of GNP. Other NATO allies average 3.5 percent of GNP for defense. Most of Latin America has low to moderate defense burdens. But South Korea, Taiwan, and Singapore carry relatively substantial defense burdens which are close to U.S. levels.

16. See sources cited in chapter 1 note 30, especially Dobson, Evans, Meyer, and Kock. Thus, moderate tariffs (before the Kennedy and Tokyo GATT Rounds were implemented) did not impede major trade expansion and world prosperity. In fact, a reasonable argument can be made that trade liberalization went a substantial step too far, with significant job losses, disruption, economic strains, and a backlash of protectionist pressures (variously handled) in Europe, the United States, and other industrial nations since that time. Since Japan did not really open most of its manufacturing markets, they suffered much less disruption.

17. GATT Article VII (valuation for customs purposes). See also sources cited in chapter 6, note 41.

18. Many respectable voices have urged a VAT for the United States. See, for example, sources cited in chapter 6 note 41.

19. For example, H.R. 4750 (cited in note 7) included a new Section 311 to the Trade Act of 1974, providing for "Mandatory Negotiations and Actions Regarding Foreign Countries Having Unwarranted Trade Surpluses with the United States." It would require annual ITC determination as to whether any "major U.S. trade partner" maintains an "excessive trade surplus." For such countries, phased reductions in trade surplus would be mandated, subject to various disciplines (including suspension of trade agreements, quotas, or tariffs, and/or new orderly marketing agreements to restrict imports). This proposal could be strengthened to limit presidential discretion and to force surcharges of 10 to 15 percent until "substantial progress" in surplus reduction is achieved. But, it should be noted that this would be powerful bargaining leverage that probably would be targeted against only a few countries (Japan, Taiwan, and perhaps South Korea, West Germany, and Canada).

Another variant of the import surcharge against key surplus countries was H.R. 1740, 98th Cong., 1st Sess. (submitted March 1, 1983, by Congressman Regula). It provided for tariff surcharges to cover cost sharing for U.S. defense assistance and U.S. military forces abroad against Japan and NATO allies that did not make a fair and equal contribution to U.S. and allied defense efforts.

20. Developing countries have been effective in using domestic-content or local-purchase requirements as a side condition for some foreign investments (by U.S., European, Japanese, or other foreign multinational corporations). Technology sharing is widely enforced to some degree. Performance requirements are sometimes imposed with respect to exports and foreign exchange earnings. Even countertrade or industrialized-country imports can be influenced this way. In most developing countries, exchange controls are significant leverage and discipline, so that MNCs (and even homebase countries) can be influenced. This whole array of pro–developing-country regulations is often referred to as a "New Bilateralism." (This is partly in recollection of the harsh bilateralism, tough mercantilist discipline, and even exploitation used by Nazi Germany against its satellites from the late 1930s through World War II.) The bargaining leverage of every country varies, and some feedback requirements are easier to enforce than others. Domestic-content or -purchase requirements, extensive training of host-country employees, and some sharing of technology has become common among developing nations. Export-performance requirements and countertrade occur less frequently, and countertrade has been objected to most strongly by MNCs and industrial countries.

These requirements are well discussed in recent international trade literature, though not easy to tabulate comprehensively (because they are imposed informally, often quietly, and with varying terms and conditions, while developing nations do not want to appear hostile or difficult for multinational and foreign investors). But, regulatory constraints are easy to enforce indirectly (within limits) for many developing nations, where exchange controls still are widely utilized. (See note 11.)

For sources on the New Bilateralism (emphasizing developing countries), see Stephen Guisinger and Associates, *Investment Incentives and Performance Requirements: Patterns of International Trade, Production, and Investment.*(New York: Praeger, 1985); C. Fred Bergsten, Etienne Davignon, Isamu Miyazaki, *Conditions for Partnership in Economic Management* (New York: Task Force Report to the Trilateral Commission, 1986); OECD, *Counter Trade: Developing Country Practices* (Paris: OECD, 1985); Pompiliu Verzariu, *International Countertrade: A Guide for Managers and Executives* (Washington, D.C.: International Trade Administration, U.S. Department of Commerce, Nov. 1984); *Countertrade in the World Economy* (New York: Group of Thirty, 1985); David Yoffie, *Power and Protectionism: Strategies of the New Industrializing Countries* (New York: Columbia Univ., 1983); Christopher Saunders, ed., *The Political Economy of New and Old Industrial Countries* (London: Butterworths, 1981); Vincent Cable, *Protectionism and Industrial Decline* (London: Overseas Development Institute-Hoddler and Stoughton, 1983); and John Black and Brian Hindley, *Current Issues in Commercial Policy and Diplomacy* (New York: St. Martin's, 1980). See also Hufbauer and Erb, Hufbauer and Schott, Shutt and Metzger (cited in note 11); Lamont (cited in chapter 2 note 15); along with Seymour Rubin and Thomas Graham, *Managing Trade Relations in the 1980's: Issues Involved in the GATT Ministerial Meeting of 1982* (Totowa, N.J.: Rowman and Allanheld, 1984).

21. Within modest limits, a great deal can be done to ease trade frictions bilaterally at the consular, embassy, and foreign ministry levels as well as to help U.S. MNCs cope with foreign mercantilism. But, larger responses to substantial policies of foreign governments (currency undervaluation, industrial development, export promotion, sector targeting, subsidies, tax relief, pricing and discounting by state enterprises, or low-cost financing by state-owned or closely regulated banking systems) are much harder for the U.S. government to deal with. Partly because it lacks a MITI of its own, the U.S. government finds it difficult to respond effectively to foreign mercantilism. But, U.S. responses are awkward for another reason. As "leader" of the Free-World alliance, the United States finds itself under special scrutiny in which favoritism and/or toughness is resented (and not easily kept confidential), at least when any U.S. trade action is believed to be the president's direct decision.

22. See chapter 6 for more complete recommendations. Laissez faire (or trusting to luck alone) will not be sufficient against modern world market competition.

23. See chapter 6 for an integrated package. While some trade-equity advocates might believe old-fashioned protectionism to be sufficient, that approach fails to recognize needs for greater efficiency and keeping up with the best available technology. On the other hand, merely encouraging high tech by itself (without offsetting foreign mercantilism, widespread subsidies, export promotion, discounting, and unfair trade practices) allows many U.S. industries to flounder and fall substantially below their proper potential. There is no sound alternative to a balanced and vigorous effort toward improved trade equity, stronger U.S. industrial policy, and meeting the challenge of world market competition. (See chapter 6, including note 45.)

24. Congressional support will be important in providing sufficient new funding for a stronger industrial policy, improved trade law remedies, and more skillful safe-guarding. But, Congress cannot provide the executive leadership, administrative follow-through, and sophisticated coordination with industry, engineering, and science that is essential for a comprehensive rejuvenation of the U.S. economy. The most important role in U.S. trade and industrial policy, if these efforts are to reach their full potential, must be played by the president and cabinet. Let us hope that U.S. politics in 1988–92 achieve that result. The best solution would be for leading candidates in both Republican and Democratic parties to recognize the need for renovating the United States's trade and industrial policy. National teamwork toward improved trade equity and stronger industrial policy is essential for the United States to maintain and improve its competitiveness.

4
Managing Debt Overloads

B y the mid-1980s, the world debt crisis was no longer seen as a brief, transitory squeeze on liquidity for some Latin American countries and their creditor banks. Comprehensive data on debt loads revealed more widespread problems in many countries.[1] Most of Latin America, most of Africa, the Western-oriented Middle Eastern nations, seven Asian nations, at least three Eastern European nations, and nearly ten Western nations (Scandinavia, Ireland, Portugal, Greece, and perhaps Australia and New Zealand) suffered significant debt overloads. At least sixty countries had excessive external debt loads. (See table 4-1.) As interest rates (including risk premiums) remained fairly high, debt-service burdens were serious for the medium term, economic recovery proceeded unevenly, and the costs of stabilization discipline were often painful. Some impasses are evident in rescheduling negotiations, with many debtor countries saying they cannot fully service outstanding debts and resume increases in economic growth without substantial relief or new credits. Multinational banks and creditor nations, on the other hand, want to keep debt service current, although more liberal, extended moratoria on principal payments, along with partial deferral or capitalization of interest payments, have become common. Capital flight and slowdowns in domestic and foreign investment are typical in the debt-overload countries, which presents a serious drag on their economic development progress. These conditions, if allowed to persist, can be politically destabilizing for many countries.

The debt-overload crisis seriously strains the world economy, greatly complicates trade and investment, and creates additional tension among nations. Fortunately, thus far, problems have been handled with reasonable skill, and the multinational banks and creditor nations have accepted significant delays in repayment. Under these circumstances, few debtors have had sufficient incentives to declare explicit default. "Open debt repudiation by delinquent sovereign borrowers is the least likely development because a debtor's objectives can be obtained without the formality of repudiation."[2] But reduced bank earnings, substantially reduced new bank credit to developing countries, strained debtor–creditor relations, and uneven world recovery are serious

Table 4–1
Debt-Overload Countries, 1985
(in $ billions)

	External Debt Load	GNP or GDP	Total Debt/Exports of Goods and Services	Debt Service/Exports of Goods and Services (Due within 1 Year)
Latin America and Caribbean				
Brazil[a]	104.5	227.3	359.9%	112.4%
Mexico[a]	97.3	177.5	325.8	124.8
Argentina[a]	48.5	67.2	487.7	232.3
Venezuela[a]	37.5	57.4	218.0	155.3
Chile[a]	21.5	20.3	441.3	105.6
Peru[a]	15.2	18.0	405.5	165.7
Colombia[a]	13.1	38.4	259.4	121.5
Equador[a]	8.7	11.1	257.0	93.5
Bolivia[a]	4.3	2.6	601.4	232.4
Uruguay[a]	4.8	5.9	362.6	166.9
Paraguay	1.1	5.3	n.a.	n.a.
Guyana[a]	1.3	0.5	n.a.	n.a.
Costa Rica[a]	4.2	3.7	n.a.	93.2
Panama	4.2	4.7	65.9	14.6
Honduras[a]	2.4	3.4	261.8	49.6
Guatemala	2.0	9.1	155.1	38.4
El Salvador	0.6	4.5	n.a.	n.a.
Nicaragua[a]	4.0	2.7	n.a.	n.a.
Jamaica[a]	3.9	2.5	296.6	95.2
Cuba	2.9	n.a.	n.a.	n.a.
Dominican Republic[a]	3.8	6.0	126.6	54.2
Trinidad and Tobago	1.6	8.9	60.1	13.1
Africa				
Nigeria[a]	19.8	74.1	153.1	104.5
Algeria[a]	17.2	50.7[b]	135.3	53.7
Morocco[a]	14.1	14.3	348.4	80.4
Tunisia[a]	5.7	8.8	179.9	40.4
Libya	n.a.	29.8[b]	n.a.	n.a.
Mauritania	1.4[b]	0.8[b]	n.a.	n.a.
Senegal[a]	2.3[b]	2.5[b]	n.a.	79.0
Sierra Leone[a]	0.4[b]	1.1[b]	n.a.	n.a.
Liberia[a]	1.0[b]	1.0[b]	n.a.	150.0
Ivory coast[a]	8.0	6.4	201.5	37.2
Ghana[a]	2.1	4.7	307.0	78.8
Cameroon	1.8[b]	8.0[b]	n.a.	n.a.
Togo[a]	0.8	0.7	n.a.	51.0
Central Africa Republic[a]	0.3	0.7	n.a.	n.a.
Congo[a]	1.3	2.1	n.a.	n.a.
Zaire[a]	5.3	4.2	229.9	33.2
Sudan[a]	8.3[b]	8.2[b]	296.6[b]	111.1[b]
Uganda[a]	1.2	3.3	n.a.	n.a.
Kenya[a]	3.5	6.0	n.a.	n.a.
Tanzania[a]	3.4[b]	4.5[b]	n.a.	53.0[b]
Mauritius[a]	0.6	1.1	n.a.	n.a.
Madagascar[a]	2.3	2.6	n.a.	n.a.
Malawi[a]	0.9	1.4	n.a.	n.a.
Zambia[a]	4.2	3.0	n.a.	n.a.
Zimbabwe[a]	2.4	6.0	211.6	57.1

Table 4–1 continued

	External Debt Load	GNP or GDP	Total Debt/Exports of Goods and Services	Debt Service/Exports of Goods and Services (Due within 1 Year)
Africa (continued)				
Botswana	0.3	0.9	n.a.	n.a.
South Africa[a]	22.5	74.0	119.5	88.3
Mozambique[a]	2.6	2.4	n.a.	59.0
Latin America and Caribbean				
Middle East				
Israel[a]	30.2	22.2	253.8	140.0
Egypt[a]	33.7	49.1	321.1	92.3
Jordan[a]	4.2[b]	4.3[b]	144.1[b]	43.3[b]
Iraq	7.0[b]	33.6[b]	n.a.	40.8[b]
Iran	8.6[b]	n.a.	n.a.	23.6[b]
Syria	3.6[b]	20.1[b]	125.5[b]	49.0[b]
Saudi Arabia	14.7	116.4	34.6	39.2
Kuwait	3.7	27.6	23.0	21.8
Lebanon	1.5[b]	n.a.	n.a.	n.a.
Bahrain	0.1[b]	4.3[b]	n.a.	n.a.
United Arab Emirates	1.5[b]	28.5[b]	n.a.	n.a.
Oman	2.0	7.4[b]	40.9	17.7
Yemen (Saana)	1.0[b]	3.9[b]	n.a.	n.a.
Turkey[a]	28.5	57.8	216.5	73.4
Asia and Pacific				
South Korea[a]	50.1	84.9	149.6	75.9
Indonesia[a]	37.4	85.4	186.1	60.8
Philippines[a]	26.3	35.0	322.2	154.9
Thailand	18.9	42.8	183.1	69.8
Malaysia	18.7	31.4	104.8	29.7
Burma	2.0[b]	6.6[b]	n.a.	n.a.
Bangladesh	4.0[b]	12.8[b]	n.a.	n.a.
Sri Lanka[a]	3.5	6.4	184.1	28.4
Pakistan[a]	14.0	35.4	233.3	40.5
India	35.8	197.2	219.6	30.8
Nepal	0.2[b]	2.6[b]	n.a.	n.a.
China	14.4	348.5	46.7	25.6
Taiwan	7.8	60.1	22.0	14.6
Singapore	3.7	18.4	12.4	6.2
Hong Kong	9.5	34.1	26.2	12.8
Japan	148.0	1331.5	67.4	21.5
Australia	51.0	185.0	180.5	64.1
New Zealand[a]	14.6	23.5	188.5	41.8
Eastern Europe				
Soviet Union	27.0	1520.3	70.3	48.1
East Germany	12.0	82.2	111.0	46.3
Poland[a]	25.8	90.1	327.1	84.3
Romania	5.6	75.5	67.9	29.0
Hungary[a]	9.7	22.0	192.4	90.8
Yugoslavia[a]	19.3	48.7	167.9	54.0
Czechoslovakia	2.8	67.3	58.7	40.3
Bulgaria	2.1	25.1	50.2	35.2

Table 4-1 continued

	External Debt Load	GNP or GDP	Total Debt/Exports of Goods and Services	Debt Service/Exports of Goods and Services (Due within 1 Year)
Western Europe				
Denmark[a]	56.6	57.7	240.4	83.4
Norway[a]	34.0	57.0	117.5	44.1
Sweden	51.5	100.0	133.9	58.3
Finland[a]	28.9	54.5	171.9	90.0
Iceland	1.9	2.7	164.5	59.4
Ireland[a]	17.6	18.6	147.6	84.5
U.K.	96.5	480.7	49.2	48.1
West Germany	120.7	678.9	51.9	37.8
Netherlands	15.9	135.8	18.2	8.3
Switzerland	28.0	105.1	58.2	32.1
Belgium	38.0	83.1	47.6	30.2
France	67.0	543.0	44.4	27.7
Spain	35.5	172.4	89.0	39.8
Italy	73.3	367.0	70.8	35.4
Portugal [a]	22.0	20.1	234.4	88.4
Greece[a]	17.0	36.9	213.7	61.4
Cyprus	0.6	2.4	n.a.	n.a.
Austria	11.3	68.8	38.2	42.0
North America				
U.S.	410.0	3988.5	114.0	69.6
Canada	122.0	332.3	116.6	45.8

Sources: "World Debt Crisis: Special Report," *Wall Street Journal* (June 22, 1984). World Bank Atlas (Washington, D.C.: World Bank, June 1986). Morgan Guaranty Trust Company, International Economics Department, *Morgan International Data* (June 1986), tables A–8, A–9. *Euromoney Trade Finance Report* (July 1986), p. 33.

n.a. = not available

[a]Debt-overload country.

[b]1984 data.

difficulties. It could be years, perhaps a decade or more, before the current international debt-overload crisis eases substantially.

The Debt-Overload Crisis

Sources of widespread debt overloads include rivalry and secrecy in private multinational banking (that facilitate tax avoidance and weaken regulation), limited accountability to central banks and creditor nation governments, and large public-sector deficits in many countries (especially since 1973 and the OPEC oil shocks).[3] Increasing prosperity from the 1950s through the early 1980s fostered confidence in this "system" and delayed awareness of debt overloads. Some critics worried about excessive tax avoidance, the risks of capital flight, thin reserves, and modest capitalization for many international banks. But most previous concern about international banking focused upon arguably excessive contributions to world liquidity and inflation in the later 1970s.

International bankers generally were confident and pointed out that banking "centers" like Switzerland, West Germany, and even Japan had low inflation rates in the later 1970s. They saw inflation as a domestic disease reflecting a lack of fiscal, monetary, and wage-price discipline, with insufficient saving, investment, and productivity in badly managed countries. Meanwhile, worldwide deposits in multinational banking increased rapidly, and the composition of lending portfolios gradually shifted to include more government debts, quasi-government corporation borrowing, and more NIC and LDC loans. Successful recycling of petrodollars from the mid-1970s, along with rapid growth among many developing nations, seemed to justify increasing confidence in the world banking network.

Deposits poured into the international banking circuit, with faster annual growth than most national economies enjoyed. Multinational banking became a glamorous bonanza. Branches proliferated around the world. Bankers enjoyed stimulating travel, prestige, and sophisticated life-styles. Even regional banks and other financial institutions came into the game through loan participations, following the leading banks. These enlarging resources had to be reinvested in "productive" loans.

How did bankers let debt loads get out of hand? In retrospect, the basic mistake was simple. Big banks failed to share adequate information on the *total* amounts borrowed by each developing nation. Country risk analysis focused mainly upon diversification of loans to different countries. As LDC debt loads increased, politicians in those countries exploited this information gap and eased growing budget deficits with foreign loans.[4] Recently, this mistake can be prevented for *future* loans through a new association of multinational banks (the Institute of International Finance), along with better IMF—World Bank—Central Bank collaboration. But, meanwhile, many countries accumulated debts beyond their capacity to service comfortably, and at least thirty-six countries already are operating under IMF-monitored stabilization and/or rescheduling programs. What was a bonanza for big banks in the 1970s, a growing international market, is now a serious strain for the world economy in the mid-to-late 1980s.

Viewed realistically, the international banking crisis is a medium-term overload problem, one appreciated too late. We must apportion the burden and risk of this excess debt and its servicing among international banks (their depositors and stockholders), multinational enterprises, debtor countries (including private enterprise, government companies, and governments), and the major creditor countries and their governments. Nobody wants to bear any significant burden. It is now rather academic to assign blame or responsibility, although press reports often take this line, usually with a parochial bias reflecting particular constituencies. Many participants played myopic parts in the game.[5] But, it is more constructive to view shortcomings systemically and get on with the task of managing an international economy with widespread overloads of debt that cannot be promptly paid and whose general default would be greatly disruptive to world trade and prosperity.[6]

A Workable Blend of Remedies

How big is the overload problem? Roughly $600 billion of the $850 billion external debt owed today by developing countries could be characterized as involving serious or aggravated overloads. (Another $150 to 200 billion is involved with "incipient" overload situations, but much of this is held by advanced industrial or developed countries.) (See table 4–1.) Maybe $300 to 350 billion is international *bank* debt in the serious overload category, with $125 to 135 billion owed to U.S. banks (mostly concentrated among its top fifteen multinationals).

For most major U.S. banks, the ultimate loss potential substantially exceeds their equity capital (normally, at least 6 percent of total assets). Total equity for the fifteen top U.S. banks is about $60 billion.) While few believe general default is likely, several major defaults among the six largest debtor nations (with $375 billion external debt outstanding) would be a nasty mess for the U.S. government, the world banking system, and international relations. Equally serious, though less obvious, is the cumulative debt-overload problem for another thirty or so smaller debtors. It is hard for banks to justify extending much new credit to these countries, but many are suffering great strain now, and widespread defaults among their ranks might be hard to handle.[7]

Alternative Outlooks on Solutions

A basic difficulty with the present world debt crisis is incomplete agreement on how to handle it. Three major camps should be distinguished, although each grouping contains a variety of emphasis. Such diversity is hardly surprising, because the debt crisis has about ten dimensions, and at least a dozen different remedies are suggested in varied mixtures. Nonetheless, it is helpful and accurate politically to break diagnosis-remedy packages into three ascending levels of multinational intervention and relief.[8]

The lowest degree of multinational support is involved in the recent pattern of international bank rescheduling, coordinated normally with the Paris Club and International Monetary Fund (IMF) stabilization programs, with occasional loans from the Bank for International Settlements (capitalized by member central banks) and/or bilateral aid from the United States to a few big debtors (such as Mexico and Brazil). This camp, while conceding that international banks make excessive loans to many countries in the 1970s and early 1980s, believes that the debt crisis is mainly a transient liquidity problem. Their primary solution package, therefore, is generous rescheduling or stretch-out relief, combined with policies designed to restore exports and prosperity quickly, so that enlarged NIC and LDC exports can carry their debt-service obligations more comfortably.

The second camp sees debt overloads more seriously for many countries, especially where aggravated inflation, heavy budget deficits, capital flight, and mismanagement make substantial export revival more problematic, or where the debt loads simply grew well beyond medium-term servicing capacity. (Some ask why the banks allowed debts in these countries to reach such excessive levels. The explanation lies, first, in a previous lack of full information sharing and, second, in too much optimism and lack of critical judgment among lenders and borrowers.) From this darker assessment, harder choices must be faced. Some degree of writedown or loss recognition in Third-World loan portfolios might be required and/or, alternatively, some kind of IMF and multinational "bailout" assistance could be desirable, at least in the form of extended bridge loans for five years or more (in some cases). Controversy follows, of course, on whether these additional loans might be necessary, desirable, or inflationary. Some within this camp would like a multinationally guaranteed secondary market for softer developing-country–loan "assets," so that these countries can get more credit and so that banks could unload their more doubtful loans. But, sufficient international consensus might be difficult, unless enough new credit is assured to the borrowing countries.

Some members of the first camp concede that bad luck could force us into harder choices, at least for a number of developing countries. Thus, for example, if U.S. and other creditor-country deficits remain very large, world market interest rates stay fairly high, and the dollar continues to be overvalued, servicing strains may be continued. Or, if economic growth proves weaker, exports revive only slowly, or excessive protectionism limits balanced trade revival, then many debtor countries will suffer greater difficulty, with stress placed on the international banking system. In any event, though, some bankers, business interests, and conservatives (including many monetarists), strongly oppose any bailout of the banks or debtor countries. They insist that default discipline is healthy and that bailouts, once begun, would tend to be inflationary and dangerous in the long run. This view is resisted by many in both camps, however, because it accepts too much risk of bank insolvencies, conceivable panic, debtor defaults, political disruptions, not to mention strain upon international trade and investment relations. Once creditor–debtor relations are seriously disrupted with explicit default or extended failure to service current obligations without rescheduling, a serious danger of aggravated mercantilism, international conflicts, import restrictions, problems for foreign investment, and reduced economic growth potential seems likely.

A third camp believes the structural crisis facing our world economy is more fundamental. Many people (mostly from developing countries) argue that larger investment and capital import "needs" must be recognized for the less prosperous nations. This implies more generous foreign aid and multinational assistance commitments, lower interest rates generally, and larger, steadier increases in international liquidity created by multinational institutions such as the IMF via special drawing rights (SDRs) or other devices. In this camp, proposals for existing loan forgiveness are more open-ended, with or without some degree of bailout to multinational banks. Many in this camp are Keynesian or post-Keynesian structuralists, who believe in a shortage of international liquidity (after years of tighter money and recession). Some doubt that inflation risks are so serious, but others prefer dealing with inflation through incomes policies and/or indexation schemes. Most economists in this camp accept a stronger role for government planning and public enterprise in the growth process. Some, though not all, are frankly socialist as well as suspicious of private-sector capitalism and banking or any generous returns to rentiers, passive investors, and entrepreneurs. (It should be noted that some Marxist-Leninist countries, while eager, perhaps, to exploit a breakdown in free-world credit, investment, and trade relations, have become active and eager borrowers in recent years. Yet, some communist or Marxist countries, most notably Poland, now are overloaded with external debt obligations. The extent to which free-world creditor countries should allow or encourage bank lending to Marxist governments is a ticklish question. But, it seems reasonable that limited or perhaps even moderate credits should be extended to many of these nations, depending upon debt-servicing performance and the degree of friendliness in overall political relations.)

Cutting across these issues is an important tactical or procedural problem. To what extent should we hope for a major breakthrough in new multinational negotiations or, as some suggest, another great Bretton Woods-type settlement? Most experts in the field of international banking doubt that sufficient consensus exists among creditors and debtors now; they predict evolution toward settlement merely by bits and pieces. Nonetheless, a considerable range of commentators and officials do urge important negotiations toward an improved multinational support system, more equitable contributions toward burden sharing, freer trade and less protectionism, greater capital mobility, and strengthened regulation of international banking. Some suggest another round of GATT negotiations, others want broader economic summit meetings, while many developing nations want a new North–South relationship to adjust basic differences. Not surprisingly, more proposals come from the second and third camps. Some urging comes as a means to add emphasis and leverage in bargaining, particularly from debtor countries reluctant to accept harsh stabilization discipline until they receive enough rescheduling or new credit relief. The Latin American debtors, in particular, are sharing information, pooling ideas, and bargaining with increased awareness of their joint influence on multinational bank rescheduling policies. Creditor banks oppose a "debtors' cartel" however and hope to rely mainly upon existing institutional arrangements, Paris Club rescheduling, and recent IMF supervision regimes.

But, even the existing arrangements, in fact, allow substantial room for incremental flexibility and a gradual relaxation of terms and conditions. Rescheduling, interest rates, fees, new credits, special assistance, stabilization discipline, and other arrangements have been altered considerably over time. These changes are watched very carefully by most participants (major international banks, central banks, treasury ministries, and multinational organizations—including the IMF, BIS, World Bank, and regional development banks, along with GATT, UNCTAD, and other groupings). A clear trend toward lower spreads, fees, and, most importantly, lower interest rates is evident. Thus, proposals for international discussions or institutional reforms should be understood as part of a bargaining process, with substantial flexibility and resiliency already demonstrated.

Alternative Specific Remedies

Among the most important elements suggested for solution packages are the following: (1) stretching out principal and/or interest obligations, (2) new bank lending, (3) additional direct foreign investment, (4) expanded export-import credits, (5) partial forgiveness or writedowns of established indebtedness, (6) limits on interest rates and fees, (7) multinational agency assistance, (8) IMF stabilization programs, (9) balanced world trade, restored growth, and expanding prosperity, (10) more stable exchange rates, and (11) stronger bank regulation. Because most observers predict incremental progress toward solutions to the world debt crisis, and some significant activity or discussion already is occurring in each of these areas, it is necessary to evaluate current trends with respect to each topic.

Stretch-out Relief. The dominant solution thus far has been to stretch out principal and interest obligations over time through successive reschedulings. Liberal relief on principal repayments (from three- to 14-year extensions), along with partial deferral or capitalization of interest payments, are allowed. This allows multinational banks to carry their soft foreign loans as "good" performing assets, and debtor nations are not so badly squeezed on use of their foreign exchange earnings.

But serious conflicts remain: (1) rates of interest and fees for older and new loans and (2) the volume of new credits and their uses. Debtor nations seek continued access to credit which, for a while, gives multinational banks enough leverage to insist upon "sufficient" interest rates (including fees). But debtor countries are refusing to maintain debt service on this basis unless they receive enough new credit or reduced servicing cost as a quid pro quo. Is this an adequate *modus vivendi*? How much longer can it last? To what extent can other measures ameliorate the debt-overload problem during the next five to ten years and beyond?[9]

Continued Bank Lending. Apart from loans rescheduled recently, there has been a substantial reduction in new bank lending to most debt-overload countries and to other LDCs. Critics say excessive stringency followed prodigality. But, with recent LDC debt buildups and servicing problems, caution is understandable (though a little late).

Naturally, this may crimp growth among some developing countries. The most overloaded nations have greater problems, with more severe retrenchment and consequent political strains. Difficulties in fully taxing themselves and limiting demand for public projects and social insurance are characteristic of new industrial societies (along with many mature ones). But international banks can no longer offer major new relief for overloaded economies (except insofar as existing debt is rolled over and rescheduled, with some capitalization of unpaid interest). New bank lending should come mainly to their stronger private enterprises and solid export operations, with something more akin to a collateralized potential for repayment (or a reliable priority in claims treatment).

How much constraint this imposes on economic development, export revival, and eventual creditworthiness varies among countries. Many believe that a substantial part of the NIC and LDC borrowing for the late 1970s and early 1980s was used rather wastefully. Expensive buildings, spending on high-priced consumer goods and appliances, government subsidies for constituency interests, and, in many instances, heavy capital flight were involved. Elimination of these credits will not do that much damage to economic growth. On the other hand, a complete blockade of new bank financing and credit could be burdensome. In most countries, continued access to modest levels of new bank lending (especially short-term trade finance), with stronger growth and exports, would be consistent with gradual reductions in external debt loads. But, one way or another, most countries must restore general productivity, healthy domestic savings and investment, and overall growth with less foreign bank credit. The foreign loan boom of the later 1970s and early 1980s is unlikely to return, because the multinational banks have become, hopefully, more realistic and careful about renewed overexposure.

Enlarged Direct Foreign Investment. Many urge enlarged opportunities and encouragement for private direct investment as a replacement for greatly reduced new bank lending to many developing countries. The Reagan administration, in particular, stressed this approach, provided that adequate investor safeguards are maintained. (The Bilateral Investment Treaty, or BIT, program of the United States is a very serious effort in this regard, and the Reagan administration's proposals at the Punta del Este conference initiating the eighth GATT round in Fall 1986, are part of this emphasis.) But, in many of the more overloaded countries, reliable repatriation of earnings and investment security is questionable. It is doubtful, in fact, that much new foreign capital would flow into the most troubled economies. Capital flight is already significant in many of them, so it is unrealistic to anticipate naive new foreign investment in any large volume. On the other hand, countries with less serious debt loads that still produce substantial economic growth and exports are good candidates for welcoming foreign investment, even though multinational banks should be more cautious. Hence, new direct investment could go mainly to the "virtuous" nations that really do not need it so much, but funds will be least available to countries in more desperate economic straits.

Nonetheless, multinational banks and MNCs want more liberal inducements to foreign direct investment. Their self-interest is obvious. Some NICs and LDCs, within limits, may be expected to respond. Since bank lending is greatly reduced and government-multilateral assistance and/or loans are limited, this route to foreign capital may be accepted, at least in some sectors. But socialist planning is common in the Third World, so that direct investment may be tied into joint venture deals and/or smaller dosage investments for tourism, trade, and light industry where government restrictions are less bothersome. International bank financing may be more accessible as an adjunct to such direct investment, and it could facilitate projects that contribute to increased productivity and export earnings. If ideological conditions change in developing countries and allow somewhat more free enterprise, these prospects may improve. But, the capital-seeking countries will have to decide for themselves that private foreign investment activity is desirable, and they must offer sufficient inducements and assurances of fair treatment and repatriated earnings.

Expanded Export-Import Credits. Considerable potential for new credit for developing countries exists, in any event, with short- and medium-term exporter credits for imports of machinery, equipment, and other supplies into these nations. Substantially higher prices will have to be charged for these goods and services to cover risk and an implied interest rate, but many manufacturers will be pleased with such sales opportunities.

Increased prices are tolerable in overload countries with a lot of inflation. In fact, competition among exporting countries is keen in a world market not fully recovered from general recession, with subsidized export credit guarantees and government insurance. Capital goods exporters (such as Japan, Germany, and others) already provide considerable new credit this way, in spite of loan rescheduling difficulties for many international banks. In addition, so long as debtor countries keep enough foreign exchange reserves and cash flow to their own central banks and financing institutions, further domestic credit for essential imports and considerable new capital equipment should still be available.

For these reasons, multinational banks and creditor nations should not overestimate their bargaining leverage or economic blockade potential in confrontations over rescheduling, interest rates, and de facto default. Overloaded debtor countries suffer already a large diminution of new bank credit, and they cannot be entirely excluded from exporter creditors. Thus, creditor nations and banks must be realistic about the additional disruption they can impose as the penalty for undue delay in payment of loans. Most debtor nations will find it inconvenient and burdensome to have cut off relations with creditor banks, but many vital imports and some credit will continue, especially if the debtors are smart enough to build up sufficient foreign exchange reserves.

Partial Forgiveness of Loans and Loss Recognition. Among overloaded debtor nations, there is broad consensus that excessive borrowing was not entirely their own fault or at least that their "innocent" general public should not suffer alone the painful consequences of drastic retrenchment. International bankers, former political leaders (and generals), and their business cronies are held largely to blame. And fat profits from previous dealings and capital flight often came back to secret tax-haven accounts in multinational banks or other properties abroad. So there is considerable resentment to be exploited against the creditor banks (and nations), which leads to a common recommendation among debtors that partial forgiveness of loans is desirable as part of a general solution to the world debt crisis.

Creditor nations and international bankers are sometimes shocked at such thinking and regard it as irresponsible. But, there is growing realization that some losses due to partial or extended failure to pay may be unavoidable. Regulatory precautions or contingency plans are already developed for U.S. banks, which allow gradual write-offs for defaulting or nonperforming international loans. In this way, the drastic, panic impact on multinational bank balance sheets through heavy, sudden recognition of losses can be minimized. These regulations also discourage debtor nations and banks alike from declaring default against each other.

But beyond gradual recognition of losses for nonperforming international loans, it is difficult for bank regulators (or multinational banks) to allocate partial forgiveness or loan write-offs.[10] How can different nations or borrowers be classified for greater or lesser write-off relief? Once some countries or classes of borrowers receive this dispensation, it becomes hard to stop this relief from spreading to other loan accounts and borrowers. And, it is against the nature of bankers to contemplate or propose such relief. Thus, the main significance of partial forgiveness thinking is not operational for bankers; it is in the psychology and politics of debtor countries. This attitude on the equities of burden sharing will affect rescheduling negotiations by governments in the future.

Reduced Interest Rates and Fees. An idea advanced by some international bankers and bank regulators—and urged widely among debtor nations—is that of a limit or cap upon interest rates charged to many developing nations. This is an element in recent proposals that there should be reconstruction or renegotiation of the contracts for floating-rate loan agreements with developing countries.

Higher interest rates in the U.S. and world markets starting in early Fall 1983, which lasted at least another year, increased the resistance of many debtor countries to paying full debt-service costs in the short run. In the initial year after Mexico's inability to meet its obligations (beginning in July 1982), many observers had looked forward to a steady easing of debt-interest burdens, so that considerably lower rates would come naturally with stretch-out relief. But, increased U.S. deficits, crowding pressures, and stubborn inflationary expectations with fear of renewed inflation actually brought real interest rates (and related world market rates) back up. Continued high real rates are a major problem for developing countries, and they increasingly object to such burdens in rescheduling.

While leading Western bankers expressed sympathy, it was difficult in fact, to select loans, countries, and situations suitable for interest rate reduction. Allocation problems are similar to partial loss recognition. What lines should be drawn in selecting "below-market" loans? It may be easier for an IMF-World Bank facility to provide limited, supplementary soft loans as part of regular rescheduling. But, the allocation process for reduced interest rates will not be all that easy (except as a bonus for success in meeting conditionality goals, and mainly with respect to older bank loans).

Nonetheless, the goal of limiting real interest rate burdens for overloaded debtors must affect regular rescheduling. The length of principal moratoria, the extent of deferral or capitalization of interest rates, and any discount lending through IMF-World Bank facilities should be influenced by this objective. While multinational banks resist any significant discounting or threats to their earnings, balance sheet soundness, or stock price values, the banks have shown relative mildness in resisting loan renewals and capitalization of interest rates. Banks bargain for rescheduling fees, if possible, but developing countries are increasingly objecting to expensive fees or risk premiums. So long as rollover and automatic capitalization of interest can be relied upon, however, bank resistance to loss of special fees may erode for their older bank loans.

Fortunately, interest rates were reduced considerably in 1985–86.[11] (See tables 4–2 and 4–3.) Whereas real interest rates remained relatively high between 1981 and 1984 in the major creditor nations (the United States, Japan, West Germany, Switzerland, and Britain), as reflected in the premium of interest rates over inflation rates, by Fall 1986, this differential had been substantially reduced. Thus, for example, real interest rates in the United States (the largest and most influential creditor country, with the biggest impact on world market rates) had eased considerably by Fall 1986. Continued softness in many commodity and industrial markets also led to increased confidence in moderate interest rates, at least for the medium term. And, while few expected the unusually low real interest rates of the late 1970s to return (they had been too generous and unsustainable), more moderate interest rates would ease debtor-servicing burdens (while maintaining savings and investment incentives) for the longer run.

Multinational Agency Assistance. IMF quotas and borrowing authority were increased substantially in 1983, and further increases are needed for 1987–89.[12] Increases in World Bank, International Development Association (IDA),

Table 4-2
U.S. Inflation Rates and Interest Rates, 1971-86

	Inflation Rate	Treasury Bill Rate	Commercial Bank Deposit Rate	Commercial Bank Prime Lending Rate	Domestic Corporate Bond Yield
1971	4.3	3.72	4.25	5.25	7.30
1972	3.3	5.21	5.63	5.75	7.33
1973	6.2	7.54	9.25	9.75	8.28
1974	11.0	7.28	9.25	10.25	9.25
1975	9.1	5.27	5.50	7.25	8.55
1976	5.8	4.41	4.70	6.00	7.35
1977	6.5	6.33	6.80	7.75	8.30
1978	7.7	9.42	10.90	11.75	9.25
1979	11.3	12.39	13.55	15.25	10.75
1980	13.5	14.87	16.25	21.50	13.00
1981	10.4	11.90	12.62	15.75	15.50
1982	6.1	8.15	8.25	11.50	11.75
1983	3.2	9.28	9.70	11.00	12.63
1984	4.3	7.99	8.35	10.75	12.25
1985	3.6	7.25	7.75	9.50	10.15
1986	0.8	5.39	5.75	7.50	8.56

Source: Morgan Guaranty Trust Company, "World Financial Markets" (Monthly). *Economic Report of the President,* transmitted to Congress Feb. 1986 (U.S. Government Printing Office) table B–59. U.S. Department of Labor, Bureau of Labor Statistics, *C.P.I. Detailed Report* (Monthly) table 2.

Note: Except for 1986, inflation rates are based on the year-to-year period and interest rates are based on December of the year. 1986 inflation is based on the first three quarters data from U.S. International Trade Commission, *International Economic Review* (Nov. 1986), statistical tables.

and regional development bank resources should be made also. Within moderate limits (allowing for periodic enlargement), multinational credit resources can help developing countries adjust to a period with substantially reduced international bank financing and more cautious foreign direct investment. Such additional resources can encourage responsible stabilization programs that reduce excessive budget deficits in developing nations and improve their growth and export performance.

But these international agencies cannot be expected to fill the entire gap created by reduced multinational bank lending. IMF resources are limited compared to outstanding debt loads, and the IMF's mandate has been primarily to ease short-term balance of payments difficulties. Although the World Bank offers concessionary loans for economic development, its resources are modest, and they cannot fully replace multinational bank lending and foreign direct investments. A major question to be resolved during the next decade is the extent to which IMF, World Bank, and regional development bank resources and liquidity creation should be increased relative to private bank capital and liquidity.

Developing countries prefer a larger role for multinational agencies, with more generous lending and better terms for them. Most multinational bankers and MNCs, on the other hand, want a more limited role and less competition in this regard. Yet recent overloads and insecurities for repayment of bank borrowing are easing this antagonism to some degree. Multinational bankers now

Table 4–3
Comparative Inflation Rates and Interest Rates, 1971–86

	Inflation Rate				Commercial Bank Prime Lending Rate				Domestic Corporate Bond Yield			
	U.S.	Japan	W. Germany	Switzerland	U.S.	Japan	W. Germany	Switzerland	U.S.	Japan	W. Germany	Switzerland
1971	4.3	6.0	5.2	6.6	5.25	7.10	7.25	7.00	7.30	7.38	7.59	5.42
1972	3.3	4.6	5.6	6.7	5.75	6.33	8.50	7.00	7.33	6.75	8.58	5.47
1973	6.2	11.8	6.9	8.7	9.75	8.07	14.00	7.50	8.28	10.73	10.33	6.55
1974	11.0	24.4	7.0	9.7	10.25	9.55	11.00	8.50	9.25	11.82	10.09	7.95
1975	9.1	11.8	6.0	6.7	7.25	8.38	7.00	7.50	8.55	9.39	8.63	7.08
1976	5.8	9.3	4.4	1.7	6.00	7.96	6.50	7.50	7.35	8.77	7.47	5.50
1977	6.5	8.0	3.7	1.3	7.75	6.34	6.00	6.75	8.30	6.36	5.92	4.96
1978	7.7	3.8	2.7	1.1	11.75	4.50	5.50	5.00	9.25	6.94	6.80	4.85
1979	11.3	3.6	4.2	3.6	15.25	6.51	9.75	5.00	10.75	8.34	8.20	5.53
1980	13.5	8.0	5.3	4.1	21.50	8.16	11.50	5.75	13.00	8.60	9.50	5.63
1981	10.4	4.9	6.3	6.5	15.75	7.00	13.00	8.00	15.50	7.70	10.50	6.60
1982	6.1	2.7	5.3	5.6	11.50	6.28	8.75	6.00	11.75	7.55	8.20	5.80
1983	3.2	1.8	3.3	3.0	11.00	5.89	7.75	6.00	12.63	7.09	8.30	4.92
1984	4.3	2.2	2.4	2.9	10.75	5.70	7.75	6.00	12.25	6.21	7.20	5.09
1985	3.6	2.1	2.2	3.4	9.50	5.71	7.25	6.00	10.15	6.90	6.90	4.93
1986	1.7a	-1.0	-1.1	0.9b	7.50	5.24	6.75	5.75	8.88	5.14	6.40	4.71

Source: Morgan Guaranty Trust Company, "World Financial Markets" (Monthly). *Economic Report of the President*, transmitted to Congress Feb. 1986 (U.S. Printing Office), table B–108. U.S. International Trade Commission, "International Economic Review" (Dec. 1986), statistics tables; IMF, *International Financial Statistics* (various issues).

Note: Except for 1986, inflation rates are based on year-to-year period and interest rates are based on December of the year. The 1986 Japanese inflation rate is based on Oct. 1985–Oct. 1986; the 1986 German inflation rate is based on Nov. 1985–Nov. 1986.

a Estimate.
b Second quarter.

favor somewhat more latitude and resources for multinational agency lending to developing countries, provided this does not undercut the reliability of long-term repayment for outstanding bank indebtedness or the security of other private foreign investments. Most bankers, however, oppose any rapid increase in multilateral agency liquidity that could refuel worldwide inflation.

Some conflicts of interest are inevitable, and a delicate role must be played by leaders of these multinational institutions, the IMF, World Bank, and regional development banks. The IMF already has a vital role in collaboration with the Paris Club in debt-rescheduling negotiations. But a feeling seems to be emerging among many, though not all, international bankers that multinational resources will have to play a somewhat larger role in the next decade for developing-nation finance. International bank lending simply became overloaded, and new bank loans and direct investment may be insufficient to sustain adequate economic growth momentum and assure certainty of repayment in many countries.

While some private international bankers might like a multinational agency bailout, loan guarantee program, or reinsurance scheme targeted mainly for their own benefit, this may be difficult to establish—at least for outstanding debt loads. But some of the new credit desired by developing nations should be doled out by the IMF, World Bank, or regional development banks in conjunction with the ongoing rescheduling process. This is a logical path for evolution. It merely requires periodic quota and capital increases for multinational institutions as well as somewhat greater latitude for borrowing and liquidity creation by the IMF and international agencies.

Another opportunity for moderate enhancement of IMF flexibility, along with another periodic increase in IMF-World Bank resources, will come during 1987–89, when continued heavy debt repayments and reschedulings are needed. Further increases will be needed in later years, but probably not in massive doses.

IMF Stabilization Programs. The rescheduling process has become standardized, in many respects, although there are differences in circumstances for each debtor country seeking relief. This routinization is a blessing for creditors and debtors alike. The process is faster, more expert, and reliable; terms are more uniform. Greater fairness, with less risk of breakdown, panic, or default has resulted. Most official multilateral reschedulings (between 1975 and October 1983, there were thirty-seven) occurred through Paris Club auspices (OECD banking-creditor countries). They are coordinated with IMF-supervised economic stabilization programs involving IMF resources and conditionality. This approach is consistent with the IMF's role in easing foreign exchange and balance of payments difficulties. The number of creditors varies considerably, but comparable treatment is a basic ground rule.

Balance of payments relief or reduced debt repayment as a share of exports has been substantial. Access to international credit usually has been maintained, although in smaller amounts. Although short-term export-import finance is normally excluded from direct rescheduling or stretch-out relief, keeping credit-worthiness is an important benefit to debtor countries.

But fiscal retrenchment in most debtor countries is needed. Even though rescheduling and stretch-out relief puts off repayment and reduces current servicing burdens, there will be less new foreign credit than before. In debtor countries, public-sector deficits are often large and excessive, forcing painful choices. Continued heavy deficits mean depreciating currencies, inflationary pressure, economic and political strains, and possible capital flight. But these countries find increased taxes and reduced government spending awkward, too.

Critics in these countries often blame the IMF and international banks for this distress, which does not make retrenchment discipline any easier. Yet without rescheduling relief and IMF assistance, disrupted trade, credit shortages, capital flight, slow recovery, and domestic inflation will normally be worse. For Marxist and some other opposition elements, this disruption may be useful politically; in their rhetoric, the IMF has become a favorite whipping boy. But radicalization or default will bring even less new credit to the debtor countries, in most circumstances.

As the debt overload-rescheduling prospect becomes longer-term (five to ten years, in many countries), more fundamental issues come under negotiation: (1) interest rate levels and fees and (2) the volume of new credits and foreign investment over this medium-term horizon. Gradually the bargaining leverage of debtor countries has increased. Much depends upon world inflation trends, fiscal discipline in creditor countries (especially the United States), interest rates, export growth, trade revival, and the maintenance of mutual confidence. Clearly, more multilateral resources are needed for the next stages in rescheduling. But thus far, the IMF–creditor–debtor rescheduling process has been largely constructive, providing a framework for more professional mutual accommodation, with less disruptive emotionalism and less conflict between creditor and debtor countries.[13]

In the next several years, however, substantial new IMF, World Bank, IDA, and regional development bank resources and credits will be needed to sustain the rescheduling process and to induce a sufficient combination of new private bank lending and direct foreign investment. As the world debt crisis matured in 1985–86, it has become evident that major debtor countries cannot (and will not) maintain heavy debt service without more significant new loans and/or investments. These countries do not want to make net capital outflows for the sake of servicing older loans. On the other hand, private international banks and foreign investors will not offer much in the way of new resources without substantial participation, reassurance, and support from multinational agencies and institutions. This is the essential quid pro quo for continued rescheduling.

Restored Growth, Balanced Trade, and Expanding Prosperity. Almost all analysts of the world debt crisis, recent inflation trends, recession in the early 1980s, and related economic strains agree that these difficulties would be greatly alleviated by a resumption of strong economic growth and prosperity. All boats rise on a tide of greater affluence. In retrospect, most of the world prospered, with substantial economic growth, though at unequal rates, during the 1950s through the 1970s. Resumption of growth and more balanced trade expansion are desirable for the mid-to-late 1980s and beyond.

There is considerable consensus among economists on policies needed for these purposes. Public-sector deficits in both creditor and debtor countries should be greatly reduced. There is growing agreement that Keynesian development-deficit strategies were carried to excess, and that modern logrolling politics creates hard-to-resist spending pressures (and reluctance to tax heavily). These problems afflict almost every nation. Sustained fiscal, monetary, and wage-price discipline is needed to bring and keep inflation rates down and to maintain sufficiently low interest rates. We must maintain reasonably open trading conditions in world markets, so that expanded exports can be imported. Both mature and developing countries will require trade growth. But somehow the massive U.S. trade deficit needs to be eliminated, and a sustainable balance restored.

Achieving this agenda will not be simple in all countries. It is easier in the more successful countries, with stronger growth, productivity and less inflation. Laggards suffer more political strains and distributional conflicts. Hence, patience and some compassion will be required. Even though major new bank credits might now flow to badly overloaded countries in distress, stretch-out and restructuring relief will be available on a regular basis. Unavoidably, though, countries with overloaded external debt obligations must suffer (and, in the end, benefit from) somewhat reduced access to foreign borrowing. Economic development progress should become more self-reliant, depending upon domestic capital formation to a greater extent. And yet, continued rescheduling by international institutions, creditors, and debtors assures adequate export-import finance and enough access to world capital markets or assistance for the higher-priority projects. In the end, debtors and creditors alike could be stronger and wiser after the excesses of 1974–81, the consequences of which must be felt through the coming decade.

Expanding trade in a more balanced way is necessary, too. Neither the United States nor its major trading partners can accept for long massive U.S. trade and current account deficits. (The former was $170 billion in 1986; the latter, $120 billion in 1986.) In order to play any appreciable role as a capital exporter, the United States must generate some blend of trade and service surplus. Recently, though, the United States has become a large net borrower, benefiting from heavy inflows of foreign deposits and investments, which allowed $387 billion in merchandise imports with only $217 billion in exports for 1986. Such imbalances are unnatural and unsustainable, undercutting the U.S. role as a creditor and significant source of net new investments to help restore world economic growth and prosperity.[14]

It will not be sufficient for the United States merely to collect large inflows of foreign investment and flight capital and recycle them into renewed investment for developing countries. These nations need to retain substantially more of their own investment resources. While some mutual diversification of investment flows among MICs, NICs, and LDCs is inevitable and desirable within limits, recent investment and trade flows for 1982–86 are abnormal, seriously unbalanced, and unsound. A more healthy and sustainable U.S. trade and current account balance will have to be restored reasonably soon.

Somehow, the recent disproportionate buildup of U.S. imports (from $250 billion to $387 billion between 1980 and 1985), with sluggish U.S. exports (holding roughly steady around $215 billion), must be turned around considerably. There must be some combination of increased U.S. exports and/or reduced imports into the United States. Most U.S. trade partners would prefer retention of their existing exports to the United States, and this applies with special emphasis to countries needing to service indebtedness to U.S. banks. But, these increased U.S. import flows cannot be sustained too much longer without enlargement of U.S. export sales.

The helpful impact of gradual dollar devaluation and appreciation of surplus-country currencies, along with long-term efforts at improving openness for U.S. exports in the eighth GATT round, remains controversial. Many free-trade enthusiasts insisted that this was all that should be done. But, even though the yen, deutsche mark, and Swiss franc had appreciated some 41 percent between early 1985 and late 1986 (and other currencies appreciated less), U.S. trade flows corrected only slowly. In this situation, considerable support was developing for stronger efforts toward improved trade equity, GATT reform, and a more comprehensive U.S. industrial policy. (See chapter 3.)

The need to correct large U.S. trade and current account deficits certainly complicated efforts to ease debt overloads and restore broad world prosperity. But, only $25 to 30 billion of the $155 billion U.S. trade deficit in 1985 actually involved major debt-overload countries (South Korea, Indonesia, Mexico, Brazil, and other Latin American nations). The great bulk—nearly 80 percent—of U.S. trade deficits in 1985 involved Japan ($50 billion), Canada ($22 billion), Western Europe ($26 billion), Taiwan, Hong Kong, and Singapore, as shown in table 3–3. This has an important implication. Most of the United States trade deficit, therefore, mainly involved problems of currency misalignment, insufficient trade equity, and U.S. industrial competitiveness. Debt servicing needs only involved some 20 percent, at most, of the deficit.[15]

Most economists agree that big U.S. budget deficits (approaching $200 billion in 1983, 1984, 1985, and 1986) were a substantial cause of overvaluation in these years, which adversely affected U.S. industrial competitiveness. But, asymmetrical trade openness, foreign industrial policies, subsidies, and trade restrictions were significant factors, too. In any event, substantial dollar misalignment, massive U.S. trade and current account deficits, and heavy investment and capital inflows into the United States had aggravated the world debt overload and slowed the recovery and restoration of more balanced international trade expansion.

More Stable Exchange Rates. Many economists believe that exchange rate instability became excessive after the early 1970s breakdown of the Bretton Woods system and fixed dollar–gold exchange rates.[16] The first and second oil price shocks in 1973–74 and 1978–80 aggravated these exchange rate variations, as did substantially divergent inflation rates around the world. This risk environment encouraged use of additional currencies for reserve purposes, beyond the dollar and gold, including the deutsche mark, Swiss franc, and others. Desire for broader reserve assets led to creation of special drawing rights by the IMF, which were also seen as a means to enhanced liquidity reserve potential.

But most economists believe that floating exchange rates were unavoidable when the dollar could no longer be sufficiently trusted as the universal equivalent of gold reserves. Sooner or later, U.S. dollars had to find partial substitutes as reserve assets. Because international liquidity and investment are increasingly mobile in most of the world's capital markets, it has been difficult for any country, including the United States, to regulate closely the dollar's value. To be sure, increased U.S. money creation and/or inflation can reduce the dollar's value, while monetary restraint and higher interest rates may increase the dollar relative to other currencies. But other world market forces also affect the dollar, especially because significant Eurocurrency liquidity (denominated in dollars or other currencies) is created separately in international banking markets.

For these reasons, among others, U.S. financial authorities have been skeptical about their ability to regulate dollar exchange rates closely in recent years, except, perhaps, to limit some "disorderly" speculation occasionally. But other countries, having more control over capital mobility or thinner markets, have tried to intervene in or regulate their currency exchanges, with some success, at least part of the time. A number of countries, including some strong exporters, took great pains to keep reasonably low currency values, so as to sustain healthy export expansion and industrial growth.

Among certain experts, mostly from countries where currency intervention seemed feasible or desirable, it has been suggested that stronger limits on exchange rate variation could be implemented. But U.S. monetary authorities, the Reagan administration, and the majority of international bankers generally remained skeptical. In these circumstances, therefore, while sophisticated suggestions are regularly made for "bands" or "limits" on exchange rate variation, they are not taken very seriously for the entire world (that is, involving the dollar). (On the other hand, the European monetary system has been just such an effort for most of Western Europe. But their capital-trade markets are more closely integrated, and such efforts seem both necessary and feasible in those circumstances.)

Taken more seriously at the world level are efforts to coordinate macroeconomic, monetary, and fiscal policies. More economists now believe that a substantial consensus can be achieved for relatively low inflation policies among most leading industrial nations, at least for a number of years. This would lead to more stable exchange rates, with less inflationary disturbance, provided that world trade is not seriously disrupted and prosperity revives for most key countries.

With hindsight's wisdom in 1987, more economists now believe that an excessive increase in the dollar's value between 1983 and 1985 was costly and disruptive, not only for the U.S. trade and payments balances, but also for many of its trade partners and allies. It is widely agreed now that massive U.S. budget deficits have become a serious strain, along with some five years of high interest rates (1981–85). But, there is less consensus lately on the proper alignment of currencies and interest rates.[17] Despite the dollar's recent decline with respect to Japan, Germany, and other strong current nations, they resist further appreciation. Meanwhile, Canada and most NICs and LDCs have experienced much less appreciation relative to the dollar. Some American economists want lower U.S. interest rates and an even weaker dollar in order to force a more rapid import-export adjustment toward balance. But Japan, Germany, and many other countries resist such a drastic change precisely because they fear just such a rapid loss of exports and jobs, with destabilizing economic and political consequences. Thus, unfortunately, while most nations now affirm the desirability of more stability in exchange rates and more policy coordination, there is rather large disagreement lately on the best alignment of exchange and interest rates for the short and medium terms.

But most nations now agree that large U.S. budget deficits should be reduced substantially, and that this would help set a better example among many developing nations. Greater fiscal responsibility all around would greatly facilitate more stable interest rates, ease inflation pressures substantially, and lessen the basic pressure behind growing debt overloads in many nations.

Stronger Bank Regulation. Increased consensus has been developed for central banks and treasury ministries in major industrial and creditor countries to regulate international banking activities more strictly, with somewhat stronger prudential safeguards. In the Basle Concordats I and II, the principle was accepted that every significant creditor nation should take responsibility for "its own" multinational banks and the external branches of other international banks located within its jurisdiction. This implies lender-of-last-resort support, failure minimization (for larger banks at least), and prudential requirements—including capital reserves, liquidity ratios, "provisioning" or loss-recognition standards, merger and holding company supervision, and any other measures considered necessary or appropriate. The bulk of multinational banking can be supervised this way, leaving a scattering of tax havens and small countries as limited loopholes. Customers dealing with independent international banks may be at some hazard in lightly regulated areas, but customers connected with major and respectable multinational banks should be adequately protected, more or less insured, and taken within the net of responsible supervision. At least, this is how the present international banking system is supposed to work, assuming that nothing serious breaks down.

A chain reaction of developing country defaults, greatly increased trade protection, and/or disruptive social revolutions in many countries could place nasty strain upon this international banking-finance-trade-prosperity system. But, the late 1980s were suffering considerable strain already from widespread debt overloads, large budget deficits, and the aggravated U.S. trade and current account deficits. Because this interdependence is widely recognized, and the lessons of economic breakdown in the 1920s and 1930s are fairly well understood among world central bankers, there is some willingness to work together in preventing such disasters.

An example of this evolving tradition is the close, confidential collaboration of major multinational bankers and/or central banks in the Paris Club, BIS, IMF, and the new Institute of International Finance (a club of over 350 multinational banks) in Washington, D.C. Increasingly, extensive data sharing is now implemented, correcting the oversight of previous years, when insufficient data was collected, shared, or utilized on debt loads and various types of default risk among developing and other nations.[18]

This system is now somewhat more resilient and shock resistant than before, with considerably better communication among central bankers. Finance ministries and political leaders are not so well coordinated, though, are often less sophisticated, and are not fully conscious of the consequences of harsh, abrupt, or selfish policies. Significant blunders can still be made by political leaders, parties, or pluralist situations that lack adequate control or responsibility. The established arrangements can never be entirely foolproof. But, if most major creditor and debtor countries are responsibly led, the likelihood of significant breakdowns probably can be kept to a bearable minimum.

But, this observation carries a significant warning. The present world debt-overload crisis is seriously disruptive in potential and needs careful attention for years to come. Complacency cannot be justified. Harsh, emotional rhetoric, recrimination, or angry conflicts could get out of hand fairly easily if the world debt crisis becomes politicized or a political football. This implies a substantive lesson, too. Neither debtor nor creditor countries should be expected to absorb too much pain, loss, or disruption at once. Debt-crisis management requires coolness, diplomacy, and realism about bearable suffering, trade equity, and rival national dignities.

Overall Prospects for Relief and Recovery

On the basis of reasonable projections for each of the specific remedies to the debt crisis, we can formulate an overall assessment of their total impact. Generous rescheduling relief should be continued and seems to be assured. But, although banks will lend some additional amounts to developing countries, a substantial net reduction in new lending seems unavoidable. This constraint can be offset, to a modest degree, by additional direct foreign investment (in the more successful debtor economies) and by export-import credits (often coming from manufacturers in the industrial nations). Debtor countries will press for partial forgiveness on loans and reduced interest rates, but multinational banks will resist these concessions—except, perhaps, to lower interest rates and eliminate fees on older loans. Debtors will be reluctant to make meaningful net repayments of older debts until such concessions are offered or significant new loans are extended. Multinational assistance through the IMF, World Bank, and regional development banks must be increased substantially, with limited bridge loans, and as a catalyst for some additional private lending-investment resource flows. But, IMF stabilization supervision will be part of the bargain that keeps the rescheduling process glued together.

Almost everyone hopes that increased world growth, balanced trade expansion, and enlarged exports will restore prosperity as quickly as possible. Ultimately, economic growth and lower interest rates are the fundamental solution for making short- and medium-run debt overloads bearable and for restoring normal creditworthiness and servicing. Reduced investment flows will be a complication, especially for the most inflation-ridden, traumatized, and insecure economics. But, much of the borrowing boom credit of the late 1970s and early 1980s was wasted on consumption and capital flight, so that considerable economic growth can still continue—so long as we avoid a general shutdown in credits, a widespread default crisis, greatly disrupted trade relations, and harsh limitations on mutual export expansion.

In time—whether five, ten, or twenty years are needed will depend upon each particular country, its politics, and its economic situation—most of the developing nations can recover and grow sufficiently to carry existing and somewhat enlarged (at a slower rate of expansion) debt-load burdens. In the meantime, multinational bank loan portfolios to many countries may remain somewhat insecure, "substandard" perhaps, with a limited quantity in the "doubtful" category. Hopefully, few countries will declare explicit default and force loss recognition directly. More frequently, in these years, periods of disrupted rescheduling will break out, for a considerable number of countries, in which bank regulators may impose loss-provisioning disciplines (contingency plans and/or reserves for the possibility of loan losses). Such loan losses should be spread over time to avoid drastic insolvency problems with large multinational banks. (The big U.S. multinational banks will continue diversification efforts and mergers, designed to spread their developing-country loan-loss risk exposure over larger blocks of assets and equity capital. Many interests will resist this effort, because of strong U.S. traditions of federalism and decentralization as well as fears of reduced competition in financial markets over the long run.)

For all these reasons, central banks (and responsible governments) must supervise international banking more carefully. (Regulatory authorities must be ready to nip panics in the bud and stand behind beleaguered multinational banks. There may be more Continental-Illinois receivership situations, though we could hope that regulators will supervise more promptly to minimize damage and dislocations in the future.)

Fortunately, most of the data-gathering needs are better recognized now than before, and central banks have closer coordination. In this way, more nations (especially among the industrial creditor group) can collaborate more effectively, which should facilitate more cohesion in macroeconomic, monetary, and fiscal policies generally. In the end, the world debt crisis of the 1980s may prove to be a worthwhile, net beneficial stimulus to more responsible banking, financial, and fiscal policies in many nations.

In any event, a fundamental lesson should be drawn by the world community about this whole debt-crisis experience. All societies must realize that heavy deficit finance (except perhaps, for major recession periods) and living beyond current means cannot last long without significant penalties—domestic inflation, increased foreign debts, and devalued currencies.[19] Other consequences normally include eroded business confidence, weakened incentives, reduced saving and investment, lower productivity and economic growth, greater sluggishness, eventual unemployment pressures, and poorer long-run performance. This realization is an important part of the overall relief and recovery effort needed to solve the world debt crisis and to restore more balanced international trade and general economic prosperity.

Notes

1. An earlier version of this chapter was presented at a conference sponsored by Stanford Law School's *Journal of International Law* in April 1985. It was published as William A. Lovett, "Managing the World Debt Crisis: Economic Strains and Alternative Solutions," *Stanford Journal of International Law* 21, no. 2 (Fall 1985), pp. 499–547. Extensive citations to the debt-crisis literature were provided, including 105 footnotes. Because so much material was referenced there, this chapter cites only the most important and more recent sources and developments.

During 1985–86, more complete data became available on more countries, world market interest rates eased considerably, and the controversy over rescheduling evolved toward somewhat greater realism. The result is a mixture of bad news and good news. (1) The bad news is that the number of debt-overload nations increased from roughly forty to sixty, and that rescheduling (in most situations) did not appreciably reduce outstanding debts. (See table 4–1.) In many nations, unpaid interest was simply added to the tab of principal outstanding, so that external debts actually got somewhat worse. For a large number of countries, there seems to be no alternative but continuing rollovers (and slightly increasing indebtedness). Where economic growth sags, full service of this debt will be difficult to restore (and, in the most overloaded countries, impracticable). This is a tough situation which will continue for years in some countries, and it places strain on many large international banks (which became overexposed in soft loans to debt-overload countries). (2) The good news is that interest rates eased substantially in world markets during 1985–86 (See tables 4–2 and 4–3.) U.S. interest rates declined 2-½ to 3-½ percent on T-bill, commercial bank deposit, prime lending, and corporate bond rates. Even Swiss, West German, and Japanese interest rates declined, though not so much. All this means lower costs in servicing large debt loads. And finally, international banks and the financial experts have grown more realistic about the limits on debt servicing, and the need for greater multilateral support and credit, and the importance of reviving economic growth on a healthy, balanced, and sustainable basis.

2. "World Banking Crisis: Is Debt Repudiation out of the Question?" *International Currency Review* (London: March 1984), p. 27.

3. See Lovett (cited in note 1), pp. 501–5 and notes 6 through 21. See also more recent works such as Benjamin J. Cohen, *In Whose Interest?: International Banking and American Foreign Policy* (New Haven: Council on Foreign Relations-Yale Univ., 1986); Philip A. Wellons, *Passing the Buck: Banks, Governments and Third World Debt* (Boston: Harvard Business School, 1987); David Lomax, *The Developing Country Debt Crisis* (London: St. Martin's, 1986); and Joe Foweraker, "What's Good for Citicorp . . .," *Challenge* (Jan.–Feb. 1987), pp. 47–50. In addition, for a significant early warning about the dangers of excessive debt buildups and undue financial dependency for developing countries, see W. Arthur Lewis, *The Evolution of the International Economic Order* (an Eliot Janeway lecture at Princeton Univ.) (Princeton, N.J.: Princeton, 1978), pp. 58–66.

4. In 1981–84, greatly increased interest rates, enlarged debt-service costs, world recession, and lower export earnings combined to substantially reduce the debt-load–carrying capacity of many developing countries.

Meanwhile, in some of these countries, private business interests—aware of growing deficits, debt loads, and currency devaluation risks—borrowed heavily abroad, often as a means toward capital flight (sometimes even labeled "self-debt").

5. We should realize that most major players—banks, governments, and many leading politicians—cannot afford to admit liability. It would be poor bargaining strategy, furthermore, to offer responsibility for one's country or other interests represented. Hence, most participants tend to understate the full scope of the debt-overload problem.

6. This does not mean, of course, that the excessive debt buildups of the late 1970s and 1980s should be ignored or forgotten. Quite the contrary! International finance, banking, and experts on foreign economic policies must understand the sources of this massive, systemic blunder of world markets in the same way that economists from the 1930s through the 1960s tried to explain and learn lessons from the 1920s and the Great Depression.

7. See table 4-1. In addition, see Lovett (cited in note 1), pp. 505–7 and notes 22 through 24. Also, see Irving S. Friedman, *Toward World Prosperity: Reshaping the*

162 • *World Trade Rivalry*

Global Money System (Lexington, Mass.: Lexington Books, 1987), pp. 46–71; Cohen, Foweraker, and Wellons (cited in note 3).

    8. See Lovett (cited in note 1), pp. 507–37 and notes 25 through 93.

    9. See Lovett (cited in note 1), pp. 513–14 and notes 34 through 36. See also the following sources, which reflect Latin American debtor countries' growing toughness and decreasing willingness to sacrifice their economic recoveries for the sake of servicing past debts. Implicit is the realization that debt-overload countries do not have to make major net capital outflows in servicing old loans, unless sufficient new lending or other advantages are received as a *quid pro quo*.

    Raul Prebisch, "The External Debt of the Latin American Countries," *CEPAL Review* 27 (Dec. 1985), pp. 53–54, argued for renewed growth, equal burden sharing between banks and debtors, and holding part of the debt-service payments in escrow to serve as a fund for renewed capital investment and economic growth. Guillermo Maldonado L., "Latin America and Integration: Options in the Crisis," *CEPAL Review* (Dec. 1985), pp. 55–77, emphasizes the slump in growth for Latin America, declining living standards in many countries, and strains of net capital outflows to service external debts (with weakened capital investment). He argues for more independent development and greater regional cooperation (with expanding intra–Latin American trade and economic integration). Fabio R. Fiallo, "A Two-Front Attack to Overcome the Payments Crisis of Developing Countries," *CEPAL Review* 27 (Dec. 1985), pp. 79–96, complains of the rising net transfers of capital from developing countries to banking-center nations between 1982 and 1984, with the burden of adjustment to the debt-overload crisis falling mainly upon debtor nations. His remedies are: (1) a new "commodity-based money or reserve asset (a device by which developing nations would receive increased liquidity resources to relieve their weakened capital positions and also receive larger multilateral lending flows and (2) much tougher trade bargaining by Latin America to force developed countries (especially the United States) into allowing greater preferential access to their markets, with more extensive countertrade and other barter-style dealings (justified under GATT articles XIX, XXII, and XXIII, despite their conflict with GATT's MFN principle) and aggressive use of "authority" derived through a voting majority in GATT to impose trade relationships more favorable to developing nations. A final Fiallo suggestion is the familiar "debtors' club" idea, using the "threat of joint repudiation," although conceding a risk of "adverse bommerang effects" (ibid., p. 93).

    The Peruvian government took the position recently that Peru must limit its foreign-debt–service payments to 20 percent of foreign exchange earnings. The international creditor banks strongly protest this harsh restriction and will greatly limit further credits to Peru until more normal rescheduling is resumed. But, Peru enjoys substantial moral support in Latin America, although no other debtor nation has gone so far in challenging the creditor banks openly.

    From a public interest (or at least "populist") perspective in the United States, the role of multinational banks in the world debt-overload crisis is also coming in for criticism. See, for example, Joe Foweraker, "What's Good for Citicorp . . ." (cited in note 3), stressing the large interest earnings of the biggest multinational banks in the debt-rescheduling process. He says that when capital flight from developing countries (especially in Latin America) is included, the big banks have net deposit liabilities outstanding to many debtor nations. Without capital flight, for example, the net debt flow of Argentina, Mexico, and Venezuela would be modest. Foweraker argues that the biggest banks have relied upon the U.S. taxpayer (ultimately) to bail them out for improvident lending; meanwhile, these banks demand higher U.S. and world market interest rates to shore up profits on these loans and capital flight from insecure countries.

All this suggests political strains from the world debt-overload crisis and the uncomfortable role of major U.S. multinational banks (although some might say, "They earned it—the old-fashioned way!"). Imprudence in banking is hardly new. See, for example, Davis, Foreman-Peck, and Kindleberger, (cited in chapter 1 note 30), Bogart, Clough and Cole, and Bowden, Karpovich, and Usher (cited in chapter 1 note 2), or John Kenneth Galbraith, *Money: Whence It Came and Where It Went* (Boston: Houghton-Mifflin, 1975). But, as Benjamin Cohen observes in *In Whose Interest? International Banking and American Foreign Policy* (cited in note 3), p. 1, high finance has become high politics, and international banking has become politicized with an involvement in scores of countries, with increasing intermixture.

10. Despite great practical difficulties for U.S. regulators in allocating "forgiveness" for Third-World borrowing, this idea keeps popping up. See Lovett (cited in note 1), pp. 517–22 and notes 45 through 49. More recently, Senator Bill Bradley (Democrat of New Jersey), among others, has been associated with this idea. "Sen. Bradley Warns Industrial Nations of Debtors' Cartel," *Wall Street Journal* (Feb. 2, 1983), p. 12; Peter Kilborn, "More Lenient Debt Aid for Third World Urged," *New York Times* (Dec. 5, 1986), Section D, p. 2. Interestingly, Latin American spokespeople have not stressed the partial-forgiveness solution recently. See, for example, Prebisch, Maldanado, and Fiallo (cited in note 9). Evidently, they believe other methods of debtor relief are more realistic and effective.

But, the Vatican urged recently (in a special report ordered by Pope John Paul II) that wealthy industrial countries should be more generous with rescheduling of debts, granting foreign aid, and allowing total remission of debts in emergency situations. The vatican document, "At the Service of the Human Community: An Ethical Approach to the International Debt Question," could add moral force to debtor-country negotiating firmness. See Associated Press dispatch, "Vatican Trying to Ease Third World Debt Crisis" (Vatican City, Jan. 28, 1987), appearing in *New Orleans Times-Picayune,* (Jan. 28, 1987), p. A–10. On the other hand, see "Citicorp's Reed Takes Firm Stance on Third World Debt; Chairman Aims to Stem Commercial Banks' Trend toward Concessions," *Wall Street Journal* (Feb. 4, 1987), p. 6.

11. See also, IMF, *World Economic Outlook* (Washington, D.C.: October 1986), chart 1, p. 3. The most relevant measure of interest-rate burdens in world credit markets is *real* rates (discounted for inflation). According to IMF staff estimates, real interest rates (for five major industrial countries) averaged close to zero percent between 1978 and late 1979, and moved up fairly rapidly (except for a dip in late spring–early summer 1980) to reach a plateau above 6 percent between 1981 and 1985. (Real long-term rates averaged somewhat higher than short-term rates in this period.) But, during 1985–86, real interest rates declined at least 2 percentage points. These interest-rate declines in 1986 are comparable to those shown in tables 4–2 and 4–3. This represents substantial, though not complete relief for debt-overload countries.

12. For good reasoning along these lines, see Friedman, *Toward World Prosperity: Reshaping the Global Monetary System* (cited in note 3), esp. pp. 269–79.

See also Lovett (cited in note 1), pp. 522–24 (notes 51 through 57). For other recent sources, see chapter 6, infra, note 54.

13. See Lovett (cited in note 1), pp. 525–26 (notes 58 through 60). But, there are limits to the IMF's leverage in stabilization agreements, and their targets, while desirable, are often left unattained. As a Latin American banking commissioner remarked to this author recently, "The IMF cannot command the impossible."

14. The biggest and most awkward challenge in restoring trade and prosperity to debt-overload countries (especially in Latin America) is the now massive U.S. trade deficit ($387 billion worth of U.S. imports versus $217 billion worth of exports in 1986). In these circumstances, the United States cannot simply turn up the "import valve" and let heavy imports flow in more strongly from debt-overload countries. The severe U.S. trade deficit puts a nasty crimp in this easy solution. Everyone's first step in an export-oriented industrial policy was to hit the U.S. market in a big way, as Japan, Taiwan, and South Korea did. Now, export expansion must be better balanced and spread more evenly. (For recently prevailing hopes in revived debtor-country exports, see Lovett (cited in note 1), pp. 526–28 (notes 61 through 67).

15. In other words, at most only 15 to 20 percent of the now massive U.S. trade deficit could be explained by the need for debt-overload countries to cut imports from the United States and increase their exports to the United States.

16. See Lovett (cited in note 1), pp. 529–32 (notes 68 through 74). More recently, see John Williamson, Institute for International Economics, "Exchange Rate Management: The Role of Target Zones," paper presented to the American Economics Association (New Orleans: Dec. 29, 1986). Williamson argues that dirty or "unmanaged floating" did not work well and that since the Plaza G-5 Agreement of Sept. 1985, it has been replaced by "managed floating." While many agree that recent experience with unmanaged floating (including the "dollar roller coaster") leaves a lot to be desired, it is not so clear that a wise "managed float" has taken its place. Current exchange rates are controversial in the United States, Europe, and Japan and among NICs and LDCs. In terms of major trade imbalances (especially involving the United States, Japan, West Germany, and Taiwan) the new system is hardly working well. Many economists believe that better fiscal and monetary coordination is essential to harmonize exchange rates, as Europe gradually learned in recent years with the European Monetary System (EMS).

17. Some believe that the dollar is too low, many insist that the dollar needs to be depreciated even further, and many (including Fed Chairman Volcker) believe that the dollar is about right for now. The Japanese and Germans worry that the yen and deutsche mark are too high, but many U.S. experts think greater appreciation is needed. Most people think NIC surplus currencies such as Taiwan's are undervalued, but not those of NICs with large external debts to be serviced. No international conference could achieve consensus now. We are left with somewhat disorderly "managed" currencies and disagreement on appropriate exchange rate alignments.

18. See Lovett (cited in note 1), pp. 531–43 (notes 75 through 105). In addition, see Benjamin Cohen, *In Whose Interest? International Banking and American Foreign Policy* (cited in note 3), on the need for greater coordination of international banking activities with high-level foreign policy. Also, see generally "Reluctantly at the Helm," *The Economist* (Sept. 22, 1984), for the challenges to central-bank leadership when national foreign policies and international economic relationships are left in disarray and pluralist confusion.

19. See Lovett (cited in note 1), pp. 540–43 (notes 100 through 105). See also John Makin, *The Global Debt Crisis: America's Growing Involvement* (New York: Basic, 1984); Benjamin M. Friedman, "Implications of the U.S. Net Capital Inflow," in R.W. Hafer, *How Open Is the U.S. Economy?* (Lexington, Mass.: Lexington Books, 1986). Finally, see chapter 6, infra.

5
International Investment: Limits and Potential

I nternational investment activity enlarged substantially since World War II, along with increased borrowing across international borders. In many respects, this was beneficial, to the extent that more widely shared economic growth and broader prosperity resulted. But, there are some limits on the security and protectibility of foreign investments as well as the degree to which host countries welcome these flows, and assure repatriation of earnings and vendability for these investments. It is important, first, to appreciate these potentialities and limitations in framing sensible national policies for industrial and trade development and, second, to understand the logic of contemporary world capital markets.

Three perspectives must be taken into account: (1) the international portfolio management outlooks of investing individuals, enterprises, financial institutions, and government agencies in world markets, (2) divergent national policies affecting these investments in LDCs, NICs, and MICs with varied mixtures of private enterprise, social regulation, and/or public ownership, and (3) conflicting global networks (free world, mixed economies, and socialist nations) for investment activity with partial overlaps and investment flows across these boundaries.

International Portfolio Management and National Regulation

From the viewpoint of investment portfolio managers—whether individuals, companies, enterprises, financial institutions, or even government agencies (in some circumstances)—the problem of investment allocation is to achieve an optimal mix in terms of yield, growth, and relative security. Investors analyze all prospective risk and return factors—to the extent that their information allows—and act accordingly. Beyond relatively low levels of assets, or business situations where the bulk of resources are tied into a single profitable venture or project, most investors try to achieve some degree of risk diversification.

This means spreading their investment eggs among different baskets of separable, independent areas for risk and return. More secure, sustainable yields and growth may be achieved, and somewhat higher levels of risk (and potential profitability) can be accepted. Better investment results can be maintained this way for their portfolios, and the total supply and boldness of investment resources for the country or countries involved may be enhanced appreciably.[1]

Within free enterprise systems, it is usually desirable to broaden the range of permissible investments and portfolio distribution, subject to reasonable regulations for domestic financial institutions and industries that promote public responsibility, soundness, competition, economic development, and national security. Some sectors of the economy may need public investment resources when private capital is limited, the projects are very large, and/or risks are hard to calculate. Other sectors may require substantial regulation when competition is significantly limited or monopolies are involved. In countries with more socialist ideologies and institutions, additional industries may be regulated or managed as state enterprises. In communist systems, most significant industries and large enterprises are state controlled, with the possible exception of handicrafts, personal services, little businesses, and small-scale agriculture and/or gardening.[2]

A basic dichotomy exists between mainly free–private-enterprise countries and the more socialist and communist nations. In private-enterprise countries, free-market forces are trusted, with broad latitude for investment diversification (subject to some reasonable regulation). The bulk of investment resources are owned privately. But, the more socialist and communist nations mistrust private capitalism, at least for significant sectors of the economy, and impose heavy regulation or state ownership and control. The state owns a major part of investment resources, if not most of them. In the evolution of many socialist and communist states, substantial expropriation of private-enterprise corporations and properties has occurred. Foreign investments were frequently expropriated or nationalized, often with limited or negligible compensation in terms of previous or potential market values. Even in some "moderate" developing countries, there have been earlier expropriations or nationalizations (often directed against foreign companies, as in oil and mining operations, railroads, transit systems, electric and gas utilities, or large agricultural plantations).

When international investment is reviewed historically in the modern era (including bond issues, bank loans, and direct investments from the nineteenth century onward), extensive political risks are evident.[3] Defaulted obligations, suspended payments, restricted repatriation of profits or interest, discriminatory regulations, and various forms of expropriation or nationalization have occurred fairly often. These disruptions are more common in periods of economic strain or crisis, when the debtor or host country is troubled and has more difficulty servicing foreign obligations. But, international conflicts, revolutions, domestic uprisings, or other major changes in government as well as serious scandals and corruption have also brought difficulties. Finally, the gradual spread of socialist ideologies, since the Bolshevik revolution in Russia of 1917 and even more after World War II, particularly in former colonial areas, led to more frequent limitations on the role, reliability, and servicing of foreign investments and lending.

Four main groups of nations have emerged with respect to international investment, capital mobility, and national regulation. In the first group, the OECD (which mostly consists of free-enterprise nations), broad investment diversification and substantial freedom is allowed, with a fairly high degree of investment reliability and integrity for debt servicing. The United States, Canada, Western Europe, Japan, Australia, and New Zealand comprise this group along with some closely related former colonies. These countries include most of the MICs plus some NICs and LDCs. A few have been substantial capital exporters and lenders since the 1950s. A majority of their multinational investments and loans have been diversified among this bloc, and this reflects two primary strategies: (1) export-related and MNC expansion into friendly world markets and (2) increased investment diversification within this bloc (for individuals, financial and investment institutions, and MNCs). The major constraints upon investment freedom relate to national laws that maintain public responsibility for companies, soundness, sufficient competition, and appropriate connections or loyalty to local communities and employees. In some respects, small countries need more "identity preservation" regulation, because their markets can be more easily dominated by outside MNCs.

The second group comprises NICs and LDCs with reasonably strong commitments to free markets, at least recently (even though they may have some state enterprises and/or earlier nationalizations in their histories). Part of Latin America, the eastern rim of Asia, part of the Middle East, India lately, and some African countries fit this pattern. These countries welcome foreign investments, within limits, and may allow some outflow of their own investment capital into world markets. Some MNEs are growing out of this group, including South Korea, Hong Kong, Singapore, Brazil, and others. These countries seemed reasonably secure for international investment, but recent debt overloads, large budget deficits, substantial inflation, capital flight, slowed growth, unemployment, and income inequalities in many countries make some of them less secure now. Unfortunately, capital flight can be hard to reverse, especially when Marxist-Leninist or other revolutionary movements (such as extreme Muslim fundamentalism) threaten political stability.

These countries, even more than MICs, need reasonable regulation of foreign investment to preserve sufficient competition, prevent dominance by large foreign MNCs, and limit dangerous capital flight. But regulating foreign exchange and capital flows is tricky, because this can easily degenerate into excessive restrictions upon repatriation of earnings that chokes off much of the incentive for new foreign investment, and domestic nervousness and capital flight may be increased by such measures in a counterproductive way.

The third group includes NICs and LDCs with mixed economies and/or less solid commitments or security for private enterprise. Much of Latin America, Africa, and the Middle East along with some Asian, Pacific, and Caribbean nations fall into this category. Foreign investment is less welcome, substantially more restricted, or less reliably protected. Because their public sectors can be sizeable, government borrowing is frequently large. While foreign aid and multilateral loans at concessional interest rates are preferred, considerable bank debt from abroad is often accumulated. While some of these nations used to be relatively secure and private-enterprise–oriented, recent political and economic strains may make them less so. Capital flight is a serious problem for many, even though supplies of domestic capital are smaller than in stronger capitalist states (MICs and NICs). Most of these countries employ substantial limitations on foreign investment to prevent undue dominance or exploitation, and joint venture deals to secure advanced technology are popular. Such constraints, however, limit the flows of foreign direct investment, while helping to explain their greater reliance upon government in their domestic capital formation and their hopes for concessional loans from "rich" countries abroad.

The last grouping is communist or predominantly socialist states, including the Soviet Union, Eastern Europe, China, North Korea, Indochina, some of Africa, several Middle Eastern countries, Cuba, Nicaragua, and a few others. Because private enterprise is greatly restricted and suspect, they allow only modest scope for foreign investment. But some of their state enterprises and banks operate abroad to a limited extent. Borrowing by socialist countries from multinational banks and institutions is more substantial, however, and they often seek trade finance from foreign MNEs. Yet, foreign investment in the heavily socialized countries is still tentative, strictly limited, and not really part of the open, free-world capital market system. Technology imports are greatly preferred to any serious opening for capitalist private enterprise, which would be disruptive and destabilizing, while offering awkward rivalry to socialist state enterprises and bureaucratic control.

In reality, the world investment, finance, and trade environment is an uneasy mix of collaboration, rivalry, and even occasional armed conflict between free-enterprise and private-capitalism nations (the OECD bloc, many NICs, and some LDCs), and the most heavily socialist and state capitalist countries (the Soviet Union, Warsaw Pact nations, and some NICs and LDCs). Many developing nations in Latin America, Africa, the Middle East, Asia, the Pacific, and Caribbean strive for a degree of nonalignment between the free world and socialist camps, but they cannot avoid significant choices between public- and private-sector investment strategies. Inevitably, some kind of investment, industrial development, and economic growth program must be put into effect.

But, these states unfortunately are not entirely left to their own devices. Many developing countries are zones of contention, with Marxist-Leninist forces and other revolutionary and terrorist groups actively seeking political and military power.[4] Liberal and free-market forces resist these challenges with uneven success. To the extent that healthy economic growth and development can be sustained, with moderate and bearable debt servicing on foreign loans, political stability may be preserved. Within limits, the developing countries seek friendly commercial, investment, and trade relations from both the free-world and socialist blocs. But, care must be taken to create and maintain adequate military forces, internal security, and political cohesiveness. One-party regimes with authoritarian features are normal in the Third World. Until a stronger, better educated, and somewhat prosperous middle class is created through economic development, the extensive political freedoms of the liberal Western democracies may be infeasible for them. "Pluralist" opportunities can be subverted by forces seeking to overthrow the government and a growing free-enterprise sector. On the other hand, harshly repressive, economically unsuccessful regimes, with widespread inequalities, unemployment, and human distress, may not survive in the world today. Their peoples want a better life and would like to see some progress for the majority.

In the widespread economic prosperity and growth of the 1960s and 1970s, most developing countries gradually increased their growth rates, industrial production, and infrastructure outlays. Foreign investment and lending activity expanded, especially in the inflationary boom of 1973–81, when petrodollar recycling and tax-haven banking enlarged the deposit resources of multinational banks. In these years, international investment and loans flowed more readily, and with a less critical eye, to the developing nations.[5] Growth rates looked better in many developing nations than in some stagflation-ridden MICs of Europe and North America.

In the 1980s, international lending and investment became more discriminating, with wariness and concern for risk limitations.[6] Multinational banks finally recognized serious debt-overload problems in 1982 and greatly reduced new credits to many developing countries. Meanwhile, a worldwide recession in 1982–83, lower commodity prices, heavy debt-service burdens, frequent capital flight (especially in Latin America), and slow or stalled growth for most countries led to more limited progress. Between 1979 and 1985, real interest rates were high, which helped lower inflation substantially for the advanced nations. But, economic recoveries were hesitant, with only a few strong performers (mostly in East Asia). International investment and lending, in these circumstances, turned more cautious and selective. Tables 5–1 and 5–2 reflect U.S. direct investment abroad and foreign direct investment in the United States from 1960 to 1985.

Improving the Environment for International Investment

A crucial requisite for improving the environment for international investment is greater realism for all participants. Capital exporters, MNCs, international

Table 5–1
U.S. Direct Investment Abroad, 1960–85
(in U.S. $ millions)

	1960	1965	1970	1975	1978	1981	1983	1984	1985
Developed Countries	19,319	32,313	53,145	90,695	120,471	163,076	155,736	157,461	172,750
Canada	11,179	15,319	22,790	310,382	37,071	45,129	44,339	46,830	46,435
Japan	254	675	1,483	3,339	4,972	6,755	7,661	7,920	9,095
Europe	6,691	13,985	25,255	49,305	69,533	101,514	92,178	92,017	106,762
U.K.	3,234	5,123	7,996	13,927	20,416	30,260	27,637	28,635	33,936
Germany	1,006	2,431	4,597	8,726	12,731	15,840	15,319	14,794	16,746
France	741	1,609	2,590	5,743	6,806	9,132	6,614	6,224	7,835
Switzerland	—	—	2,631	5,152	8,615	12,509	14,099	14,865	16,230
Netherlands	283	686	1,550	3,097	4,685	8,813	6,613	6,201	7,046
Developing Countries	11,129	15,177	21,448	26,288	40,399	56,182	45,746	50,131	54,474
Latin America	7,481	9,440	12,252	16,394	21,467	30,020	24,113	25,229	29,479
Middle East	1,139	1,536	1,617	-4,040	-2,194	1,992	4,451	5,032	5,127
Africa	639	1,390	2,614	2,414	3,175	4,228	4,123	4,752	4,994
Asia and Pacific	984	1,366	2,457	5,747	6,757	11,099	13,039	15,119	14,874
Total	31,865	49,474	78,178	124,050	167,804	226,359	207,203	212,994	232,667

Source: U.S. Department of Commerce, Bureau of Economic Analysis, *Survey of Current Business* (Sept. 1974, Oct. 1974, Aug. 1980, June 1985, Aug. 1986) and *Revised Data Series on U.S. Direct Investment Abroad, 1966–78.*

Table 5–2
Foreign Direct Investment in the United States, 1960–85
(in U.S. $ millions)

	1960	1965	1970	1975	1978	1981	1983	1984	1985
Europe	4,707	6,076	9,554	18,534	29,180	72,377	92,936	108,211	120,906
U.K.	2,248	2,852	4,172	6,331	7,638	18,585	32,156	38,387	43,766
Germany	—	—	680	1,408	3,654	9,459	10,845	12,330	14,417
Switzerland	713	940	1,545	2,138	2,879	5,474	7,464	8,146	11,040
Netherlands	947	1,304	2,151	5,347	10,078	26,824	29,182	33,728	36,124
Canada	1,934	2,388	3,117	5,352	6,180	12,116	11,434	15,286	16,678
Japan	88	118	229	591	2,749	7,697	11,336	16,044	19,116
All other areas	181	214	370	3,135	4,326	16,524	21,356	25,046	26,251
Total	6,910	8,797	13,270	27,662	42,471	108,714	137,016	164,583	182,951

Source: U.S. Department of Commerce, Bureau of Economic Analysis, *Survey of Current Business* (Aug. 1983) and *Selected Data on Foreign Direct Investment in the United States, 1950–79* (December 1984).

banks, and governments must be more understanding about local country needs and legitimate concerns about excessive foreign influence. Outside investment capital is welcome, within limits, and represents helpful collaboration (especially when beneficial technology comes along). But, excessive flows can spoil a good thing. Foreign investment should be diversified among many capital-exporting countries and companies.[7] Local partners (in one form or another) are highly desirable, and a low profile may be prudent. On the other hand, host countries must appreciate that foreign investment requires at least world market interest rates and some risk compensation. While there is a limited role for international charity, military assistance to allies, and modest educational, engineering, agricultural, and scientific aid (bilateral and multilateral), any larger flows from the free-world economies need sufficient incentives. Developing nations, if they want foreign investments from free-enterprise nations, must provide sufficient incentives for these inflows, repatriation of earnings, and debt servicing. Tax concessions, higher capital gains, and extra profit potential are normal incentives used to lure direct investment resources. Bank lending requires reliable interest and debt service, including reasonable spreads and fees. Naturally, free-world economies feel more comfortable if there is healthy, expanding private enterprise in the host country. This entails not merely potential for quick deals, but a growing and respected class of property owners, farmers, and business and professional people. As economic development prospers, this class broadens fairly rapidly under wise regulation. Thus, sound economic development really involves broader enterprise partnership—shared and expanding benefits within the host country—which enlarges with productive and restrained foreign investment and lending activity. Tables 5–3 and 5–4 show U.S. banks' liabilities to foreigners and claims on foreigners from 1974 through 1986.

Adequate military security and political cohesion are essential to keep order, protect property and investment interests, and prevent disruptive violence or terrorism from destabilizing groups.[8] This is a necessary charge on every nation's resources, although friends and allies should be reasonably generous (whenever possible) in helping to resist external aggression or subversion against each other. The lessons of collective security from the 1930s through the 1950s still apply. But, as the Chinese Civil Wars (1911–49), Vietnam War (1946–74), troubles in the Philippines (1946–87), and many other areas demonstrate, there must be enough social justice, leadership, and vitality to encourage majority support. Responsible partnership and shared benefits in economic progress are needed, over the long run, to sustain military security and political collaboration in every culture.

Increased Multilateral Liquidity to Sustain World Credit Markets

Some sixty nations became seriously overloaded with external debts in the late 1970s through the mid-1980s, and most suffered substantially from inflation strains and

Table 5–3
U.S. Bank Liabilities to Foreigners, 1974–86
(in $ millions, end of period)

	1974	1978	1981	1983	1984	1985	1986[a]
Canada	3,264	4,607	10,250	16,026	16,059	17,426	22,359
Europe	48,619	85,169	91,275	138,072	153,145	163,829	162,986
Germany	9,560	17,286	7,645	3,599	3,358	4,835	5,645
France	4,257	9,214	8,486	9,441	12,701	15,540	19,986
U.K.	7,580	14,125	28,286	60,683	68,671	76,728	78,081
Switzerland	9,940	12,343	18,716	32,246	31,740	28,742	28,640
Latin America	11,850	23,670	85,223	140,088	153,381	167,792	178,937
Japan	10,904	14,616	20,750	18,079	21,640	23,077	33,469
Other Asia	5,571	6,893	16,080	27,515	32,743	34,671	44,054
Middle East (oil-exporting countries)	4,717	8,979	12,992	12,976	10,804	14,523	12,296
Africa	3,546	2,535	3,180	2,827	3,396	4,883	4,041
Other countries	2,827	1,297	1,419	8,067	5,684	3,347	2,924
International organizations	3,992	3,274	2,721	5,957	4,454	582	3,974
Total	95,290	166,877	243,889	369,607	407,306	435,368	465,041

Source: Board of Governors of the Federal Reserve System, *Federal Reserve Bulletin* (Monthly), table 3.17.
[a] 1986 data through July.

Table 5–4
U.S. Bank Claims on Foreigners, 1974–86
(in $ millions, end of period)

	1974	1978	1981	1983	1984	1985	1986[a]
Canada	2,609	5,152	9,193	16,341	16,109	16,476	18,232
Europe	7,728	24,232	49,262	91,927	99,014	106,407	99,804
Germany	526	845	940	1,284	1,306	1,267	1,461
France	836	3,735	4,127	8,766	9,157	9,124	9,604
U.K.	800	10,172	23,849	47,364	56,185	62,560	55,676
Switzerland	300	1,283	2,213	1,863	2,123	3,171	2,614
Latin America	14,911	57,567	138,347	205,491	207,862	202,663	202,492
Japan	12,749	12,671	26,797	30,354	29,066	31,249	41,898
Other Asia	4,338	9,590	21,473	32,529	32,206	30,665	31,390
Middle East (oil-exporting countries)	714	3,125	1,581	4,954	5,044	4,298	2,910
Africa	1,183	2,221	3,503	6,154	6,615	5,407	4,817
Other countries	717	988	1,376	2,898	3,447	3,390	3,110
International organizations	8	56	56	164	800	1,030	493
Total	44,958	115,603	251,589	291,312	400,162	401,585	405,144

Source: Board of Governors of the Federal Reserve System, *Federal Reserve Bulletin* (monthly), table 3.18.
[a] 1986 data is through July.

heavy deficit financing.[9] Tough stabilization and interest rate discipline imposed by the United States and other leading creditor nations between late 1979 and 1984 led to general recession, price declines in many commodities, and a slump in world growth and trade. For typical debt-overload countries, a hiatus in economic growth substantially aggravated debt-overload and debt-servicing problems. (See figure 5–1.) Debt-servicing costs escalated during 1979–84, but economic growth slowed drastically. In figure 5–1, the dotted line of external debt load burdens rose above the solid line of economic growth and debt-carrying capacity, with a substantial excess (point x) in debt overloads realized between 1982 and 1984 for different countries. At this stage, three options existed:

1. *Default or write-down of debt load.* This was not feasible for multinational banks or the creditor countries. Major banks would have failed. Financial disruption, possible crisis, and political embarrassment would follow for leading creditor governments.
2. *Servicing and rescheduling with negligible new loans.* This was the initial compromise solution, but it greatly reduced economic growth in debt-overload countries.
3. *Servicing and rescheduling with increased new loans.* This allows more economic growth for most developing nations, a stronger recovery for the world economy, and a more balanced trade revival and expansion.

It became increasingly clear during 1986 that option 3 (renewed new lending, stronger economic growth, and broader trade revival) is better for free-world countries (including both creditor and debtor nations). (This is depicted as line $c'c''$ in figure 5–1.) Widespread default and/or major debt write-down (option 1) is too disruptive, very costly for the banks, and risks financial crisis in the creditor countries. Rescheduling and servicing with negligible new loans and greatly constrained economic growth (option 2) could only be an emergency makeshift. A continued halt in growth causes too much damage to the free-world economy (both debtor and creditor countries) and risks widespread political destabilization. The practical problem is how to finance renewed credits and investment in a context of widespread debt overload.

The Baker Plan proposal of September 1985 (increased World Bank, IDA, and regional development bank credits to developing countries, combined with more new loans from the private multinational banks) was broadly supported. But, during the next year, the Reagan administration concentrated on getting a tax reform bill through Congress, while its chief foreign policy concerns were Central America, strategic weapons, and summit talks with the Soviet Union. By October 1986, the major implementation of the Baker Plan was more generous rescheduling with Mexico, using more new bank credits, together with substantial IMF, World Bank, and U.S. government assistance. Most observers saw this as an important breakthrough and encouraging precedent, but many complained that not enough new credit was being extended to other debt-overload countries suffering adjustment problems, weak recoveries, and inadequate growth.

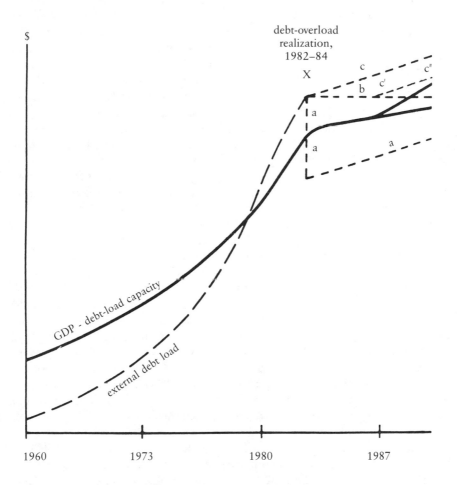

Note: In the late 1970s, many debt-overload countries were approaching their limits of debt-serving capacity. During 1979–84, real interest rates increased substantially, while economic growth and commodity prices slumped. Many debt overloads were realized in 1982–84 (point X). Three options existed: (a) default and/or write-downs of debt load (not desirable or allowed by creditors); (b) servicing with negligible new loans (greatly reduced economic growth); (c) servicing with some new lending and renewed economic growth.

Figure 5–1. Typical Debt-Overload Strains for Many Developing Countries, 1960–87

Additional investment and lending to restore strong economic development must come through four channels: (1) expanded multilateral resources (IMF, World Bank, and regional development bank capital and enlarged borrowing), (2) domestic saving, investment, and a return of flight capital, (3) new lending from private international banks, and (4) more direct foreign investment through MNCs and other portfolios.[10] In typical debt-overload countries, a blend of all four sources is needed, with new multilateral loans and IMF stabilization packages serving as the catalyst to reassure other creditors and investors. The Paris Club of major international banks generally makes its rescheduling and new loan agreements contingent upon IMF conditionality, so that these crucial channels of support are interlocked. IMF and Paris Club policies favor reduced government budget deficits, a substantial effort to lower inflation, realistic exchange rates, and adequate incentives for savings and investment, so that domestic and international business confidence can be restored. This does not require abandonment of all public-sector activities, but greater efficiency, some retrenchment, reduced subsidies, and competitive pricing discipline are strongly encouraged. All these structural reforms provide an environment for improved economic growth, gradually restored confidence, and a revival of domestic business activity. Foreign investment by MNCs and others can be revived in such a climate, once the bridge loans from multilateral institutions and banks combine with domestic policies and capital to assure reasonable profit prospects.

Marxist-Leninist and anticapitalist elements, however, attack and try to undermine IMF conditionality discipline as well as the encouragement for private saving, investment, and enterprise (domestic and foreign).[11] They seek more drastic social revolution, expropriation of private companies, debt default, and a restructuring of institutions toward state enterprise. This comes more easily if developing nations founder in stagnation, capital flight, demoralizing inflation, increased unemployment, and distress. But, if market-oriented recovery programs succeed, the case for radical revolution will be undercut. Obviously, private business interests as well as conservative and moderate political outlooks should welcome a more liberal recovery scenario and favor IMF support and stabilization efforts (provided that enough multilateral institution and bank resources can be obtained).

Deciding, first, just how much IMF, World Bank, and other multilateral assistance is desirable for each country and, second, how much new international bank lending can be raised are delicate problems. The existing debt-load structure for that country and its economic potential, business conditions, and political prospects are all part of the equation. Understandably, the United States and other key creditor nations will concentrate bilateral aid on the biggest debtors and those with the most strategic importance for them. Mexico, Brazil, and the Caribbean basin, among other areas, receive special U.S. attention. There is a real danger, however, that some small backwater countries, ones with limited significance in the short run, may be neglected. These debt-overload nations (parts of Africa and scattered island nations, for example) represent convenient targets for subversion by Marxist-Leninists or other revolutionaries. Over the long run, significant shifts in geopolitical balance could occur through a chain of revolutions, guerilla activities, and military beachheads spreading from these areas.

For all these reasons, the United States and other leading OECD nations should realize that larger multilateral resources are essential for the IMF, World Bank, and regional development banks. More generous capitalization (including bigger IMF quotas), and more SDRs or "multinational liquidity" must be provided if Baker Plan revival packages are to be widely employed for many developing countries. It is clearly in the longer-run geopolitical interests of the United States, most other OECD nations, and many developing countries that bigger bridge loans be mobilized to carry the world economy through a serious debt-overload crisis (and recovery from anti-inflation discipline in the 1980s).

Some worry about the risk of excessive SDR creation and the danger of renewing major worldwide inflation.[12] Obviously, SDRs would depreciate in value and usefulness if expanded too rapidly. But, with large U.S. budget deficits (approaching $200 billion), the Americans cannot be too generous with IMF quota increases or bilateral aid. Nor will other OECD nations be much more generous than the United States. Accordingly, a significant portion of enlarged multilateral resources should come from SDRs (international "currency"), in addition to bigger IMF and World Bank quotas and capitalization and increased borrowing on world capital markets by the multilateral institutions and regional development banks.

For the medium term, at least, it seems that international commodity price (or scarcity) inflation has abated, with slow growth and slump for many nations. A moderate revival of world monetary growth to ease widespread debt-overload strains does not present a danger of serious inflation in these circumstances. And, we should bear in mind that for most countries, the major source of inflationary pressure is still large and sustained government budget deficits (which tend to be monetized because excessive real interest rates cannot be suffered too long). Thus, the main danger of inflation stems from the domestic political disease of failing to provide adequate tax revenues for public-sector spending, and excessive deficit finance. The problem is quite serious today in many MICs, NICs, and LDCs. Current IMF and Paris Club stabilization-rescheduling packages properly emphasize the need for stronger fiscal discipline. The United States must really get its own budget deficits down to modest levels, both for its own economic health and to serve as a better example to developing countries and those getting rescheduling relief under Paris Club and IMF auspices.

Finally, we come back to the fundamental requisites for saving and investment in any society. Somehow, substantial resources must be set aside, saved, and invested from current consumption. This saving and investment must be mobilized by adequate private funding, encouraged by sufficient interest rates and profit returns, or these resources must be mobilized in the public sector. Governments can only raise these funds (1) with borrowing at market interest rates, (2) by increasing taxation and limiting consumption, or (3) through indirect taxation via excess budget deficits, inflationary finance, and "forced saving" by loss of consumer purchasing power.

Inflation experience for many countries in the 1970s and 1980s shows that business confidence, domestic savings, and investment are eroded by high and sustained inflation.[13] In other words, healthy private enterprise development, which can provide vigorous incentives, broad popular enthusiasm, and wide prosperity over the long run, does require low to moderate inflation, generally speaking. Forced saving strategies through large and sustained public-sector deficits (whether employed for reasons of compassion, political weakness, or impasse, or in order to subvert established governments) will undermine liberal and free-enterprise societies, leading eventually to more socialist or dictatorial regimes. Only repressive governments can impose a regular regimen of inflation, forced saving, and reduced purchasing power upon their peoples. Ultimately, even these governments cannot be too harsh, because their peoples may rebel. But in the meantime, liberal institutions can be destroyed. It can take a long time, perhaps generations, to rebuild individual liberties, broadly shared property rights, sensible regulation, and the social cohesion needed for healthy free-enterprise nations.

Investment-Guarantee Programs and Limitations

Assurances for foreign capital investment come mainly from the host or receiving country. Export-credit guarantees, political-risk insurance, tax subsidies, and other forms of encouragement (or discouragement) also may be significant for the capital-exporting nations (and the IMF and World Bank). But the strongest assurance for foreign inflow is a healthy, secure domestic economy in the host country, with solid growth prospects and no significant risk of discriminatory regulation or expropriation. (The Reagan administration is an example. Most of the OECD bloc fits this category in many respects.) When foreign investors, companies, and enterprises are commingled with local business activities, under favorable and fair treatment, they share in the general economy's prosperity.

Where host country regulation merely protects reasonable competition, financial responsibility, and national security and/or encourages economic development (including by infant-industry or "rejuvenation" tariffs and subsidies), foreign investors can still share in the business opportunities provided. So long as foreign enterprises or investors participate comfortably in the local environment, considerable net inflows may occur. (These capital flows depend upon differential exchange rates and earnings potential in their source countries, with appropriate discounts for cost and risk of transfer.) Further restrictions can be justified to prevent undue foreign dominance in the host country or excessive concentration from particular source nations (such as the United States or Japan). While such regulations could be burdensome or even encourage flight of foreign investment capital, negative impacts need not materialize. If constraints are kept within reasonable limits, foreign investment may still feel welcome and prosper in a healthy manner.

In fact, a smaller volume and lower visibility for foreign investment often helps survivability. This applies with special force to recent U.S. overseas investments, which had become large and a target of nationalist resentment in many nations during recent decades. A recent weakening of U.S. capital exports, with the United States becoming a net debtor, could really be beneficial in easing antagonisms. Mutuality of cross-investment between nations is helpful, too.

But when the host country is insecure and/or the climate for foreign investment becomes unreliable or threatening, new foreign inflows will be greatly reduced. While existing foreign properties and operations cannot be withdrawn quickly, outside investors and MNCs tend to reduce their entanglements. A precautionary technique is to restrict major new financing to host-country banks or local sources. On the other hand, exchange controls are normally used by insecure countries to restrict capital flight and to retain liquidity. But these restrictions (including economic performance requirements) are often ineffective, and their use signals a warning to foreign investors. Even so, investments in extractive industries (mining, petroleum, timber, or plantation crops) or branch plant manufacturing could still be profitable when the primary profits come out of resulting exports. This requires, however, adequate continuity for these activities and a sufficiently secure political environment to sustain them.

Actually, many developing countries live in an extended environment of partial insecurity, with continued exchange controls. While these are not ideal circumstances for outside investors, when liberal tax concessions are offered by the host government, substantial investments for extractive industries and low-wage branch plants may still be encouraged. Where significant host country financing can be employed (through local partners or low-interest bank credits), the proportion of outside capital is limited substantially, and the resulting enterprise will be more secure and attractive. If the local government is firmly established, a substantial amount of economic development and growth can be fostered this way. In the most successful NICs and LDCs (Japan, Taiwan, South Korea, and Singapore), the economy may graduate eventually into a stable, prosperous free-enterprise condition with open capital markets.[14] Thus, "winners" in the economic growth scramble can become full members in the OECD "club." But some developing countries that are more politically and economically troubled find it difficult to grow out of their insecurities. They often remain in a limbo condition—with mixed economies, considerable private enterprise, some foreign investment (frequently welcomed), extensive exchange controls (with significant leakages for the influential parties), and corruption in government. A crucial question for the latter type of countries is how much economic growth can be achieved. With some progress, continuity may be sustained; but economic stagnation or decline undermines political stability.

Established international law and custom gives broad latitude for each host country to regulate its own internal affairs, domestic industries, economic development, and foreign investment activities. Discrimination in access to local markets is allowed and even encouraged by the GATT for developing countries. But, once foreign investments and property rights are established in the host country, these interests should not be seized or taken without a public purpose and just compensation; there should also be no unfair discrimination against foreigners.[15]

But there is substantial disagreement on implementing these standards of fair treatment. Creditor nations and MNCs believe that just compensation in expropriation cases should be equivalent value, in useable form, within a reasonable time. For many years, the U.S. government has urged "prompt, adequate, and effective compensation," with market rates of interest taken into account. Many developing nations, however, reject these guarantees and insist upon "economic self-determination," especially for their natural resources. In 1974, the U.N. General Assembly adopted a Charter of Economic Rights and Duties of States (with 120 nations in favor, 6 against, and 10 abstentions), which affirmed the right of every state to nationalize or transfer ownership of foreign property with "appropriate compensation" to be "settled under the domestic law of the nationalizing State and by its tribunals." The opposition came from creditor nations. While many settlements between investors and governments have been reached, only modest compensation has been granted in some situations. As the International Court of Justice stated in the Barcelona Traction Case (1970), such settlements are *sui generis* and provide no guide to international practice. The U.S. Supreme Court has observed that "there are few issues in international law today on which opinion seems so divided as the limitations of a state's power to expropriate the property of aliens."[16]

Since the mid-1970s, the United States and other creditor countries have increasingly employed bilateral investment treaties (BITs) to provide more reassurance for their investing nationals and MNEs. BITs normally require national or MFN treatment for investing interests in the host country and promise fair adjudication and access to arbitration for dispute settlement.[17] BITs sought by the Reagan administration provide "prompt, adequate and effective compensation" equivalent to fair market value immediately before expropriation becomes known, along with commercially reasonable rates of interest. In addition, to prevent creeping expropriation or unduly harsh exchange controls, the Reagan administration wants guarantees for free and open transfers of foreign earnings, returns, and profits in convertible currencies. Such provisions, especially those limiting exchange controls, are felt to be onerous by many developing countries, and relatively few have acceded to the U.S. BITs so far.

European bilateral investment treaties, by contrast, are more ambiguous and less demanding, so they have been accepted by a wider variety of nations. Nonetheless, U.S. government officials insist that strong guarantees are desirable for international law, in order to secure a more reliable, free movement of capital and finance in world markets. And, to the extent that U.S. BITs help change international practice, the position of MNCs and other foreign investors is strengthened.

Exchange controls are widely employed by developing countries, most of whom use such controls to some degree.[18] Characteristic devices are separate exchange rates to encourage exports, to subsidize productive imports, and to discourage low-priority and luxury imports. Tourism often receives favorable rates, although very attractive areas (convenient to many travelers) may set rates that "exploit" tourism. Capital transactions are commonly regulated. The majority of nations also regulate payments for current transactions.

While the IMF tries to discourage exchange controls for current transactions (at least in theory) under Article VIII, and regular IMF surveillance and reporting is maintained on exchange controls, their use remains prevalent in developing countries and among more socialist states.[19] All debt-overload countries have been forced to use exchange controls. The list of countries not using such controls is now fairly short. (Open-exchange countries include the United States, Canada, Britain, the Netherlands, West Germany, Switzerland, Austria, Italy, Saudi Arabia, Kuwait, the United Arab Emirates, Japan, Hong Kong, Singapore, Malaysia, Australia, New Zealand, and a few small and island nations closely interlocked with major trading nation economies.) Obviously, the open-exchange economies are especially suitable as banking or funds-transfer centers and as free-market capital exporters.

International investors, MNCs, and banks involved in other countries try to protect their interests with contractual provisions, choice of law, and arbitration agreements. Within limits, and to the extent that assets are available in creditor nations against which to assert claims or attachment, these remedies may prove effective. But, if a host-country government is willing to risk reduced-access foreign borrowing or investment, remedies under international law can be slow, expensive, and of limited value. Another danger, widespread recently, is an overload of external debts and foreign exchange obligations that simply exceeds a nation's ability to service them in convertible currencies or other liquid reserves. Here, rescheduling of debt service, foreign exchange rationing, and/or other disruptions may be unavoidable (even without any special antagonism against outside investments or MNCs). But as IMF-Paris Club stabilization-rescheduling packages enforce significant fiscal discipline, government spending retrenchment, and economic hardships, the role of foreign investment can become more controversial and lead to tighter restrictions.

Because heavy debt loads are now so common among developing countries, especially for Latin America and Africa (see table 4–1), with exchange control restrictions prevalent, the potential for limiting repatriation of earnings from foreign investments is serious and widespread. This is why MNCs and other multinational investors should try to make good connections with local partners, maintain political influence in host countries, and hope that these relationships will withstand periods of economic and political stress. Extractive industries, export-oriented manufacturing, and local assembly and marketing operations linked to strong MNCs and their technology and international marketing may offer enough to developing nations to ensure reasonable viability. But, it now seems clear that excessive presence and visibility for MNCs (and particular source countries) in host nations is unwise and may attract political opposition and/or restrictive measures.

Finally, the ultimate limitations on foreign investment and MNCs are political.[20] So long as reasonable economic growth and expanding prosperity are maintained, foreign investment opportunities provide a basis for mutually beneficial profit sharing between host countries and international investors. But, when MNCs become too powerful or their host countries fall into economic difficulties or distress, foreign investors should become uneasy. High inflation, serious unemployment, severe inequalities, capital flight, and demoralization provide the best prospects for Marxist-Leninist revolution and other radical changes that can greatly limit the role for international investment and lead to costly expropriations and other losses. This means that foreign MNCs and investors might be wise to take a long-term stake in developing countries, setting limits on their involvement, but also helping these nations to evolve stronger, more durable institutions and sustainable economic expansion. Too often, perhaps, foreign investors have merely looked for quick deals and high profits. This has worked for some in the past, but this is not the best way for many MNCs and international banks, which will be better off to play a steady, solid role in continuing economic development, thereby earning a reasonably secure place for themselves with constructive contributions. There is a growing roster of source countries with large, respectable MNCs and banks to serve this function—including the United States, Japan, West Germany, France, United Kingdom, the Netherlands, Sweden, Switzerland, Italy, and even some NICs, South Korea, and Singapore.

The competition from these many companies and exporting nations affords a growing resiliency to the supply of foreign investment resources and enterprise, provided that host countries allow enough latitude and security of earnings and trading activity for them. But, host countries can be expected to measure the worth and contributions of their resident foreign investment communities and to expect mutuality of benefits. All this means that international investment and trading relationships can and will become more diversified. Somewhat greater competition may be unavoidable, but this should prove beneficial in the end. An era of predominant U.S. industrial, banking, and marketing leadership clearly has closed. Mercantilist subsidies, regulation, and preferences to strengthen national economic development can never be entirely suppressed, whether for LDCs, NICs, or MICs. Thus, nations at every stage of the economic-development ladder must realize that "hands-on" influence from governments is a normal part of the game. MNCs from countries with insufficient government support at home and in world bargaining may encounter difficult challenges from nations with tougher blends of government–industry collaboration.

Notes

1. An expanding literature on multinational business has flourished in recent years. See, for example, Michael E. Porter, ed., *Competition in Global Industries* (Boston: Harvard Business School, 1986); J. Orlin Grabbe, *International Financial Markets* (New York: Elsevier, 1986); United Nations Centre on Transnational Corporations, *Transnational Corporations in World Development,* third survey (New York: United Nations, 1983); Jack N. Behrman, *National Interests and the Multinational Enterprise: Tensions among the North Atlantic Countries* (Englewood Cliffs, N.J.: Prentice-Hall, 1970); John Williamson, *The Open Economy and the World Economy* (New York: Basic, 1983); Charles Kindleberger and David Audretsch, eds., *The Multinational Corporation in the 1980's* (Cambridge, Mass.: MIT Press, 1983); Toyohiro Kono, *Strategy and Structure of Japanese Enterprises* (Armonk, N.Y.: M.E. Sharpe, 1984); Joseph Grunwald and Kenneth Flamm, *The Global Factory: Foreign Assembly in International Trade* (Washington, D.C.: Brookings, 1985); William R. Cline, *Exports of Manufacturers from Developing Countries: Performance and Prospects for Market Access* (Washington, D.C.: Brookings, 1984); Charles Lipson, *Standing Guard: Protecting Foreign Capital in the Nineteenth and Twentieth Centuries* (Berkeley: Univ. of California, 1985); Volcker Bornschier and Christopher Chase-Dunn, *Transnational Corporations and Underdevelopment* (New York: Praeger, 1985); Rhys Jenkins, *Transnational Corporations and Industrial Transformation in Latin America* (New York: St. Martin's, 1984); Jeffrey A. Frieden, David M. Lake, *International Political Economy: Perspectives on Global Power and Wealth* (New York: St. Martin's, 1987); Richard P. Mattione, *OPEC's Investments and the International Financial System* (Washington, D.C.: Brookings, 1985); Louis T. Wells, Jr., *Third World Multinationals: The Rise of Foreign Investment from Developing Countries* (Cambridge, Mass.: MIT Press, 1983); Rajiv Lall, *Multinationals from the Third World* (Oxford, England: Oxford Univ., 1987); Richard J. Herring, *Managing International Risk* (Cambridge, England: Cambridge Univ., 1983); James Kelder, *How to Open a Swiss Bank Account* (New York: Crowell, 1976); Ingo Walter, *Secret Money: The World of International Financial Secrecy* (Lexington, Mass.: Lexington Books, 1985); Howard M. Wachtel, *The Money Mandarins: The Making of a Supranational Economic Order* (New York: Pantheon-Random House, 1986); Jonathan David Aronson and Peter F. Cowhey, *Trade in Services: A Case for Open Markets* (Washington, D.C.: American Enterprise Institute, 1984); Richard Dale, *The Regulation of International Banking* (Cambridge, England: Woodhead-Faulkner, 1984); and Marcia Stigum, *The Money Market, Newly Revised* (Homewood, Ill.: Dow-Jones-Irwin, 1983), with its much

greater emphasis on international finance recently. See also standard international economics texts such as Ethier, Caves and Jones, Lindert and Kindleberger (cited in chapter 1 note 1).

2. See sources cited in chapter 1 note 35.

3. See sources cited in chapter 4 note 7, particularly Davis, Foreman-Peck, Kindleberger, Bogart, Clough and Cole, Galbraith, Cohen, and Bowden, Karpovich, and Usher.

4. For the current military power balance in world affairs, see *The Military Balance, 1985–1986* (London: International Institute of Strategic Studies, 1985). (And see table 3-2.) We should not forget that the Soviet Union exports large quantities of arms to its client states and various revolutionary movements around the world.

5. For the excesses of multinational lending in recent years, see Cohen, Wellons, and Foweraker (cited in chapter 4 note 3) and Lovett (in chapter 4 note 1), pp. 503–7 (notes 11 through 23).

6. This reduction in new lending was a natural, albeit belated response to widespread debt overloads and threatened defaults, especially after the Latin American debt crisis of 1982–83. See Lovett (cited in chapter 4 note 1), pp. 514–16 (notes 37 through 39).

7. A growing diversification of source countries for MNCs, with reduced U.S. dominance (and a more equal role for Japanese, European, and even Third-World MNCs) will help ease antagonisms in many host countries. See, for example, sources cited in note 1, including Porter, Kono, Grunwald and Flamm, Lipson, Mattione, Wells, and Lall. Also, growing foreign investments in the United States (see tables 5–1 and 5–2) will ease tensions over unbalanced investment flows and excessive dependency, at least among NICs and LDCs that clearly share in the expanding global investment network (and benefit from it).

8. Prosperity is never secure without effective military security and/or an absence of dangerous foreign powers. Political cohesion for healthy economies must be founded upon a reasonably broad sharing in prosperity (without extensive deprivation or injustice).

9. See chapter 4, especially tables 4–1 and 4–3.

10. A crucial catalyst in most countries plagued by debt overload and capital flight is significant new multilateral loans, which provide an essential keystone function in restoring bridges of renewed domestic and foreign capital investment flow. More liberal rescheduling and gradually reduced interest rates are important, too. But, in the more seriously overloaded countries, domestic and foreign confidence must be restored before significant private capital flows and economic growth can be revived. Multinational banks and MNCs will not invest significant new lending and direct investment resources without some reassurance. And, the domestic capital that has moved abroad can only be coaxed back gradually.

Ultimately, private international banks will help to mobilize greater multilateral (IMF, World Bank, and regional development bank) lending, because of increased debtor-country resistance to significant net capital flows for debt servicing that cripples any revival in their economic growth. See sources cited in chapter 4 note 9 (especially from Latin America), along with Irving Friedman and Benjamin Cohen (cited in chapter 4 note 7). See also Lovett (cited in note 1), pp. 522–24 (notes 52 through 57).

11. This author recalls vividly a charming, rather demogogic, but effective speech by former Prime Minister Michael Manley of Jamaica (a notable left-oriented socialist), before a Union of Radical Political Economy (URPE) American neo-Marxist session in

New York at the December 1985 meetings of the Allied Social Sciences Association. Manley likened the multinational banks to drug pushers, who force excessive and addictive overloads of debt onto the borrower countries in the Third World. But, the final joke is on these greedy international banks, he argued, because the debtor countries owe so much they cannot really pay. Manley's solution is general debtor default and repudiation to provoke worldwide financial crisis, so that widespread "structural revolution" can come more easily. Fidel Castro has been preaching this line for debtor countries, too, although Cuba has been careful to keep servicing its own *postrevolutionary* financial obligations. (This reflects an amusing double standard—repudiation for moderate countries to spoil any healthy capitalist recovery, but more prudent debt management for the Marxist faithful.)

12. Certainly, the risk of worldwide inflation (as in the 1970s) must be borne in mind. There should be reasonable limits to renewed international liquidity creation. But, widespread slump in economic growth produced an extended surplus in many commodity markets. For some time, at least, renewed world liquidity expansion seems reasonably safe (provided that most countries can reduce excessive budget deficits and domestic monetary expansion).

13. The lesson of the 1970s inflation is that domestic fiscal, monetary, and wage-price discipline must be maintained in countries wanting to keep inflation low. For an extensive review of that experience and literature, see William A. Lovett, *Inflation and Politics: Fiscal, Monetary, and Wage-Price Discipline* (Lexington, Mass.: Lexington Books, 1982). See also, sources cited in chapter 1 note 6, particularly those dealing with recent stabilization efforts in Argentina, Bolivia, Brazil, and Israel.

14. See, for example, sources cited chapter 2 notes 5 through 8, chapter 5 note 1 (particularly Kono, Lall, and Wells), and preface note 1 (Hofheinz and Calder).

15. This summary of established international law and custom is based upon *The Restatement of the Law, Foreign Relations Law of the United States (Revised)*, tentative final draft (July 15, 1985), vol. 3, parts V–IX (Philadelphia: American Law Institute, 1985), esp. pp. 1108–58.

16. *Banco de Cuba* v. *Sabbatino*, 376 U.S. 398, 428 (1964).

17. For a convenient summary of recent BIT developments, see Pamela B. Gann, "The U.S. Bilateral Investment Treaty Program," *Stanford Journal of International Law* 21, no. 2 (Fall 1985), pp. 373–460. In addition, see Charles Lipson, *Standing Guard: Protecting Foreign Capital in the Nineteenth and Twentieth Centuries* (Berkeley: Univ. of California, 1985).

18. See *Annual Report on Exchange Restrictions, 1986* (Washington, D.C.: IMF, 1986), "Summary Features Exchange and Trade Systems in Member Countries."

19. Under the Articles of Agreement of the IMF, second amendment, April 30, 1976, especially Articles IV, VI, VIII, and XIV, member states must report and furnish information on exchange rate policies to allow surveillance and appropriate consultations. All members may regulate international capital flows, but those accepting Article VIII discipline are not supposed to regulate exchange for current transactions without IMF supervision and approval. And yet, fully two-thirds of the sixty-two Article VIII countries (including Argentina, Bolivia, El Salvador, Jamaica, Mexico, Nicaragua, Peru, South Africa, and Venezuela) use some kind of capital or current-transactions controls. Meanwhile, nearly one hundred countries still reserve general exchange-control authority for themselves under Article XIV. Hence, the great majority of nations, in fact, still use exchange controls to some degree.

20. The most sophisticated MNCs and international banks fully understand that they must accommodate to many political environments to sustain their operations. Accordingly, they develop multinational staffs, legal counsel, and lobbying networks, and they try to maintain influential friends in high places wherever possible. Meanwhile, host countries and home-base–headquarters nations attempt to supervise, regulate, and tax these enterprises in a sensible way. See, for example, George W. Ball, "CosmoCorp: The Importance of Being Stateless," in Friedmen and Lake, cited in note 1.

6
U.S. Economic Renewal and International Responsibility

T hree major efforts are needed to rejuvenate U.S. industry and export competitiveness and to promote a healthy, balanced economic recovery for international trade and finance. First, the United States must restore fiscal discipline, greatly reduce government deficits, and strengthen incentives for savings and productive investment throughout its economy. Wasteful practices and weakened accountability grew with affluence and became entrenched with excessive pluralism and splinter-group politics. Government is fatter (from civilian programs through defense contracting), but often feeble, timid, or entangled in litigation and red tape. Business enterprises and corporations need greater vitality, along with broadly shared incentives. High living standards can only be maintained in a world of industrial rivalry and technological progress by tougher education standards, creative work efforts, and skillful collaboration between government and industry to keep up with the strongest foreign competition.

Second, the United States must restore international trading equity, eliminate large trade and current account deficits, and implement a more comprehensive, productivity-oriented trade and industrial development policy. U.S. trading partners increasingly realize that heavy trade surpluses with the United States are unsustainable. The United States cannot rely indefinitely upon capital flight, investment inflows, and sale of existing business assets and real estate properties. While the United States should seek more trade openness abroad for the long run, it is unrealistic to expect significant changes soon in foreign subsidies, trade restrictions, and support for their major industries (and skilled employees). This means that the United States must strengthen unfair trade practice law enforcement, employ more extensive safeguarding for key industries, and fashion reasonable offsets to foreign mercantilism. It must maintain technological excellence and some skilled production capacity in most important sectors of the economy to sustain viability for the long haul. The United States should emulate its toughest international competitors and develop better collaboration between government and industries. An overriding theme should be creating industrial vitality and accepting the realities and challenge of world market competition in an era of increasing potential for innovation.

Third, the world financial system needs multilateral strengthening, greater supervision, and more realistic exchange rates. Capital and borrowing authority must be increased for the IMF, World Bank, and regional development banks, allowing these multilateral institutions to sustain the rescheduling-stabilization process. Private international banks must offer new loans, under Paris Club-IMF auspices, to continue rescheduling momentum and to secure older loan investments in debt-overload countries. As more countries benefit from financing and stabilization discipline, their domestic and foreign investment can be revived. But, excessive exchange rate fluctuation, especially for the dollar (the key reserve currency) in recent years, brought disruption to U.S. industry and exports as well as strain for the world economy. Clearly, large U.S. budget deficits and high interest rates between 1983 and 1986 were partly to blame. But, a further problem has been widespread currency intervention (or multiple exchange rates) by many countries to stimulate exports. Greater economic-policy coordination and fiscal discipline is needed for realistic exchange rate policies and increased stability. U.S. monetary authorities also should be tougher and act independently to offset and counter foreign exchange manipulation that may adversely affect U.S. interests, exports, and prosperity.

While the United States should defend firmly its interests and industries in world trade and finance, we must appreciate the lessons of increased interdependence since World War II. Beggar-thy-neighbor policies, heavy protectionism, and a return to economic isolation would be mutually damaging for the Free World and most developing countries. But OECD financial and industrial leaders generally understand these realities. No real prospect exists for any drastic retrogression. The relevant range for adjusted relations is far narrower, compromising mainly some latitude for the United States, Japan, Western Europe, Canada, Australia, and New Zealand to achieve better "trade equity"—more closely similar industrial and trade development policies. (Compare figure P–1 and figure 6–1.) Because Japan and Europe cannot achieve complete openness and they will not abandon efforts to promote exports, improve technology, or safeguard vital industries (including agriculture), the United States should do the same. Greater protection, subsidy, and mercantilism will continue in the majority of NICs and LDCs. And yet, the United States could press the most successful NICs, (such as Taiwan, South Korea, and Brazil), into more openness, especially when they enjoy large trade surpluses vis-à-vis the United States. Limited further opening might occur also in some strongly socialist and communist nations, but major changes are not likely to come quickly in Marxist countries.

Fiscal Discipline and More Productive Investments

A top priority for U.S. policy is to reduce excessive budget deficits. While tax cuts in the early 1980s were popular and even desirable to some extent (offsetting

Communist and heavily socialist countries
Largely state-controlled economies—modest openness, tightly regulated access, substantial borrowing, and technology imports. Subsidized exports to earn foreign exchange.

Newly industrialized and less developed countries
Growing openness substantially protected with considerable subsidy and mercantile regulation to encourage new industries, expand exports, and limit competing manufacturers. Technology transfer encouraged, but carefully regulated foreign investment.

Japan
Somewhat more open markets—limited subsidies and export-oriented financing. Strong tradition of government–industry collaboration, administrative guidance, and national strategy for export manufacturing and imports of raw materials. Growing capital exports and skillful blend of new plants abroad, both for low-wage components and assembly in export markets.

European Economic Community and European Free Trade Area
Substantially open markets, but protected agriculture, considerable subsidies for manufacturing, and considerable use of voluntary restraint agreements to limit excessive imports and industrial job losses. Moderate capital exports, with diversified overseas investment.

United States
Substantially open markets, but more extensive safeguarding. Occasional protection and limited subsidies, with moderate rejuvenation tariffs and offsets to foreign mercantilism. Greatly reduced trade deficits, with much less deindustrialization. Capital exports gradually restored, partly through continued capital inflows from abroad. Overseas investment becoming more diversified.

Figure 6–1. Improved Trade Equity for the World Economy (Realistic Prospects)

accumulated "bracket creep"), the Reagan administration and Congress found it difficult to achieve comparable spending reductions. (See Tables 6–1, 6–2, and 6–3.) This led to unusually large federal deficits, averaging about $200 billion for 1983–1987, or roughly 5 percent of GNP each year. These are the largest sustained peacetime budget deficits in U.S. history. Consequently, the national debt doubled from $1,000 billion to more than $2,000 billion between 1980 and 1987. Annual service charges on federal debt increased from $79 to $139 billion. If the United States continued excessive deficits of this magnitude, debt-service "waste" would grow, and greater economic problems are almost inevitable. Some combination of increased inflation pressure, more monetary restraint, higher interest rates, reduced competitiveness for domestic industry, and/or weaker economic performance would be hard to avoid.[1]

The consensus among financial, banking, and economic experts in the United States and elsewhere is that U.S. political leaders must get their house in order, close ranks somehow, and end fiscal looseness. The Gramm-Rudman Act of 1985 reflected this realization, although its timetable for gradual reduction in deficits was rather slow.[2] Recent U.S. fiscal irresponsibility stems from too much partisanship. Both conservatives and liberals had unrealistic hopes for retrenchment on their own special terms and tried to maneuver each other into taking responsibility for politically painful proposals.

In the early 1980s, the Reagan administration insisted upon substantial defense-spending increases, which many moderates (both Democrats and Republicans) supported. But conservatives wanted considerable retrenchment in civilian outlays, too. Accordingly, supply-side tax cuts in the early 1980s were proposed, not merely as economic stimulus (which some conservatives knew was overstated), but as fiscal discipline to force reductions in the size of "welfare-state" activities. Democratic leaders in the House of Representatives quickly realized that the Reagan tax cuts would lead to large deficits, unless substantial civilian and social security cuts followed promptly. Yet, they understood that political support for widespread retrenchment was weak, and they hoped Reagan and the Republicans could be defeated as a result. Democrats figured that either Reagan deficits would refuel inflation or the administration would have to raise taxes. By Fall 1981, both conservatives and liberals were feeling good about their respective prospects.

Moderates worried, however, and their ranks included Paul Volcker, head of the Federal Reserve. Seeing increased budget deficits between 1981and 1985, the Fed kept monetary reins tight as an offset to fiscal looseness, in order that anti-inflation discipline could be sustained.[3] Higher real interest rates resulted, and for a long period, 1981–1985 altogether. This led to a bigger, worldwide recession than anyone really wanted. But, deflation proved more successful in greatly reducing inflation than many anticipated. While developing-country debt-overload problems were aggravated, the Federal Reserve's toughness under Volcker rescued Reaganomics. Although the recession of 1982–1983 was severe for the United States, with unemployment peaking at 12 percent, public acceptance followed. U.S. inflation was reduced from 12 to 13 percent down to 3 to 4 percent, and a solid economic recovery ensued during 1983–1984 (from the trough of recession).

While Democrats won substantial gains in November 1982, elections to the House of Representatives, the "Reagan" economic recovery (with greatly reduced inflation) proved hard to beat in November 1984. Walter Mondale, the Democratic presidential candidate, made things worse for himself by volunteering to raise taxes. President Reagan replied that the last thing he wanted was to increase taxes (a popular line with voters). A landslide victory followed for Reagan and Bush over Mondale and Ferraro, though little realignment occurred in Congress.

During 1985, the principal fiscal development was the Gramm-Rudman Act, a Congressional compromise to gradually reduce excess federal budget deficits over five years. This enactment supposedly forced "automatic" across-the-board spending cuts (with major exclusions for social security and a few other areas) in both defense and civilian spending if Congress did not meet the schedule of deficit reductions. Reagan, the Federal Reserve, and most financial commentators endorsed Gramm-Rudman (although many felt its deficit reduction was too slow). But, the Supreme Court held unconstitutional a crucial element of Gramm-Rudman—the delegation of setting budget-reduction amounts to the General Accounting Office. This led to uncertainty about further implementation, as Congress was not willing to accept the Reagan administration Office of Management and Budget (OMB) calculations as the basis for automatic percentage spending cuts. Congress would have to make these specific calculations itself. During 1986, Congress tried to comply with Gramm-Rudman's scheduled reductions—and did so, at least technically (with some controversy over sales of government assets and other gimmicks used in part to achieve the targeted deficit reductions).[4]

Meanwhile, another important development was the greatly enlarging U.S. trade deficit, from $123 billion in 1984 to $148 billion in 1985, and $170 billion in 1986. Another effect of U.S. monetary policy (and higher interest rates in the United States than in Japan, West Germany, or Switzerland) between 1983 and 1985 was a substantially overvalued dollar which, together with U.S. recovery, greatly enlarged foreign imports into the United States from $270 to $387 billion from 1983 to 1986, while U.S. exports were held back as they became more expensive. The dollar did not begin falling toward more realistic levels until Summer and Fall 1985, although during 1986, more substantial correction occurred.

Foreign investment into the dollar and the United States grew substantially during 1982–1986. This reflected flight capital from developing nations, diversification investments from Europe, and Japan's need to invest export surpluses. Comparatively high U.S. interest rates were an important incentive for

Table 6–1
U.S. GNP, Government Deficits, Inflation, and Unemployment, 1929–86
(in current $ billions)

	GNP	Government Deficits [a]	Inflation [b]	Unemployment Rate
1929	$103.4	$ 1.0	—	3.2%
1933	55.8	− 1.4	− 24.4% [d]	24.9
1939	90.8	− 2.2	7.2	17.2
1940	100.0	− 0.7	1.0	14.6
1941	124.9	− 3.8	5.0	9.9
1942	158.3	− 31.4	10.7	4.7
1943	192.0	− 44.1	6.1	1.9
1944	210.5	− 51.8	1.7	1.2
1945	212.3	− 39.5	2.3	1.9
1946	209.6	5.4	8.5	3.9
1947	232.8	14.4	14.4	3.9
1948	259.1	8.4	7.8	3.8
1949	258.0	− 3.4	− 1.0	5.9
1950	286.2	8.0	1.0	5.3
1951	330.2	6.1	7.9	3.3
1952	347.2	− 3.8	2.2	3.0
1953	366.1	− 6.9	0.8	2.9
1954	366.3	− 7.1	0.5	5.5
1955	399.3	3.1	− 0.4	4.4
1956	420.7	5.2	1.5	4.1
1957	442.8	0.9	3.6	4.3
1958	448.9	− 12.6	2.7	6.8
1959	486.5	− 1.6	0.8	5.5
1960	506.0	3.1	1.6	5.5
1961	524.6	− 4.3	1.0	6.7
1962	565.0	− 3.8	1.1	5.5
1963	596.7	0.7	1.2	5.7
1964	637.7	− 2.3	1.3	5.2
1965	691.1	0.5	1.7	4.5
1966	756.0	− 1.3	2.9	3.8
1967	788.6	− 14.2	2.9	3.8
1968	873.4	− 6.0	4.2	3.6
1969	944.0	9.9	5.4	3.5
1970	992.7	− 10.6	5.9	4.9
1971	1,077.6	− 19.4	4.3	5.9
1972	1,185.9	− 3.3	3.3	5.6
1973	1,326.4	7.8	6.2	4.9
1974	1,434.2	− 4.7	11.0	5.6
1975	1,549.2	− 63.8	9.1	8.5
1976	1,718.0	− 36.5	5.8	7.7
1977	1,918.0	− 18.3	6.5	7.0
1978	2,156.1	− 0.2	7.7	6.0
1979	2,413.9	11.9	11.3	5.8
1980	2,627.4	34.5	13.5	7.0
1981	3,052.6	− 29.7	10.4	7.5
1982	3,166.0	− 110.8	6.1	9.5
1983	3,401.6	− 130.8	3.2	9.5
1984	3,774.7	− 108.5	4.3	7.4

Table 6–1 continued

	GNP	Government Deficits [a]	Inflation [b]	Unemployment Rate
1985	3,998.1	– 136.4	3.6	7.1
1986 [c]	4,234.3	– 156.9	1.7	7.0

Source: *Economic Report of the President* (Feb. 1986). *Historical Statistics of the U.S. and Colonial Times to 1970* appendix tables. U.S. Department of Commerce, *Survey of Current Business,* national income and product account tables (Dec. 1986), tables I–1, I3.2, I3.3.

Note: Federal deficits since 1981 were as follows: $78.9b. in 1981, $127.9b. in 1982, $207.8b. in 1983, $185.3b. in 1984, $211.9b. in 1985, and $220.7b. (estimated) in 1986. Fiscal year basis in 1985 and 1986 deficit are based on Treasury Department, "Final Monthly Treasury Statement of Receipts and Outlays of the United States Government," Sept. 30, 1986, table 1.

[a] Consists of federal, state, and local government deficits. Lack of a minus sign indicates a surplus.

[b] Based on percent change in Consumer Price Index during year.

[c] Estimates.

[d] Decline in Consumer Price Index from 1929 to 1933.

some investment, but a desire for the security and growth prospects of the United States was significant, too. By 1984–86, net foreign investment into the United States was running over $100 billion annually. The United States became a net debtor nation during 1985. This means 2½ to 3 percent of the U.S. GNP could be traced directly to foreign capital inflows. This propped up the dollar and U.S. prosperity, while helping to offset heavy U.S. budget, trade, and current account deficits. Few believed, however, that such large foreign investment flows could be relied upon indefinitely to bail out fiscal looseness by the U.S. government.[5]

Somehow the United States should restore normal and prudent fiscal discipline and bring government deficits down to levels compatible with reasonable low-inflation growth potential. A sensible guideline (based upon post–World War II experience) would be:

1. *During full employment with modest excess capacity:* government deficits limited to 0 to 1 percent of GNP,

2. *During substantial recession with considerable excess capacity:* government deficits no larger than 3 to 4 percent,

3. *During limited growth with considerable slack and unemployment:* government deficits limited to 1 to 2 percent.

This guideline policy would not enlarge public debt as a share of GNP (over the long run) and would stimulate reasonable growth without significant inflation pressure.[6] Reasonable monetary policy should be combined with this fiscal guideline. This means "relative ease" with recession, "relative tightness" in boom periods and incipient inflation, and "normal" interest rates otherwise, with a positive real return to 1 to 3 percent (over inflation) for demand, short-term, and medium-term deposits, respectively. Such a fiscal-monetary regime

Table 6–2
U.S. Federal Spending, Revenues, Deficits, Debt, and GNP, 1913–86
(*in $ billions; fiscal year*)

	Spending	Revenues	Deficits	Debt	GNP	Debt/GNP
1913	0.7	0.7	—	1.2	39.6	3.0%
1929	2.6	3.8	1.2	16.9	103.4	16.3
1933	4.0	2.7	− 1.3	22.5	55.8	40.3
1940	9.5	6.5	− 2.9	50.7	100.0	50.7
1944	95.5	41.0	− 54.5	201.0	210.5	95.5
1945	92.7	45.2	− 47.6	260.1	212.3	122.5
1946	55.5	38.4	− 17.1	269.4	209.6	128.5
1952	66.0	65.1	0.9	259.1	347.2	74.6
1960	92.2	92.5	0.3	290.9	506.0	57.5
1968	178.1	153.0	− 25.2	369.8	873.4	42.3
1974	263.2	269.4	− 6.1	486.2	1,434.2	33.9
1980	590.9	517.1	− 73.8	914.3	2,627.4	34.8
1981	678.2	599.3	− 78.9	1,003.9	3,052.6	32.9
1982	745.7	617.8	− 127.9	1,147.0	3,166.0	36.2
1983	600.6	808.3	− 207.8	1,381.9	3,401.6	40.6
1984	851.8	666.5	− 185.3	1,576.7	3,774.7	41.8
1985	946.0	734.1	− 211.9	1,827.5	3,998.1	45.7
1986	989.8	769.1	− 220.7	2,139.0	4,234.3	50.5

Source: *Statistical Abstract of the United States,* 1946, 1986 (Washington, D.C.: U.S. Bureau of the Census). *Economic Report of the President, Feb.* 1986. *Treasury Department, Monthly Statements of the Public Debt of the United States* (monthly). Treasury Department, *Final Monthly Treasury Statement of Receipts and Outlays of the United States Government for Fiscal Year 1986, through September 30, 1986 and other periods. Historical Statistics, Colonial Times to 1970,* (Washington, D.C.: U.S. Bureau of the Census, 1977).

would yield fairly steady growth in the monetary aggregates over the medium and long run, while facilitating business growth planning.

As labor markets reach full employment and excess capacity is eliminated, noninflationary guidelines for wage settlements and large corporate price increases may be desirable.[7] Guidelines were useful in some concentrated industries (without enough domestic or foreign competition) in the 1950s through the 1970s. With recent slack and higher average unemployment, greatly weakened unions, and more foreign competition (aided by the high dollar), wage-cost pressures abated in the 1980s. Inflation momentum has not been entirely eliminated, though, and it survives in sectors insulated from competitive rivalry. But for a few years, it seems the inflation spiral has been greatly reduced. This is a good opportunity to consolidate major progress against the worldwide inflation trend from the 1970s and to restore fiscal responsibility with limited monetary growth.

Ideally, the United States should reduce current budget deficits from 5 percent of GNP to 2 to 3 percent (in other words, from $220 to $100 billion) rather quickly and bring them down further as economic growth, employment, and capacity utilization improve.[8] Several approaches make sense: (1) proportionate spending cuts, say $50 to 75 billion, combined with across-the-board tax increases of $40 to 60 billion, (2) proportionate spending cuts of $50 to

Table 6–3
Growth in U.S. Federal, State, and Local Government
Spending and Debt Loads, 1913–86
(in $ billions)

	GNP	Total Government Spending	Federal Debt Service	Federal Debt	State and Local Government Spending	State and Local Debt Service	State and Local Government Debt
1913	39.6	2.5	.02	1.2	1.6	.17	4.4
1929	103.8	12.3	.66	16.9	7.4	.66 (1927)	14.8 (1927)
1939	91.3	18.6	1.04	40.4	9.9 (1938)	.78 (1938)	19.4 (1938)
1940	100.0	20.4	1.10	50.7	11.2	.79	20.2
1946	208.5	79.7	5.35	269.4	14.0	.56	15.9
1949	256.5	59.8	5.60	252.7	19.7	.54 (1948)	24.0
1960	503.7	137.5	9.31	290.9	53.0	2.02	70.0
1969	930.3	316.6	17.09	367.1	113.0	4.40	133.5
1974	1,295.0	494.4	31.30	486.0	226.0	8.84	206.0
1977	1,918.3	644.2	46.40	709.1	323.0	14.04	259.0
1980	2,631.7	959.0	78.9	914.3	432.0	17.60	326.0
1986	4,234.3 [a]	1581.1	138.2	2,214.8	565.1	43.06 [a]	695.0 [a]
	(Oct. 1986)	(1986 FY)			(1986 III)	(1985 FY)	

Source: U.S. Department of Commerce, U.S. Census Bureau, Historical Statistics of the U.S., 1789–1945, and Colonial Times to 1970 (Bicentennial ed.). Statistical Abstract of the U.S., 1916, 1931, 1953, 1976, 1980, 1984, 1986. Federal Budget, 1931, 1941, 1951, 1962, 1971, 1977. Economic Report of the President (January 1976, February 1986). Economic Indicators, prepared for the Joint Economic Committee by the Council of Economic Advisors (October, 1986). U.S. Department of Commerce, Bureau of the Census, Governmental Finance in 1984–85, (Dec. 1986) tables 1 and 25. Survey of Current Business, (Dec. 1986), table 3.3. Prospects for Financial Markets 1987 (New York. Salomon Bros., Dec. 16, 1986).
[a]Estimate.

75 billion, combined with VAT waiver correctives and 10 percent revenue tariffs, or (3) a 10 to 15 percent federal VAT (coordinated with state and local sales taxes) to generate $100 to 125 billion in new revenues. Each approach requires collaboration between the Reagan administration and Congress. Unbalanced spending cuts are probably unrealistic in this political environment, but a blend of items (1) and (2) might be achievable during 1987–88. Hopefully, the 1988 elections will bring a more cohesive presidential and Congressional combination into office, even if the opportunity for major deficit reduction is not achieved between 1987 and 1988. Reducing excessive deficits would help improve national productivity by reducing waste and needless debt-service charges. The route selected should be consistent with an "optimal" tax and expenditure load. Options (1) and (2) involve federal spending cuts of 5 to 7 percent, while option (3) involves no spending sacrifice. One way or another, these measures should harmonize with improved trade equity and a stronger U.S. industrial policy.

Other general steps to improve U.S. national productivity include the following: (1) tax reform that encourages greater saving and more productive investment, while eliminating unjustified giveaways or subsidies, (2) reducing excessive corporate merger and takeover activity associated with undue debt

loads, eroded competitive vitality, and weakened long-run enterprise performance, (3) improving financial institution regulation to strengthen capitalization, supervision, and prudence in lending, (4) increasing use of profit-sharing
and employee stock ownership plans to foster more teamwork and partnership enterprise, and (5) increasing efforts for high-quality technical education
and boosting R&D for process efficiency, new products, and innovation. Some
progress has occurred along these lines recently, but more can and should be
effected. Yet, all this will take considerable time and political evolution; dramatic
results cannot be expected in these channels quickly. The long-term payoff can
be quite handsome, but (like most economic growth efforts) the larger yields
come with increased momentum and continuity.

Tax Reform

As public revenues take a growing share of GNP for various public services,
social security, national defense, and administration, the problem of allocating
the tax burden becomes more serious. Overall tax loads should be somewhat
progressive and be related reasonably to income and wealth differentials. But
when about one-third of the GNP is spent through the public sector, the majority of revenue must come from general taxation (taxation not only against
the wealthy). If the top tenth earns 30 to 35 percent of GNP, no more than
a third of public revenue can really come from this class. At least the remaining two-thirds (or more) of revenue must be levied against the great majority.
Accordingly, most modern industrial societies (with large public sectors and
social security programs) employ a medley of income, payroll, corporate,
property, sales, VAT, and excise taxes, plus user fees to generate revenues. As
public revenues grow as a share of GNP (and as middle class income levels
have increased in many countries), there has been a tendency to reduce progressivity by increasing reliance upon consumption, payroll, and user fees and
limiting the burdens of progressive income, capital, and property taxes. The
need to sustain savings and investment and to promote economic growth is
operative in free-enterprise societies, and the middle class wants some latitude
for wealth accumulation, too. (Only in heavily socialist and Marxist countries
is this constraint relaxed. There the state performs most or all of the capital
formation, saving, and investment functions through government enterprise
and finance.) Typical devices to encourage private savings and investment include lower rates for capital gains, investment credits, depreciation and depletion allowances, liberal deductions for business expenses, and deferral of income and capital gains recognition, along with special tax exemptions by local,
state, and federal governments.

Inevitably, modern high-tax systems are forced into complexities. Spe-
cial-interest lobbying proliferates. Supervision and enforcement become difficult.
The U.S. tax load increased dramatically during the 1930s and World War II,

and as a share of GNP, it remained substantially higher than before.[9] (See table 6–2.) Taxes increased gradually from 25 to 31 percent of GNP during the 1950s and 1960s, with income tax bracket creep plus increased payroll, sales, and property taxes (taking into account all levels of government). But corporate taxes receded in importance.[10] (See table 6–4.) Business became more experienced in tax avoidance, and tax preferences for some types of saving, investment, and sheltering became significant. Unfortunately, anomalies and divergent tax incidence grew also. U.S. industry and business were forced into

Table 6–4
U.S. Federal, State, and Local Taxes and Other Revenues by Major Sources, 1982

Major Source	Revenues[a] (billions)	Percentage of Total Revenue
Federal government		
Individual income tax	$296.7	50.4
Corporation income tax[b]	31.3	5.3
Excise tax	32.4	5.5
Estate and gift taxes	7.6	1.3
Payroll tax	204.5	34.7
Other	16.2	2.8
Total	912.6	100.0
State and local governments		
Individual income tax	$51.8	16.0
Corporation income tax[b]	12.7	3.9
Sales tax	95.5	29.5
Estate and gift taxes	2.6	0.8
Payroll tax	4.0	1.2
Property tax	86.5	26.7
Other	71.0	21.9
Total	324.1	100.0
All levels		
Individual income tax	348.5	38.2
Corporation income tax[b]	43.8	4.8
Sales and excise taxes	127.9	14.0
Estate and gift taxes	10.2	1.1
Payroll tax	208.4	22.8
Property tax	86.5	9.5
Other	87.3	9.6
Total	912.6	100.0

Source: *Survey of Current Business* 63 (July 1983), tables 3.2, 3.3, 3.4, 3.6. *Economic Report of the President* (Feb. 1982), table B–83. Reproduced from Albert Ando, Marshall E. Blume, Irwin Friend, *The Structure and Reform of the U.S. Tax System* (Cambridge, Mass.: MIT Press, 1985). With permission © 1985, Massachusetts Institute of Technology.

[a]Revenues are defined as receipts in the national income accounts less contributions for social insurance other than payroll taxes. Federal grants-in-aid are not included in state and local receipts.
[b]Federal Reserve profits are deducted from corporate income tax receipts at the federal and local levels.

sophisticated tax planning for all investment and major enterprise decision making. In effect, corporate and business tax law became a powerful de facto industrial policy. But unlike the coherent industrial and trade expansion policies of Japan (and some other nations), U.S. tax policy was far less cohesive and more a jumble of regional, industrial, and interest-group infighting and log-rolling politics. Public confidence in the fairness of taxes declined, and underreporting of taxable income increased.

President Carter called the U.S. tax system a disgrace, but only modest reforms came in his administration. In President Reagan's agenda, income tax reduction received top priority in 1981–83; he sought further reform and lowering of higher individual income tax rates in 1985–86. After much controversy and uncertainty, Congress and the Reagan administration enacted a Tax Reform Act in October 1986.[11] Maximum individual rates were reduced to 33 percent for upper-middle incomes, and to 28 percent for higher incomes, but capital gains rates were raised from 20 percent to 28 percent. Personal exemptions were increased; lower-income families were given modest relief. Because substantial individual income tax cuts were granted, increases in corporate and business taxes were required as well. Chief benefits claimed for these reforms in 1986 were somewhat greater uniformity in tax rates for different kinds of investments; reduced tax sheltering, loopholes, and distortion of investments; and enhanced incentive for higher-income recipients. On the other hand, some complained about short-term disruption for many business investments, less incentive for capital equipment and building outlays, and insufficient response to foreign tax laws and industrial policies in other countries. Other complaints concerned insufficient progressivity and an explicit hump of higher marginal rates for upper-middle–class incomes. Some feared net revenue losses and aggravated budget deficits, though it would take several years before the full revenue implications of these changes were known.

Whether the 1986 reforms will have lasting impact remains unclear, but in any event, budget-deficit reduction is now a major priority for Congress. Some blend or proportionate spending cuts with sensible revenue enhancement will be needed. Taxes can be increased proportionately or concentrated upon consumption (through foreign VAT waiver correctives, general revenue tariffs, safeguard tariffs for vital industries, or a federal value-added tax). But, it seems doubtful that major new taxes could be imposed against business, and middle class resistance against any higher income tax loads will be strong. In this respect, the Reagan "tax revolt era" could have some permanence and enjoy wide support in a younger generation which wants to accumulate capital for good housing, educating children, and supplementary retirement income.

While somewhat higher income tax rates for the truly wealthy probably would be sought by a subsequent Democratic administration, for reasons of equity, capital gains rates cannot be increased very heavily without sacrificing some saving and investment incentives. (Substantially higher income tax rates with significantly lower capital gains rates could bring back business pressures to expand loopholes and tax shelters as well as repeat the post–World War II evolution in U.S. tax policy. Even a moderate increase in very-high–income tax rates—say, to 35 percent—which could be justified on equity grounds would provide incentives again to take income in the form of capital gains if capital gains rates remained at 28 percent. Whether a return to mild progressivity would do much damage to savings and investment is more doubtful.[12] In fact, many would argue that lower rates for capital gains investment may be healthy in fostering long-term industrial and property development incentives.) In any event, a likely prospect for change in a subsequent Democratic administration would be to eliminate the 33 percent hump in the upper-middle income rate structure. This hump anomaly is clearly objectionable on equity grounds, but its removal (by reducing these marginal rates to 28 percent) would entail some revenue loss. Coupling these two equity-related corrective changes should be revenue-neutral. These moderate further changes would not substantially alter the 1986 Tax Reform Act and its effort toward simplification, lower rates, and more incentives for savings and investment.[13]

Merger and Takeover Limits

Larger mergers and extensive corporate takeovers can lead to weakened competition, dangerously increased private indebtedness, and reduced enterprise vitality. Cutting back on the "antisocial" excesses will improve business productivity. While many mergers may be helpful to business efficiency, enhance management quality or success, and facilitate business economies or retrenchment, other mergers and takeovers can be costly to society. Mergers and takeovers that should be prevented, corrected, or undone include: (1) mergers that may substantially threaten competition, (2) takeovers that result in corporate looting, waste, depletion of pension funds, and/or serious weakening of enterprises, and (3) mergers and takeovers that lead to undue dependence on foreign suppliers and weaken domestic industry, technological vitality, and growth potential.

Extensive merger activity swept the U.S. economy between 1887 and 1903, in the 1920s, and during the 1950s through the 1980s. Some anticompetitive and financial excesses clearly occurred in the first two merger movements, but Theodore Roosevelt's early antitrust enforcement and then the Great Depression brought them to a halt. More recently, however, antitrust enforcement under Section 7 of the Clayton Act (originally enacted in 1914 and amended in 1950), together with reasonable vigilance by the SEC and banking regulators in policing securities markets, had kept these problems within reasonable limits. But, a major relaxation of antitrust and regulatory supervision came in the 1980s under the Reagan administration. Because antitrust authorities have brought hardly any Section 7 complaints lately, the only serious defenses to mergers and hostile takeovers in recent years have been developed by the resisting managements of target companies.[14]

A whole new lexicon and kit bag of ploys now enrich business literature. Shark repellent, supermajority, white knight, lock-up, selling crown jewels, fat man, scorched earth, kamikaze, blank check, poison pill, countertender, and pac-man defenses found popularity (often in combination). While these tactics worked well enough in many situations, they often aggravated corporate weakness. Merger mania and defensive-mindedness enhanced widespread tendencies toward short-run profit performance in U.S. industry, increased debt loads, and the neglect of long-run innovation and growth. Fast-buck artists, corporate raiders, and manipulators became fashionable, even heroes. Many respectable investment banks and major commercial banks found it profitable to participate in speculative merger and takeover mania. Junk bonds became state-of-the-art in corporate finance. Debt loads enlarged substantially in many industries, and many corporations leveraged up. More of the U.S. economy became financially strained—not to mention vulnerable to cyclical slump, reduction of export sales, or increased foreign competition—with increased commitments to service debt obligations. Business failures, organizational instability, and reduced reliability for long-term teamwork became more common. Excessive freedom and fashionability for corporate mergers and takeovers were part of a weakening in U.S. industry. All this occurred when U.S. business should have been more concerned with the need to strengthen engineering quality, international competitiveness, and export growth in world markets.[15]

The best ways to eliminate anticompetitive mergers and excessive corporate takeover activity are through restored antitrust enforcement, improved banking and financial regulation, and stronger remedies in corporate law. Section 7 of the Clayton Act provides ample authority and tradition to deal with anticompetitive mergers. We merely need a revival of serious supervision and enforcement at the Federal Trade Commission and Department of Justice's Antitrust Division. While the 1968 Merger Guidelines were not entirely satisfactory (being overly stringent with small mergers, but incomplete with respect to large conglomerates), the 1982 and 1984 guidelines (as enforced) are now too lenient and require some strengthening. The Merger Guidelines need revision also to foster stronger U.S. companies in world markets and to offset foreign industrial policies and mercantilism. The realities of increased foreign import competition in many fields (estimated now to reach at least 70 percent of U.S. manufacturing) must be taken into account. But this does not imply antitrust oversight and enforcement should be emasculated or dismantled. Quite the contrary! In fact, the challenges for competent antitrust investigation of industrial markets have increased. Competitive evaluations of industrial structure, conduct, and performance must often include the world market. Greatly increased sharing of data, discovery, and investigative effort is needed between the antitrust agencies, ITC, Department of Commerce, and USTR. In industries needing retrenchment and consolidation for healthy revival, the antitrust and trade agencies should collaborate skillfully for prompt action. Delay and confusion are costly in world markets. Other leading nations (including Japan and West Germany) make antitrust and industrial-trade policy decisions more smoothly, with reasonable foresight, and long-run perspectives. U.S. industry and its regulators need more teamwork and collaboration, competitive discipline, and sensible oversight for the long haul of industrial progress.[16]

Financial Strains and Prudence

Financial institution risks and vulnerability have increased substantially in recent years.[17] Strains accumulated from a buildup of inflationary momentum and expectations in the 1970s, with artificially high nominal business profits and interest payments, followed by substantial monetary restraint (1979–84) and even higher real interest rates. Serious recession followed for the world economy and much of domestic U.S. manufacturing. While the U.S. service sector recovered fairly well, many manufacturing industries suffered from reduced exports and increased imports. Continued agricultural, raw materials, oil, and gas surpluses in world markets brought lower prices and regional distress to many farming regions, mining areas, and the oil patch states. Overbuilding and undue real estate speculation added more difficulties in many areas, and national growth prospects slowed during the mid- to late-1980s for the U.S. economy.

Meanwhile, the debt-overload crisis for international banking added great strains for the largest U.S. multinational banks and some big banks of other nations (along with the debt-overload countries themselves).[18] The problems of multinational banking and finance were so large and urgent that leading creditor nations (the United States, Japan, West Germany, Switzerland, and the Netherlands), the Paris Club (of multinational banks), BIS, and IMF gave priority attention to the larger banks. Not seen seriously enough were strains among regional and community banks along with thrift institutions. (The latter suffered badly from a 1979–83 squeeze on earnings, with long-term mortgage rates not moving up as rapidly as short-term deposit rates.)

Partial deregulation and more lax supervision for financial institutions further complicated matters. Previous banking history in many nations proves the need for continuing examination, prudential safeguards, lender-of-last resort assistance, and mandatory deposit insurance. The United States suffered frequent bank failures along with recurrent panics and slumps, as in 1819, 1837, 1857, 1883–84, 1893, 1907, and 1929–33. But tougher federal regulation and FDIC insurance brought a new era of stability, minimum failures (fewer than ten banks per year, with all depositors fully protected), and greatly increased confidence for U.S. financial institutions generally. But, during the late 1970s and early 1980s, attitudes among some (though not all) bankers and regulators relaxed, reflecting overconfidence and rather naive faith in profitability and "market discipline" as the sole means of enforcing financial responsibility. Under relaxed standards, some institutions became overeager for growth and neglected traditional requirements for loan quality and adequate collateral.[19]

Between 1980 and 1985, the debt load of U.S. credit markets increased significantly to twice the GNP, as the United States leveraged up. By contrast, between 1950 and 1970, debt growth was lower and fairly stable, continuing in direct proportion to nominal GNP.[20] During the 1980s, the U.S. bank failure rate went up sharply, averaging 150 banks annually between 1984 and 1986. According to Federal Deposit Insurance Corporation (FDIC) Chairman Seidman, there were 1,450 banks on the troubled list, or 10 percent of the nation's banks.[21] Savings and loan institutions were worse off, proportionately, with hundreds of insolvent thrifts kept going because regulators could not afford to exhaust the limited FSLIC reserve funds still available. Obviously, FSLIC reserves must be increased (though it is difficult to allocate these costs, in part because recently liberalized regulation fostered wider real estate and development speculation in many sick thrifts, which led to unsound loan portfolios).[22] Financial regulators, fortunately, were returning to traditional wisdom about the need for serious examination and supervision discipline. Capitalization requirements were stiffened, too, though somewhat belatedly (since leading U.S. multinational banks had been allowed to squeeze capital down to 3 to 4 percent by the early 1980s).[23] Continued vigilance will be needed for the financial sector in the United States and many other countries in the coming years.

Reduced budget deficits and greatly improved fiscal discipline will help substantially in easing strain on financial institutions. This will allow a more stable monetary policy and more continuity in lower interest rates. But, if the Reagan administration and Congress cannot cut the deficit significantly, greater risks and uncertainties will afflict monetary policy and interest rates. Large U.S. deficits undermine international confidence and could combine with a weakening dollar and more inflation to force tighter U.S. money policy and higher rates, while complicating management for banks and other financial institutions.

Profit Sharing and ESOP Expansion

Improved teamwork, morale, and work efforts are important elements in strengthening the productivity of U.S. industry. A recent trend toward more employee stock ownership plans (ESOPs) and profit sharing needs to be strengthened, because this will broaden incentives and foster a more collaborative environment in the workplace.[24] Traditional unionism in the United States has been weakening. Young people are less alienated from management and want more of a share in the action. Recent studies of ESOP and other profit-sharing companies are showing better performance, on the average, than in other enterprises. Employees work harder and take more responsibility and pride when they receive a direct share of the proceeds, capital accumulation, and partnership rewards. Properly managed ESOP and/or profit-sharing companies show greater concern and responsibility for their employees. The resulting teamwork reduces conflict and enhances productivity. And, workers and their families gain considerable capital value from joint efforts, which improves wealth distribution and the morale of industrial society.

Although ESOPs and profit sharing significantly help improve efficiency and work discipline, they cannot, in and of themselves, guarantee business success for the companies involved. Adverse technological trends, product obsolescence, or business cycle slumps may prove difficult for these companies. Heavy foreign competition subsidized by governments abroad and/or utilizing substantial marginal-cost discounts or dumping—or simply involving much lower wages— can be a tough challenge. Yet, ESOP and profit-sharing arrangements provide the best incentive system and morale builder to foster high tech efficiency and innovative responses to foreign competition. Work forces will be leaner under these arrangements, but this is appropriate, because a high-wage labor force can only survive by maximizing output per worker.

ESOP and related profit-sharing arrangements have been growing rapidly in recent years. Many young companies have used these plans—the number approaches 7,000 firms with some 10 million workers enrolled in ESOPs or PAYSOPs—while 367,000 companies (with 22 million workers involved) employ some form of profit sharing.[25] In a considerable number of recent situations, companies in trouble have sold off plants to newly recapitalized companies with substantial worker ownership (or ESOPs); to save jobs, these arrangements were often embraced with enthusiasm. But, the full potential for ESOPs and profit sharing remains to be developed.

Three substantial policy efforts can be implemented for this purpose.[26] (1) Tax incentives of ESOPs and substantial profit-sharing should be liberalized. (2) ESOP companies (and companies with substantial profit sharing for their employees) should be given fast-track, special treatment in access to safeguarding remedies and unfair trade practice proceedings. (3) ESOPs or profit sharing can be required of all larger and medium-sized U.S. companies on a long-term twenty to twenty-five–year phase-in schedule. In 1973, U.S. pension plans were greatly strengthened with the Employee Retirement and Income Security Act (ERISA), which improved vesting, expanded coverage, and greatly increased funding for pension plans over a 25-to-30–year phase-in period. Vesting was further liberalized under the Tax Reform Act of 1986, which requires (after Dec. 31, 1988) that all qualified employee benefit plans (pensions or ESOPs) achieve vesting within five years. (ERISA allowed 10-to-15–year vesting delays.)

Neither organized labor (the AFL-CIO and other unions) nor employers and trade associations should feel threatened by this evolution toward greater employee stock ownership and profit sharing. ESOPs and the desire for more employee partnership and equal dignity are natural trends, based upon broadening education and sophistication—for both workers and corporations. Old-fashioned and dictatorial paternalism is out of date. More and more people, especially the younger generation, want a more honest, fair, and cooperative relationship in the workplace, with flexibility for movement and changing family situations. The most progressive and enlightened employers, professional groups, and labor organizations already understand this trend and seek to make the most of it.

Technical Education, R&D, and Progress

The United States has been slacking off in recent years on many aspects of international rivalry in technological progress. It came out of World War II and the early Cold War with strong efforts (public and private) on a broad front of R&D that led the world (2.9 percent of U.S. GNP being devoted to R&D in 1960). By 1983, however, U.S. R&D had slumped somewhat to 2.3 percent of GNP, and a large chunk of that is now defense-related (including SDI or "Star Wars").[27] U.S. 1986 federal budget outlays were projected for research, development, and testing as follows (a rather unbalanced R&D program):[28]

National defense	$34.0b.
Atomic energy defense	4.3b.
Space science technology	2.1b.
National Science Foundation basic research	1.5b.
Department of Energy general science	.7b.
Energy supply conservation	2.6b.
Environmental research	.15
Agricultural research	.8b.
Department of Commerce research	.3b
Aeronautical research (transportation)	.6b.
National Institute of Health research	4.7b.
Other health research	.5b.
Total	$52.2b.

By contrast, Japanese R&D efforts (as a share of GNP) grew from 1.2 percent in 1960 to 2.6 percent in 1983, and its government R&D efforts are projected to reach 3.5 percent of GNP in the next ten years.[29] Civilian R&D in the United States is particularly revealing, with such efforts having declined to only 1.5 percent of GNP. Meanwhile, civilian R&D efforts as a share of GNP are larger now in Japan, West Germany, and even France.[30] (Considering relative pay scales and overhead costs for R&D in these countries, recent U.S. efforts may be even less intensive.)

Japan has twice as many engineers per capita as the United States. In Japan, the Soviet Union, and West Germany, annual output of engineers per capita is higher than in the United States.[31] Among leading countries, American students (except for a limited minority) have fallen significantly behind in math education. There is more emphasis on liberal arts, business, and legal education in the United States lately with a relative decline in many areas of technology (except health care and medicine). It is evident that the United States is not making as strong or as comprehensive an effort today as Japan and a few European countries to keep up with the best R&D technology, or engineering progress. If this trend continues, the United States cannot maintain itself as a leading high-income society, or as a nation with increasing productivity. Living standards may erode, as they have in Britain during the later post–World War II era.

Take agriculture as an illustration of the productivity challenge and opportunity.[32] For many years, the government (including the Department of Agriculture, state research programs, and state agricultural colleges), agribusiness, and farmers collaborated in greatly improving techniques, crops, animals, and overall productivity. The number of active farmers and farm workers declined drastically between 1940 and 1986, but output expanded generously. Agriculture became the United States's strongest suit in comparative advantage and exports. The heart of this success story was comprehensive, joint public-private sector efforts, with strong incentives and reasonable regulation (to limit excess surpluses and destructive competition). The United States generously supplied surplus commodities to many poor countries and helped with the "green revolution" that enlarged output in developing countries. These efforts, over the long haul, have been so fruitful, ironically, that U.S. exports are less in demand and now suffer greater competition. But the secret of sustained productivity improvement was technological progress, achieved by long-term public-private sector collaboration involving universities, research groups, and both large and small business enterprises.

Very serious questions are raised by these contrasting developments. A criticism can be fairly made that the United States recently has been coasting along with an obsolescent and incomplete technology system, with more R&D in the defense sector and civilian R&D neglected recently as part of gradual deindustrialization, with more industries being phased back, moved abroad, or simply abandoned.[33] Even in defense and aerospace, concerns are frequently expressed about waste, boondoggling, and declining productivity. Soviet defense and military outlays are substantially larger for weaponry, and U.S. technology no longer claims superiority in many categories.

Viewing these long-term trends realistically, the time has come for the United States to expand more comprehensively the range and quality of its research and development efforts to achieve greater efficiency, lower costs, increased output, new products, and innovation generally.

This can be done in three ways.[34] (1) Tax incentives should be strengthened to foster more civilian R&D efforts. In Japan, marginal tax credits were increased recently from 20 to 30 percent for general research and to 50 percent for basic research in certain areas. For the United States, which lacks comparable encouragement, a catch-up tax credit of 50 percent on civilian R&D outlays could be justified. (2) Engineering, the sciences, and mathematics should get more support from the federal government and the business community. A balanced program of encouragement is needed at the high school, college, graduate, and research levels. Additional spending should begin with at least $5 billion annually and move up steadily until U.S. engineering, science, and math establishments reach rough equivalence to Japan or the Soviet Union (whichever is stronger) in each major category of technology. (3) Industrial support and employment for a big portion of this enlarged technology establishment should be worked into industry rejuvenation programs for most applied areas of engineering and manufacturing. Coordination for this effort should be led by a new Department of Industry, Technology, and Trade, as discussed in the next section. Total U.S. R&D efforts (as a share of GNP) should reach at least 3.5 percent of GNP within six years. But, strong collaboration should be encouraged between academic institutions, industry, and government for this program, with a large portion funded as (a) industrial expansion projects and/or (b) international engineering, science, and technology catch-up programs. Wherever possible, technology should be promptly put into practice in U.S. enterprises, often in conjunction with foreign joint venture companies (from the OECD bloc and elsewhere). DITT policy should ensure that some manufacturing and/or research effort is maintained by U.S. companies or institutions in almost all significant areas of technological progress. (Complete national self-sufficiency is not necessary or even desirable in many areas. But, the United States should maintain quality participation in almost every area of industrial activity and/or technology.)

Trade Equity and Stronger Industrial Policy

The United States must confront the reality of unequal trading conditions and unbalanced trade openness, especially with massive trade deficits ($123 billion for 1984, $148 billion for 1985, and $170 billion for 1986). Most agree that an overvalued dollar (caused by heavy U.S. budget deficits and higher interest rates) aggravated the competitiveness problems of U.S. manufacturing and exports and made foreign imports more attractive. Debt overloads and servicing costs in many overseas markets also weakened exports. High U.S. wages and production costs have been a real problem in some sectors, although wages are approaching parity with West Germany, Japan, and other industrial countries. Some NICs, however, have considerably lower labor costs than the United States, Europe, or Japan.

But unequal trading conditions and unbalanced trade openness, along with substantial foreign subsidies and export promotion, are also a significant problem for many industries.[35] This imbalance grew more pronounced in recent years. U.S. unfair trade practice laws (administered by the president, USTR, ITC, and Department of Commerce) failed to stop a great increase in imports. In fact, access to these remedies remains very difficult. Meanwhile, Europe (in contrast to the United States) somewhat increased the use of voluntary restraint agreements, industrial subsidies, and government support. While European practice varies among countries, its agriculture is heavily protected, and Europe generally is more mercantilist and less open than the United States. Japan continued a successful combination of R&D subsidies, low-cost financing, export promotion, and expanded low-wage branch plants abroad to keep itself competitive, and its export machine kept on growing. But Japan's cultural loyalties, difficult language, domestic marketing practices, and administrative guidance serve to greatly limit Japanese imports of competing foreign manufacturers. Most developing countries (NICs as well as LDCs) have become even more restrictive in recent years, reflecting foreign exchange shortages, external debt-service needs, and, in some countries, strong industrial-development policies. Developing countries, as a whole, are more mercantilist and less open than Japan or Europe. And, the most state-controlled socialist and communist nations are the least open markets in the world trade bazaar. (Compare figure P–1 and figure 6–1.).

The United States should press now for more effective reciprocity. To a limited extent, greater openness can be achieved abroad, but progress in this direction is inherently constrained and slow-going. The reasons include: entrenched attitudes favoring local industrial development in developing countries (along with debt-service needs); strong unionism and resistance to job losses in Europe, Canada, Australia, and New Zealand; and powerful momentum for successful industrial policy and mercantilism in Japan. Certainly, large U.S. trade deficits lately should be used to justify improved access to foreign markets. But restricted openness, extensive subsidies, and protection for domestic agriculture are strongly established (and legitimate) in many countries. These mercantilist practices are rooted in tradition; they are reinforced by nationalism, along with resource insecurities and economic development strategies.

It would be unrealistic to believe most mercantilist practices abroad will quickly disappear. Even more naive is a U.S. bargaining strategy based upon a standstill against further unfair trade practice remedies, safeguard relief, or offsets to foreign mercantilism or industrial policies.[36] This merely "locks in" present asymmetry. A U.S. standstill response that guarantees continued access to U.S. markets (on an unequal basis) removes any serious pressure to reduce foreign mercantilism. More importantly, a standstill policy loses important corrective benefits to U.S. industry, skilled labor, and technology that flow from appropriate use of U.S. unfair trade practice remedies, reasonable safeguard relief, and offsets to foreign mercantilism. While everyone should appreciate standstill as a lobbying objective desired by foreign exporters, importers into the United States, and other interests dependent upon current international trade, a standstill policy is really unsound for U.S. national interests. It is weak trade-bargaining strategy. It fails to correct unequal trade conditions and unbalanced openness. It neglects the need to rebuild and strengthen U.S. industrial technology and production capability. Standstill will guarantee further U.S. industrial deterioration and relative economic decline.

On the other hand, it would be wrong and ill considered for the United States to retreat into economic isolationism, drastically increase trade barriers, or install Smoot-Hawley–style high protective tariffs.[37] While strongly protectionist policies could restore employment in some U.S. industries, an overall decline in world trade might follow. Many countries in East Asia, Europe, and Latin America might lose sizeable chunks of their exports. While big U.S. trade deficits allow considerable latitude for "corrective action" by the United States, drastically protectionist policy involves overkill and risk of backlash. U.S. exports could suffer from retaliation against big tariff increases. Moreover, recent economic revival for many nations could be reversed. Most importantly, political relations with many U.S. allies could be adversely affected by a return to Smoot-Hawley–style protectionism. Although the United States can and should act firmly now to achieve effective reciprocity, equalize trading conditions, and renew U.S. industrial strength and technology, it should avoid undue disruption for world markets.

More Extensive Safeguard Relief and Stronger Unfair Trade Practice Remedies

Existing safeguards and unfair trade practice remedies under U.S. law, from the standpoint of industries suffering increased competition and decline, have proven weak and unreliable. Faith in free trade has been dominant among most officials administering these laws in recent years. Hope for occasional relief was held out as a safety valve and shock absorber for protectionist pressures. But concessions were held to a minimum, so as to maximize free trade, and presumably benefit international prosperity, or at least those interests (such as MNCs and multinational banks) involved in international trade or lending.[38] Not recognized as serious dangers were additional deindustrialization; continued movement of jobs, manufacturing, and technology to NICs and LDCs; increased U.S. unemployment; and stagnant or declining real wages in many sectors. For years, it was assumed that advanced industrial nations would continue moving up the technology, productivity, and prosperity ladder; LDCs and NICs would merely follow, with everyone gaining in the bounty of multilateral trade. But in recent years, the North of Britain, Smokestack America, and lately, much of U.S. agricultural, mining, and "oil patch" regions are suffering economic trouble, with widespread unemployment and sluggishness. While considerable high tech, service, and rentier interests may prosper, others are being dumped off the train of progress. A crucial problem, therefore, for most MICs, is how to ensure that the great majority of their citizens keep moving forward in productivity or at least maintain living standards, while keeping the number and fraction of losers as small as possible.

Two rather obvious mistakes should be avoided. The first is total protection of the status quo—"lemon socialism." This strategy is a palliative and guarantees increased costs in a competitive world market. The second is naive faith in a completely benign, untrammeled free international market. The world reality is competing national industrial policies, strong export promotion, widespread manufacturing surpluses, declining cost curves, mercantilist import restrictions, unequal trading conditions, and unbalanced openness. Failure to understand this reality is dangerous and foolhardy, especially for nations such as the United States with a great deal to lose in widespread deindustrialization. But we can avoid both blunders of extreme thinking.

Sensible safeguarding measures and realistic unfair trade practice relief should be integrated with a long-term strategy of industrial rejuvenation, with stronger R&D, that recognizes the importance of sustaining efficient participation in most areas of manufacturing and technology (with appropriate retrenchment and reduced labor forces in some areas). But, to dismantle and throw away entire industries, with their long-accumulated teamwork and know-how, would be stupid.

U.S. trade policy must stop treating its domestic manufacturing industry and labor force as "the enemy" of free trade. Instead, U.S. trade policy agencies (Department of Commerce, USTR, ITC, and the White House) should start working with domestic industry, agriculture, and labor (including ESOP representatives) to revive U.S. productivity.[39] Each significant U.S. industry should be encouraged to develop revival plans (on a long-term ten-year basis), with sufficient flexibility for improving technology and changing world market competition. Large foreign importers should be encouraged to build new U.S. plants for assembly, component manufacture, and repair as well as to form technology exchanges and joint ventures with U.S. partners. Failure to participate in such relationships should be considered prejudicial in remedial negotiations and arrangements for settlement of unfair trade practice and safeguard proceedings.

Existing unfair trade practice laws (antidumping, countervailing duty, and Sections 301, 337, and 406) should be broadened to cover all forms of subsidy (direct or indirect) and discounting or indirect price discrimination, as well as to allow aggregation of such conduct (of various types) from many countries. Records from unfair trade practice complaints and proceedings in relevant industries should be incorporated into broad records for Section 201 safeguard relief and industrywide rejuvenation packages. Remedial options (safeguard and unfair trade practices) should be enlarged to include quotas, tariffs, financing for domestic industry rejuvenation, orderly marketing arrangements (OMAs), VRAs, domestic-content requirements, and joint ventures and/or technology exchanges with major foreign importers. A new Department of Industry, Technology, and Trade should take over and revitalize the Department of Commerce. DITT should develop long-term rejuvenation programs and technology-improvement campaigns (including export promotion and selective retrenchment). The U.S. antitrust agencies (FTC and Department of Justice Antitrust Division) must be brought into the clearance process. But, all rejuvenation and improvement packages should receive expedited review. Speed, decisiveness, and results are essential. Any significant market distortions, price increases, shortages, disruptions, or exceptional profits should receive prompt attention on a continuing basis. Congressional oversight must be welcomed as normal and constructive criticism.

In all unfair trade practice, safeguard, and rejuvenation proceedings, there should be a commitment to upgrading U.S. industry, improving technology, and expanding exports (where possible). Foreign competition is a helpful prod to accomplishment, and MNCs from abroad have become part of the U.S. industrial scene. This is legitimate. But, foreign MNCs must be good U.S. corporate citizens (just as U.S. companies abroad are expected to be good citizens in their host countries).

An outdated "free-trade–protectionist" dichotomy no longer provides an adequate guideline for U.S. industrial-trade policy.[40] Instead, U.S. government policy should become more like Japanese policy, a consensus tradition of government–industrial teamwork dedicated to goals of strong industrial performance, healthy economic growth, minimum inflation, and full employment.

General Offsets to Foreign Mercantilism

Even though stronger safeguards and unfair trade practice relief will be helpful in many industries, they should be combined with more general offsets to foreign mercantilism, widespread subsidies, lower-cost financing, and cheap labor. The best offsets to foreign mercantilism, subsidies (in all forms), and low wages would be the following: (a) VAT waiver correctives (to offset the foreign waiver of value-added taxes) on exports into the United States and (b) moderate revenue tariffs (say, 10 percent ad valorem).

VAT waiver correctives make sense in removing an anomaly under rival taxation systems.[41] Europe, Japan, and many NICs use VATs (in the 12 to 15 percent range, most frequently). Not charging this tax for exports into the U.S. market confers an indirect subsidy on their export sales. Perhaps $20 to 30 billion in VAT waivers on U.S. imports may be involved in 1986. Meanwhile, U.S. domestic manufacturers must pay normal federal and state income taxes on their production. A VAT waiver correction can be considered a tax-harmonization measure. More comprehensive tax harmonization would be a federal U.S. VAT enactment, let us say at the 12 to 15 percent level. This could generate enough revenue to close most of the federal fiscal deficit. To deal with objections from state and local governments that a VAT crowds their sales tax revenues, the federal VAT could be shared with states and localities under a revenue-sharing formula. Of course, a U.S. VAT does increase the overall tax burden and reduces consumption by the public. While some would complain about insufficient progressivity in a VAT, the overall U.S. tax load (federal, state, and local) is no longer very progressive (especially after the Tax Reform Act of 1986).

A solid case can be made for revenue tariffs (say, in the 10 percent range). The United States employed comparable import levies (or even higher tariffs) through most of its industrial development and to some extent into the 1950s. Although real wages were traditionally higher in the United States, many industries benefited, and technical progress was broad-based, at least until recently. Revenue tariffs are not very distortive, but provide a reasonable degree of buffering to offset lower wage costs and/or widespread foreign subsidiaries, export promotion, and discounting. A 10 to 12 percent revenue tariff seems fair as an estimate for the amount of offset needed for widespread foreign subsidies, export promotion, or limited discounting. Large discounts from abroad can then be more easily detected as possible unfair trade practices. A further justification is industrial rejuvenation (part of the infant-industry rationale), although this reasoning might also justify higher, protective levies (say, 25 to 30 percent) during the renewal stages for some industries. National security and defense arguments apply, especially as against those U.S. allies that carry much lower burdens of proportional defense outlays. (See table 3–2.) Certainly, the revenue effect of 10 percent import levies (say $30 to 40 billion annually) will be helpful in closing the U.S. budget deficit. Finally, an administrative oversight argument makes sense, namely, that it will be easier to enforce U.S. unfair trade practice and safeguard remedies if regular data is collected through a general revenue tariff on most import flows.

Principal responses by free-traders are as follows: (a) Revenue tariffs could limit trade somewhat. But, where only modest 10 percent levies are involved, the gains-from-trade forgone cannot be very large. In these conditions, the offset is not significantly distorting. And, the benefits outweigh modest trade losses. Major benefits include sizeable government revenues, industrial rejuvenation, fuller employment, more social harmony, enhanced national security, greater economic growth, reduced market instability, and more effective limits on foreign unfair trade practices. (b) U.S. revenue tariffs would encourage similar tariffs among major trading nations or at least between countries that do not form close-knit customs unions or economic communities. This is probably correct, but as previously indicated, the gains-from-trade forgone are limited. And, the offset benefits stated above outweigh these modest losses in gains-from-trade.[42]

Import surcharges would be another offset to correct trade imbalances, large current account deficits, and substantially undervalued currencies (or failure to appreciate surplus currencies). Import surcharges were employed for this purpose with some skill by the Nixon administration in 1971, to correct an overvalued dollar (and insufficient appreciation of other major currencies); a serious dollar disequilibrium probably existed in 1983–85. But with a more substantial decline of the dollar in 1986, the need for import surcharges as a U.S. corrective measure has weakened to a considerable degree. In these recent circumstances, it is more doubtful now that import surcharges should be added to revenue tariffs and/or VAT waiver correctives. But import surcharges should be kept in reserve as a tool to deal with serious currency misalignment.[43]

Domestic content laws have been urged (especially by organized labor and the AFL-CIO) as responses to foreign subsidies, discounting, and industrial policies. Requirements might be developed that manufactured products sold in the United States have 25, 40, 50, 60, 75, or 90 percent domestic content. The most extreme domestic-content requirement is a "buy American" law or domestic-purchase obligation. These requirements are really quotas and are more strongly protectionist than mild revenue tariffs. Inevitably, their trade distortion and restrictive impact is greater. This—their protectionist power— is the lobbying appeal of domestic-content laws. But it is hard to draw lines between industries, and such laws' overall impact is more seriously protectionist and disruptive of trade. It is better to use domestic-content requirements mainly in their more traditional role as national security safeguards, for vital public utilities, and in defense contracting. But domestic-content requirements would be helpful as optional relief in unfair trade practice and safeguard proceedings, and specific authority for this should be added to existing U.S. trade laws (antidumping and antisubsidy remedies, together with Sections 201, 301, 337, and 406 of the Trade Act of 1974).[44] Strengthening U.S. trade remedies in this way would give American trade negotiators more clout and enhance their bargaining leverage and flexibility.

Stronger Industrial Policy

The key to strengthening U.S. economic performance is understanding the challenge of competing national industrial policies and their link to multinational export development and trade relations. The United States cannot maintain high living standards, reasonably full employment, and broad prosperity without revitalizing its engineering, manufactures, productivity, and output on a wide front.[45] There are important economies of integration and scale in the snowballing progress of industrial and technological growth. Dynamic engineering and creative design teams as well as joint efforts for industry and marketing flourish in an environment of expansion. General forward momentum encourages prospering careers and enterprise in many fields. Yet, the opposite tendency operates, too. A country with a lot of closing factories, moribund communities, and economic stagnation erodes its elan and could easily fall into general decline. When a business-managerial elite becomes passive, rentier-minded, and/or preoccupied merely with financial gains and short-term profits and it loses the enthusiasm for industrial expansion and technical development, that nation is in serious economic trouble.

The United States has slipped gradually into greater passivity and a rentier mentality. We have seen decreasing industrial dynamism in the past ten to fifteen years. The United States must shake itself out of this slump. A broad-based national effort toward industrial and technological rejuvenation is essential. The country enjoyed a tradition of vigor and progress through most of its history. Energetic response to challenge was the American hallmark. The time for an industrial renewal movement in the United States has come.[46]

A strong New Industrial Policy requires appropriate government organization and broad collaboration with U.S. industry. There must be an American MITI and a long-term partnership of government and industry for broad economic and technological progress.[47] The most direct solutions are the simplest and can be most productive. The U.S. Department of Commerce should be revamped into a vigorous Department of Industry, Technology, and Trade (DITT). The existing Department of Commerce (founded in 1903) is a legacy from an earlier era and ranks among the older branches of U.S. government administration. It includes the old Patent Office (which screens applications for patents and new inventions), the Bureau of Standards (a small technical staff with limited responsibilities), and the Bureau of the Census (with extensive statistical and data-gathering responsibilities). More recently, an international commerce and trade staff was established (primarily with data-gathering functions). These agencies are essential as the data base for a New Industrial Policy, and they should be expanded with more industry collaboration worldwide.

But, a crucial new role for DITT is systematic coordination, consensus building, and networking with industry and technological elites. This requires an overlay of higher-quality leadership cadres for DITT. But, the larger part of this effort and talent should come easily from industries, trade associations, lobbyists, and law firms. It could be supplied readily by the private sector.) Engineering schools, research institutes, economists, and international experts must be mobilized for R&D, technological monitoring, and market analysis. Substantially enlarged endowments, grants, and research projects will be needed for these purposes. Fortunately, the entire Department of Commerce budget was only about $2 billion annually in 1984–86, so that a great expansion of technology monitoring plus consensus building and networking should cost less than $1 to 2 billion. (The 1985 Department of Commerce budget breaks down as follows: General Administration, $38 million; Census and Statistics, $205 million; Patents and Trademarks, $100 million; Bureau of Standards, $120 million; International Trade Administration, $170 million; Travel and Tourism, $230 million; Economic Development and Enterprise Assistance—Domestic—$350 million; and National Oceanic and Atmospheric Administration, $1,133 million.[48]

A program of industrial R&D support, loans, and stronger tax incentives should be developed, which could absorb another $5 to 10 billion annually, but this should be expanded slowly and prudently to avoid wasteful boondoggles. These R&D projects should be coordinated closely with government-industry task forces and subjected to independent technology monitoring. A new agency for technology monitoring is desirable, with distinguished academic and industry leaders serving as its board of trustees. There should be extensive peer review, openness, and publicly available reports (with limited restrictions for national security). The Bureau of Standards could be used in this effort. But, a far more comprehensive, up-to-date technology monitoring effort clearly is needed, one closely associated with the nation's engineering and scientific education system. Extensive research grants and frequent conferences should be supported for these activities and shared with select U.S. allies on a reciprocal basis.

DITT should be responsible for organizing and maintaining a complete network of government-industry councils that incorporate participation from almost every significant area of U.S. industry, engineering, and technological development. Each council should develop up-to-date "Industry and Technology Status and Problem Reports" with recommendations for stronger U.S. achievements and assessments of foreign competition and potential. Economic and market development analyses must be included, along with policy discussions. Industrial trade associations and academic experts should participate and help review these reports in their annual meeting and committee work. This tradition of expertise and collaboration would be very helpful in dealing with foreign unfair trade practices, subsidy programs, financing, and export promotion. Competitive responses, countermeasures, safeguard relief and adjustment assistance, and/or proceedings under U.S. trade laws can be developed and analyzed effectively in these networks.

Ultimately, the DITT, USTR, and White House should formulate appropriate programs for each sector's government-industry improvement, rejuvenation, safeguard and adjustment relief, and/or unfair trade practice proceedings. Remedies should be sought in those sectors with serious trouble, underachievement, or difficulty in meeting world market competition.

Antitrust agencies, the Federal Trade Commission, and Department of Justice Antitrust Division should provide independent review and competitive analysis for these recommendations and policies. While industry–government collaboration can be very helpful to economic development over the long run, there is a danger of cartels, trade restraints, and combinations to raise prices and limit rivalry. Therefore, watchdog review and regular investigations by the antitrust agencies, along with the General Accounting Office (GAO), Office of Technology Assessment (OTA), and various committees of Congress is essential. In this way, market-stabilizing measures, retrenchment plans, mergers, joint ventures, R&D collaboration, and trade practices can be kept consistent with reasonable domestic competition policy.[49]

All this does not imply, of course, the substitution of government decision making for a competitive marketplace.[50] Nor is this a program for centralized targeting or picking winners by politicians and their favorites. The scope for supplementary action and corrective policy is carefully and rationally confined. Unfair trade practice proceedings and safeguard relief concern industries under stress, with significant losses in sales in foreign and/or domestic markets. Technology reviews and status reports merely expose and recommend responses to lagging productivity and foreign improvements or breakthroughs. The primary thrust of government–industry collaboration is to deal with growing challenges for U.S. industry in world-market rivalry. The purpose of U.S. New Industrial Policy is to facilitate stronger and more equal competition in international markets by U.S. enterprises.

Labor representation and participation is important in these activities. Broader consensus, employee backing, and public understanding can be developed this way. The Departments of Labor and Agriculture should participate actively in developing government-industry councils, along with their staff recruitment. Relevant professional associations, labor unions (AFL-CIO and others), ESOP groups, and other employee interest groups should enjoy access, participation, and rights to independent commentary. A U.S. industrial policy that ignores the contribution of working families, organized labor, and professional associations would suffer from mistrust and limited public support. On the other hand, substantial inputs from labor and professional organizations will help fashion stronger policies, better work discipline, and higher productivity.[51]

Properly understood, modern U.S. industrial policy should revamp public outlooks, enterprise planning, and the government oversight process. More coherent and better coordination is needed to compete successfully with highly networked industrial export "machines" such as Japan or West Germany today. Decentralized initiative and free enterprise are still valuable, but they are no longer the whole story for success in world trade, technology, and industrial development. Extensive teamwork and collaboration with government is needed to sustain high tech living standards, economic growth, reasonably full employment, and broad prosperity for a nation's citizens.

Multinational Finance, Investment Guarantees, and Trade Negotiations

Every nation, including the United States, is primarily responsible for its own fiscal integrity, domestic savings and investment, incentives, productivity, and a sensible industrial-trade development strategy. But the multinational finance, investment, and trade order can be strengthened to the general advantage of most countries. The highest priority is additional capital resources for the IMF, World Bank, and regional development banks, so that widespread debt over-loads in many countries can be rescheduled with as little strain and reduction in economic growth as possible.[52] Greater supervision and coordination for international banking is appropriate to facilitate rescheduling and avoid further blunders of excessive borrowing. More safeguards for investment security are desirable, along with guarantees against unjust expropriation or unreasonable burdens upon productive investment. And, with respect to international trade and GATT, we should move toward improved trade equity and reciprocity as a means to eliminate unsustainable trade deficits and/or surpluses.

Mutual surveillance and coordination of exchange rates will be constructive in this regard, but all nations should be responsible for their own finances. While multilateral influence may help discipline wayward currencies, over-valuation, or undervaluation, greater national responsibility is desirable. This applies with special force to the United States, which should have limited budget deficits and dollar overvaluation more wisely in recent years. But, the United States can be tougher now in defending its own vital trade interests and intervene more actively with respect to undervalued foreign currencies that both subsidize disproportionate imports to the United States and limit U.S. exports abroad. (The U.S. Federal Reserve and Treasury Department should buy undervalued foreign currencies more aggressively by selling more dollars and use the hard-currency proceeds to enlarge the United States's foreign exchange reserves.)[53]

Multinational Finance and Capital Flows

Because the United States is less predominant and more equal in productivity to other industrial countries (Europe, Japan, the Soviet Union, and others), the need for multinational finance and liquidity increases. Widespread debt overloads affect some sixty nations now. These loans form a sizeable part of the asset portfolios in major multinational banks. Loans to debt-overload countries exceed equity capital of many leading international banks. Default or failure to service these loans could be greatly disruptive to these banks and awkward for creditor countries and their governments. The risk of default or breakdown in the rescheduling process has been real, although skillfully averted so far by the IMF–Paris Club rescheduling process. The key to coping with widespread and growing debt overloads since the early 1980s is adequate IMF, World Bank, IDA, and regional development bank capitalization and borrowing authority. These institutions provide the bridge loans that encourage new bank lending, enable additional foreign investments, and allow the growth process to resume in a healthy manner. IMF-supervised stabilization plans also help restore fiscal responsibility and reduce inflation in debtor countries. After a hard period of world deflation and recessions—as was necessary to reduce inflation—the international economy needs another round of pump priming and liquidity to promote more vigorous recoveries.[54]

The U.S. economy can no longer provide sufficient investment resources (public or private) to meet all these needs. The United States ran record federal budget deficits averaging $200 billion annually (roughly 5 percent of GNP) from 1983 to 1987, and during 1985, the United States became a net debtor nation. While Japan, West Germany, Switzerland, Taiwan, and some other nations have prospered recently, with sizeable net surpluses and increased investment abroad, the banks and MNCs of these nations cannot provide sufficient liquidity for the entire developing world, their own domestic economies, and the borrowing demands of the U.S. economy. There is no real alternative to additional multilateral liquidity; it is essential for a strong international recovery.

A round of increased IMF and multinational institution capital resources occurred in 1983–84. This served well enough as an emergency stopgap in the early world-debt–crisis rescheduling process, when tougher anti-inflation discipline was still vital. But, as world growth slumped and surpluses grew in many markets, the need for greater liquidity to restore economic progress is now evident. The Baker Plan of 1985 proposed somewhat increased multinational resources and substantial new lending by private international banks, along with renewed foreign investment and the repatriation of flight capital. Most observers support this effort (along with the debt-rescheduling process), but a majority believe now that the Baker Plan must be expanded with more generous resources and that another sizeable increase in multilateral institution capital and borrowing is necessary.

While some debtor countries and commentators seek partial debt cancellation as a way to ease the world debt-overload crisis, this approach is less practical.[55] It would disrupt the renewal of investment and bank lending that must flow to enable stronger recovery among developing countries. Administrators would find it difficult to select the debtor countries, particular loans, and creditors suitable for cancellation. How can lines be drawn between deserving and undeserving debtors and/or creditors? Once begun, a sizeable debt-cancellation process is hard to limit. However apportioned, the cancellation or failure to service debts greatly weakens creditor confidence and must constrict additional lending and renewed capital investment.

Rescheduling generosity is far preferable to cancellation as a debt-overload remedy. With major declines in key interest rates, outstanding debt loads can be carried more comfortably. Continued rescheduling allows more bridge loans, renewed foreign investment, and additional bank credits that would largely dry up with partial cancellation or debt default. And, IMF stabilization agreements are largely constructive as a means to encourage fiscal responsibility, greatly reduced deficits, and lower inflation in debt-overload nations. These countries cannot really restore healthy investment markets, eliminate capital flight, or obtain full access to borrowing and overseas investors without restoring financial respectability and creditworthiness.

The need for macroeconomic coordination, tougher monetary discipline, greater fiscal responsibility, and lower inflation has been widely recognized in recent years. Substantial progress has been made among industrial nations with reduced inflation, and the rescheduling-stabilization process must be extended among developing countries. The United States really needs more fiscal responsibility, too, and must halt the growth of its debt burden before things get out of hand. When federal debt was only $1,000 billion or 28 percent of GNP in 1980, the United States enjoyed some leeway for increased borrowing. But, federal debt exceeded $2,000 billion or about 50 percent of GNP in 1986 (not to mention another $700 billion of state and local debt). The United States is approaching its overall borrowing limits and in recent years has added excessively to federal debt-servicing charges (which increased from $79 billion in 1980 to $139 billion in 1986).[56]

Assurances of fair treatment of foreign investment will be helpful in broadening international recovery. Bilateral investment treaties (BITs) have become fashionable in recent years and are a good method for developing countries to provide more confidence.[57] Combined with IMF–Paris Club rescheduling and stabilization, BITs contribute significantly to an environment that can bring renewed capital investment to many nations. But balanced industrial growth and economic development programs are needed for the long run. This requires broad, incremental progress in education, employment, economic opportunities, and social mobility. Many developing countries have progressed greatly since the late 1940s. Their success demonstrates that more nations could make comparable achievements with a sensible blend of government guidance, sound industrial policies, and healthy marketplace incentives.

More Balanced Trade and International Negotiations

The most important requirement for world trade at this stage is to achieve more realistic balance, equal trading conditions, and effective reciprocity.[58] (See figures P–1, 6–1, and 6–2.) The United States led many of its allies toward more open markets in the post–World War II era, with a policy of "trade not aid" to foster economic recovery in Europe and Japan and to spread industrial progress among developing countries. This effort was largely successful. Western Europe and Japan have reached near parity in living standards, industrialization, and advanced technology. (See table P–2.) Many developing nations are doing well, and their success shows the way for others. But an unintended by-product of this forty-year evolution is a trading network with substantial asymmetry and inequality of access. Most countries use industrial-trade-development

Sources of the Problem

1. Overvalued dollar rising from 1980 to 1985
   - Finally receding against major currencies by fall 1986 nearly to 1980 levels
   - Enlarged U.S. imports and restricted U.S. exports
2. Big U.S. budget deficits
   - Averaging $200b. annually (1983–87)
   - Roughly 5 percent of GNP
   - Raise interest rates
   - Add to debt-service burdens
   - Weaken long-run growth
3. Substantial world debt overloads
   - For many developing nations, especially in Latin America
   - Reduce U.S. exports plus sales
   - Strain world economy

   } Macroeconomic imbalance problems need relief (medium run).

4. Unequal trading conditions and asymmetrical U.S. openness
   - Foreign industrial policies— widespread subsidies, export promotion, and discounting
   - More import restrictions abroad
5. Decline in U.S. competitiveness
   - Increased foreign competition
   - Reduced demand for U.S. agricultural surpluses
   - High U.S. wages (low NIC wages)
   - Reduced U.S. edge and uniqueness

   } Structural problems require basic reforms (long run).

Solutions to the Problem

1. Greatly reduce U.S. budget deficits and improve incentives
   - Enlarge savings and investment
   - Real tax reform
   - Financial strengthening
   - Responsible corporations and reduced takeover activity
   - More profit sharing and employee stock ownership plans
   - Lower interest rates
2. Ease world debt overloads
   - More multilateral credit and liquidity
   - Lower interest rates
   - Expanded "Baker Plan" relief
   - Avoid debt default or debt cancellation
   - Appreciation of surplus currencies

   } Improved macro-economic policies and world debt relief.

3. Improved trade equity
   - Stronger unfair trade remedies
   - More safeguard relief
   - Offsetting restrictions against foreign mercantilism
4. Stronger U.S. industrial policy
   - Department of Industry, Trade and Technology
   - Broader R&D efforts
   - Government–industry cooperation for renewed productivity
   - Stronger incentives, investment, and productivity

   } Structural reforms assist trade equity and industrial revival.

Figure 6–2. Sources and Solutions for the U.S. Trade Deficit Problem

policies with more mercantilism than the United States, that is, extensive sub-sidies, greater export promotion, discounting, and tougher trade restrictions (in one form or another). And the United States is significantly more open to imports than other major markets.

Unequal trading conditions and unbalanced access are now a serious struc-tural problem and a cause of the worsening of U.S. trade and current account deficits during the 1980s. In 1986, U.S. imports approached $387 billion, and U.S. exports were only $217 billion. While some improvement is expected, most experts believe these flows will change slowly. Exchange rate prospects are not entirely clear, with Europe and Japan fearing additional currency appreciation, reduced exports, and job losses. Meanwhile, most NICs experienced little (if any) appreciation in their currencies, and their exports still benefit from much lower wage rates.

While the United States should try to open more markets for its exports abroad, significant constraints limit results in many areas. Foreign industrial policies are well entrenched, with substantial export biases. There are wide-spread subsidies that promote exports, support discounting, and bail out troubled industries. Imports are extensively restricted: (1) Agriculture is heavily protected by many countries, and surpluses have increased. (2) Industrial manu-factures are commonly protected by NICs when they produce comparable prod-ucts. Other advanced industrial nations use more nontariff barriers (NTBs), safeguard measures, and/or voluntary restraints.

Wage rates are lower in many foreign markets, which further limits U.S. export potential for manufactures. Big gains in U.S. exports cannot come easily. While some hope for increased service earnings by the U.S. abroad, there are limits in this direction, too. U.S. capital exports abroad have slowed, while foreign capital inflows have increased substantially. The United States became a net debtor nation in 1985. Thus, net earnings or capital investments do not look so promising. Some seek more U.S. earnings from patents, trademarks, copyrights, and computer software, but the U.S. lead in many areas is declining, and intellectual property cannot support a large trade deficit. Others want earn-ings from banking, insurance, or other financial services. But most countries jealously restrict foreign influence in their financial sectors, so no large net earn-ings should be expected from these activities. After careful review, the ines-capable conclusion seems to be that U.S. growth potential for merchandise and service exports in the near future is not strong and that it suffers from power-ful mercantilist restrictions and rivalry abroad.[59]

U.S. negotiators must not be deceived by friendly assurances embroidered with free-trade idealism. Many foreign economists share belief in an ideal model of a truly open, free-world economy with total factor mobility (labor, capital, and technology), and a complete absence of trade restrictions and subsidies. (But academic agreement on this theoretical ideal is largely irrelevant.) The real world, we should realize by now, is a regime of competing national industrial policies, with unequal trading conditions and asymmetrical openness. (Compare figures P–1 and 6–1.) Most countries employ extensive de facto mercantilism with powerful historical and legal momentum plus reinforcement by strong national interests, skillful administration, and entrenched political constituencies. While lip service and vague promises to open markets abroad are easily obtained from foreign negotiators, the United States would be foolish to put much faith in them.

Instead, the United States should alter its trade policies and adapt to a world of rival industrial policies, with increasingly tough foreign competition, and a reduced competitive edge. The United States got by for an extended period with strong headstarts in technology and productivity, which were lengthened substantially by World War II and the disruptions suffered by Europe and Japan. For many years in the postwar era, the United States could afford unequal openness. But gradually, the U.S. margin of superior technology and productivity eroded, as Europe, Japan, and other nations eventually caught up in an environment of unequal trading conditions, generous technology sharing by the United States, and increasingly open U.S. markets after the Kennedy and Tokyo Rounds of 1967 and 1979, respectively.

Basically, the United States should withdraw its excessive, naive, and, to a great extent, unilateral trade openness to become more like modern Europe and Japan (its major industrial and trade rivals).[60] (See figures 6–1 and 6–2.) It is foolish and self-destructive for the United States to continue (or perhaps even accelerate) a dangerous process of deindustrialization, with large-scale relocation of manufacturing plants to low-wage countries. Another ten to fifteen years of current trade policies would substantially weaken the U.S. economy, erode its manufacturing base within many sectors, and, in some respects, do permanent damage to the competitive position of the United States.

Another GATT round (initiated in Fall 1986 at Punta del Este, Uruguay) cannot accomplish a lot for U.S. trade, although modest gains might be feasible.[61] Foreign industrial policies, mercantilist habits, and patterns of subsidy are well entrenched, and U.S. wage costs are much higher than most LDCs and NICs. Negotiating positions already taken by many nations suggest little room for general agreement. The EEC clearly is determined to maintain its strongly protectionist Common Agricultural Policy, and hardly any change is likely in their subsidies, export promotion, voluntary restraints or NTBs. Japan will be accommodating, polite, and sympathetic in rhetoric. But, few expect Japan to change its basic export-growth orientation, dismantle MITI, eliminate NTBs, or suddenly welcome foreign manufactures on a large scale. And, the NICs and LDCs have made it clear that they reject reciprocity or any significant changes in GATT, and many want considerably more generalized preferences (GSP). While separate negotiations have been accepted for finance, insurance, and intellectual property, few expect more than limited gains for the United States in this direction (even though advantages could be substantial for a limited number of U.S. multinational banks, securities firms, and insurance companies, such as Citicorp, Merrill-Lynch, or Prudential-Bache).

The United States must begin to limit its imports rationally and in a gradual manner, without unduly disrupting world trade or general economic recovery.[62] Fortunately, massive U.S. trade imbalances in the mid-to-late 1980s provide an ideal opportunity and ample justification for independent U.S. action.

	1983	1984	1985	1986
U.S. imports	$270b.	$341b.	$355b.	$387b.
U.S. exports	$220b.	$217b.	$213b.	$217b.

The United States should go forward with a logical, moderate, and limited program of responses to foreign mercantilism and industrial policies. The best U.S. policy package, building upon existing U.S. unfair trade law and in line with the country's historical experience, is the following:

1. Strengthen unfair trade practice remedies and enforcement.

2. Use more extensive safeguarding for its vital industries and important technology, while preserving viable competitors in most industries (although allowing retrenchment in many areas).

3. Develop appropriate offsets to foreign mercantilism, widespread subsidies, discounting, and restrictive practices. The most logical offsets are VAT waiver correctives, and a 10 percent revenue tariff on most imports.

But the United States cannot rely upon other nations to protect its vital trade interests. Other countries, quite naturally and properly, concentrate upon protecting their own trade interests (promoting exports, strengthening industrial development, and limiting imports that threaten their industries or employment). This is why a U.S. standstill policy (locking in the established trade inequity and unbalanced openness) would be foolhardy and irresponsible.

The United States stands at crossroads in economic history. For most of its 200-year history as a constitutional republic, the United States focused upon its own economic, agricultural, and industrial development. U.S. trade policy usually employed revenue tariffs, with considerable periods of higher protection which were often stringent from the Civil War through World War II (1861–1945). Foreign trade was mainly limited (1) to articles and commodities clearly in surplus for the United States and exported abroad at competitive prices and (2) to imports not readily available at home. After World War II, the United States broke with isolationist tradition and consciously assumed "leadership" of the free world. The United States tried to lead the world toward freer trade by opening its own markets more generously. "Trade not aid" was a guiding slogan that helped rebuild Europe and Japan and provided assistance to many developing nations—some of which are now vigorous and rapidly growing NICs. All this U.S. historical development made good sense and requires little or no apology.

But now that Europe and Japan have caught up in manufacturing, technology, and productivity, it no longer makes sense for the United States to be unequally open and disproportionately generous in giving up manufacturing markets to its allies.[63] The United States should now take better care of its own vital industrial interests, protect its technological base, and strengthen long-term productivity. Special care should be taken to restore full employment. From the 1940s through the 1960s, the United States enjoyed relatively low unemployment and stronger economic growth. This is a feasible objective today, provided the United States abandons excessive and unequal trade openness. But, a policy of serious unfair trade practice enforcement, more extensive safeguarding, and moderate offsets to foreign mercantilism and subsidies is now required.

The United States needs to put its economic affairs in order. Fiscal responsibility must be restored, with greatly reduced budget deficits. Savings and productive investment should be strengthened. Real tax reform should be implemented. Corporate business should emphasize long-term productivity and economic growth and be less distracted with short-term gains and financial manipulation. Trends toward greater profit sharing and widespread use of ESOPs should be accelerated to improve work incentives and morale. More balanced fiscal policy will allow lower interest rates consistent with low inflation. The world financial order needs strengthening, with additional multinational resources to ease the world debt crisis and promote broader recovery. And, responsible steps toward improved trade equity and balanced trading conditions should be put in place promptly by the United States.

Notes

1. For a wide consensus on U.S. budget deficit reduction, see Council of Economic Advisors, *The Economic Report of the President, 1984* (written under the chairmanship of Martin Feldstein); Paul Samuelson, "Evaluating Reagonomics," *Challenge* (Nov.–Dec. 1984); Peter Peterson, *Fortune* (Sept. 17, 1984); Paul Volcker, in repeated public statements between 1981 and 1987; Herbert Stein, *Presidential Economics* (New York: Simon and Schuster, 1984), pp. 345–54; John Makin, *The Global Debt Crisis* (cited in chapter 4 note 19); Paul McCracken, "Toward World Economic Disintegration," *Wall Street Journal* (Feb. 9, 1987), p. 14; Benjamin Friedman, "Implications of the U.S. Net Capital Inflow" (cited in chapter 4 note 19); Ernest Hollings, "The Deficit Is a Drug, Too," *New York Times* (Sept. 28, 1986); David Stockman, *The Triumph Of Politics* (cited in chapter 1, note 65); David Broder, "An Epitaph for Gramm-Rudman," *New Orleans Times-Picayune* (Nov. 25, 1986), editorial page; James Reston,

"Holidays: A Time for Reflection," *New Orleans Times-Picayune* (Dec. 26, 1986), editorial page.

2. "Congress Enacts Strict Anti-Deficit Measure," *Congressional Quarterly Almanac* (cited in note 1).

3. U.S. and world market "real" interest rates increased substantially as a result of tighter federal monetary policy; they remained high between 1981 and 1985. See *World Economic Outlook* (Washington, D.C.: IMF, Oct. 1986), chart 1 on p. 3.

4. See Jonathan Feurbringer, "Washington Talk: Whither the Budget Balancing Law," *New York Times* (Oct. 14, 1986), p. 6. Also see "Budget Deadline? What Deadline?" *New York Times* (Oct. 14, 1986), p. 34.

5. See, for example, sources cited in note 1 (especially Friedman, McCracken, Hollings, and Broder).

6. See Lovett, *Banking and Financial Institutions Law* (St. Paul, Minn.: West, 1984), with respect to monetary and fiscal policy guidelines (pp. 61–97). See also T.R.G. Bingham, *Banking and Monetary Policy: Trends in Banking Structure and Regulation in OECD Countries* (Paris: OECD, 1985); Thomas Mayer, James Duesenberry, and Robert Aliber, *Money, Banking and the Economy* (New York: W.W. Norton, 1984).

7. For the importance of wage-price discipline in overall inflation and stabilization policy, see Leon Lindberg and Charles Maier, eds., *The Politics of Inflation and Economic Stagnation* (Washington, D.C.: Brookings, 1981). See also William A. Lovett, *Inflation and Politics: Fiscal, Monetary, and Wage-Price Discipline* (Lexington, Mass.: Lexington Books, 1982); Robert Flanagan, David Soskice, and Lloyd Ulman, *Unionism, Economic Stabilization, and Income Policies: The European Experience* (Washington, D.C.: Brookings, 1983); William Fellner, *Essays in Contemporary Economic Problems, Disinflation,* 1983–84 ed. (Washington, D.C.: American Enterprise Institute, 1984). Yet, compare Gottfried Haberler, *The Problem of Stagflation* (Washington, D.C.: American Enterprise Institute, 1985).

8. This would be consistent with the moderate guidelines summarized in sources cited in note 6.

9. Concerning the increase in U.S. tax load (especially since the 1930s and World War II), including the gradual increase in the 1950s–1970s, see William A. Lovett, *Inflation and Politics,* (cited in note 6), pp. 62, 187–90; Albert Ando, Marshal/Blume, and Irwin Friend, *The Structure and Reform of the U.S. Tax System* (Cambridge, Mass.: MIT Press, 1985), p. 24. See also Paul Studenski and Herman Kroos, *Financial History of the United States,* 2nd ed. (New York: McGraw-Hill, 1963).

10. Thus, in 1952, corporate taxes represented one third of federal tax receipts (see Studenski and Kroos [cited in note 9], p. 496). In 1982, corporate taxes were under 6 percent of federal tax receipts. (See table 6–4.)

11. For recent works on tax reform issues, see Ando et al. (cited in note 9); Joseph Pechman, *Federal Tax Reform,* 4th ed. (Washington, D.C.: Brookings, 1984); "The Principles and Politics of Tax Reform," *The Cato Journal 5*, no. 2 (Washington D.C.: Cato Institute, Fall 1985).

12. Earlier versions of the Tax Reform Act of 1986 (including Bradley-Gephart) featured mild progressivity. See also "Tilting at Tax Reform," *Time* (June 3, 1985), pp. 18–21.

13. Whether substantial changes in the Tax Reform Act of 1986 can be made quickly is doubtful. First, the Reagan administration will resist alteration of a major

"achievement." Second, many leading Democrats, including Congressman Dan Rostenkowski, were co-opted into the enactment of 1986 tax reform. Only a new presidential administration in 1989, with considerable Congressional support, could make appreciable tax changes. Perhaps at this stage, the budget deficit could be dealt with more seriously.

14. See U.S. Department of Justice *Merger Guidelines* (1982 and 1984). For recent evolution of U.S. antitrust law, see Phillip Areeda, *Antitrust Analysis: Problems, Text, Cases,* 3rd ed. (Boston: Little, Brown, 1984, with 1986 Supplement); ABA Antitrust Section, *Antitrust Law Developments,* 2nd ed. (Chicago: ABA Press, 1984); Eleanor Fox, "The New Merger Guidelines—A Blueprint for Micro-economic Analysis," *Antitrust Law Bulletin* 27 (1982), pp. 521–91; Kenneth M. Davidson, *Megamergers: Corporate America's Billion Dollar Takeovers* (Cambridge, Mass.: Ballinger, 1985); "Deal Mania: The Restructuring of Corporate America," *Business Week* (Nov. 24, 1986), pp. 74–96; Allen Michel and Israel Shaked, *Takeover Madness: Corporate America Fights Back* (New York: Wiley, 1986); Willard F. Mueller, "The New Attack on Antitrust," paper presented at Conference in Honor of Robert F. Lanzillotti, Univ. of Florida (April 4, 1986); Walter Adams and James Brock, *The Bigness Complex: Industry, Labor, and Government in the American Economy* (New York: Pantheon-Random House, 1986), pp. 158–208, 372–73; William A. Lovett, "Where Antitrust Is Going Wrong?" *Antitrust Law and Economic Review* 15, no. 4 and 16, no. 1 (1984–85); and Robert Wills, ed., *Issues after a Century of Federal Antitrust Policy* (Lexington, Mass.: Lexington Books, 1987).

15. See "Deal Mania," Michel and Shaked, and Adams and Brock (cited in note 14).

16. Unquestionably, a revival of antitrust and merger enforcement is needed to some extent, and this would receive broad support from small business, consumers, and those concerned about long-run competitiveness and economic vitality in the United States. See Areeda, Mueller, Adams and Brock, and Lovett (cited in note 14). But, serious damage has been suffered by some important U.S. manufacturing industries during the high-dollar period of 1982–86, when U.S. export growth was crippled, and substantial new import penetration occurred. Some retrenchment and consolidation seem inevitable in the most weakened U.S. industries. But, this merger activity should be carefully supervised by the U.S. antitrust authorities to minimize long-run damage to competitiveness within U.S. industry. See, for example, James T. Halverson, Robert B. Peabody, J. Paul McGrath, Robert Pitofsky, and Malcolm Baldrige, panel discussion, April 9, Washington, D.C., "U.S. Industrial Competitiveness and Section 7 of the Clayton Act: Are They Compatible?" *Antitrust Law Journal* 55, no. 1 (Chicago: American Bar Association Sect. of Antitrust Law, 1986).

17. See "Deal Mania," *Business Week* (cited in note 14), esp. p. 1. See also Henry Kaufman, *Interest Rates, the Markets, and the New Financial World* (New York: Times Books-Random House, 1986), esp. pp. 34–50; Howard M. Wachtel, *The Money Mandarins: The Making of a Supranational Economic Order* (New York: Pantheon-Random House, 1986); Henry Kaufman, "Debt: The Threat to Economic and Financial Stability," *Economic Review, Federal Reserve Bank of Kansas City* (Dec. 1986), pp. 3–9; "The Casino Society," *Business Week* (Sept. 16, 1986), pp. 78–90. For a speculative tease, see also Paul Erdman, *The Panic of 1989* (New York: Doubleday, 1987)—a somewhat realistic novel.

18. See John Makin, *The Global Debt Crisis: America's Growing Involvement* (New York: Basic, 1984); Lovett (cited in chapter 4 note 1); and table 4–1.

19. The need for continuing bank regulation in the midst of considerable financial consolidation is explained by Irvine H. Sprague, *Bailout: An Insider's Account of Bank Failures and Rescues* (New York: Basic, 1986); William Lovett, *Banking and Financial Institutions Law* (St. Paul, Minn.: West, 1984); Richard Dale, *The Regulation of International Banking* (Cambridge, England: Woodhead-Faulkner, 1985); Mayer, Duesenberry, and Aliber, *Money, Banking and the Economy* (cited in note 5); George Kaufman, *The U.S. Financial System: Money, Markets, and Institutions* (Englewood Cliffs, N.J.: Prentice-Hall, 1986); Richard Timberlake, *The Origins of Central Banking in the U.S.* (Cambridge, Mass.: Harvard Univ., 1978); George Benston et al., *Perspectives on Safe and Sound Banking: Past, Present, and Future* (Cambridge, Mass.: American Banker's Association-MIT Press, 1986); John Cooper, *The Management and Regulation of Banks* (New York: St. Martin's, 1984); Jane Welch, *The Regulation of Banks in the Member States of the EEC,* 2nd ed. (The Hague: Martinus Nijhof, 1981). And see Studenski and Kroos, *A Financial History of the United States* (cited in note 9); John Kenneth Galbraith, *Money* (cited in chapter 4 note 7).

20. See sources cited in note 17.

21. Leonard Silk, "Economic Scene," *New York Times* (Nov. 14, 1986), p. 30.

22. S&L industry strains came from a double whammy. (1) Regulation Q deposit rate regulation held down the cost of deposits for a while in the 1970s, which allowed mortgage loan rates to be somewhat low. But, as inflation worsened in the late 1970s, greater competition for deposits (especially from money market mutual funds) and rate deregulation raised the cost of thrift industry deposits well above their mortgage loan portfolio returns. A nasty squeeze on earnings resulted, which led to broader lending freedom as relief, and access to some emergency borrowing. (2) Unfortunately, many thrifts got into additional trouble with speculative lending, widespread recession, and a real estate slump in the 1980s. So many thrifts are insecure now that FSLIC reserves need replenishment. The problem (not a simple one) is how to allocate increased premium charges? Among thrifts alone? Among thrifts and banks together? And with how much responsibility from the U.S. Treasury due to mismanaged macroeconomic policies?

23. See Lovett (cited in note 19), pp. 106–9, 124–28. More recently, there has been some modification of capital adequacy requirements to take account of different levels of risk in various bank assets.

24. See Corey Rosen, Katherine J. Klein, and Karen M. Young, *Employee Ownership in America: The Equity Solution* (Lexington, Mass.: Lexington Books, 1986); "ESOP's Improve Corporate Performance: New Study Established Definitive Link," *The Employee Ownership Report* 6, no. 5 (Arlington, Va.: National Center for Employee Ownership, Sept.-Oct. 1986), p. 1; Martin L. Weitzman, *The Share Economy: Conquering Stagflation* (Cambridge, Mass.: Harvard Univ., 1984); William Foote Whyte et al., *Worker Participation and Ownership: Cooperative Strategies for Strengthening Local Economies* (Ithaca, N.Y.: New York State School of Industrial and Labor Relations-ILR Press, 1983); William A. Lovett, "Profit Sharing and ESOP's: Improved Incentives and Equity," in Arthur S. Miller and Warren Samuels, eds., *Corporations and Society* (Westport, Conn.: Greenwood, 1987). See also Studs Terkel, *Working* (New York: Avon, 1975); "The End of Corporate Loyalty?" *Business Week* (Aug. 4, 1986), pp. 42–45.

25. See Rosen and Lovett (cited in note 24).

26. See sources cited in note 24, particularly Rosen, Weitzman, and Lovett. The relationship of industrial and trade policy to broader profit sharing and employee stock ownership is significant. If American working people, companies, and industries are to be enrolled in a stronger teamwork effort, they have a right to expect more support from their own government against foreign industrial policies, mercantilism, restrictive practices, subsidies, and frequent discounting in world markets.

27. See Lester Thurow, *The Zero-Sum Solution: Building a World-Class American Economy* (New York: Simon and Schuster, 1985), pp. 148, 273.

28. *Budget of the United States Government,* Executive Office of the President, Office of Management and Budget (fiscal year 1986).

29. See Thurow (cited in note 27), pp. 88, 273.

30. See ibid., pp. 273–77, 292–93.

31. See ibid., p. 88; Charles J. McMillan, *The Japanese Industrial System* (Berlin: Walter de Gruyter, 1984), p. 12; Edward B. Fiske, "U.S. Pupils Lag in Math Ability, 3 Studies Find," *New York Times* (Jan. 11, 1987), p. 11.

In addition, The National Research Council reported in 1980 that 46 percent of all U.S. doctoral degrees in engineering went to non-U.S. citizens (1,149 out of a total of 2,479 awarded). Of these Ph.D. recipients, 299 (12 percent) held permanent visas, while 850 (34 percent) held temporary visas. See also "U.S. Science and Engineering Education and Manpower," Report by the Congressional Research Service, Library of Congress, for the Subcommittee on Science, Research and Technology Committee on Science and Technology, U.S. House of Representatives, 98th Cong., 1st Sess. (April 1983).

32. See Thurow (cited in note 27), pp. 270–73. In addition, see the appraisal of John Kenneth Galbraith, *The New Industrial State,* 2nd ed. (Boston: Houghton Mifflin, 1971), note at pp. 190–91. See also John Kenneth Galbraith, *Economics and the Public Purpose* (Boston: Houghton Mifflin, 1973), pp. 46, 73–77, 131–32, 282–83, 294. (Remember that when Galbraith went to Harvard he was, and remained for many years, a distinguished agricultural economist.) For more sources on agriculture, see note 61 infra.

33. "Goldplating" and waste in defense contracting is widely discussed, but has been difficult to control. It is a serious national problem, especially when expensive weapon systems cost too much and fail to yield good performance. See, for example, Merton J. Peck and Frederic M. Scherer, *The Weapons Acquisition Process: An Economic Analysis* (Boston: Harvard Business School, 1962); Stephen Enke, ed., *Defense Management* (Englewood Cliffs, N.J.: Prentice-Hall, 1967); Edwin Mansfield, *Defense, Science and Public Policy* (New York: Norton, 1968); William Proxmire, *Report from Wasteland: America's Military-Industrial Performance* (New York: Praeger, 1970); Arthur T. Hadley, *The Straw Giant; Triumph and Failure: America's Armed Forces* (New York: Random House, 1986); Gary Hart with William S. Lind, *America Can Win: The Case for Military Reform* (Bethesda, Md.: Adler & Adler, 1986).

34. See Thurow (cited in note 27), pp. 126 and 273. But, see Kenneth M. Brown, ed., *The R&D Tax Credit: Issues in Tax Policy and Industrial Innovation* (Washington, D.C.: American Enterprise Inst., 1984). In trying to strengthen and rejuvenate U.S. industry and technology and broaden R&D efforts, we must remember the need for follow-through incentives. People (workers, engineers, scientists, managers, and

investors) and companies require long-term market opportunities for serious investments in manufacturing to implement R&D and make it pay off. Allowing foreign imports excessive freedom and displacement potential in U.S. markets undercuts these efforts. Therefore, strong trade equity policies—including offsets to foreign mercantilism, widespread subsidies, restrictive practices, and price discounting are essential. See chapter 3 and subsequent sections of this chapter.

In addition, see Stephen S. Cohen and John Zysman, *Manufacturing Matters: The Myth of the Post-Industrial Economy* (New York: Basic, 1987); Richard R. Nelson, *High Technology Policies: A Five Nation Comparison* (Washington, D.C.: American Enterprise Inst., 1984).

35. For extensive cross-references, see chapter 3 note 11. In addition, for more background on export promotion and subsidy efforts, see *The Export Credit Financing Systems in OECD Member Countries* (Paris: OECD, 1982); Michael R. Czinkota, ed., *Export Promotion: The Public and Private Sector Interaction* (New York: Praeger); C.V. Platt, *Tax Systems of Africa, Asia and the Middle East* (Aldershot, England: Gower, 1982); and detailed country articles in *Euromoney Trade Finance Report* (London: monthly).

36. Unfortunately, Reagan administration policies with respect to the current GATT round reflect this approach. See, for example, the House testimony of Clayton Yeutter and other sources cited in chapter 1 note 71.

37. It must be emphasized that extemely high protective tariffs (50 to 100 percent), which preclude access for most imports against domestic competition, enjoy little support. Needless to say, moderate and responsible trade equity policies that merely bring the United States into rough equivalence or conformity with de facto European commercial policies cannot be considered comparable or even mildly close to the severity of Smoot-Hawley Tariff walls.

38. Many free-trade advocates and lobbyists representing MNC and international banks that benefit from the existing system (with its asymmetrical openness) see a need to preserve a modest opportunity for protest against "unfair" import practices. However, their purpose is not to facilitate relief, but to grant it as sparingly as possible. In this way, "free trade" (for their purposes) can be maximized.

39. An essential reform is to restructure political influence upon U.S. trade policy. It should be more truly representative of American working people, communities, industries, and the long-run interest of society in a strong economic base of diverse industries, technology, and talent. Existing U.S. trade policy has become largely captive to a limited set of MNC and international banking interests, some of which are losing their identity as elements of American society and becoming really transnational or global. The most ardent protectionists in current U.S. trade policy are the well-organized and extremely well funded lobbyists for multinational interests fighting hard to maintain dominance. Many leading academics in the United States have become co-opted and integrated into this multinational "establishment." When we appreciate the lopsidedness of current trade-lobbying efforts, however, the resulting asymmetry of U.S. trade openness is easier to understand.

40. The old free-trade–protectionist (white and black) dichotomy is out of joint with reality. (1) Most countries operate in the large, grey middle ground between the extremes of total protection and complete free access (without any subsidies or restriction). Most countries have developed a mixed industrial-trade strategy, with substantial

elements of mercantilism and yet considerable room for maneuver enjoyed by their companies, industries, and state enterprises (which frequently collaborate in some degree). (2) In recent U.S. trade policy, the free-trade or multinational interests are dominant and trying to protect and secure the "globalist" system in their favor. In a political sense, therefore, the multinational interest network is vigorously "protecting" itself. But, it would be a misuse of terminology to label only part of a complex political equation as protectionist. In the end, trade policy affects many diverse business, labor, agricultural, regional, and political interests. Hopefully, broader prosperity, economic growth, reasonably full employment, and a strong industrial-technological system should be the predominant goals of each nation as a whole.

41. The most integrated economies of Europe (and Japan) found it desirable to enact VATs to conform their business cost structures more closely. As the United States becomes more closely integrated with Europe and Japan, similar logic operates. For VAT literature, see the following: National Economic Development Office, *Value Added Tax* (London: Her Majesty's Stationery Office, 1971); Norman Ture, *The Value Added Tax* (Washington, D.C.: Heritage Foundation, 1979); J.P. Timmermans and G.T.J. Joseph, "Value Added Tax (V.A.T.): National Modifications to comply with the Sixth Directive of the Council of the European Communities," *European Taxation* 20, no. 2 (Amsterdam: International Bureau of Fiscal Documentation, 1980); Richard Lindholm, *The Economics of VAT: Preserving Efficiency, Capitalism, and Social Progress* (Lexington, Mass.: Lexington Books, 1980); Henry Aaron, ed., *The Value Added Tax: Lessons from Europe* (Washington, D.C.: Brookings, 1981); William Turnier, "Designing an Efficient Value Added Tax," *Tax Law Review* 39 (1984), pp. 435–72; Treasury Department Report to the President, *Tax Reform for Fairness, Simplicity, and Economic Growth*, Vol. 3; *Value Added Tax* (Washington, D.C.: Office of the Secretary, Treasury Department, Nov. 1984); Alan Schenk, "The Business Transfer Tax," *Tax Notes* (Jan. 27, 1986), pp. 351–60; Richard Gordon et al., "The Business Transfer Tax—A VAT by Any Other Name," *Tax Notes* (Feb. 24, 1986); "Is a Tax Hike Coming: It Seems Inevitable. The Only Questions Now Are What Kind and When," *Business Week* (Feb. 3, 1986), pp. 48–53; Robert Kuttner, "A Tax Everybody Could Live With," *Business Week* (Sept. 22, 1986), p. 12. See also J.A. Stockfisch, "Value Added Taxes and the Size of Government," *National Tax Journal* 38 (Dec. 1985), which finds no significant relationship between VATs and the rate of growth in government or tax load.

42. See in chapter 3, the section "Offsetting or Equivalent U.S. Trade Restrictions" and notes 13, 14, and 16. See also the final section of chapter 2.

43. In chapter 3, see "Import Surcharges" and "Graduated Offset Responses," particularly note 19 and table 3–2.

44. In chapter 3, see "Domestic-Content Laws" and note 20.

45. A full-scale revitalization of U.S. manufacturing cannot be achieved without reasonable offsets to foreign industrial policies, mercantilism, subsidies, export promotion, and widespread discounting (especially in industries with considerable excess capacity). See, for example, the eloquent summary by Robert Peabody (president of the American Iron and Steel Institute), *Antitrust Law Journal* 55, no. 1 (1987), pp. 8–12.

What caused the U.S. steel industry, that in 1950 was universally recognized as the benchmark for the world, to get into such a sorry condition that it is now smaller in size than the steel industry of the Soviet Union, Japan, or the European Community, and getting even smaller?. . .

The real reasons for the domestic steel industry's current problems can be found in government policies—both foreign and domestic. In the 1960s, foreign steel imports averaged about 2.3 percent of the market. This climbed to about 10 percent in the 1960s, to about 15 percent in the 1970s, and so far, in the 1980s, to about 23 percent. This market penetration has been chiefly the result of two factors: unfair trade, plus the role of foreign governments in building, owning, subsidizing, guiding, directing, and protecting their steel industries. What has happened is that the private sector, shareholder-owned steel companies in this country, have been competing—in the United States—with steel producers which are, in effect, creatures of their government's political, social and economic policies. . . .

The major European steel producers, including those not actually owned or controlled by governments, have been, with only slight exception, creatures of the political and social policies of the European Community. In fact, having lost more than twenty-one billion dollars in the past ten years, Europe's state-owned and managed steel companies would not even be in business today were it not for the more than twenty-five billion dollars in government funding they received in that period. Moreover, for many years the European Community has protected its steel industry. Agreements with all significant steel exporters, for example, limit the amount which enters that country, and specify the minimum import price as well. . . .

As Dieter Spethmann, chairman of Thyssen, commented in 1983, "No private enterprise can in the long run compete against the combined Ministers of Finance of Europe."

In Japan, it was, and is, done differently. Following the split-up of the government-owned Japan Steel Company after the war, throughout the 1950s and 1960s MITI (the Ministry of International Trade and Industry) targeted steel as a "chosen" industry with the goal of making the industry not only internationally competitive but capable of dominating world export markets. To accomplish that goal, the steel industry was "guided" in its investments, mergers were facilitated, and the companies [were] given guaranteed access to cheap and plentiful capital for modernization and expansion purposes. As a result, Japanese steelmaking capacity increased in twenty-five years from 5.9 million tons to 143 million. To protect the industry domestically, the government for twenty-five years (the phenomenal growth period of the country) kept such a tight lid on steel imports that at no time during that period did Japan import as much as one million tons of steel. Similarly, in the developing world, the governments of so-called "newly industrializing countries" such as Brazil and South Korea decided early in the 1970s that their national interest would be served by an enormous buildup of steelmaking capacity. . . .

Fifteen years ago, Korea had no iron ore, no metallurgical coal, no history of industrialization, and no developed infrastructure on which to base a steel industry. What it did have—and has had during the fifteen years its steel industry has been under government-forced development—was a willing and able work force, a military government with a vision to "out-MITI" the Japanese, a good group of Army engineers, and relatively unlimited access by its government to foreign funds to relend at concessionary rates to the government-owned and -managed steel industry. . . .

Pohang Iron and Steel Company (POSCO) was established, funded, managed by Army generals, and given the mission of becoming a world-class steel producer. In fifteen years or so, POSCO has become roughly the same size as the Canadian or British steel industry. Without minimizing in the slightest this technical achievement, what has been accomplished is the result of massive foreign aid and the application of military discipline to a low-paid, non-organized, very able work force. Stated another way, using government-supplied debt and political/military leverage, a world-class competitior has been created which operates in this marketplace. With only slight modification, the story in Brazil is much the same, and exists on a smaller scale in other developing countries around the world. Today governments throughout the developing world either own or control nearly all integrated steel production facilities. They were aided initially (as indeed they still are) by government credit and subsidized financing of the plant and equipment—primarily from Japan and Europe. Having been built regardless of economic conditions, they are protected in their home markets, but the overbuilding many cases created a mountain of foreign debt, growing operating losses, more subsidies, and the continuing need for steel exports at any price, primarily to the United States market. . . .

Consequently, for twenty years or more, immense quantities of dumped and subsidized foreign steel were forced into this market at almost any price, coming from countries whose steel facilities had to operate for social or political reasons, or to obtain foreign exchange. The effect was brutal on domestic steel producers. In an industry that has—and it is no different around the world—high fixed costs, the loss of cash flow had a very serious effect on the ability to fund new and improved facilities. . . .

United States public policies generally have not recognized the reality of this new competition and its effects on American industry."

(Peabody's remarks appeared as part of a panel discussion in April 1986, at the Spring meeting of the Antitrust Section of the American Bar Association in Washington, D.C. This lawyer has nearly thirty years experience with the U.S. steel industry.)

But, the U.S. marketplace has by now recognized the inadequacy of realizable profits in domestic manufacturing, *in the current environment of unequal trade openness, with widespread mercantilism and industrial policies abroad, further encouraged by low wages in most NICs.* See, for example, Thomas J. Lueck, "Venture Capitalists Shifting Focus from High Technology," *New York Times* (Feb. 6, 1987), p. 1. The U.S. venture capital industry is switching emphasis away from technological innovation and related manufacturing. In 1986, more than a third of $3.4 billion raised as venture capital was used for leveraged buyouts of existing companies and assets. As a businessman active in this field observed, "It may not be good for the country, but the fact is that technology has not been as rewarding as other forms of investment" (ibid).

46. *Competitiveness* became a magic buzzword in politics for 1987. But, the Japanese, Koreans, and Taiwanese have taught the world in recent decades that industrial and trade-development success requires long-term teamwork and sustained government–industry collaboration. And, the younger generation is realizing that their own careers and lifetime income prospects are tied in with overall economic growth and industrial prosperity.

47. Americans must abandon a naive and excessively adversarial concept of industry–government relations. The United States cannot effectively compete, match, respond, and deal with foreign industrial policies, mercantilism, subsidies, export promotion, and widespread discounting, unless it creates appropriate government organization. A U.S. DITT is now essential and really overdue. (See *Report of the President's Commission on Industrial Competitiveness* (cited in note 51), pp. 51, 57.)

48. *Budget of the United States Government,* Executive Office of the President, Office of Management and Budget (Fiscal Year 1986).

49. The Reagan administration proposals have been flawed in this area, because they unduly weaken antitrust and domestic competitive disciplines, and they do not respond sufficiently to the needs for improved trade equity and offsets to foreign industrial policies, mercantilism, subsidies, export promotion, and widespread discounting (especially in industries with considerable excess capacity). Antitrust and other government agencies have a vital watchdog role to play on both fronts in dealing with problems of inadequate and unfair competition at home *and* in world trade.

50. One of the worst misleading "attacks on strawmen" (or irrelevant caricatures) in the trade policy controversy is the idea that "industrial policy substitutes government for the marketplace." Needless to say, this misrepresentation bears no relation to the success of Japanese, Korean, Taiwan, or West German industrial development in the post–World War II era. (See chapter 2.)

51. People understand when they are benefiting from industrial growth and economic development. It is a sad commentary upon industrial moral that "only 9 percent of American workers felt they would benefit directly from the increased productivity of their companies, while a similar survey of Japanese workers showed that 93 percent felt they would benefit from such improvements." Report of the President's Commission on Industrial Competitiveness, *Global Competition: The New Reality* (Washington, D.C.: Jan. 1985), p. 9.

52. See chapters 4 (especially sections "Multinational Agency Assistance" and "IMF Stabilization Programs") and 5.

53. This purchase of undervalued foreign currencies by the United States (selling dollars for such currencies) was appropriate during 1984–85, especially against the yen, deutsche mark, and Swiss franc, when the dollar became increasingly overvalued. A large U.S. reserves hoard of these hard currencies could have been built up and purchased at discount prices, which would have eased competitiveness problems of U.S. exports and somewhat limited excessive U.S. imports. A cynic might wonder whether Federal Reserve policy through 1984 was influenced by the Reagan-Mondale election campaign and the Reagan administration's contention that a strong dollar was an international vote of confidence in Reaganomics.

In any event, the U.S. dollar declined substantially between Feb. 1985 and early 1987. Whether the U.S. monetary authorities now should sell more dollars is controversial. Many experts (including Fed Chairman Volcker) insist the dollar is about right for now. Others believe that the dollar needs further decline, but even these want a soft landing. But, it seems the best opportunity to sell off dollars and offset foreign undervaluation of currencies was 1984. Thus, U.S. intervention efforts came somewhat belatedly, mainly since late summer 1985.

54. See in chapter 4, "Reduced Interest Rates" and, in chapter 5, "Improving the Environment for International Investment." See also Peter Kenen, *Financing, Adjustment, and the International Monetary Fund* (Washington, D.C.: Brookings, 1986); Richard Goode, *Economic Assistance to Developing Countries through the IMF* (Washington, D.C.: Brookings, 1985); "African Symposium," *Challenge* (Jan.–Feb. 1987); Carol Lancaster and John Williamson, eds., *African Debt and Financing* (Washington, D.C.: Inst. for International Economics, May 1986); "Trends in Foreign Aid, 1977–86," Study Prepared by the Foreign Affairs and National Defense Division, Congressional Research Service for the Select Committee on Hunger, U.S. House of Representatives, 99th Cong., 2nd Sess., Nov. 1986; Celso Furtado, *No to Recession and Unemployment: An Examination of the Brazilian Economic Crisis* (London: Third World Foundation for Social and Economic Studies, 1984); Robert E. Looney, *Economic Policymaking in Mexico: Factors Underlying the 1982 Crisis* (Durham, N.C.: Duke Univ., 1985); John Sewell et al., eds., *U.S. Foreign Policy and the Third World: Agenda, 1985–86* (Washington, D.C.: Overseas Development Council-Transaction, 1985); Robert Girling, *Multinational Institutions and the Third World: Management, Debt, and Trade Conflicts in the International Economic Order* (New York: Praeger, 1985); David Obey and Paul Sarbanes, "A Marshall Plan for the 1980's? Recycling Surpluses to the Third World," *New York Times* (Nov. 9, 1986), p. B–3. Finally, contrast Rudiger Dornbusch, "International Debt and Economic Instability," and Rimmer de Vries, "Commentary on 'International Debt and Economic Stability'," *Economic Review* (Federal Reserve Bank of Kansas City, January 1987).

55. See, in chapter 4, "Partial Forgiveness of Loans and Loss Recognition" note 10.

56. See tables 6–1, 6–2, and 6–3. As the U.S. federal, state, and local government debt approaches annual GNP, its debt-service load becomes an increasing strain and diversion from other public-sector responsibilities (including national defense). In recent years, the U.S. transformed itself from the world's largest creditor to the biggest debtor nation. Further mismanagement along these lines can only be considered a historic tragedy.

57. See chapter 5, esp. the section "Investment-Guarantee Programs and Limitations" and note 17.

58. Trade imbalances for the U.S. illustrated in appendix table A–15 are unsustainable and must be eliminated reasonably soon.

59. There are some who assert that U.S. policy should emphasize only export expansion, but this fails to take account of strongly entrenched foreign mercantilism, industrial policies, export promotion, widespread subsidies, considerable discounting, and various import restrictions that make the growth of U.S. exports and earnings abroad slow and difficult. Lip-service and verbal concessions to free trade are not enough to make large changes in world trade flows.

60. The lessons of British history in the 1920s and the subsequent decline of industrial Britain after World War II should serve as a grave warning to Americans. (See chapter 1.) Fortunately, Japan, West Germany, and other industrial rivals of the U.S. have only caught up with the United States lately. But, for the United States to continue unequal and asymmetrical openness, to neglect its industrial and technological vitality, and to allow further erosion of manufacturing competitiveness would be irresponsible economic policy. (See chapters 2 and 3 and, particularly, note 45 of chapter 6.)

61. Some naively believe that merely talking about free trade with other nations is sufficient to achieve open markets abroad quickly. Alas, as this book demonstrates, the real world has much stronger momentum of its own. Foreign industrial policies and mercantilism (along with extensive subsidies, export promotion, extensive discounting, selective import restrictions, and a wide variety of NTBs) are well entrenched, with powerful political alliances and national ideologies in support. Some U.S. export gains can be made, but more as a result of tough bargaining and better use of the heavy leverage of massive U.S. imports. Incantations of free-trade idealism will not cut many deals.

Of special importance for U.S. trade negotiations is agriculture, which had been the United States's strongest suit in comparative advantage. See the following to understand limits on U.S. agricultural export growth: "Japanese Import Barriers to U.S. Agricultural Exports" and "The Common Agricultural Policy of the European Community and Implications for the U.S. Agriculture Trade," studies prepared for Republican members of the Joint Economic Committee, Congressional Research Service, Library of Congress, 99th Cong., 2nd Sess. (Oct. 1, 1986); Rosemary Fennell, *The Common Agricultural Policy of the European Community* (London: Granada, 1979); John Marsh and Pamela Swanney, *Agriculture and the European Community* (London: George Allen & Unwin, 1980); Simon Harris, Alan Swinbank, and Guy Wilkinson, *The Food and Farm Policies of the European Community* (Chichester, England: John Wiley & Sons, 1983); Allen Bucknell, David Harvey, Kenneth Johnson, and Kevin Parton, *The Costs of the Common Agricultural Policy* (London: Croom Helm, 1982); Francois Duchene, Edward Szczepanik, and Wilfrid Legg, *New Limits on European*

Agriculture, Politics and the Common Agricultural Policy (Totowa, N.J.: Rowman & Allanheld, 1985); Brian E. Hill, The Common Agricultural Policy; Past, Present and Future (London; New York: Methuen, 1984); Hartwig de Hoen, Glen Johnson, and Stefan Tangerman, Agriculture and International Economic Relations (New York: St. Martin's, 1985); Robert Paarlberg, India, the Soviet Union, and the United States (Ithaca, N.Y.: Cornell Univ., 1985); Joel Solkoff, The Politics of Food (San Francisco: Sierra Club, 1985); Alex McCalla and Timothy Josling, Agricultural Policies and World Markets (New York: Macmillan, 1985); C. Peter Timmer, The Scope and Limits of Agricultural Policy (Ithaca, N.Y.: Cornell Univ., 1986); David Balaam, Food Politics: The Regional Conflict (Totowa, N.J.: Allanheld, Osmun, 1981); C. Ford Runge, ed., The Future of the North American Granary (Ames, Iowa: Iowa State Univ., 1986); and Bruce L. Gardner, U.S. Agriculture Policy: The 1985 Farm Legislation (Washington, D.C.: American Enterprise Inst., 1985).

The other big export strength of the U.S. economy used to be higher technology manufacturing. In this area, too, the United States's lead has eroded and needs significant rejuvenation efforts. (See figure P–3.) Also, see Herbert Fusfeld and Richard Langlois, eds., Understanding R&D Productivity (New York: Pergamon, 1982); Herbert Fusfeld and Carmela Haklisch, Industrial Productivity and International Technical Cooperation (New York: Pergamon, 1982); Donald A. Hicks, Automation Technology and Renewal: Adjustment Dynamics in the U.S. Metal Working Sector (Washington, D.C.: American Enterprise Inst., 1986); Richard Nelson, ed., Government and Technical Progress (New York: Pergamon, 1982); Edwin Mansfield, Technology Transfer, Productivity, and Economic Policy (New York: W.W. Norton, 1982).

62. The United States, however, must be responsible and careful. A drastic, rapid slash in U.S. imports would be misunderstood and very costly to many allied governments, with too much economic dislocation and unemployment.

63. The United States assumed the burden of Free-World leadership and economic aid for many allies in the post–World War II settlement. This supportive role had two primary elements. (1) In the Bretton-Woods dollar–gold exchange system, U.S. money and banking was the primary reserve for the Free World and most developing nations. By the late 1960s, this dollar–gold exchange system came under increasing strain, and between 1971 and 1973, it collapsed. In subsequent years, the world evolved a multiple–reserve-currency system, with somewhat "dirty free floating" and independent interventions to suit the export (or import) policies of various nations.

(2) In the GATT "freer-trade" system, the United States served as the most open and welcoming major import market. Under the slogan "trade, not aid," economic recovery and prosperity were fostered for Europe, Japan, and an increasing number of NICs. But, this unbalanced trade regime is under increasing strain now, with massive and unsustainable U.S. trade deficits between 1983 and 1987. The asymmetrical openness and overvalued dollar (especially between 1983 and 1985) of this trade regime cannot continue much longer. It must be succeeded by a more realistic, sustainable, and balanced trade regime in the 1990s and beyond. This new trade regime should feature a world of competing industrial policies, with partial openness, but some continuing mercantilism. There must be concern within all industrial nations (and most LDCs) to nurture and maintain adequate, highly efficient industrial machines, with extensive technology sharing, reasonable stability, and balanced interdependence. Every

nation should strive more comprehensively for good economic growth (taking care for its natural environment), reasonably full employment, and the upgrading of human talent and technological capacities. The main outlines of sound national policy efforts have been demonstrated in many nations, including Japan, West Germany, South Korea, and Taiwan in recent years. But, the world trade regime must be adapted more realistically, with far better balance in the coming years. See, in this connection, Paul McCracken, "Toward World Economic Disintegration," *Wall Street Journal* (Feb. 9, 1987), p. 14; Lester Thurow, "America, Europe and Japan: A time to Dismantle the World Economy," in Frieden and Lake (cited in chapter 5 note 1), pp. 385–94; and "Rewriting GATT's Rules for a Game That Has Changed," *Economist* (Sept. 13, 1986), pp. 63–69.

There is an important role for MNCs and international banks in this evolving, more equal, and better balanced world economy. MNCs from many countries will share in the growth process. Technology sharing, cross-licensing, and trade in goods and services will take place within and among these MNCs and their respective headquarters and host countries. But, national politics and consumer demand in most countries require more equitable participation in MNC activities. There is a long-run, natural, and largely inevitable prospect of evening out world opportunities, productivity, and incomes. In retrospect, a predominance of MNCs from one or a few countries (such as the United States, Japan, or West Germany) can only be a transient phenomenon. The evening-out process will prevail over time and could help secure more genuine comity among the peoples of our world.

Appendix Tables:
Country Comparisons

Table A-1
Steel Production by Nation, 1946–84
(1,000 metric tons)

	1946	*1950*	*1968*	*1980*	*1984*
U.S.	60,421	87,848	119,262	101,456	82,716
Soviet Union	13,300	27,600	106,537	147,941	153,996
Japan	564	4,839	66,893	111,395	105,588
West Germany	2,555	12,121	41,159	43,838	39,384
U.K.	12,899	16,554	26,277	11,277	15,120
France	4,408	8,652	20,410	23,176	19,008
Italy	1,153	2,323	16,963	26,501	23,076
Sweden	1,203	1,437	5,069	4,231	4,704
Spain	641	817	4,971	12,553	13,572
Netherlands	137	490	3,707	4,959	5,736
Norway	58	7	812	853	888
Belgium	2,296	3,777	11,573	12,321	11,304
Yugoslavia	202	428	1,997	2,306	1,956
Hungary	353	1,022	2,902	3,766	3,744
Poland	1,219	2,315	11,007	18,648	16,536
China	—	606	15,000	37,120	43,320
South Korea	7	4	372	5,760	5,016
Taiwan	16	14	474	3,651	5,627
India	1,314	1,461	6,495	9,427	10,344
Canada	2,111	3,070	10,161	15,901	14,700
Mexico	251	332	3,270	7,003	7,284
Brazil	343	789	4,453	15,752	18,384
World total	98,040	160,800	512,000	695,457	653,000

Source: United Nations, Statistical Office, *Monthly Bulletin of Statistics* (June 1951), table 14; (June 1969), table 38; (July 1951), p. 2; (Apr. 1953), table 28; (May 1986), table 38. Roger A. Clarke and Dubrovko J.I. Matko, *Soviet Economic Facts* (New York: St. Martin's), table 23, Council for Economic Planning and Development, Republic of China. *Taiwan Statistical Data Book (1985)*, table 5–6b. United Nations, Economic Commission for Asia and the Far East, *Statistical Yearbook for Asia and the Far East, 1972*, China, table 12, p. 76. United Nations, Statistical Office, *Statistical Yearbook, 1956; 1954,* table 109; *1972,* table 124; *1982,* table 147. Willy Kraus, *Economic Development and Social Change in the People's Republic of China* (New York: Springer-Verlag, 1982), table A.8.

Table A–2
Motor Vehicle Production by Nation, 1946–84
(in thousands)

	1946	1950	1968	1974	1980	1984
U.S.	3,090	8,003	10,746	10,253	8,042	10,698
Soviet Union	102	363	801	1,848	2,201	2,136
Japan	—	0.6	4,108	6,556	11,042	11,110
West Germany	23	302	3,110	3,105	3,893	4,052
U.K.	365	784	223	1,534	1,313	1,134
France	93	357	2,075	3,463	3,992	334
Italy	29	127	1,662	1,773	1,612	1,598
Sweden	14	18	245	374	317	404
Spain	—	0.3	391	838	1,194	1,206
Belgium	—	0.3	173	183	260	250
Yugoslavia	—	—	14	154	252	242
China	—	—	27	121	222	64
South Korea	7	—	23	32	121	258
Taiwan	—	—	8	107	133	171
India	—	15	80	88	113	181
Canada	—	172	391	1,425	1,570	1,375
Mexico	—	22	144	352	444	308
Brazil	—	—	473	899	1,168	920
World total	3,805	10,057	28,340	34,540	28,999	41,771

Source: United Nations, Statistical Office, *Monthly Bulletin of Statistics* (June 1951), table 23; (June 1969), table 45; (Nov. 1985). Roger A. Clarke and Dubrovko J.I. Matko, *Soviet Economic Facts* (New York: St. Martin's), table 35. Altshuler, Anderson, Jones Roos, Womack, *The Future of the Automobile* (Cambridge, Mass.: MIT Press 1984). Council for Economic Planning and Development, Republic of China, *Taiwan Statistical Data Book (1985)*, table 5–5a. Willy Kraus, *Economic Development and Social Change in the People's Republic of China* (New York: Springer-Verlag, 1982), table A.8. Motor Vehicle Manufacturers Association, *World Motor Vehicle Data, 1984–85 Edition*, pp.11, 56, 171, 234. Crain Automotive Group, *Automative News, 1985 Market Data Issue*. pp. 3–4. United Nations, Statistical Office, *Statistical Yearbook, 1954*, table 118; *1972*, table 135; *1982*, table 137. U.S. Department of Commerce, Domestic and International Business Administration, *World Motor Vehicle and Trailer Production & Registration, 1974–75* (Jan. 1976), table 1.

Table A–3
Crude Petroleum Production by Nation, 1946–84
(in thousand metric tons per month)

	1946	1950	1968	1980	1984
U.S.	21,198	22,510	37,489	35,350	36,010
Soviet Union	1,808	3,158	25,700	50,267	51,019
Japan	16	25	65	36	3
West Germany	54	93	665	386	338
U.K.	5	4	7	6,576	10,103
France	4	10	224	118	172
Italy	0.9	0.7	126	150	186
Spain	—	—	11	102	188
Netherlands	5	59	179	2,046	1,690
Norway	—	—	—	107	258
Yugoslavia	2	9	208	443	378
Hungary	57	93	150	169	167
Poland	9	15	40	22	27
China	6	17	1500	8,829	9,542
India	26	21[a]	481	783	2,329
Canada	82	312	4,265	5,867	5,883
Mexico	587	858	1,731	8,328	11,946
Brazil	.7	3	650	757	1,933
World total	29,630	40,400	158,750	248,250	226,750

Source: United Nations, Statistical Office, *Monthly Bulletin of Statistics* (June 1951), table 20; (March 1953), table 13; (June 1969), table 9; (May 1986), table 15; (July 1951), p.2. Roger A. Clarke and Dubrovko J.I. Matko, *Soviet Economic Facts* (New York: St. Martin's), table 20. United Nations, Economic Commission for Asia and the Far East, *Statistical Yearbook for Asia and the Far East, 1972*, China, table 27, p. 27. B.R. Mitchell; *European Historical Statistics, 1950–1970*, p. 373. United Nations, Statistical Office, *Statistical Yearbook, 1946–1950*, p.147; *1951*, pp. 140–41; *1954*, p. 119; *1958*, pp. 121–22; *1972*, p. 181.
[a]1949 data.

Table A–4
Coal Production by Nation, 1946–84
(thousand metric tons per month)

	1946	1950	1968	1980	1984
U.S.	44,938	42,063	41,379	54,199	62,522
Soviet Union	13,667	21,750	49,500	41,077	40,360
Japan	1,698	3,205	3,881	1,502	1,387
West Germany	4,495	9,230	9,334	7,874	7,003
U.K.	16,094	18,366	13,684	10,841	4,271
France	3,930	4,237	3,492	1,683	1,383
Italy	97	86	30	13	0
Sweden	41	26	1.6	1.4	—
Spain	897	919	1,024	1,096	1,261
Netherlands	685	1,021	179	0	—
Norway	8	46	28	24	33
Belgium	1,898	2,275	1,233	527	525
Yugoslavia	63	88	70	32	32
Hungary	60	125	353	255	214
Poland	3,914	6,500	10,719	16,093	15,933
China	190	4,300	23,500	49,667	61,350
South Korea	536	—	835	1,545	1,720
Taiwan	88	117	918	215	354
India	2,516	2,709	5,901	9,092	12,064
Canada	1,230	1,280	662	1,681	2,672
Mexico	82	79	130	417	—
Brazil	158	163	197	437	622
World total	94,090	106,900	169,500	227,333	249,750

Source: United Nations, Statistical Office, *Monthly Bulletin of Statistics* (June 1951), table 6; (May 1953), table 9; (June 1969), table 11; (May 1986), table 11. Roger A. Clarke and Dubrovko J.I. Matko, *Soviet Economic Facts* (New York: St. Martin's), table 19. Council for Economic Planning and Development, Republic of China, *Taiwan Statistical Data Book (1985)*, table 5–6a. United Nations, Statistical Office, *Statistical Yearbook, 1951*, p. 135; *1954*, table 38; *1972*, table 52; *1982*, table 15.

Table A–5

Electricity Production by Nation, 1946–84

(million KWH monthly average)

	1946	1950	1968	1980	1984
U.S.	18,598	27,416	119,416	196,199	201,359
Soviet Union	4,048	7,602	53,200	107,917	124,417
Japan	2,200	3,236	22,778	48,127	48,368
West Germany	2,576	3,663	16,994	30,731	32,857
U.K.	3,437	4,580	18,429	23,745	23,531
France	1,848	2,623	9,782	20,274	25,210
Italy	1,457	2,057	8,497	15,478	15,028
Sweden	1,183	1,529	4,694	7,786	9,967
Spain	450	523	3,765	9,193	9,755
Netherlands	221	456	2,802	5,400	4,971
Norway	938	1,444	5,010	7,008	8,885
Belgium	520	707	2,209	4,470	4,555
Yugoslavia	167	201	1,720	4,945	5,481
Hungary	89	242	1,096	1,989	2,168
Poland	551	829	4,625	10,155	11,275
China	—	—	—	25,052	31,137
South Korea	19	34	500	3,332	4,469
Taiwan	—	378	817	3,401	4,107
India	336	425	3,651	9,929	12,808
Canada	3,478	4,242	14,619	31,460	35,404
Mexico	276	368	1,900	5,580	6,624
Brazil	169	238	2,963	11,624	14,643
World total	48,820	69,900	342,583	687,250	748,250

Source: United Nations, Statistical Office, *Monthly Bulletin of Statistics* (June 1951), table 2; (Jan 1953), table 35; (June 1969), table 48; (May 1986), table 48; (July 1951), p. 2. Roger A. Clarke and Dubrovko J.I. Matko, *Soviet Economic Facts* (New York: St. Martin's), table 21. Council for Economic Planning and Development, Republic of China. *Taiwan Statistical Data Book (1985)*, table 5–6a. Willy Kraus, *Economic Development and Social Change in the People's Republic of China* (New York: Springer-Verlag, 1982), table A.8. United Nations, Statistical Office, *Statistical Yearbook, 1949–50*, table 122; 1954, table 121.

[a]1948 data.

Table A–6
Merchant Shipping Fleet by Nation, 1946–82
(1,000 gross tons)

	1946	1951	1968	1976	1982
U.S.	40,882	27,331	19,668	14,908	19,111
Soviet Union	—	—	12,062	20,668	23,789
Japan	1,200	2,182	19,587	41,663	41,594
West Germany	413	1,031	6,528	9,265	7,701
U.K.	13,340	18,550	21,921	32,923	22,505
France	1,216	3,367	5,796	11,278	10,771
Italy	321	2,917	6,624	11,078	10,375
Sweden	1,462	2,113	4,865	7,971	3,788
Spain	899	1,216	2,821	6,028	8,131
Netherlands	1,563	3,235	5,268	5,920	5,393
Belgium	219	493	933	1,499	2,271
Denmark	733	1,344	3,204	5,143	5,214
Norway	2,809	5,816	19,667	27,944	21,862
Greece	1,027[a]	1,272	7,433	25,035	40,035
Yugoslavia	—	—	1,267	1,944	2,532
China	—	—	766	3,589	8,057
South Korea	—	—	474	1,796	5,529
Taiwan	649[a]	633	763	1,297	2,481
India	317[a]	452	1,945	5,094	6,214
Singapore	—	—	134	5,482	7,183
Canada	1,870	1,647	2,403	2,639	3,213
Mexico	—	168	404	594	1,252
Brazil	511	688	1,294	3.096	5,678
Argentina	246	979	1,197	1,470	2,256
Panama	834	3,609	5.097	15,631	32,600
Liberia	—	595	25,720	73,477	70,718
Saudi Arabia	—	—	—	589	4,320
World total	72,918	87,245	194,200	372,000	424,742

Source: U.S. Department of Commerce, Bureau of the Census, *Statistical Abstract of the United States, 1953,* table 1105; *1969,* table 1265; *1978,* table 1572; *1985,* table 1503. S.G. Sturney, *British Shipping and World Competition* (London: Athlone, 1962), table 20. United Nations, Economic Commission for Asia and the Far East, *Statistical Yearbook for Asia and the Far East, 1972,* Singapore, table 25, p. 353. United Nations, Statistical Office, *Statistical Yearbook, 1954,* table 137; *1972,* table 151; *1982,* table 176.

[a]1947 data.

Table A–7
Average Real Growth Rates in Manufacturing by Nation, 1947–83

	1947–52	1950–60	1960–65	1965–70	1970–75	1975–80	1980–83
U.S.	4.0%	3.4%	6.3%	3.8%	3.3%	4.1%	0.1%
Soviet Union	—	—	8.4	8.6	7.2	—	—
Japan	28.0	18.3	11.5	16.3	2.9	6.6	1.6
West Germany	28.0	9.8	5.7	6.5	1.6	3.3	−1.4
U.K.	6.0	3.5	3.4	3.0	0.5	1.5	0.4
France	11.0	6.8	5.5	9.6	2.8	3.3	−0.7
Italy	10.0	9.3	6.3	7.3	3.0	5.0	−3.3
Sweden	3.0	3.0	7.4	4.9	2.0	—	—
Spain	—	8.8	12.6	10.1	7.9	2.9	0.2
Belgium	7.0	4.1	6.3	6.0	2.6	2.8	−0.2
Poland	—	6.8	8.7	8.9	10.7	—	—
China	—	24.5	1.8	15.6	11.6	10.2	—
South Korea	—	16.4	13.9	25.6	23.5	13.0	4.7
Taiwan	—	15.4	13.6	21.0	13.3	13.8	6.7
India	4.0	6.6	9.0	2.8	4.6	—	—
Canada	5.0	3.5	6.3	4.9	3.7	3.3	−1.5
Mexico	—	7.0	9.6	8.4	5.9	6.0	1.0
Brazil	—	9.1	3:7	10.4	9.6	7.4	−1.3

Source: World Bank, *World Tables*, Comparative Economic Data (Baltimore, Md.: John Hopkins University Press 1980), table 1. United Nations, Statistical Office, *Monthly Bulletin of Statistics* (April 1953), p. xi. Council for Economic Planning and Development, Republic of China, *Taiwan Statistical Data Book (1985)*, table 5–2b. *The Europa Yearbook, 1969*, Vol. 2, "China Statistic Survey," p. 339. Organization of American States, *Statistical Bulletin of the OAS* 4, no. 1–2 (Jan.–June 1982), pp. 185–86. United Nations, Economic Commission for Latin America and the Caribbean, *Statistical Yearbook for Latin America, 1984*, p. 167. United Nations, *Economic and Social Survey of Asia and the Pacific, 1982*, table I–10. Willy Kraus, *Economic Development and Social Change in the People's Republic of China* (New York: Springer-Verlag, 1982), table A.8.

Table A–8
Unit Labor Cost for Manufacturing by Nation, 1950–83
(in U.S. $)

	1950–55	1955–60	1960–65	1965–70	1970–75	1975–80	1980–83
U.S.	48.4	57.1	59.6	64.1	78.0	106.8	141.2
Canada	50.9	57.1	57.1	55.4	56.9	101.3	132.6
Japan	31.9	31.4	32.3	38.3	63.9	105.8	107.9
West Germany	23.0	24.8	30.5	35.5	64.5	113.7	126.5
France	46.1	46.1	45.1	45.7	47.8	117.0	131.9
U.K.	34.3	42.7	48.5	51.3	72.5	131.6	191.7
Belgium	—	—	35.4	41.6	62.0	109.0	114.0[a]
Denmark	25.1	28.7	33.7	40.4	63.7	110.2	108.8
Netherlands	20.8	24.2	30.3	38.1	62.7	109.9	115.6
Norway	17.2	20.8	24.7	30.6	52.4	103.0	117.9
Sweden	24.3	28.7	33.0	38.0	57.4	124.2	105.1
Italy	30.5	31.9	37.7	43.5	71.3	113.6	130.0

Source: U.S. Department of Labor, Bureau of Labor Statistics, *Handbook of Labor Statistics* (June 1985), table 129.

1977 = 100.

[a]1980–82 data.

Table A–9
Annual Average Unemployment Rate by Nation, 1960–85

	1960–65	1965–70	1970–75	1975–80	1980–85
U.S.	5.5%	4.0%	5.9%	7.1%	8.1%
Canada	5.7	4.3	6.0	7.6	9.9
Japan	1.3	1.2	1.4	2.0	2.4
West Germany	0.9	1.1	1.9	4.3	6.9
France	1.0	1.9	2.9	5.2	8.4
U.K.	1.7	2.1	3.0	5.4	11.4
Sweden	1.5	1.8	2.1	1.9	2.8
Italy	4.8	5.6	5.8	7.1	9.7
Australia	2.1	1.7	2.7	5.7	7.7

Source: U.S. Department of Labor, Bureau of Labor Statistics, *Handbook of Labor Statistics* (June 1985), table 126. U.S. Department of Labor, Bureau of Labor Statistics, *Monthly Labor Review,* "Current Labor Statistics, International Comparisons Data" (May 1986), table 46; (June 1986), table 45.

Table A–10
Population by Nation, 1946–84
(millions)

	1946	1950	1968	1980	1984
U.S.	141.2	151.7	179.3	227.7	236.7
Soviet Union	193.0	193.0	208.8	265.5	275.1
Japan	73.1	82.9	98.3	116.8	120.0
West Germany	45.3	47.6	56.2	61.6	61.4
U.K.	47.2	50.6	52.7	56.0	56.0
France	40.0	41.9	49.8	53.9	54.9
Italy	45.6	46.3	49.9	56.5	57.0
Sweden	6.7	7.0	7.8	8.3	8.3
Spain	27.2	28.3	30.4	37.5	38.4
Netherlands	9.4	10.1	12.7	14.1	14.4
Norway	3.1	3.3	3.8	4.1	4.1
Belgium	8.4	8.6	9.6	9.9	9.9
Poland	23.8	25.0	32.3	35.6	36.9
Yugoslavia	15.7[a]	16.1	20.0	22.3	23.0
Hungary	9.0	9.2[b]	10.2	10.7	10.7
China	455.6	463.5	582.6	983.4	1,031.6
South Korea	19.4	29.5	29.2	39.6	42.0
Taiwan	7.0	9.0	13.4	17.8	19.1
India	310.6	358.0	435.5	685.1	746.4
Canada	12.3	13.8	20.0	24.1	25.1
Mexico	22.8	25.4	34.9	70.1	77.7
Brazil	46.7	52.1	70.1	122.4	134.4
World total	2,351.0[c]	2,536.0	3,483.0	4,451.0	4,766.3

Source: United Nations Statistical Office, *Monthly Bulletin of Statistics* (Sept. 1948), table 1; (Mar. 1953), table 1; (June 1974), table 1; (May 1986), table 1. U.S. Department of Commerce, Bureau of the Census, *Statistical Abstract of the United States, 1952*, table 1077; *1970*, table 1251; *1985*, table 1475.

[a] 1947 data.
[b] 1949 data.
[c] 1948 data.

Table A–11
Foreign Exchange Rates, 1960–87

	Canadian Dollar	Japanese Yen	German Mark	French Franc	Swiss Franc	British Pound
1960	102.04	0.28	23.98	20.36	23.17	280.58
1961	96.62	0.28	25.15	20.41	23.18	278.78
1962	92.42	0.28	25.06	20.41	23.18	280.82
1963	92.76	0.28	25.13	20.41	23.11	280.03
1964	92.51	0.28	25.16	20.41	23.17	279.10
1965	92.74	0.28	25.04	20.40	23.11	279.59
1966	92.27	0.28	25.15	20.19	23.11	279.02
1967	92.52	0.28	25.01	20.38	23.12	240.67
1968	92.80	0.28	25.05	20.19	23.17	239.35
1969	92.86	0.28	25.49	19.30	23.19	239.01
1970	95.80	0.28	27.42	18.09	23.20	239.56
1971	99.02	0.29	28.77	18.15	24.33	244.42
1972	100.94	0.33	31.36	19.83	26.19	250.08
1973	99.98	0.37	37.76	22.54	31.70	245.10
1974	102.26	0.34	28.72	20.80	33.69	234.03
1975	98.30	0.34	40.73	23.35	38.74	222.16
1976	99.01	0.34	42.37	20.12	40.82	170.36
1977	91.74	0.42	47.39	21.23	50.00	190.47
1978	87.73	0.48	49.87	22.22	56.28	191.84
1979	85.39	0.46	54.56	23.50	60.12	212.24
1980	85.53	0.44	55.09	23.69	59.70	232.58
1981	87.41	0.45	44.36	18.49	51.03	202.43
1982	81.10	0.40	41.19	15.20	49.20	174.80
1983	81.14	0.42	39.16	13.12	47.61	151.59
1984	77.20	0.42	35.14	11.45	42.55	133.66
1985	73.22	0.42	33.99	11.14	40.73	129.74
1986	71.96	0.59	46.07	14.44	55.62	146.77
1987[a]	73.50	0.65	53.78	16.13	64.04	150.54

Source: U.S. Department of Commerce, Bureau of the Census, *Statistical Abstract of the United States* (annual). Board of Governors of the Federal Reserve System, *Federal Reserve Bulletin* (monthly); *Federal Reserve Statistical Release* (Nov. 28, 1986, Jan. 30, 1987).

Note: U.S. cents per unit of foreign currency (monthly averages).

[a]As of end of January 1987.

Table A–12
U.S. Balance of Payments, 1978–86
(in billions of SDR)

	1978	1980	1983	1984	1985	1986[a]
Current account	−12.5	1.5	−143.5	−105.2	−115.4	−67.9
Merchandise exports	113.3	172.4	188.7	214.6	211.1	109.9
Merchandise imports	−140.5	−192.0	−251.3	−326.1	−332.8	−180.8
Trade balance	−27.2	−19.6	−63.2	−111.5	−121.7	−70.9
Other goods, services, and income (inflow)	62.2	90.8	124.3	138.7	143.7	73.2
Other goods, services, and income (outflow)	−42.9	−64.0	−95.7	−120.5	−122.0	−63.3
Balance of services, other goods, and income	19.3	26.8	28.6	18.2	21.7	10.0
Total balance (goods, services, and income)	−8.0	7.3	−34.6	−93.3	−100.4	−60.9
Official aid and transfers (excluding military)	−3.8	−5.0	−8.0	−10.5	−13.1	−6.3
Investment and capital account						
Direct investment (net)	−6.5	1.8	6.1	17.5	−2.2	−12.2
In U.S.	6.3	13.0	11.2	21.9	16.1	—
Abroad	−12.8	−14.8	−5.1	−4.4	−18.4	—
Portfolio investment	−0.3	2.2	4.6	28.6	62.0	42.7
Bank deposits	−13.7	−23.4	14.2	18.7	30.0	7.7
Net errors and omissions	10.2	19.2	15.6	30.0	32.5	17.6
Total change in reserves	1.25	−6.19	−0.68	−2.48	−4.85	−3.36
Conversion rates: U.S. $ per SDR	1.2520	1.3015	1.069	1.025	1.0153	1.1776

Source: IMF, *Balance of Payments Statistics* (monthly), United States, table 1. *International Financial Statistics* 39, no. 11 (Nov. 1986), United States.

[a]First half of 1986.

Table A–13
Balance of Payments in Japan, 1978–86
(in billions of SDR)

	1978	1980	1983	1984	1985	1986[a]
Current account	12.9	−8.3	19.6	34.3	49.2	35.8
Merchandise exports	76.0	97.4	136.3	164.3	174.0	97.1
Merchandise imports	−56.6	−95.8	−106.7	−121.0	−118.0	−58.8
Trade balance	19.5	1.7	29.6	43.3	56.0	38.3
Other goods, services, and income (inflow)	14.9	24.2	35.2	41.1	45.5	25.4
Other goods, services, and income (outflow)	−20.8	−32.9	−43.7	−48.7	−50.7	−26.7
Balance of services, other goods, and income	−5.9	−8.7	−8.5	−7.6	−5.2	−1.3
Total balance (goods, services, and income)	13.5	−7.1	21.0	35.8	50.8	37.0
Official aid and transfers (excluding military)	−0.3	−1.0	−1.3	−1.3	−1.4	−0.9
Investment and capital account						
Direct investment (net)	−1.9	−1.6	−3.0	−5.8	−5.8	−4.7
Portfolio investment	−2.2	7.2	−2.8	−23.6	−41.8	−37.6
Bank deposits	−1.3	9.8	−7.3	8.6	9.7	15.6
Net errors and omissions	1.2	−2.4	1.9	3.7	4.5	4.6
Total change in reserves	−6.56	−4.50	−2.35	−3.46	−0.3	−7.3
Conversion rates: Yen per SDR	263.47	295.11	253.90	243.46	220.23	194.30

Source: IMF, *Balance of Payments Statistics* (monthly), Japan, table 1. *International Financial Statistics* 39, no. 11 (Nov. 1986), Japan.
[a]First half of 1986.

Table A–14
Balance of Payments in West Germany, France, and the United Kingdom, 1985–86
(in billions of SDR)

	West Germany		France		U.K.	
	1985	*1986*[a]	*1985*	*1986*[a]	*1985*	*1986*[a]
Current account	13.4	6.1	0.7	− 0.6	4.1	2.3
Merchandise exports	170.9	47.1	94.3	28.7	99.2	25.4
Merchandise imports	− 142.9	− 36.9	− 98.8	− 30.1	− 101.6	− 28.0
Trade balance	28.0	10.2	− 4.5	− 1.4	− 2.4	− 2.6
Other goods, services, and income (inflow)	48.9	12.6	57.6	15.8	97.2	25.4
Other goods, services, and income (outflow)	− 53.0	− 14.1	− 49.8	− 13.9	− 86.3	− 22.1
Balance of services, other goods, and income	− 4.1	− 1.6	7.8	1.9	10.9	3.3
Total balance (goods, services, and income)	23.8	8.6	3.3	0.5	8.6	0.7
Official aid and transfers (excluding military)	− 6.9	− 1.7	− 1.3	− 0.7	− 4.3	− 0.4
Investment and capital account						
Direct investment (net)	− 2.9	0.1	0.3	− 0.6	− 4.4	2.2
Portfolio investment	3.1	8.0	6.8	− 0.1	− 14.4	− 5.9
Bank deposits	− 9.5	2.2	− 2.5	—	12.4	—
Net errors and omissions	3.4	− 1.2	− 0.4	0.5	0.6	0.6
Total change in reserves	− 0.70	− 0.03	− 2.86	− 0.08	− 0.73	− 1.0
Conversion rates	2.9891[b]	2.6394[b]	9.1231[c]	8.1187[c]	0.79120[d]	0.76636[d]

Source: IMF, *Balance of Payments Statistics* (monthly), various countries. *International Financial Statistics* 39, no. 11 (Nov. 1986), various countries.
[a]First quarter of 1986.
[b]Deutsche marks per SDR.
[c]French francs per SDR.
[d]Pound sterling per SDR.

Table A-15
Regional Trade Balances, 1985
(in $ billions)

	Japan		EEC		Germany		France	
	Imports	Exports	Imports	Exports	Imports	Exports	Imports	Exports
U.S.	26.36	66.54	49.24	62.21	10.96	19.03	8.15	8.39
Canada	4.85	4.56	5.54	7.24	1.22	1.87	0.78	1.06
Western Europe	12.44	25.38	398.11	403.32	101.35	121.30	66.99	59.87
Japan	—	—	21.42	7.66	7.12	2.69	2.99	1.20
China	6.56	12.64	2.82	4.99	0.87	2.23	0.50	0.78
Other Eastern Asia	30.90	34.02	21.15	20.88	6.43	6.18	2.91	3.36
Total Eastern Asia	37.46	46.66	45.39	43.53	14.42	11.10	6.40	5.34
Latin America	6.07	7.25	19.45	10.31	6.11	3.75	2.92	1.93
Near East	29.73	11.03	22.80	27.81	2.65	7.05	5.11	3.87
Africa	3.58	4.57	45.67	33.43	9.58	6.86	10.33	10.54
Australia and Oceania	8.87	6.88	5.44	6.90	1.16	1.87	0.94	0.83
Eastern Europe	0.31	0.51	9.76	8.05	3.40	3.73	1.27	1.00
Soviet Union	1.43	2.79	15.46	9.01	4.63	3.60	2.45	1.90
Total East Bloc	1.74	3.30	25.22	17.06	8.03	7.33	3.72	2.90
World total	131.30	177.22	625.08	614.39	157.59	183.31	107.15	97.01

Table A–15 continued

	U.K.		EFTA		Canada		Australia		Taiwan	
	Imports	Exports	Imports	Exports	Imports	Exports	Imports	Exports	Imports	Exports
U.S.	13.02	15.06	7.65	9.82	54.63	68.28	5.25	2.35	4.75	14.77
Canada	2.14	2.19	0.87	1.24	—	—	0.47	0.25	0.37	0.94
Western Europe	69.10	58.76	82.43	77.79	9.22	6.07	6.28	3.31	2.44	2.98
Japan	5.34	1.31	5.22	1.98	4.48	4.23	5.43	6.31	5.55	3.46
China	0.40	0.51	0.31	0.81	0.30	0.94	0.29	0.87	—	—
Other Eastern Asia	5.61	5.32	2.90	3.57	3.44	2.26	2.44	4.17	4.94	6.02
Total Eastern Asia	11.35	7.14	8.43	6.36	8.22	7.43	8.16	11.35	.49	9.48
Latin America	2.05	1.38	8.43	6.36	2.89	1.73	0.27	0.24	0.44	0.17
Near East	2.05	6.28	2.20	4.06	0.19	0.49	0.98	1.74	—	—
Africa	5.00	5.44	3.54	3.79	0.81	1.06	0.16	0.56	0.52	0.56
Australia and Oceania	1.79	2.35	0.45	1.11	0.44	0.64	1.15	1.73	0.88	0.90
Eastern Europe	1.11	0.83	3.19	2.69	0.17	0.18	0.76	0.19	—	—
Soviet Union	0.94	0.70	5.13	4.34	0.02	1.18	0.008	0.59	—	—
Total East Bloc	2.15	1.53	8.32	7.03	0.19	1.36	0.77	0.78	—	—
World total	109.92	101.54	117.57	115.02	76.86	87.36	23.51	22.63	20.10	30.72

Source: Department of Economics and Statistics, *Monthly Statistics of Foreign Trade* (Paris: OECD, May 1986). Council for Economic Planning and Development, Republic of China, *Taiwan Statistical Data Books, 1985*, tables 10–10 (a–d), 10–11 (a–c).

Index

About the Author

William A. Lovett is Professor of Law and Economics at Tulane University in New Orleans and Director of the Program in International Law, Trade and Finance at Tulane Law School. He has practiced law with a Wall Street firm and has worked in Washington, D.C., as a Federal Trade Commission economist, lawyer with the Department of Justice Antitrust Division, and lecturer in economics at the National War College. Since 1969 at Tulane he has specialized in problems of economic regulation. Over the years, his teaching and writing have covered international trade, finance, and banking; financial institutions; antitrust and regulated industries; labor relations; energy and law-economics issues. His latest books are *Inflation and Politics: Fiscal, Monetary, and Wage-Price Discipline* (1982) and *Banking and Financial Institutions Law* (1984). He has published many articles in scholarly journals. In recent years, Prof. Lovett has lectured, taught, or visited in Britain, France, Germany, Switzerland, Italy, Greece, Japan, Korea, Taiwan, Hong Kong, Thailand, Philippines, Singapore, Mexico, and Canada. His students at Tulane have come from more than fifty countries.